Lyric Complicity

PUBLICATIONS OF THE WISCONSIN CENTER
FOR PUSHKIN STUDIES

David M. Bethea
Series Editor

Lyric Complicity

*Poetry and Readers in the
Golden Age of Russian Literature*

Daria Khitrova

THE UNIVERSITY OF WISCONSIN PRESS

The University of Wisconsin Press
728 State Street, Suite 443
Madison, Wisconsin 53706
uwpress.wisc.edu

Gray's Inn House, 127 Clerkenwell Road
London EC1R 5DB, United Kingdom
eurospanbookstore.com

Copyright © 2019
The Board of Regents of the University of Wisconsin System
All rights reserved. Except in the case of brief quotations embedded in critical articles and reviews, no part of this publication may be reproduced, stored in a retrieval system, transmitted in any format or by any means—digital, electronic, mechanical, photocopying, recording, or otherwise—or conveyed via the Internet or a website without written permission of the University of Wisconsin Press. Rights inquiries should be directed to rights@uwpress.wisc.edu.

Printed in the United States of America

This book may be available in a digital edition.

Library of Congress Cataloging-in-Publication Data

Names: Khitrova, Daria, author.
Title: Lyric complicity : poetry and readers in the golden age of Russian literature / Daria Khitrova.
Other titles: Publications of the Wisconsin Center for Pushkin Studies.
Description: Madison, Wisconsin : The University of Wisconsin Press, [2019] | Series: Publications of the Wisconsin Center for Pushkin Studies | Includes bibliographical references and index.
Identifiers: LCCN 2018046040 | ISBN 9780299322106 (cloth : alk. paper)
Subjects: LCSH: Russian poetry—19th century—History and criticism.
Classification: LCC PG3051 .K45 2019 | DDC 891.71/309—dc23
LC record available at https://lccn.loc.gov/2018046040

ISBN 9780299322144 (pbk. : alk. paper)

For my parents,
YULIA AND MIKHAIL,
and my brother,
ALEXEY

Contents

Preface	ix
Introduction: Outside the Book	3

PART I
Functions and Uses

1 Lyric as Speech Act and Literary Fact	21
2 Functions: How to Do Things with Verse	47
3 Situations and Occasions	76

PART II
One, Two, Many: To Whom Poems Speak

4 The Extended Self: "I" to "I" and "I" to "We"	125
5 You and I: Love Elegy and How to Use It	161
The Art of Epilogue: Critique of the Golden Age in *Eugene Onegin*	203
Notes	247
Bibliography	271
Index	287

Preface

The way in which historical material is arranged and presented in this book can be described as a step-by-step cut-in. I owe this structure to a century-old methodological debate between scholars advocating a slow and close perusal of literary texts, and those who would prefer to look for clues *between* texts—that is, explore literary contexts. "That slow reading method!" Yuri Tynianov is remembered to have once exclaimed. "The scholar must read works the way ordinary readers do—cursorily, or else they are bound to read into them what isn't there."[1] On the one hand, Tynianov had a point. The process of reading is akin to performance: here as there, timing matters. On the other, his objection—or, for that matter, any demurral of the kind—does not rule out the slow reading method. Rarely in the course of such debates (recently reinvigorated in connection with Franco Moretti's defiant defense of distant reading) do we hear a voice in favor of *both* approaches, instead of backing one at the expense of the other—as if a literary study could not be distant and sweeping at one point, and slow and myopic at another. I use both kinds of optics in this study. It begins with a wide cartographic view of an epoch, showing various currents of literary thought and the various front lines of literary struggles; and ends up with a slow and careful examination of how these lines and currents refract, as in a drop of water, in Pushkin's *Eugene Onegin*.

I would like to express my gratitude to the Davis Center for Russian and Eurasian Studies for buying me extra time—a sabbatical semester, no less!—to complete the writing; and to the Anne and Jim Rothenberg Fund for Humanities Research for its generosity as well. I am also indebted to Ugly Duckling

Presse and Rawley Grau for their permission to use Grau's splendid translations of Evgeny Baratynsky's poems.

My thanks to my editor Avram Brown, whose sense of style and skill with words helped make my prose sound as right as it possibly could; and to Geoff Cebula, Alex Droznin, Marlyn Miller, Sheila McMahon, and Ainsley Morse for their considerable editorial/translation assistance. I am also very grateful to Gwen Walker, executive editor at the University of Wisconsin Press, for her patient guidance and incisive suggestions, and to the series editor, David Bethea, for his support of my book.

My warm gratitude goes also to my Harvard colleagues who read the manuscript and suggested corrections and improvements: Julie Buckler, Stephanie Sandler, and William Mills Todd III. I spent my formative years as a scholar in conversations with colleagues whom I mostly met, year by year, at conferences in Moscow, Petersburg, Tartu, and Rezekne: Alina Bodrova, Aleksandr Dolinin, Liubov' Kiseleva, Roman Leibov, Ekaterina Liamina, Andrei Nemzer, Aleksandr Ospovat, Kirill Rogov, Tatiana Stepanishcheva (Fraiman), and Mikhail Velizhev. I include in this list only fellow early nineteenth-century scholars, but I am no less grateful to all other participants (and, of course, organizers) of the biannual Tynianov conferences in Rezekne, the Pushkin conferences and Lotman seminars and congresses in Tartu, the Lotman conferences in Moscow, and the Etkind conferences in Petersburg. This scholarly milieu gave me more than any university program could possibly give.

I also thank my domestic companions, all dear to my heart: Yuri and Vari, without whom nothing would be possible, and our cat, Perchik, to whose footwork on my keyboard I owe some of the most exquisite samples of transrational poetry.

Last but not least, I want to thank my parents, Yulia and Mikhail, and my brother, Alexey, who made, shaped, and have supported me all my life. I don't know how many times over the years at our family celebrations I would make toasts with a promise to dedicate my first book to them. I thus dedicate this, my first book, to them.

Lyric Complicity

Introduction
Outside the Book

"Can't you see I'm reading?" Reading, we get used to thinking from an early age, equals being alone with a book. Since the late nineteenth century, the established idea of what poetry is has been predicated on such time-honored dichotomies as writing versus reading and authors versus audiences; on the notion, that is, of poetry as expression and readership as reception.

While a figure hunched over a book was as emblematic of literature in Russia as anywhere else in the Gutenberg galaxy, early nineteenth-century Russian lyric was not limited to the medium of print. Open the book, savor your Pushkin, put the book back on the shelf. This is about all that our present-day bookworm diet requires of us. In Pushkin's time, his verse could have reached you in a variety of forms: as a handwritten copy, enclosed in a letter, inscribed in a personal album, recited at a private dinner, performed as a song at a family party, or whispered in your ear. Each of these—a handwritten copy of a poem, for instance—provided you with a number of follow-up ideas. You may have been moved to recopy your copy, in order to keep or repost it; amend a line or two and send it back to Pushkin (assuming you were a friend of his); or set it to music. Poetry operated in a participatory, interactive, and performative environment—as a unifying network. Doing poetry in the first third of the nineteenth century, also known as the Golden Age of Russian literature, involved social networking avant la lettre. Rather than serving as a target of literary circulation, you, the reader, *became* the circulation, replicating and replaying the behavior of the poet, or of the reader before you.

Poet, poem, and reader—in Russian literature's Golden Age the relationship within this familiar triad was differently configured. The distinction is important. At stake here is more than a mere historical adjustment of cultural and literary roles. Contrary to what common sense might suggest, poetry does not amount to poems written by poets for readers to enjoy or reflect upon. We often refer to "the medium of poetry." In early nineteenth-century Russia, that term would have to be applied in the broadest sense possible: as a habitat, human environment, the medium of daily life. In this perspective, poet and reader alike are internal rather than external to poetry; in some cases, the latter is as personally involved in the production and circulation of poems as the former. What an old poem means includes what it *meant*: what it was made for, and what people made of it. If meaning encompasses use, then recovering old uses is tantamount to discovering new layers of meaning in poems we thought we understood so well.

Poets write to depict, express, communicate; poems are read, interpreted, responded to—such, broadly speaking, are the default settings for thinking of poetry today. But poetry's leverage, cultural and social, was more complex and ramified in nineteenth-century Russia than it would seem in our present-day hindsight. Functions were more wide-ranging; distinctions, less distinct; roles, less scripted. A pleasant pastime or a smart career move could furnish as valid a motive for writing a poem as high hopes to see it published would today; amid the poetic competence of the educated, poets' readers were more like poets' peers; and such was the mutual osmosis of poetry and everyday speech that the classic formalist distinction between "poetic" and "practical" languages proves easier to declare than detect. Or, a poem—typically, a lyric one—could have been written with an eye toward its reader cutting it up into lines or stanzas to serve in the doublespeak of love. If what a poem means includes how it is used, poetry's many uses should be examined. To restore that long-lost configuration—poetry's former uses and functions; a forgotten occasion that occasioned unforgettable verse; life situations that moved people to quote or perform a specific passage from a poem—is the goal this book aspires to.

All of Them Are Poets

Who were the poets who shaped the image and character of the period this book examines? Two opposite answers to this question can be glimpsed in two different labels traditionally applied to the epoch—one synecdochic, the other metaphorical. One school of literary studies preferred to call the time the "Age of Pushkin" (*pushkinskaia epokha*), as if asserting the motto "one for all." The title is well deserved, but the devotee of Fedor Tiutchev or Mikhail Lermontov might object: what about the others? And what of Vasily Zhukovsky, Konstantin Batiushkov, Evgeny Baratynsky?—an informed student of poetry will add. Not to mention Anton Del'vig, Nikolai Iazykov, Petr Viazemsky. And others.

The point is well taken. The epoch often remembered as "Pushkin's" indeed consisted of not one but many names, each associated with an individual face and style. Yet it is also true that many people living in Russia at the dawn of the nineteenth century, and many more who would later look back on this historical moment, tended to picture the time as one in which homogeneity and coherence reigned. In their eyes, the epoch was "all for one" rather than "one for all." It may have been this sense of wholeness that moved the critic Petr Pletnev in 1824 to dub the epoch of Zhukovsky, Batiushkov, and Pushkin "the Golden Age of Russian literature."[1] Dismissed at the time as precious and pompous by the very poets that had earned their epoch this distinction, the "Golden Age" appellation was dropped—until later literary critics picked it up and ran with it.

Needless to say, the Golden Age metaphor is not unproblematic. Some of its glow is bound to spill over onto the historical period it labels—as Bulat Okudzhava shows, with tender irony, in "The Battlefield Canvas" ("Batal'noe polotno"), written (and sung) in the 1960s:

Вслед за императором едут генералы, генералы свиты,
Славою увиты, шрамами покрыты, только не убиты.
Следом—дуэлянты, флигель-адъютанты. Блещут эполеты.
Все они красавцы, все они таланты, все они поэты.[2]

[In the emperor's wake ride the generals, the generals of the train / Wreathed by glory, covered in scars, all but killed. / After them come the aides-de-camp—the duelists. Epaulettes are gleaming. / All of them are handsome, all of them are talented, all of them are poets.]

Indeed, as a historical model, the Golden Age has its advantages and pitfalls. Among the latter, most popular is what Okudzhava's nostalgic canvas parodies here: in the hands of too avid a devotee, the epithet "golden" is likely to bleed over from poetry to culture and society at large—a slippage that is far from harmless. Applied to the wider world beyond that of letters, the phrase "all of them are poets" makes one wonder what happened to everyone else.

The illiterate majority of nineteenth-century Russia, or its ethnic and religious minorities—these masses of people seem to have disappeared. An anecdote I heard from a Tartu University alumnus serves well to illustrate this point. A student freshly enamored with the image of the Golden Age is said to have asked Professor Yuri Lotman: did he ever wish he had been born in the epoch whose ways and works he knew so well? Without missing a beat, Lotman replied: "In what shtetl, sir [*sudar'*]?"[3]

On the other hand, if we narrow Okudzhava's "all of them are poets" to focus on the realm of writing and writing only, the phrase can be of help as a (hyperbolic) heuristic to describe how Russian poetry functioned in the age we now call Golden. To be a poet—what did this role mean to, entail for, and require of educated Russians around two centuries ago? And what did it take to be a reader of poetry in those days? To read, copy, memorize, perform, comment on, and reply in verse—given the scope of this impressive job description, where are we supposed to draw a line between being a reader and a poet? Is there a line at all, or is it more like a continuum?

Poetry and Performance

Explicitly or not, any study of poetry comes up with its own definition of this art form and its environs. For a grammarian like Roman Jakobson, poetry spins forth from the language it inhabits; for a literary theorist like Jonathan Culler, poetry is a continuous tradition across languages, centuries, and poets; and for an expert in versification like Mikhail Gasparov, poetry is a poem taken in its countless connections to every other poem. The list of answers will undoubtedly grow if we ask what poetry is for a rhetorician, a student of readership, or a humanist at large.

To define what poetry is for the purpose of this study, I would begin by changing *is* to *was*. The relationship I focus on is not between poetry and poems, poetry and poets, or poetry and language but between poetry and its verbal ambiance, the contemporary speech with which poets and poems used to interact. This, in itself, is nothing new. No student of old poetry can get by without some consideration of the everyday language of the given period. The difference consists in the purpose of inquiry. While normally, we go to poetry's textual surroundings in order to get a sense of historical semantics—an obsolete turn of phrase, say, or an obscure allusion—this book looks at poetry through the lens of historical pragmatics: what people *did* with poetry that we no longer do.

Viewed through this lens, Golden Age poetry comes into focus as a set of interactions—between poets and their poems, poets and their readers, readers and *their* poems. What made a reader claim a poem, recognize someone's lyric speech as their own? In his 1822 *Brief Outline of Literary Theory* (*Kratkoe nachernatiie teorii iziashchnoi slovesnosti*) the poet and theoretician Aleksei Merzliakov came up with an answer to this question. An elegy, he writes, is only as strong as its ability to relate to its reader's life, to draw him or her into complicity with it.[4] It was Merzliakov's notion of *souchastie* (complicity, participation) that prompted the main title of this book; his theory merits further consideration, and I will return to it in chapter 3.

If there is one thing that all lyric poems have in common regardless of provenance and epoch, it is that they can be both written and performed. In nineteenth-century Russia, as, arguably, in any other country in the world, poets used to read poems in public and publish them to be read by others. Poetry recitals took place in Soviet Russia, as they do in Russia today. Nothing, it would appear, has changed on this front. But if we take a more detailed look, another system, a *different* one, emerges. Did poetry readings take place in private homes or public venues? Were these ticketed affairs, or was no entrance fee required? Were all willing listeners admitted, or was it by invitation only? Was the audience anonymous, or did the poet have to know the attendees socially? And, as for publishing: was this act seen as a natural outcome of writing a poem, its consummation, or was it considered a questionable choice?

None of these questions strike us as epoch-making and poetry-defining, and yet, from the standpoint of poetry's Golden Age, they were. "*Tempi passati!*" (These times are long gone!), exclaimed one grumpy observer in 1899, looking back on an age he wished had never passed. "Happy times for literature, when ... they used to read and write much and publish little, [read and write] thoughtfully and unhurriedly, and not for the mob, but for those who could read and write!"[5] We need not sympathize with the haughtiness implicit in such complaints, but neither can we afford to ignore them as historical evidence—they are the timeworn looking glass in which, if darkly, a bygone system of literary values is reflected.

Reading as Networking

There are no writers without readers, modern literary theory reminds us. Compared to traditional literary studies, which focus on writers, the study of readership presents us with new challenges and tasks. Writers have names, whereas the reader is a construct, a concept, an analytical tool. Some reader-concepts from the tool kit of readership theory are applicable to the period examined in this book. Such, for instance, is the statistical reader constructed by sociology from numbers of works published or sold—a figure to which we owe the informative curve of Pushkin's rise to fame.[6] Or take the "fictional" or "implied" reader, the textual surrogate explored by reader-response theorists.[7] One could hardly find a more rewarding work for a reader-response theorist to tackle than Pushkin's *Eugene Onegin*, whose in-text readers come in every grammatical person: the informal *Ty*-reader to whom the author bids farewell at the end of his novel-in-verse; a formal *Vy*-reader (*blistali, moi chitatel'*) to whom the author introduces the novel's hero; plus the famous third-person reader, the one who impatiently waits for the hackneyed rhyme *morozy-rozy* (frosts-roses). Lastly, there is the "historical" (or "intended") reader, that holy grail of Russian philology's retrospective hermeneutics, the quest for which has brought us so many insightful commentaries and studies.[8]

The readership that concerns me here is of a different variety. To distinguish this reader from those just mentioned, let me first change the singular to plural. Mine is not *the* reader, but *readers*, each with a name, residence, and dates of life: the poet's audience as a community whose ways of handling poetry were unique to Russia's Golden Age. It is this perspective—specific to the period—that makes the network model of readership heuristically useful. When we say, "the poet and the reader," we place the latter at the receiving end of a one-way literary chain: the poem originates with the poet and ends up with the reader, period. Conversely, the network model of readership invites us to explore the life of a poem after it has been read. What becomes of a poem when it changes readers' hands? And what happens when a line or a thought from a poem spreads, like a catchy tune, or a textually transmitted disease, across a community of readers?

Today, we tend to think of poet, poem, and reader in retail terms. Imagine a bookstore: next to the cash register lies a collection of verse; behind the counter stands the poet, in front of it, a reader. In the early nineteenth century, the poet-to-reader relationship was configured differently. As Viktor Shklovsky observed in 1929: "When Pushkin was writing, it was typical in his aristocratic milieu to know how to write poetry, that is, almost every lyceum classmate of Pushkin's wrote poetry and competed with him in ladies' albums and so on. Back then, that is, being able to write a poem was as usual a thing as is nowadays being able to read. And yet these were not professional poets. This was an environment of people who understood the technique of writing—the environment that could produce a Pushkin."[9] In the eye of Shklovsky's technocentric poetics, the world of poetry in the Golden Age was not like a bookshop but rather like a workshop—a shop without a counter, a place where reading equaled learning from or filching from your friends. Not only the readership, but the whole of Golden Age poetry was a tightly knit fabric binding all to all. Rather than drawing a line between poet and reader, I think of readers-as-poets—a heuristic hybrid that provides a better understanding of the poetry of the Golden Age than does the retail model imported from our conception of literature in later epochs.

While books and bookstores were integral to Russia's literary infrastructure, Golden Age poetry was not consigned to their walls and covers. Our historical lens must be accordingly adjusted. To reformulate a slogan associated with creative problem-solving: Think outside the book. Why outside, if the book is the thing? Indeed, a time-tested analogy suggests we conceive of literature as an immense library whose books, when arranged in succession, form what we call literary history. Historians, exegetes, and theorists come to this virtual library to do what they have been doing here for ages: cull phrases, images, and lines of poetry from books, and then connect them, as in a dots-and-boxes game, into causal or philosophical configurations. Thinking outside the book means thinking in more than one dimension. What if literary history is, rather, three different histories in one? One is the history of texts. Another is how, differently in different epochs, texts have been handled, made use of, handed down by people; call it the personal dimension of literary history. Still another history is that of literature from the standpoint of media—the continuously evolving tool kit found on your desk as a poet (and the desk itself, seeing as the earliest forms of poetry predate the first systems of writing) and in your hands as a reader—from the clay tablets of paleography to the e-tablets so many bed-and-sofa readers nowadays prefer. The text, the human, and the means are the three coordinates to reckon with if we want to observe Russian Golden Age poetry in the round.

As tools change, so does our relationship with texts. An illustrative parallel would be music, a medium whose reliance on tools (not just musical instruments, but also sheet music or recordings) is obvious. What if you happen to be a great fan of Mozart but were unable to attend a performance of his Piano Sonata No. 9 at a concert hall last week? You might compensate by listening to a recording—an option that media technologies of the Golden Age were, of course, unable to provide. But educated Russians of that period may well have undertaken something that we in our age of media omnipotence would be unlikely to consider: performing it. Playing music was, in nineteenth-century Russia (as in the rest of Europe), part of a liberal-arts education. To listen to Mozart, you would have sent for a score, not a recording, put it on your piano, and played it yourself to yourself. Or to someone whose heart you hoped to win.

As in music, so in poetry. Poetry's life outside the book in the Golden Age was closely tied to people's life at home—speaking, of course, of Russia's educated classes, mainly urban or rural nobility. In such households, lyric poetry and music were, if not sisters, then frequent roommates, met with in drawing rooms where the piano stood, and where, when eye-to-eye with the object of one's romantic hopes, poetry helped you say things too risky for prose. Poetry, in fact, lived in more rooms than one. A secrétaire in your bedroom or a desk in your study was where you kept to yourself with your poetic exercises; the dining room, full of guests, was yet another place where poets and poetry were welcome. One, two, many: whatever the number of people in the room, poetry found itself a space.

Pragmatics and Poetics: Uses of Poetry in Early Nineteenth-Century Russia

"Uses of Poetry"—the phrase found in the subtitle of this section—echoes two earlier efforts to view art and literature from the standpoint of their pragmatics. One is *The Use of Poetry and the Use of Criticism*, a series of Norton Lectures delivered by T. S. Eliot at Harvard University in 1932–33, in which a number of assessments and definitions of "what poetry is, and does, and is for," ranging from the Elizabethan period to Eliot's own day, are examined "not merely as a catalogue of successive notions about poetry, but as a process of readjustment between poetry and the world in and for which it is produced."[10] The other is *The Uses of Images* (1999) by E. H. Gombrich, whose chapter titles alone—"Paintings on Walls," "Paintings for Altars," "Pictures for the Home"—signal an approach that is, mutatis mutandis, similar to mine. Louis H. Sullivan's "form follows function," originally conceived as a credo for architecture, has more than once been found to apply to the visual arts and poetry as well.

The moment one asks about uses one enters the sphere of pragmatics, be it of poetry or art. *Verse is another way of saying things*—while not unsound, such a definition is too broad to outline what is specific about poetry's pragmatics. That a poem grows out of the language used to compose it, rather than from feelings or ideas, was arguably the most important discovery of twentieth-century poetics. Different poetries have been shown to arise from grammatical peculiarities of their host languages and its lexical ambiguities; attempts have even been made to draw a connection to the graphic form of the written characters used.[11] Some theorists of poetry will locate poetry *inside* language; others define the language of poetry *against* the practical language; but common to their approaches is a determination to juxtapose poesy and praxis.[12]

The difference between poetics and pragmatics is in the angle of inquiry. Unlike most studies in poetics, the pragmatic approach is not confined to poems or poetry per se. Neither does it strive to set apart the poetic and practical languages. Rather, my goal is to track the language of poetry on the fly—in transit, between literary facts and quotidian speech acts. Some boundary or other always exists between poetry and everyday life, but part of what made Golden Age poetry unique was that here the border was porous enough to allow an intense traffic in verbal goods. Quotidian usages of language—courting, toasting, praying, letter-writing—were imported into poetry to crystallize as its subgenres (elegies, drinking songs, epistles); conversely, felicitous turns and figures of speech coined in the mint of lyric poetry would be snatched away to resurface later in private conversation or public circulation. The Golden Age community of readers perceived the language of poetry as *their* language, not poetry's alone. If you liked someone's poem you simply walked off with it—a pragmatic move with emotional consequences, as we learn from an 1824 lyric epistle Evgeny Baratynsky addressed to his younger friend Lev Pushkin.

Titled "To L. Pushkin" ("L. Pushkinu"), Baratynsky's epistle opens with an assuagement from which we infer that its addressee is jealous of the author, not least because he knows the power of Baratynsky's love lyric.

Поверь, мой милый! твой поэт
Тебе соперник не опасный!
Он на закате юных лет,
На утренней заре ты юности прекрасной.
Живого чувства полный взгляд
Уста цветущие, румяные ланиты
Влюблённых песенок сильнее говорят
С душой догадливой Хариты.[13]

[Trust me, my dear man! Your poet / Is not a dangerous rival to you! / He is in the twilight of his younger years; / You are at the dawn of your beautiful youth. / Your glance, alive with feeling, / Your blooming lips, your blushful cheeks / Speak stronger to the soul of a quick-witted Charis [*Kharita*] / Than lovesick songlets will.]

These lines sound more ambiguous in the original than my translation could convey. In the absence of articles in Russian, there is no certainty as to whether Baratynsky's "quick-witted Charis" refers to *a specific* Charis, or just *a* Charis, a mythopoetic nickname that stands for feminine beauty, youth, and grace. We do not know who the Kharita of this poem was; perhaps, the name stands for an archetypal female, the generic *she*.[14]

At the same time, generic as this image might have been, Baratynsky's *Kharita* is also Golden Age specific. She reads and judges poetry; speaks highly of Baratynsky's poems; and, in addition, does so with a lover's stratagem in mind.

Когда с тобой наедине
Порой красавица стихи мои похвалит,
Тебя напрасно опечалит
Её внимание ко мне:
Она торопит пробужденье
Младого сердца твоего
И вынуждает у него
Свидетельство любви, ревнивое мученье.

[When a beauty, alone with you, / Will, on occasion, praise my poems, / Let her attention to me / Not grieve you in vain: / She is [merely] urging / Your young heart to awake, / And is exacting from it / A pang of jealousy—the evidence of love.]

Many verse epistles, much like familiar letters, used to be written half in jest.[15] Our poem is no exception. The kind of love triangle it imagines—between an acknowledged poet who pronounces himself too old to contend for a beauty's love (Baratynsky was all of twenty-four when he wrote this); Lev Pushkin, his junior by five years (whose verses, unlike his brother's, were not considered anything special in the circle Baratynsky used to shine in); and a quick-witted, mischievous, conspiring reader named *Kharita*—resembles a sketch for some comedy of manners. On the other hand, the poem can be read as Baratynsky's heartfelt tribute to the peculiar ethos of the Golden Age, the time when supplying a line of poetry for someone else's use was seen as the touchstone of poetic merit:

> Что доброго в моей судьбе,
> И что я приобрёл, красавиц воспевая?
> Одно: моим стихом Харита молодая,
> Быть может, выразит любовь свою к тебе!

[What good is there in my fortune, / And what has hymning beautiful women gotten me? / Just one thing: perchance, a youthful Charis / Will use my verse to express her love for you!]

Baratynsky's is a poem about poetry, and, as such, harks back to the ars poetica tradition. At the same time, unlike the meta-poetic exercises of Boris Pasternak, Archibald MacLeish, or Horace himself, Baratynsky's poem appears less interested in what poetry *is* or how it is *made* than in what poetry can *do*. Call it love poetry's ideal job description. A "songlet" can buy you love; a serious poem, a lady's praise; yet the ultimate good, the top prize you as a poet can hope to win, is when someone runs off with your poem to appropriate, customize, and reenact it; in other words, makes *your* poetry's language *their* own. In this sense, Baratynsky's "To L. Pushkin" is ars poetica and *ars pragmatica* at once.

"The Golden Age": A Comparative Footnote to the Name

Some epochs are remembered by dates; others, by names. As a name for an epoch, the expression "the Golden Age" and the image harbored therein sounds almost too intuitive to call for a rigorous definition. This must be one of the reasons why literary scholars often seem hesitant to use such tags as "Golden Age" to define literary periods—and not of Russian literature alone. Another good reason to be wary of applying this term is the trace of value judgment present in the phrase—as if we agreed that a hierarchy existed in the succession of literary epochs. No such well-founded concern should ever be discounted; but the name "Golden Age" can be productive—provided we agree to understand the word "golden" as a classifying rather than qualitative adjective.

Historical epochs cannot technically be held "accountable" for their historiographic nicknames, but there is no harm in asking: when we look at people who used to produce and use poetry in early nineteenth-century Russia, what is it that casts our thoughts back to Hesiod's and Ovid's race of mythopoetic mortals said to have lived in harmony with nature and in agreement with each other, devoting their life to merrymaking and feasting? What do these two "golden" epochs—one metaphorical/real, the other literal/imagined—have in common? In neither of the worlds they describe would you find much in the way of solitude: a secluded retreat, a place to be alone. When we look at a painting titled *The Golden Age*—for instance, by Lucas Cranach the Elder (ca. 1530) or Jean-Auguste-Dominique Ingres (1862)—the first thing we notice is how crowded it is. Every figure is shown socializing with somebody or something—another human, a rabbit, a fish, or a deity. The prototypical Golden Age, much like its Russian namesake, was a busy place.

Another motif common to many depictions of the Golden Age is dance. In Cranach, its naked inhabitants encircle an apple tree in a round dance—a visual equivalent of the idea of harmony. This is not to suggest that Russian Golden Age poetry was somehow harmonious or carefree. This was, after all, an epoch in which duels and exile decided poets' fates. But in the wisdom of hindsight, Cranach's round dance now looks like the Ur-form of networking in art. Fortuitous and transhistorical as it may at first appear, this resemblance swayed me to stick to the term "Golden Age."

Our default idea of how literature operates—and, we tend to presume, always has—is akin to how one experiences the music performed at symphonic concerts. The orchestra and the audience are seated separately, the former playing, the latter listening; there is no trespassing the line between the two. The way poetry worked in the Golden Age was more like what takes place in a ballroom or on a dance floor. Here, everyone is, at least potentially, a dancer: you can try your luck and ask someone for a dance or (to jump sides) be asked for a dance and benevolently condescend. As in dance, so in poetry: here, you read, write, are written to, copy, show to others, discuss what you read, or gossip about whoever wrote it. Participation was essential. Russian literary culture of the time was, no doubt, a realm of books and journals; most poems were written in order to be printed—and many were. But a poem of note was seldom consigned to the solitude of being read alone. In the Golden Age, there was no such thing as a poem in itself. The real life of poetry began outside the book.

Like any epoch or any given moment in literary history, the Golden Age was far from monolithic. As Russian formalists show, literary history is more about fights and clashes than peaceful growth and development. Still, any efficient system has clashes and contradictions, actions and counteractions, checks and balances, wired into it. Golden Age poetry, as a network, constituted just such a system of relationships between poets, poems, and readers.

Chronologically, the Golden Age of Russian poetry falls within the space of roughly forty years, from the mid-1790s to the mid-1830s; it would be counterproductive to tie it to more specific dates. The Golden Age did not start with a datable literary landmark; rather, it was first *imagined* by literary visionaries like Nikolai Karamzin. A literary movement—to invoke a mantra of the formalists—can survive anything except its own triumph. The Golden Age of Russian poetry truly existed while it remained a project; the moment the project was realized, the age was over. As a utopia of ubiquity, the Golden Age was destined to become dystopian: the wished-for omnipresence of poetry proved to be a flood of versifying. By the mid-1820s, as many critics agreed, Russian as a poetic language had advanced to the point where writing good verses was no longer a problem—and this, in turn, turned the writing of good poems into a problem. When, for instance, the critic Petr Pletnev proposed calling his time a "Golden Age," he added the following cautionary proviso:

> In a word: here is [Zhukovsky], the first poet of our literature's *Golden Age* (if every literature must indeed have its own Golden Age). He turned poetry into the easiest and, at the same time, the most difficult of arts. For every genre, beautiful poetic forms are available; everyone nowadays can write a number of light, harmonious, even powerful lines. But whom are their works going to impress, next to the sample [of works] by all our newest poets?[16]

Of the "golden ages" in European literatures, Russian was one of the youngest. It coincided in time with what can be called a poetry boom across Europe and North America. By "boom" I mean not a grand parade of names, from Pushkin to Victor Hugo to Henry Wadsworth Longfellow. Rather, a "boom" is when poetry expands—into streets, politics, and domestic life; a boom not only of poetry as writing but also of poetry's readership or, to add here the oral and audial dimensions, of poetry's audience. Russian poetic culture of the early to mid-nineteenth century shared many poetry practices with European and American literatures: from a rich song culture, to album inscriptions, to occasional verses. The difference is that in Russia, the poetry boom *became* the Golden Age of national literature.

Scholars may give up using terms like "the Golden Age," but the historical narratives of national literatures do not yield their foundational myths lightly. Every European literature we know of has its *before* and *after*, a pivotal figure like Goethe in Germany or a golden epoch—like the Elizabethan reign in England or the age of Louis XIV in France. How different scholars approach and explain the early nineteenth-century poetry boom in their national cultures depends on its place on the timeline of literary history. When Michael Cohen in the first chapter of his recent study *The Social Lives of Poems in Nineteenth-Century America* examines occasional verses written and printed in the late eighteenth and early nineteenth century by New England peddlers, he treats them as extraliterary phenomena. Peddlers' verses, Cohen insists, were too unrefined to be considered literature, let alone poetry. The "pure" reading of poetry (the practice that Virginia Jackson has termed "lyric reading") must, according to Cohen, be kept apart from such transpoetic activities as copying or singing (in our terms, performance).[17] To rely on Perry Miller's eponymous anthology, in the early nineteenth century, the Golden Age of American literature was still ahead; hence, the culture of broadsides and scrapbooks insightfully analyzed in Cohen's book appertains to "preliterary" times. On the other hand, Corinne Legoy, pointing to the ubiquity of poetry in the daily life of early nineteenth-century France, calls for studying the social uses of poetry, without isolating "pure" poetry from occasional verses, songs, and the like.[18] In the French literary chronology, the poetry boom comes not *before*, as in America, but *after* the Golden Age, as a product of a mature poetic culture, not as a precursor to one.

Was it by mere chance that in Russia—unlike in France or the United States—the boom of poetry and the Golden Age of literature coincided in time? It was and it was not. It was, because it is easy to see how, as times changed, the status of the Golden Age in Russia could have been assigned to the epoch of Lev Tolstoy and Fedor Dostoevsky—as indeed, it frequently is by Western readers. (Why and how the title stayed with Pushkin and his age could be the subject of a separate study.) And it was not—because the Golden Age did not happen all by itself. It was handmade by people who saw it in the future. In 1825, surveying Russian literature of 1824—the year in which Pletnev deemed his current age a golden one—Aleksandr Bestuzhev declared that Russia had no literature at all.[19] It was yet to be built. What was to be built had to be twofold, as critics tirelessly repeated from the 1790s on: writing and reading; authorship and readership, the two inseparable halves of literary life. Pletnev's essay was a desperate plea for Russian readers to take note of the Golden Age poetry that was happening right around them. The paradox inherent in idylls, and the myth of the Golden Age *is* the ultimate idyll, is that people who live in them do not know they do. As long as our Golden Age figures felt a lack, felt the need to build—to construct a future literature and its readership; to usher in, that is, the Golden Age—then the Golden Age was (invisibly) present. As soon as the Golden Age grew visible—and Pletnev's claim was but a first sign of this coming—it slipped from the present to the past, where all Golden Ages belong by definition.

Is poetry a thing in itself (to venture a term reminiscent of Kantian metaphysics) or a thing for others, grounded in reality and usable in life? No two opinions on this could differ more than those expressed by Goethe and John Stuart Mill in the period covered by this study. Goethe's is practical and down-to-earth: "All my poems are occasional poems [*Gelegenheitsgedichte*], suggested by real life, and having therein a firm foundation."[20] By contrast, Mill, writing in 1833 of the "poet's utter unconsciousness of a listener," removed other people from the equation entirely: "Poetry is feeling, confessing itself to itself in moments of solitude."[21] On the one hand, in the Golden Age, Russian poetry's "solitude" was actually quite loud and crowded; on the other, it was Pushkin who, in a letter to Zhukovsky, declared that the aim of poetry was poetry.[22] Our task as literary historians is not to choose or, worse, defend this or that position, but to examine their mutual dynamics. No definition of poetry, whether by Goethe, Pushkin, or Mill, can be accounted for other than in conjunction with their multiple alternatives. To study a poem historically is to relate what it says to what it does—its properties as a stand-alone text to its different purposes and uses.

PART I

Functions and Uses

1

Lyric as Speech Act and Literary Fact

One day in the late 1860s, Varvara Olenina made the following entry in her notebook:

An anecdote, humorous but also true to life. The loving wife of a state official once embroidered a fire screen for His Majesty Alexander I, adding a poem to her beautiful gift:

Я шью овцу
Отечества отцу.
От сих причин,
Чтоб мужу дали чин.

[I embroider [this] sheep [the screen's pattern], / For the father of the Fatherland, / For the reason that / My husband be given a rank.]

His Majesty, in return, sent her a lovely gift, but ordered that two lines of verse be appended to it:

Отечества Отец
Не дает чинов для овец.

[The Father of the Fatherland / Gives no ranks to sheep].[1]

Leaving aside the obvious fact of this little narrative's status as pure (didactic) fiction meant to celebrate the wit and wisdom of the emperor of Russia, two sets of questions suggest themselves. Some will pertain to the gift's inherent meaning. Why, for instance, did the embroideress choose to represent, of all animals, a sheep? One plausible explanation will have to do with the symbolism of the good shepherd and the loyal flock; another might point to the humorous rhyme *ovtsu-otsu, otets-ovets*. And so on.

The other questions will concern the situational meaning of the art involved. No historian (even if pursuing a narrow focus—say, the history of royal fireplace appurtenances) will likely ignore the fact that, as the story goes, the needlework presented to His Majesty came accompanied by a poem declaring unequivocally the practical interest behind the whole affair. In other words, the screen with a sheep on it must be studied in context—in tandem with its verbal companion piece. The variety of questions that may be asked about context knows no limits. We are entitled to know why the emperor, having accepted the embroidered screen and even reciprocated with a gift, refused to follow up with precisely the step the sheep's giver had hoped he would take. Did the anecdote mean that, when it came to promotions, Alexander I was incorruptible, or that shallow materialism never pays? More broadly, what rules and games, of ethics and semantics, defined the communication, in verse, between subject and sovereign, men and women, or among friends in early nineteenth-century Russia? This second series of questions concerns contextual meanings—in other words, it involves pragmatics.

The term *pragmatics*, applied to poetry in this study, has its own history of usage. The related *pragmatism, pragmatist,* and *pragmatic* recall the philosophical debates that took place in the United States at the turn of the nineteenth to twentieth century. In the second of a series of lectures titled "Pragmatism: A New Name for Some Old Ways of Thinking," delivered at the Lowell Institute (Boston) in 1906, William James offered the following historical sketch:

> The term is derived from the same Greek word πρᾶγμα, meaning action, from which our words "practice" and "practical" come. It was first introduced into philosophy by Mr. Charles Peirce in 1878. In an article entitled "How to Make Our Ideas Clear," in the *Popular Science Monthly* for January of that year Mr. Peirce, after pointing out that our beliefs are really rules for action, said that, to develop a thought's meaning, we need only determine what conduct it is fitted to produce: that conduct is for us its sole significance.[2]

Pragmatism, as understood by Peirce and James, set a new—operational—criterion of truth. "Is the world one or many?—fated or free?—material or spiritual?" Pragmatism, James contends, offers a tiebreaker solution to such otherwise irresolvable metaphysical debates. "The pragmatic method," James notes, "is to try to interpret each notion by tracing its respective practical consequences. What difference would it practically make to any one if this notion rather than that notion were true? If no practical difference whatever can be traced, then the alternatives mean practically the same thing, and all dispute is idle."[3]

Is the world one or many? Inconsequential as questions like this may be to our pursuit of truth, in the hands of a poet they can become instrumental. "It is always best to discuss things by the help of concrete examples," James announced in lecture eight of the 1906 series. "Let me read therefore some of those verses entitled 'To You' by Walt Whitman—'You' of course meaning the reader or hearer of the poem whosoever he or she may be."[4] "There exist, according to James, "two ways of taking [the poem], both useful."[5] One is a monistic way (your "you" remains intrinsically and inalienably good, for all its flaws and failures), the other a pragmatic (or pluralistic) one: "The you so glorified, to which the hymn is sung, may mean your better possibilities phenomenally taken, or the specific redemptive effects even of your failures, upon yourself or others."[6] While either way of reading Whitman's poem is "noble," James maintains, the pragmatic one "sets definite activities in us at work,"[7] in other words, factors in the effect of the poem on its reader.

Related but not identical to pragmatism are two pragmatic models of language and speech proposed in the late 1950s by Roman Jakobson and J. L. Austin. The latter's study *How to Do Things with Words* identifies a special group of utterances—"performative speech acts"—which, rather than state, narrate, or describe facts, act upon the world we inhabit, causing things to happen: ordering, inviting, swearing, or bequeathing. Performative speech acts cannot be deemed true or false; we evaluate them, rather, on the strength of their practical effect, something Austin terms "felicity."[8] The sentence "I give and bequeath" is only felicitous when (and if) the speaker's last will and testament takes effect after their death. The (in)felicity of an order is in its (un)fulfillment.

The Pragmatics of Allo-speaking

The question of whether or not the theory of speech acts is applicable to literary texts was initially posed by Austin himself in *How to Do Things with Words*. Austin thought it was not. Discussing the scope of "performative utterances"—

verbal equivalents of action—Austin restricted their power "to do things" to the here and now of the real world. When used as a line in a poem or said by an actor on the stage, his treatise says, a performative utterance will be bereft of its performative force.[9]

Austin's austerity notwithstanding, different scholars, at various times, have weighed and tested the possibility of applying his speech-act model to literary texts, most recently (and closest to our field) Jonathan Culler in his 2015 *Theory of the Lyric*. Here, Culler poses a question that has been preoccupying theorists for the last hundred years. What makes lyric speech functionally, rhetorically, and linguistically different from the way people speak in everyday life? Early on in the twentieth century, formalist poetics saw as its task studying the difference between "poetic" and "practical" language; in 1970, Viktor Shklovsky came up with a neologism that highlighted indirectness as a trait that distinguished love lyric from non-lyric speech: *inakogovorenie*, or allo-speaking. The distinction Culler foregrounds is lyric's extravagance, the special status of a lyric poem as a performative event. While Culler cautions against thinking of poetry in terms of performative—illocutionary—speech acts whose effect is always predefined by a set of linguistic and social conventions, his theory of the lyric does embrace Austin's notion of the perlocutionary: "effects such as moving readers, provoking reflection, leading them to act differently—all perlocutionary consequences that cannot be [linguistically and socially] predicted."[10] In light of this, my approach to Golden Age poetry sits well with Culler's theory.

I also agree with Culler when he cautions against conflating the performative momentum inherent in lyric poems with performance in a dramatic sense. The analytical tradition, which Culler traces back to New Criticism, encouraged students of lyric to approach a poem as if it were a fragment of a character's direct speech—even if no indication of this is given by the poem's author. Indeed, the lyric speaker is a role for the reader to jump into, rather than a dummy for us scholars to construct for the sake of our interpretive convenience. To posit the existence of a dramatic "I" whose physiognomy and current situation the reader allegedly infers from a poem's "inner voice" impoverishes the way we interact with lyric. Where I am less inclined to follow Culler is when his critique of assigning to poems this or that dramatis persona calls into question the whole idea of relating lyric texts with acts of ordinary speech. What ordinary, sane speaker, Culler asks, will address the west wind as Percy Shelley's "Ode" does? In the context of real-life speaking, such an address would sound embarrassing at least.[11]

A distinction exists, and is important to my study, between a lyric poem being associated with a theatrical mask, and the idea of relating the poem to speech acts—language being, of course, the native medium of poetry. We must be careful not to throw the baby out with the bathwater. Why can a lyric poem not be a poem *and* an act of speech all at the same time? To be fair, Shelley was hardly counting on the West Wind answering him with a nod; but someone serenading their love interest in the window might well be hoping for a response.

Neither is it easy to agree when Culler deems the language of lyric extravagance (especially evident in apostrophic poems) native to poetry, yet too embarrassing to be assimilated by the language used in ordinary life. It stands to reason that no one in their right mind would start conversing with wild winds; however, such colloquial expressions as the Russian "razrazi menia grom!" ("strike me, thunder") or the English "holy smoke!" (or, for that matter, the ordinary "oh my God!") do testify to the contrary. There are plenty of niches for the uncommon in our common speech. Of course, most of these are faded metaphors, but some of the most extravagant expressions that took root in the Russian language were seeded by the poetry of the Golden Age. These seeds did not fall by chance: linguistic gardening was listed as one of poetry's pragmatic aims.

When we say "ordinary speech," we are not necessarily characterizing it as listless or inexpressive. This particularly applies to performative speech genres, namely, utterances whose goal is not to convey information but to produce an effect: strong language, spells, prayers, or lullabies.[12] What links such verbal acts with lyric poetry is their sonic and pragmatic otherness and oddness. Here, speech as sound does more than serve as a vehicle for meaning, and the effects these speech acts are meant to achieve—to put a baby to sleep, to invoke a divinity—lie beyond the power of everyday language. We do not command our toddler to sleep, we lull her to sleep. Some things cannot be done with ordinary words; in these cases, ordinary speech becomes extraordinary.

All this, of course, does not mean my aim is to deny or obliterate the distinction between practical and poetic language. The latter is always a special, salient, conspicuous, self-conscious, and defamiliarized type of speech—a buskin, a stage, an elevation. Yet I wonder if Culler's distinction between "extravagant" and "ordinary" speech does justice to the fluidity between what counted as poetry and what did not in the Russian Golden Age—the fluidity that made its poetry unique. Think of it as *extraordinary* speech: a type of speech whose otherness is perceived as (nevertheless) related to the ordinary. This perspective makes it easier to fathom how lyric speech could be used in ordinary situations without ceasing to be lyric.

Culler's theory of the lyric embraces the performative element and foregrounds lyric as act rather than representation. Culler is nevertheless apprehensive of the idea of linking or likening lyric poems to ordinary speech precisely because his theory comes close to the borderline between the two. At stake, in his view, is the lyric's literary status. Each lyric poem, by the very virtue of its existence as such, constitutes an event. An ordinary speech act like "please join us for dinner" is voided the moment the invitation is (or is not) accepted. The lyric performance, by contrast, is anything but ordinary or fleeting; it "succeeds as it acts iterably through repeated readings, makes itself memorable."[13] "The extravagance of poetry," Culler writes, "includes its aspiration to what theorists since classical times have called the 'sublime.'"[14]

Extravagance—uncommonness, salience, sublimity—are indeed frequent concomitants of lyric; but to suggest it as a sine qua non of a lyric poem would mean to consign lyric to an essentialist definition. In the epoch under discussion, lyric extravagance was a tenet of only one ("archaist") camp on the map of contemporary literary struggles. Not that early nineteenth-century poets lacked fascination with the sublime, but their newly developed interest gravitated toward the other side of the spectrum: to test and question the boundaries between poetic enunciation and functional speech act. How to do little things with verse? What does it take for a poem to work as an everyday speech act, or for a speech act to suddenly function as a poem? Consideration of these questions, like others regarding the liminal states between poetry and speech, literature and practical life, may benefit from recourse to Jakobson's model of language and its functions, and Yuri Tynianov's notion of the literary fact.

There exist, among the multitude of verbal utterances, some that manage to capture our attention precisely as utterances, irrespective of the information they transmit. Thus, "I like Ike," the one-liner used during the 1952 presidential campaign, is memorable regardless of whom you were inclined to vote for. To account for such utterances, Jakobson in a 1958 talk posited the existence of the "poetic" function of language. That "I like Ike" fulfills the poetic function, Jakobson specifies, does not yet make it a poem. Which raises the question, what would? Two possible ways of addressing this have been suggested. Jakobson's answer is text-internal: for a linguistic utterance to become a poem, the poetic function must be dominant. Tynianov's answer is contextual: literature evolves by redefining the facts of language as literary facts.[15] In either case, it is taken for granted that, to become a poem or a literary fact, facts of speech must transcend their mundane linguistic duties. Now, consider changing "fact" to "act," and you discover a whole family of cases in which a text in verse functioned both as a poem—a full-fledged lyric act— and as a speech act, depending on the pragmatic situation. The extravagance of gastronomic detail in Gavriil Derzhavin's "Invitation to Dinner" ("Priglashenie k obedu," published in 1798) may be explained by the fact that the poem was initially written on the occasion of a dinner held at Derzhavin's home in 1795—presumably, to serve as an actual invitation, complete with menu preview;[16] by the same token, Ivan Dolgorukov's last will and testament was written in verse, and included a stipulation that this ultimate poem be performed in its author/testator's dying hour.[17] Eccentric as these two cases may appear, they lay bare the central tendency of the age, in which a felicitous poem could be felicitous on two fronts, poetic and pragmatic. In this study, I call this phenomenon the dual felicity of verse.

Live Address and Dual Felicity

Why attend to the *dual* felicity of texts like "Invitation to Dinner" if, as we know, Derzhavin's lavish still life in verse became deservedly well-known as a poem? Why bother with its prior incarnation as a menu? The question is legitimate and merits consideration. Undeniably, every poem, by virtue of being conceived as one, is born with a plan of literary immortality. "Not only did he like to compare himself to Ovid," Ivan Liprandi wrote in his reminiscence of Alexander Pushkin's early years, "he also loved it when someone praised his works and recited for him a line or two thereof."[18]

Young Pushkin, indeed, took solace (even pride) in sharing an exile destination with Ovid; he got into the habit of bowing to "Ovid's lyre" and, in 1821, authored an epistle to him. "Perhaps, then, one should say that literary discourse achieves felicity only insofar as it is published, received as literature, disseminated, inscribed in memory, and repeated by others in acts of reading," suggests Jonathan Culler, noting how many poets, across the long history of the lyric, have laid claim to equaling Sappho, Ovid, or Nicolas Boileau-Despréaux in fame.[19] But on the other hand, Pushkin also addressed poems to Nikolai Gnedich, Anna Kern, or Count Khvostov—people who, as he counted on, would read his (their) poem and, differently in each case, respond to it.

A response, a plea for a response, its possibility or denial—this alone justifies looking into that other, short-run felicity of poetry. To return to Derzhavin: instead of the sonorously exotic "kaimak [a scalded cream] and borsht," the original, what's-on-the-table version of the "Invitation" had indicated the more down-to-earth "beef and cabbage soup" (*goviadina i shchi*); more importantly, one particularly illustrious invitee, Prince Platon Zubov, at the time Catherine's favorite, failed to show, in his "regrets" note citing the urgency of remaining by the empress's side. In response, the final stanza in Derzhavin's poem commends, tongue-in-cheek, (unnamed) Zubov's virtuous restraint from food. Thus, Zubov's no-show to Derzhavin's dinner was incorporated, as Derzhavin's counter-response, into his "Invitation to Dinner." To put it in terms of pragmatics, the infelicity of a quotidian speech act echoed as a felicitous poetic act. Dual felicity, then, is hardly inconsequential to poetics. To have a full view of poetry's eternal self, we must account for its flip side: selfish and momentary felicity.

We have been taught to imagine lyric poems as monolithically monological. Philosophically, this idea has been espoused by Mikhail Bakhtin on the one hand (with one possible caveat brought to our attention by Stephanie Sandler in her *Distant Pleasures: Alexander Pushkin and the Writing of Exile*[20]), and the current of thought known as New Criticism on the other.[21] But such an assumption could only result from an examination of poetry in isolation from its uses. A long-standing critical tradition ascribes the expressiveness of lyric exclusively to the speaking subject. An alternative theory is found in Yuri Tynianov's 1927 study of ode in relation to oratory. Rather than being intrinsic to the poet as a person or persona, Tynianov suggests, the qualities we tend to perceive as "expressive" or "subjective," including the inimitable "intonation" of a verse, depend on the *genre* of speech and the *listener* implied thereby. Konstantin Batiushkov's erotic poems, for instance, speak not of the author's interest in the subject but of his search for a new poetic language (as enounced, Tynianov reminds us, in Batiushkov's speech "On the Influence of Light Poetry on Language"); likewise, "sentimental" themes were introduced not under the pressure of sentiments and emotions, but in order to shift poetry's orientation toward a "'personal' (conversational or melodious) intonation capable of revitalizing the live address of poetic discourse, thus foregrounding its relatedness to common speech and, through it, to extra-literary events (salons); this was the new track literature had to swerve into, given the necrosis of the odic, oratorical orientation previously related to celebratory speeches and, through them, to extraliterary events, in this case official celebrations."²²

The shift Tynianov refers to here should not be mistaken for a depiction of poetry's progress from conventionality to increasing "realism." What Tynianov defines as the "live address of poetic discourse" (*zhivoi adres poeticheskogo slova*) is, first and foremost, a function, a tendency ingrained in "conversational and melodious" genres of speech. But Tynianov never asks what happens next—after the poem has been "dispatched," reaching (or failing to reach) its living addressee. Did it accomplish what it was meant to? What used to happen upon receipt? Did the receipt of your poem entail a response (a reciprocal verse, a thank-you note, a benevolent glance) on the part of the person your verse addressed? All these, of course, are canonical questions of pragmatics.

In terms of infrastructure, Golden Age poetry hinged, to no small degree, on literary albums and postal correspondence. Albums and letters are resonant mediums. Mailed off with a letter, or inscribed in a hostess's album, a poem to a live address envisaged a live reaction to it, and itself often constituted a reaction to something else. In this sense, Russian lyric could be described, pace Bakhtin, as an essentially dialogic genre of speech. A madrigal was, quite often, a gallant response to a hostess gesturing toward her album; an epistle in verse, a response to a verse epistle to you. Mutual courtesies of this sort were sometimes begrudged as a nuisance, but hardly ever neglected. When, on 7 September 1833, passing through Kazan, Pushkin paid a visit to Karl Fuchs, the latter's wife, Aleksandra, herself a poet, showed him her album covered in poems, among them one recently inscribed by Evgeny Baratynsky. In a letter written five days later, Pushkin (expert nonpareil in the rules of album courtesy) informed his wife with a mix of relief and surprise: "Baratynsky wrote her a verse, extolling, with astounding shamelessness, her beauty and talent. Sure as I was that I would be forced to inscribe a poem to her, God had mercy on me; but she took down my address, and is threatening correspondence and a visit to P[eters]B[urg], on which I congratulate you as well."²³

In the context of familiar correspondence, it was as imperative to reciprocate a live-address poem in kind as it was a letter with a letter. Late in 1832, Pushkin began writing "To Gnedich" ("Gnedichu"), a poem designed to serve as his "poetic manifesto"²⁴ and at the same time also as a response to Nikolai Gnedich's just-published "To A. S. Pushkin, Upon Reading His *Tale of Tsar Saltan*, etc." ("A. S. Pushkinu, po prochtenii skazki ego o tsare Saltane i proch").

That Pushkin left his epistle unfinished was, as Vadim Vatsuro points out, simply because, early in 1833, Gnedich died.[25] From today's point of view, an epistle in verse is first and foremost a poem masquerading as a letter; but to Pushkin, his "To Gnedich" was, no less vitally, an act of real communication. Here, the logic of dialogic correspondence seems to have overridden that of literature "proper." Why keep up a correspondence if there is no one to respond?

In "Ode as an Oratorical Genre," Tynianov contrasts the speech genres, equipped as they are with a live address, to rhetorically oriented (and loud) odes—the genre of lyric that, Tynianov argues, had been predominant in eighteenth-century Russian literature. This juxtaposition, however, should not blind us to the fact that celebratory odes, in their own way, more often than not used to be addressed to a living person: a newborn or newly crowned monarch, or a commander fresh from his latest victory in war. An ode-writer (*odopisets*) was also entitled to a response, which often, though by no means invariably, took the form of a gift. For one of his odes, Pavel Golenishchev-Kutuzov was awarded a colonelcy and a golden snuffbox; Mikhail Lomonosov, the unheard sum of 2,000 rubles—enough to pay off all his debts; Derzhavin, in the thirty-plus years of his fame, was known to have landed a veritable collection of royal snuffboxes and finger rings.

A method devised by the resourceful Aleksandr Suvorov, Russia's most famous field marshal, attests to the importance attached in his day to acknowledging a congratulatory ode. Every new victory he won drew a fresh bombardment of odes. With no budget for snuffboxes or finger rings to repay them all, Suvorov employed an eloquent staffer ("my little Demosthenes," as he called him) whose primary job was to respond to odes with letters of acknowledgment.[26]

The live address was thus a crucial component of lyric poetry in both ages. The difference Tynianov stresses was in the vector, the directionality of the address. Even while the odic writer claims a sublime position within the world of the poem (e.g., on the top of mount Parnassus), in social space oratorically oriented poetry was directed, so to speak, bottom-up: from me thy subject to Thee my sovereign. As poetry moves into the Golden Age, the live address palpably changes course. Formerly ascending, the vector of speech becomes increasing horizontal: from equal to equal, friend to friend, peer to peer or, in cases of diatribes and epigrams, foe to foe.

The live address criterion could be used as a critical tool. Whether your poem succeeds as a poem is contingent on whether it works—attains its goal, *does* things—as a speech act, and vice versa. Such, for instance, was how Petr Viazemsky, in a notebook entry from 1831, substantiated his critique of Pushkin's jingoistic diatribe "To the Slanderers of Russia" ("Klevetnikam Rossii"). The eponymous "slanderers," whom Pushkin addresses in the second person plural, were not Russia's enemies in the abstract but rather historically specific deputies of the French parliament who had officially condemned the empire's brutal suppression of the Polish uprising of 1830. In making his case, Viazemsky proceeds from the premise that no French deputy is likely to read Russian. In other words, vis-à-vis its live address, "To the Slanderers" is patently infelicitous. This makes the whole poem ethically dubious (this was, we should keep in mind, also the golden age of calling and being called out to duels): Pushkin's challenge is ungentlemanly, Viazemsky concludes, precisely because his opponents are unable to challenge *him*: "He is aware of the fact that [the French deputies] will be unable to read his poem, and will not, therefore, be able to respond. . . . And should these 'people's tribunes' ever find out about Pushkin's poem and his sublime talent, their answer to him would be short and plain: we hate, or, better, despise you all because, in Russia, a poet of your stature is not ashamed of writing and publishing a poem like yours."[27] (Not to exonerate Pushkin, but merely to give *him* a chance to defend his honor: his irate ode "To the Slanderers" *was* translated into French by Elizaveta Khitrovo and others, which fact, at least technically, gave them an option to respond.[28])

Unless your poem is good enough as a poem, it will hardly succeed as a speech act. As it happened, fifteen years before Viazemsky used his ad hominem argument to disavow Pushkin's invective, his own poem, addressed to his wife, Vera Viazemskaya, incurred a somewhat similar criticism from Konstantin Batiushkov. Titled "To My Soulmate" ("K podruge"), Viazemsky's 1815 epistle in verse contrasts the rustic joys of his ancestral home to the vanity and pomp of city life.

Простись с блестящим светом,
Приди с своим поэтом,
Приди под кров родной,
Под кров уединенный,
Счастливый и простой,
Где счастье неизменно
И дружбой крыл лишенно
Нас угостит с тобой![29]

[Take leave of brilliant society, / Come, together with [me,] your poet, / Come [live] under the ancestral roof, / Under the secluded roof, / Happy and simple, / Where constant happiness, / Deprived of its wings by friendship, / Shall entertain us both!]

Upon finishing the poem, Viazemsky, as was customary in the Golden Age, sent handwritten copies to his friends, asking Batiushkov and Vasily Zhukovsky for comments and amendments. Each replied, Batiushkov rather harshly, particularly regarding the passage just cited: "'Oh my beloved soulmate.' ... Were you calling me under your roof, stringing together such a quantity of epithets in the course of the conversation,—believe me, I would never come. Correct this, for God's sake! Tell your imagination that 'ancestral roof' says it all, what does 'secluded' and 'simple' add to it? And then, 'happy'; and then, as if 'happy' were not enough, 'constant happiness'! Replace this with depictive [*zhivopisnye*, or 'scenic'] verses."[30]

This is, once more, an *ad feminam* (or perhaps *ad pragmaticam*) argument. In order to expose what he sees as flaws in Viazemsky's epistle, Batiushkov assumes the viewpoint of its live addressee. His counterfactual argument—were your invitation-verse addressed to me, I would not come—deems Viazemsky's poem infelicitous exactly as a speech act. Too many epithets will oversell your case; do not just praise your home, Batiushkov advises, *depict* it. Symptomatically of the Golden Age, Batiushkov's critique of Viazemsky's verse conflates pragmatics (will she respond as hoped?) and poetics (change your verse, and she may). A key word in Batiushkov's assessment is *conversation*. An agglomeration of epithets and rhetorical repetitions was appropriate in an ode. Love lyric, to return to Tynianov's study quoted above, is oriented "towards 'personal' (conversational or melodious) intonation." Indeed, to get a sense of Batiushkov's critique, we should pause to take another look at Yuri Tynianov's theory of literary evolution.

Literary Orientation and Literature's Environment

During the fifteen years of their existence as a group, Russian formalist theorists kept coming up with terms and concepts to match the new problems and challenges they faced. Some of the best-known of these—*fabula* and *siuzhet* (a distinction between diegetic and discursive sequencing of narrative events), defamiliarization (*ostrannenie*),[31] and *device*—emerged relatively early. Tynianov's *orientation* was a late addition, born in the course of—and in response to—bitter political/academic debates around formalism as a method and a school of thought. From 1923 on, formalist theoretical positions were besieged, on the one flank, by critics and politicians of the Marxist camp and, on the other, by stand-alone thinkers like Mikhail Bakhtin and Boris Engelgardt. The stock charge was that formalism underrated the social stratum of literature—its links with reality and the "undeniable" fact that works of art are reflections of life.

The reaction, on the formalist side, was twofold. When given the floor during a public debate, or a chance to respond in print, formalist scholars would do their best to pinpoint how this or that aspect of their theories had been misunderstood or misrepresented, and attempt to clarify the original intent and meaning of terms used in formalist poetics.[32] One "advantage" of being put on the sociopolitical defensive was the extra impetus it provided to substantiate issues, to give extra thought to problems so insistently thrown at formalists by others. Each in his own way, Boris Eikhenbaum and Yuri Tynianov took on the "art and reality" question as scholars must—not as a poisoned polemical arrow, but as an interesting theoretical challenge. If, indeed, such a thing as "real life" exists, it must somehow dovetail with literature and literary evolution. If so, we must figure it out.

There was another—internal—reason to give reality a second thought. Around the mid-1920s the Sturm-und-Drang period in the formalist movement was coming to a close. Earlier on, formalism had marched under the banner of independence. In its view, literature was an autonomous organism or system, not a manifestation of social thought (as late nineteenth-century criticism, in particular, had insisted) or socioeconomic conditions (as Marxist dogma would have it). A literary work was more than the sum total of its author's ideas, ergo, to study literature, it was not enough to dabble in generalities; it took knowing how *literature* worked. The very fact that two leading Marxist ideologists—Leon Trotsky in 1923 and Anatoly Lunacharsky in 1924—decried in print the formalist movement's claim to independence in a sense signaled that that independence had been (temporarily) won. Perhaps now was the time for formalism to interrogate the interface between literature and life.

Unwilling to either consign literature to life, or to insist, as Shklovsky had at the dawn of formalism, on the immanence of literary studies, Eikhenbaum and Tynianov now contemplated the question of where and how literature and life may, indeed, cohere. The first problem on this front was how to avoid the classic trap of mimesis—the temptation of relating art to life analogically, as it were. There should be a way of tackling questions of art without wondering what it reflects, represents, or manifests. Eikhenbaum's idea of a workable interface—a buffer zone—between literature and reality was what he termed "literature's everyday environment" (*literaturnyi byt*): a network of period-specific infrastructures, from literary circles and salons to journals, the historical examination of which, Eikhenbaum believed, should clarify for us the interdependence between literary texts on the one hand and their social functioning on the other. The approach proved productive. Before the debate *about* formalism descended into a state-backed campaign *against* it, Eikhenbaum's disciples managed to publish a number of studies on literature's social environment, specifically in the epoch this book examines; subsequent analyses of literary institutions, most recently Joe Peschio's *The Poetics of Impudence and Intimacy in the Age of Pushkin*, have taken up the tool kit formalists had been commanded to discard.[33]

This brings us to Tynianov's proposition. Like Eikhenbaum's *literaturnyi byt*, Tynianov's *ustanovka* (orientation) addressed the give-and-take between literature and life. The latter of the two, however, was less of a believer in literary institutions and infrastructures. Literary systems—a work, a genre, a movement—correlate with social reality, Tynianov suggests, through the agency of speech. The way we speak is hardly ever neutral. We sound different at a rally, behind a pulpit, or in a parlor, boudoir, or nursery. While no literary system can ever be treated as a subsystem (or "superstructure") of a religious, political, or other ideology, the historian of literature must reckon with the existence of different speech genres privileged within this or that ideological framework. Here is where the concept of "orientation" comes in. According to Tynianov, literary genres differed depending on what genre of extraliterary speech and what kind of communicative situation each tended to evoke (were *oriented toward*).

What made the concept of orientation particularly important for Tynianov was its usefulness in exposing the mechanisms of literary evolution. How did it happen that, on the cusp of the nineteenth century, Russian poetry, which had previously privileged thundering imagery and larger-than-life subject matter, was upended by its stylistic opposite—the domestic-sounding epistles and melodic elegies peculiar to the Golden Age? In a series of articles Tynianov explained this turn using the concept of literary orientation.[34] The ode—the dominant genre of eighteenth-century poetry—was oriented toward oratory as a speech genre. Oral by their very name, oratorical speeches are public and stentorian, hence the articulatory and rhetorical saliency of odes.³⁵ But in the formalist view, no dominant orientation remains dominant forever; its very dominance is what brings it down eventually. The engine of literary evolution is powered by two currents: innovation and fatigue. Once odes, whose main asset, or built-in felicity, was to be perceived as sublime and elevated speech, grew into a set standard of poetic devices routinely employed to achieve this felicity, their exuberance and vigor began "wearing off" (*iznosilas'*, as Tynianov puts it), and were increasingly perceived as empty bombast. At the turn of the centuries, as Tynianov shows, a "shift" (*smena*) in orientation occurred—from the "worn off" oratory to intimacy (*kamernaia ustanovka*).

Not that poets ceased celebrating occasions, such as coronations, with apposite verse contributions; the shift was in literary values and generic attributes. As Luba Golburt shows in *The First Epoch: The Eighteenth Century and the Russian Cultural Imagination*, turn-of-the-century ode did not simply erode but rather changed by integrating non-odic elements into its structure: elegiac, sentimental, personal attitudes were sneaking into what previously was the sublime-only terrain of celebratory ode.³⁶ Court poetry in general found a new home base. In the early nineteenth century, due to Alexander I's lack of interest, court poetry was relegated to the so-called "small courts" (*malye dvory*)—most notably, to that of the Dowager Empress Maria Fedorovna and, later on, *le petit cour* of Grand Duchess Alexandra Fedorovna, who cultivated domesticity, not odic grandiosity, at their courts.³⁷

Even before that, the decline of the odic principle began with a split within the odic form. Hyperbolic and emblematic, the culture of court jubilations (of which an appropriate ode was a vital component) required that the celebrated one be praised, literally, to the sky. From the day of her coronation in 1762, for instance, Catherine II had been allegorized as "Minerva Triumphant"—a sobriquet that was echoed, sometimes ironically, in poems (including Nikolai Karamzin's, of which more later). Catherine, whose carefully crafted self-image increasingly shifted away from royal grandeur, is known to have had as little patience for odes "packed with names of fabled deities" as she did for their festive entourage: decorative design featuring, in her words, "the Janus Temple and Bacchus Temple, a Temple to Who-Knows-What-Devil, all these foolish, intolerable allegories of enormous size, fruit of extraordinary efforts to produce something senseless."³⁸ This explains, in the view of modern historians and in the eye of contemporary observers, the sudden success (with the empress as well as with the public) of Derzhavin's 1782 "Felitsa."[39] This was an ode and anti-ode at once. In terms of pragmatics, "Felitsa" was a proper ode glorifying Catherine II; its themes and tone, on the other hand, were anything but odic: personal, tempered with self-irony, suave, and savvy.[40] Much like Batiushkov wished Viazemsky had done in addressing his soulmate, Derzhavin, instead of hymning his empress, engaged her in a conversation.[41] If Derzhavin's "Felitsa" was, indeed, the first step in literature's evolution from the epoch of odes toward the Golden Age, this was an evolution from above.

This shift, to return to Eikhenbaum's model, was also an institutional and infrastructural one. As William Mills Todd III describes it, "instead of a subservient relationship to his patron, the writer now enjoyed by convention a position of social and cultural equality with his (or her, we may now add) immediate audience, and, indeed, the roles of addressers and addressees ideally coalesced in this institutionalization of literature."[42] They did, but the coalescence, ideal in theory, was not fully carried through. In fact, patronage continued to coexist with the network of "familiar associations" or, to put it more accurately, "familiar associations" were not always free from the notion of hierarchy (Aleksei Olenin's position toward Ivan Krylov and Nikolai Gnedich, say, can be described as "familiar patronage"). What *had* changed was the prevalent mode of poetic address. Whereas formerly, the address worthy of a poet was supposed to ascend along the vertical axis—from here to divinity, to the hero or monarch, this universal verticality making poetry inherently public—now poets tended to be conversing with their readers and addressees in horizontal intimacy, which radically changed the relationship of poetry and the reading public.

This was not a development many saw coming, and some found it difficult to stomach when it did. In 1818, Zhukovsky, whose wartime "Bard in the Camp of Russian Warriors" had already earned him a lifelong pension from the emperor, wrote (or, rather, freely translated from Alemannic) "The Summer Evening" ("Letnii vecher")—a picturesque ballad that flaunted a folkloric, childlike diction. Three years later, when the poem appeared in the widely read *Syn otechestva* (Son of the fatherland), Viazemsky, himself ambivalent about the poetic merits of Zhukovsky's pastorale, had serious misgivings about a reaction it might cause among the public. "What does the crowd [*tolpa*] think [poetry is for]?" Viazemsky asks rhetorically. To appreciate the caustic answer he then provides, it should be kept in mind that, in imperial Russia, the number of horses a functionary was allowed to put in front of a carriage was governed by the owner's rank.

They envision poetry by ranks. You begin by riding a carriage-and-pair; then, a coach-and-four, still later, a coach-and-six. What they are not able to understand is that one horse can sometimes be worth six harness horses. "How is it," they say, "that [Zhukovsky], who in the past used to write odes and poems addressed to the Most Radiant prince [*svetleishemu*], and was even entrusted the honor of addressing, in verse, the Most Devout, All-Powerful Monarch, has now lapsed into writing verselets about the dear little sun [*solnyshko*]: "Even the dear little sun can be ill-fated: / Never does it get along with its son" [i.e., the moon]. "It's like being a priest one day, a deacon the next," [people think].[43]

Such a change would, of course, be quite a demotion, a career nosedive. Zhukovsky's swing from writing poems like his 1815 "Epistle to Emperor Alexander" ("Poslanie k imperatoru Aleksandru") to "fooling around," as Viazemsky calls it elsewhere in his letter, was an act of downshifting, even if the "dear little sun" in the poem did allegorize the dowager empress.[44] The overwhelming (even for Viazemsky) intimacy of a poem whose lexis was colored by vernacular Russian and whose stylistic locus was a nursery rather than a throne room could bewilder the public in precisely the way that Viazemsky feared. Why publish nursery nonsense? What happens in familiar space must stay in familiar space.

New Poetry: Topography and Languages

Contemporary observers found one aspect of this shift especially intriguing: changes in what might be called the pragmatic topography of poetry. The newfound intimate (literary, "chamber") orientation (*kamernaia ustanovka*) entailed not just new poetic forms but, quite literally, new chambers for poetry to move in. Lomonosov's odes required resonant halls, but the conversational lyric now migrated from public to social and domestic spaces. Writing in the early 1820s, Petr Pletnev linked this process with poetry's newfound propensity to engage its readers and listeners in a semblance of conversation.

> The all-embracing Lomonosov, valiant Petrov, inimitable Derzhavin have enriched our poetry with their lofty, perhaps unique works, but failed to conquer [our] self-willed language. Everyone admired [those] poets, but only a few read their poems. It took Dmitriev's genteel and playful muse [for poetry] to be accepted in everyone's rooms [*kabinety*]. Inveterate literati, idle swanks, demi-French ladies [*polu-frantsuzhenki zhenshchiny*]—everyone started conversing

with her. Around that time two persons appeared that came to master the language of poetry perfectly.... I am talking of Zhukovsky and Batiushkov.[45]

What Pletnev must have meant by *kabinety* were studies and parlors—private spaces to which visitors were admitted on social calls. And when he refers to "demi-French ladies," he means the enlightened Russian hostesses of such premises who, indeed, preferred to converse and read in French.

How to do things with verse? Dmitriev's "genteel muse," according to Pletnev, had already managed to change poetry's very habitat and the social demography of its users during the 1790s. Pletnev's account was, in part, wishful thinking. Two years after this fragment was published, in his letter to Countess Sofia Sollogub published in the *Severnye tsvety na 1825 god* (Northern flowers for 1825), Pletnev tried to convince his addressee and the Russian female readership at large that Russian poetry could replace their "beloved Lamartine" in their parlors (this was the very letter in which Pletnev proclaimed that Russian poetry was experiencing its Golden Age). In 1825, as in the 1790s, the contested issue remained the linguistic preferences of the Russian reading public.

The linguistic landscape available to educated (especially urban) nobility in early nineteenth-century Russia is routinely described as Russian-French bilingualism.[46] At the same time, it is important to keep in mind the presence in this landscape of a third language, namely Church Slavonic, which was used in church services and religious texts. The presence of a language does not always mean that everyone has command of it. Not everyone understood Church Slavonic, but the language, or rather its remnants, had been salient for poetry ever since Lomonosov had decreed that the sublimity of the high style, especially in odes, required as many borrowings from Church Slavonic as the poet could manage, as the language was elevated by its very nature. Despite a number of mid-eighteenth-century attempts on the part of Lomonosov's main rival Aleksandr Sumarokov and his followers to institute a literary language based on the "speech of polite society," the Lomonosovian axiological scale remained mainly intact until the end of the century. This, to believe Pletnev, was good for poetry, yet less so for the reading public.

In the 1790s, Karamzin approached the problem from the opposite end. He found it hard to imagine how the "speech of polite society" could aid instituting the literary language, while the members of polite society, in fact, used mainly French, not Russian, when socializing with each other. It is literature that ought to create language, not the other way around. The writers' task thus became to turn Russian into an idiom rich, light, and flexible enough to accommodate social discourse, and for the Russian language to, if not replace, then at least compete with French as both a society language and the language of reading. In Russia, despite selfless publishing endeavors on the part of eighteenth-century enlighteners like Karamzin's mentor Nikolai Novikov, the reputation of French remained that of the language one *reads* in, both for fun and for intellectual purposes. As a Russian writer and a publisher, Karamzin was keenly interested in educated readers. But to get them to read in Russian, it was not enough to satirize Russian nobles' Gallomania (a commonplace of comedy and journalism since the mid-century); on the contrary, this readable and sociable Russian had to become "a new French," that is, to shoulder the tasks of a literary language.[47]

Karamzin's project had not only its opponents but also its skeptics. No one doubted that the Russian language was capable of producing sublime oratory, but the notion that Russian poetry could be used to produce a perfect language, suave and nuanced enough to vie with French, while intriguing to many, struck others as a feat of linguistic engineering well-nigh impossible, as Filipp Vigel' describes in his memoir: "It seemed to me that, between the boring ponderous language of our Church and [odic] poetry, and the ugly language spoken by our simple folk, lay an immeasurable empty space, and in the middle of this space, like a barely visible speck stood Karamzin. What prose, what poems could there be, I thought; what is there to discuss at all?"[48]

Champions of Karamzin's endeavor were no less aware of the potential pitfalls. To serve as a literary language, to become the new lingua franca of polite society, the new Russian would have to be embraced and accepted by women—those whom Pletnev somewhat flippantly calls "demi-French," and their young daughters whose ears it was the mothers' duty to protect.[49] To these ears, the Russian of the street sounded vulgar, and its liturgical brother Slavonic barely comprehensible. Would-be literary Russian had to learn to navigate between the Scylla of coarseness and the Charybdis of boredom. This is how Vigel' summed it up, using, again, the spatial metaphor of middle ground:

> Before [Dmitriev], men and women of society had no habit of reading Russian verse, and those who did had no understanding of it. There was no middle: on the one hand, Lomonosov and Derzhavin, on the other, Maikov and Barkov; either the ecstatic and bombastic or the vulgar and obscene; the ode "God" ["Bog"], or else "Elisei, or Bacchus Annoyed" ["Elisei, ili razdrazhennyi Vakkh"]. . . . [Dmitriev's] "Fashionable Wife" ["Modnaia zhena"], "Castles in the Air" ["Vozdushnye zamki"], and even his many songs were what ladies began learning by

heart. He brought his muse down from the unattainable heights, but set her well above the putrid swamp in which the likes of Pankratii Sumarokov composed their works. In other words, he introduced her to drawing rooms.[50]

Both Pletnev's and Vigel's stories of Dmitriev's career are essentially success stories, the type of narrative that a historian finds suspicious by nature. But what Vigel's description, perhaps inadvertently, reveals is that it was, more specifically, the story of a successful downshifting.[51] It is important for us to keep in mind the risk run by Karamzin, his friend Dmitriev, and like-minded writers in taking poetry into a registerial nosedive. There was always the danger that, rather than landing in living rooms, their muses would drop out of poetry altogether. It is precisely the precariousness of such a trajectory that Vigel' underscores with regard to two poems ("Ermak," 1794, and "The Liberation of Moscow" ["Osvobozhdenie Moskvy"], 1795), both singing the glory of Russia's past, that marked the takeoff of Dmitriev's poetic career: "Having asserted himself . . . in the lyric genre, it was not ineptitude [*ne ot bessiliia*] that led [Dmitriev] to what may at first appear an easier genre."[52] In many eyes, writing for the drawing rooms spelled a poet's powerlessness to handle higher realms.

The conventional wisdom of poetic pragmatics, challenged at the turn of the century, was, simply put, as vertical as the hierarchy of the empire: the higher your aim, the loftier your poetic goals, the higher will be your standing as a poet. In the wake of the odic culture that Harsha Ram characterizes as the *imperial sublime* there was a predictable political touch to this wisdom. Aleksandr Shishkov, the president of the state-sponsored Russian Academy and the head of the anti-Karamzinist camp, addressed members of the Academy in order to defend "the advantage of academic activities over private authorial pursuits," Aleksandr Turgenev informed Dmitriev in a letter dated 9 January 1820.[53] A denunciatory letter sent to the minister of internal affairs by Vasily Karazin (not to be confused with Karamzin!), another champion of poetry's loftier goals, outlines in greater detail what renders the private pursuit of literature objectionable. Poets ought to devote their efforts to manlier matters than the sighing of fairy-tale lovers, charades, seductive elegies, or album verses. Hostile toward art that does not nourish the mind with useful truths but merely serves as an "amusement" amid "domestic conversations" (*zabava domashnikh besed*), Karazin's report castigates those poets who eschewed more elevated goals, and thus shirked their civic duty.[54] The mere fact of writing for living rooms rather than on (and for) history on the grand scale betrayed a defiant attitude not inconsequential for a poet's reputation for political trustworthiness.

The question of whether the Karamzinists succeeded in attaining their sociolinguistic goals is beyond the scope of this study. One goal was certainly achieved as a result of the Karamzinist campaign: a new, conversation-oriented poetry, which, alongside its many other functions, could be (and was) used in the course of social interactions. Lamenting once again (as late as the late 1820s!) society's aversion to using Russian in socializing, Baratynsky wrote to Viazemsky apropos the latter's translation of Benjamin Constant's 1816 novel *Adolphe*:

> I feel how difficult it is to translate the genteel [*svetskii*] *Adolphe* into a language not spoken in society circles [*svet*], but we need to keep in mind that this language will eventually be spoken, and that the expressions that sound recherché today will sooner or later sound ordinary. We must not, it seems to me, be afraid of uncommon expressions. With time, these will be accepted and will enter the everyday language. Remember that those of us who speak Russian speak the Russian of Pushkin, Zhukovsky, and you—the language of poets; this means that it is we who must teach the public, not the other way around.[55]

While, in Baratynsky's view, poets do teach the public, they do so not in the moral or civic sense. More ambitiously, poetry teaches the public to communicate, to make *use* of language.

To Women, with Friendship

Apprehensions like Shishkov's and Vasily Karazin's may not have been entirely unfounded. Humility can, to recall the Russian proverb, be more defiant than hubris. When Batiushkov, a poet of genius, exclaims—speaking of his poetic self as *he*—"Alas, his talent is minor [*nichtozhen*]," what the poet is questioning is not, in fact, his talent, but our thoughtless readiness to treat lightness as insignificance. Indeed, in the same stanza Batiushkov compares his talent to a "little bee" (*pchelka*)—which might seem like a gesture of humility, if not for the contrasting trope found next to it: "He, like a little bee, cannot / Follow the intrepid flock of eagles."[56] Refusing to fly the martial airways preferred by the heraldic birds of Russia is exactly the hubris behind humility.

For the new poetry to become newly useful, its pragmatic premises had to be rethought: goals lowered, subject matter downscaled, readership re-gendered.

What must the new poet be? What is the new readership? How to build the new language of poetry? Karamzin's early—and programmatic—"Epistle to Women" ("Poslanie k zhenshchinam," 1795) poses precisely this series of questions. We would do well to take a closer look at this profoundly articulate piece, whose three thematic strands—autobiography, cultural policy, and ars poetica—interweave, offering us a useful picture of how Karamzin intended to do things with words.

To be a poet takes more than mastering versification. Being a poet calls for certain behavior, a particular sort of conduct. Karamzin's "Epistle to Women" presents the reader with three biographical snapshots of himself: as a little boy climbing a tree to impress a little village belle; at seventeen, dreaming of such military laurels as might be exchanged for a lady's kiss; and lastly, as a warrior-turned-writer. This latter step, as Karamzin describes it, sounded as unconventional in 1795 as the slogan "Make love, not war" would in 1965:

О вы, для коих я хотел врагов разить,
Не сделавших мне зла!
. . . .
Для коих после я, в войне добра не видя,
В чиновных гордецах чины возненавидя,
Вложил свой меч в ножны ("Россия, торжествуй,"—
Сказал я,—"без меня!") . . . и, вместо острой шпаги,
Взял в руки лист бумаги,
Чернильницу с пером,
Чтоб быть писателем, творцом,
Для вас, красавицы, приятным.[57]

[It was for you [o women], that I was willing to smite enemies / That had done me no harm / . . . / It was for you that, later on [in my life], seeing no good in war, / [And] having grown to hate the official proudlings and their ranks, / I sheathed my sword ("O Russia, triumph!" / I said, "Without me!") . . . and took up, instead of the sharp blade, / A sheet of paper, / An inkwell and a pen, / In order to become a writer, a creator / Pleasant to you, beauties.]

What Karamzin outlines here is akin to what behavioral scientists call choice architecture. In the period under consideration, a young nobleman like Karamzin had two standard career options: service in the military or as a state official. Neither path, in theory, precluded one from writing poetry, or from being known primarily as a poet; in practice, as recent studies show, balancing poetry and service was not an easy task for people like Ivan Dmitriev and Mikhail Murav'ev, two early champions of light poetry.[58] In Karamzin's "Epistle" and in his own life trajectory, becoming "a writer, a creator" entailed bidding farewell to arms and rejecting statesmanship. For Karamzin, to be a poet is not "also," but "instead"; his choice is a gesture, an act of civil relinquishment. Becoming "a writer, a creator" in Karamzin's sense presupposes choosing to be an independent—private—person.[59]

Karamzin's "creator" targets—or should we say creates—a very specific set of readers. His "Epistle" is a pragmatic manifesto that leaves no doubt as to his audience's demographic composition, what new poets can learn from their expected readers, and what poets can do to cater to their needs. Punctuated by the rhetorical "O you," the "Epistle" is addressed to women. Here an important peculiarity should be kept in mind. As distinct from Karamzin the boy or Karamzin the warrior, what Karamzin the writer hopes to win is not a woman's love ("Frolicsome Cupid / Has signed my resignation") but women's friendship ("Instead, I gain true friends in you," 178). Friendship with women is mutually profitable. Poets must learn compassion and charity from their female readers; women, per Karamzin, are also endowed with a unique "instinct for the truth" (*chuvstvo istiny*, 175). (In a footnote to the poem, Karamzin credits his acquaintance, theologian and physiognomist Johann Caspar Lavater, with this phrase). It is only when a lady is present that male philosophical conversations become palatable and lively:

Скажите, отчего мудрец Сократ милее
Всех прочих мудрецов? учение его
Приятнее других, приятнее, сильнее
Нас к мудрости влечет? Я знаю—оттого,
Что граций он любил, с Аспазией был дружен. (176)

[Tell me what made wise Socrates / Lovelier than other wise men? why is his teaching / More pleasant, why does it attract us to wisdom / More strongly than other [teachings]? I know: because / He loved the Graces and was friends with Aspasia.]

Reciprocally, to be of use to their women friends, poets must create a language refined and flexible enough to capture the richness and sensitivity of women's emotional worlds. "To depict for you the shades / Of happy and unhappy passions, / In a clean style, intelligible to the heart" (170)—such, in a nutshell, is the built-in pragmatic program of the "Epistle to Women." As Karamzin describes it, a successful poem is a performative act whose projected result—the sought-after felicity—would constitute a collective acknowledgment, by womankind, of the poet's endeavor. It is no longer a village girl admiring your tree-climbing skills, or a young lady rewarding your heroic service to the fatherland with a kiss; now, women acknowledge the things you as a poet can *do for them* with words. To be a writer, Karamzin proclaims, is to have your women friends say to each other:

Он, право, мил и верно переводит
Всё темное в сердцах на ясный нам язык;
Слова для тонких чувств находит! (170)

[He is truly a darling, and translates faithfully / All that is obscure about hearts into a language clear to us; / He finds words for subtle feelings!]

What should the new language of poetry be like? We touched on this issue earlier, with regard to Karamzin's language project in the light of literary evolution. To phrase it in Tynianov's terms, Karamzin's idea was to reorient poetry toward the tones and themes characteristic of a friendly conversation, in this particular case, in the form of a letter.

Я к вам хочу писать послание стихами.
Дам волю сердцу: пусть оно
С своими милыми друзьями
Что хочет говорит!
Не нужно думать мне: слова текут рекою
В беседе с тем, кого мы любим всей душою.

[I want to write my epistle to you in verse. / I'll set my heart loose: let it / Say whatever it wants / To its dear friends! / No need for me to think: words flow like a river / When you converse with someone you love with all your soul.]

Here, more clearly than anywhere else in the poem, Karamzin casts the new poetry as speech struggling out of (and with) conventional strictures. A poem, like speech in the course of a conversation, must be sincere ("let my heart speak"); impromptu ("no need to think"); natural ("flow like a river");

and—importantly—incautious ("say whatever it wants")—for what, if not a liberal-minded joke, enlivens a parlor conversation? "O Russia, triumph without me!"—the exclamation from the "Epistle" quoted earlier—is a case in point. This was, as Yuri Lotman points out, a risky, not to say challenging, phrase to include in your poem—particularly so in the initial version, which ran: "Minerva, triumph without me"—*Minerva Triumphant* being, as we recall, Catherine the Great's mythological sobriquet.[60] What renders Karamzin's unpatriotic outburst ingenious and poetry-specific is the clever use of enjambment—the technique whereby a sentence runs over the metric divide between adjacent verses. When a phrase like "O Russia, triumph" is placed, as in Karamzin's poem, at the end of a line, we read it as odic eulogy; when, having stepped over (*enjambé*) to the next verse, the sentence ends with "I said, 'without me!,'" it turns out to be a parlor witticism.

Literary values are relational. In literature, sincerity (simplicity, clarity, spontaneity—or any other item from Karamzin's wish list) is not an integral component of style but a dynamic device employed in a literary struggle. Karamzin is no exception. A clear and simple poem is only perceived as clear and simple so long as we remember that poems can easily be neither. Karamzin's enjambment would hardly work if not for odic echoes that ring in the phrase "O Russia, triumph—." In terms of Tynianov's conception of literary evolution, for a poem to strike us as artless and sincere, it must harbor the ghost of its factitious and flamboyant other.

One way to conceive of the dynamics successfully exploited by Karamzin and his movement pertains to what we might call pragmatic distance. How far from (or close to) the poem's "I" is its imagined "you"—the being (or thing, in the case of apostrophe) the poet intends to address? Needless to say, the rhetorical equipment of your poem will depend on how distant a target it is designed to reach—the eternal deity somewhere up there; or a nearby young lady with her eternal album. From the standpoint of the contemporary user, poetry had two communicative profiles, each facing an opposite direction. On the one hand, poetry could be seen as the divine language, the language spoken to (and by) gods. Thus understood, it went without saying that the language the poet spoke had to be very different from ours: formidable, forbidding, extravagant in Culler's sense of the term, and loud enough to reach the outmost ear. On the other, one could see poetry as a language in which people speak to people, no voices raised. This is where Karamzin and his followers come in.

Literary struggle, as the formalists understood it, is a seesaw—the kind of game that is never won for good. To define itself, poetry needs something to define itself *against*, and the game lasts as long as the opposite side of the plank is occupied: once you win, you lose. When, in an 1839 poem on poetry, Karolina Pavlova defines her poetic voice as a "wailful whisper, secret talking," she asserts that it is on a par with the "sonorous torrents of songs / And stately words."[61] And yet, no whisper, nor for that matter any particular decibel level, can dominate poetry forever: sooner or later, values flip. When, around 1930, Vladimir Mayakovsky conceived of a programmatic poem to be titled, tellingly, "At the Top of [My] Voice" ("Vo ves' golos"), he took care in the prologue to assure us of his opposition to whispery poetry: "I am / not used to caressing / the [maiden's] ear / with words."[62] In poetry, as on a seesaw, your relevance depends on the weight of your literary vis-à-vis.

2

Functions
How to Do Things with Verse

TYNIANOV WROTE ON THE dynamics of literary evolution: "In the epoch when a certain genre disintegrates, it shifts away from the center [of the literary system] to [its] periphery, while a new phenomenon, formed of literary trifles, floats in from the outskirts and lowlands of literature to take its place."[1] This way of describing epochal literary upheavals sounds perhaps too cataclysmic to wholly apply to what was happening at the turn of the nineteenth century in Russia. No deluge lifted trifles from outskirts and swamplands to rain them down upon the literary center. Rather, where the center was, and what counted as its periphery, had been gradually redefined as a result of incessant and invisible ideological work. Part of this involved a rethinking and reassignment of values, some of which anticipated, in its simple ingenuity, Tom Sawyer's method of whitewashing the fence. In 1794 Nikolai Karamzin published his first book, *My Trifles* (*Moi bezdelki*), a two-volume collection of poems and prose works, not all of them necessarily trifling affairs. A year later, Ivan Dmitriev followed suit with *his* collection, called *My Trifles Too* (*I moi bezdelki*). One thing literature can do for language is change the public's attitude toward words. In common parlance, trifles are a negligible nuisance; framed by the cover of a book, *Trifles* turned out to be a big deal.

Aurea mediocritas—the old Horatian ideal of the golden mean—became influential as poetry's new ideological window; viewed through it, a number of facts mentioned in the previous chapter may be situated in a coherent landscape. The *middle* language—not high-flown, but not vulgar either—that the poetry of the Golden Age aspired to deliver; young Karamzin's refusal to climb the official social ladder; Batiushkov's portrayal of his own talent as a bee, a little busybody that neither crawls, nor soars, but hovers in midair:

these phenomena were not isolated, but rather aligned along one and the same axis. Where must a poet set the thematic horizon of their work? Should poetic endeavor appear heroic, or remain within human reach? Who is the projected reader of a poem: a sovereign, an unknown descendant, Ovid, or a friend? None of these choices were taken independently of one another. Thematics (what about), poetics (how), and pragmatics (what for, and for whom) were interrelated parts of the ideological configuration.

When, in 1824, Wilhelm Küchelbecker chastised Russian poets for their neglect of the odic genre, Vasily Ushakov comforted the reading public with the consideration that such an attitude simply betokened a time of peace: "The ode, in this country, is not forsaken. Upon the thundering of the storm of war, the poets shall take up their lyres."[2] For most of the poets, however, whom Küchelbecker was trying to awaken to the odic calling (Pushkin and Baratynsky included), the magnitude of poetry was no longer seen as proportionate to the grandeur of its themes or the sublimity of its subjects. Instead, poetry strove to dissociate itself from ideals too lofty, heroes too dignified, or palaces too opulent.

The thematic megalophobia of Golden Age poetry is reflected, in particular, in poems about ancestral homes. More often than not, such a residence was depicted as a humble rustic hut in which to hide from the vain glories of the world. "Warmed by my quilted dressing robe," Anton Del'vig confides in his "My Hut" ("Moia khizhina"), "not only counts and princes / But the sultan himself shall I refuse to recognize as a brother."[3] In Viazemsky's "To My Soulmate," the list of reasons for him and his wife to escape to *their* familial abode occupies sixteen lines: living-room quarrels, gossip, and disputes; self-important fools, bothersome merrymakers, blind critics, and "Pathetic shepherd-boys [*zhalkikh pastushkov*] / Sighing in their sonnets / By women's toilet tables."[4]

Both Del'vig's (1818) and Viazemsky's (1815) poems owe the rebukes just quoted (and, potentially, the very fact of having been written) to Batiushkov's "My Penates" ("Moi penaty," 1811–12, published in 1814), whose abode is an ancestral hut from which our poet disinvites wealth and vanity, corrupt courtiers, and pale puffed-up princes. In their stead, lines of invitees from different epochs and walks of life pass through the hub that is Batiushkov's mythopoetic hut: an old war veteran; Horace and Pindar, followed by Karamzin, Dmitriev, Viazemsky, and other Russian poets; and, at night, the true star of the show knocks at the door, a young beauty named Lileta, cross-dressed as a Roman warrior:

Вошла—наряд военный
Упал к ее ногам,
И кудри распущенны
Взвевают по плечам,
И грудь ее открылась
С лилейной белизной.

[Enter then, thou soldier sweet! / Throw thy mantle at my feet; / Let thy curls, so brightly glowing, / On thy ivory shoulders flowing, / Be unbound: thy lily breast / Heave, no more with robes opprest!] (Translated by John Bowring, 1821[5])

As a place to live, Batiushkov's hut is rather basic: "[By] the window stands a table, / Three-legged, tott'ring, with a cover, / Gay some centuries ago, / Ragged, bare and faded now."[6] Such is the model home for you as a poet to revisit—regardless of how the ancestral home you had (or did not have) looked in real life. Take Del'vig, who had none. Or take Ostafievo, a few hours' ride from Moscow, to which Viazemsky, we recall, was so impatient to go with his wife Vera. Unlike Batiushkov and Del'vig, Viazemsky never calls his country home a hut; but even so, in his "Soulmate" it is presented as "our humble refuge" (*smirennyi nash priiut*) and "simple shelter" (*krov prostoi*)—despite the fact that, as most people likely to read the poem knew, Prince Viazemsky's Ostafievo, a sizable neoclassical palace complete with a colonnade and wings, was anything but humble. No reader protested: at times, literary values override those of reality and realty.

Indeed, poetry, in the Golden Age, became less and less willing to depend on borrowed values. "There, a hard and creaking bed," Batiushkov points as he guides the readers among his Penates; this bed "in higher love I hold, / Than sofas rich with silk and gold."[7] Not that the poet was promoting asceticism: as the reader knows, the mores of his Penates are more Horatian than monastic. Nor is it a matter of the ethics of the poor. Much of Batiushkov's "My Penates" is the new poetry's *pro domo sua*. My Penates—my poems—must not look overfurnished: nowadays, sofas, silk, and gold are a debased literary currency, devalued both as items of the poetic diegesis and as words, the raw material of style. The latter point—style—does not come across (and scarcely could have) in John Bowring's otherwise masterful translation of 1821. In English, the choice is between two classes of furniture, bed and sofa; in Russian, between *postel'* and *lozhe*, two different ways, domestic and majestic, of naming one and the same thing.

From majestic to domestic—such, in a nutshell, was the trajectory of values that defined the dynamics of poetry in the Golden Age. Domestic poetry, formerly entertained in select, highly enlightened households, became a widespread fad in the 1810s–20s. "Those [were] happy times for literature... when poems flowed freely and harmoniously on any occasion, trivial or important,"[8] Baratynsky's nephew Sergei Rachinsky wrote in his 1899 commentary to a printed edition of old manuscripts, important and trifling, discovered, fittingly enough, in his family nest. Indeed, a hasty note, a congratulatory speech, or an invitation card now afforded many the chance to try their hand at poetry.

Domestic verse was a subculture with its own domestic celebrities. Vasily Pushkin, for instance, confided his literary endeavors primarily to family members, friends and friends' friends, and society acquaintances—concentric circles ultimately encompassing a good half of Moscow's beau monde, literary and otherwise. Domestic thematics were in favor; as were domestic little dogs. When in 1821, at the request of the salon hostess Sofia Ponomareva, Anton Del'vig composed the lament "On the Death of the Dog Mal'vina" ("Na smert' sobaki Mal'viny"; a lapdog remembered by history, together with her companion Hector, for her fierce dislike of her mistress's suitors), it began with an invocation of weeping graces, cupids, and Aphrodite herself, and ended with an allusion to Catullus's "On the Death of Lesbia's Sparrow."[9] Ancient gods and ancient poets, Del'vig's poem reminds us, were sympathetic toward small pets. In the poem's fatalistic (and optimistic) finale, Del'vig describes the little dog Mal'vina's arrival in the underworld, where Catullus, long since dead, is shown listening to Lesbia's deceased sparrow chirping in his hand. Even the realm of Hades had gone domestic.

WRITE, DRINK, TALK: POETRY'S PRAGMATIC CONTINUUM

Form follows function. A light poem on a small subject or petty occasion had to look casual—much as, at home, especially in the morning, one was supposed to dress casually, not formally—even if dressing informally took longer. "I am sincerely grateful for your fatherly instructions on how to write poetry," wrote Batiushkov to Zhukovsky in June 1812, "but I will not be able to make use of them. I do not write much, and I write slowly; but to pause on every word, or every line, rewriting, erasing, crossing out... no, my dear friend, it's not worth it: poems are not worth the time you waste on them [*pogubish za nimi*], and I know how to put my time to better use: thank goodness, I have wine, friends, and tobacco."[10] (The true number of corrections and revisions that "effortless" style could cost a Golden Age poet would become clear only later, when literary archives allowed access to handwritten drafts and rough copies.)

Spend time on poetry, or with friends? The alternative Batiushkov sketches in his letter to Zhukovsky was no either/or dilemma. In Batiushkov's poetic self-image, poetry, friends, wine, and tobacco formed a continuum of pleasures, among which it was wise to distribute your time evenly. In an early poem, "To Kaverin" ("K Kaverinu"), Pushkin adds two more—philosophy and gambling: ". . . One can live amicably / With verses, gambling, Plato, and a glass of wine."[11] My book of poems is poetry for friends, Batiushkov declares in the dedicatory piece "To Friends" ("K druz'iam"), which opens the hand-copied, hand-bound collection that Batiushkov, indeed, sent to be circulated among his friends and later published, after a series of painstaking revisions, as a second volume of his 1817 *Opyty v stikhakh i proze* (Essays in poetry and prose). The dedication is expressly self-effacing.

The book, he says, may want for artful rhymes and words; what his circle of friends (*druzhestvo*) will find in it instead is just a "diary" (*zhurnal*) of his carefree living and feelings. The sole felicity Batiushkov claims for his book is that its friendly readers shall conclude: "He lived exactly as he wrote . . . / Neither well, nor poorly!"[12] Even while, as a book, Batiushkov's *Opyty* was too ambitious and, as a poem, Batiushkov's "To Friends" too well rhymed and worded for anyone to be fooled by its self-abasing closure, the Golden Age was also the age of the golden mean, in which the most sophisticated dishes had to be presented modestly and simply. True poetry must be oblivious of being such.

A good poem could afford to sound artless but never awkward. Distinct from the "grand genres" (*bol'shie rody*) of poetry that engross readers in the depiction of passions, Batiushkov wrote in his programmatic 1816 "Rech' o vliianii legkoi poezii na iazyk" (Speech on the influence of light poetry on language),

> from poetry's light genres the reader demands maximally possible perfection, purity in expression, harmony in style, flexibility and smoothness; he also demands truthfulness in feelings and strict propriety in all respects. Here, the reader instantly becomes a stringent judge, for his attention is not distracted. The beauty of style is necessary here and cannot be replaced by anything. The secret of [this beauty] lies in poetic gift and permanent attention to a single

subject, for poetry, even in minor genres, is a difficult art that needs all your life and efforts.[13]

Batiushkov's "Speech" (delivered by Fedor Kokoshkin before Moscow University's Society of Lovers of Russian Literature on the occasion of Batiushkov's election as member) was, from more than one point of view, a brave paradoxical endeavor to set the pyramid of genres on its tip; he calls light poetry "the luxury" of literature, thus, seemingly, reducing "grand genres" to bare necessities. Its eponymous thesis sounds ironic: how can the fate of Russian language and, with it, the nation and society at large depend upon, or be influenced by immaterial trifles like light poetry?[14] Or take the very idea of delivering a gravely serious oratory on lightness in front of university savants. Not that Batiushkov cared much about what the Moscow professors thought, or so we can infer from his letter to Gnedich in which the event is accounted for by using a line from Derzhavin with the word "asses" replacing Derzhavin's "Tsars": "Я истину ослам с улыбкой говорил" ("With a smile I spoke of truth to asses").[15] But the thesis voiced in the excerpt was no less challenging—that light poetry (under whose banners Batiushkov puts works by a majority, if not all, contemporary top-tier Russian poets, from Derzhavin to Zhukovsky) demands all the attention and perfection you can give it on the strength (or is it weakness?) of its lightness, for verbal perfection is all it has to its name.

Indeed, poetry's shift in orientation from public speech genres toward private, intimate, or society talk did not mean that verbal skills were now in less demand. Quite the opposite: through the lips of a skillful master, an ordinary causerie became a work of art, an act of verbal performance that, according to the famed French conversationalist Madame de Staël,

> animates the spirits, like music among some people, and strong liquors among others. That sort of pleasure which is produced by an animated conversation does not precisely depend on the nature of that conversation; the ideas and knowledge which it develops do not form its principal interest; it is a certain manner of acting upon one another, of giving mutual and instantaneous delight, of speaking the moment one thinks, of acquiring immediate self-enjoyment, of receiving applause without labor, of displaying the understanding in all its shades by accent, gesture, look; of eliciting, in short, at will, the electric sparks which relieve many by the very excess of their vivacity, and serve to awaken others out of a state of painful apathy.[16]

How you spoke, in Russian or in French, was as integral a part of what you were—your social self—as how you looked or wrote. As part of their education, young gentlemen were taught *Colloquia scholastica*, and young ladies— the arts of domestic and social conversation: what phrases a young lady must use when meeting a guest of the opposite gender, how to see him out, how to accept an invitation to the mazurka, or how to receive or visit her grandparents.[17] Pushkin is said to have been a mesmerizing interlocutor. As Dolly de Ficquelmont, hostess of a Petersburg salon, wrote in her diary: "When he speaks, you forget his lack of whatever might render him handsome: he speaks so well, his conversation is so interesting, sparkling with witticisms and devoid of any pedantry."[18]

Can we posit conversations as literary facts—on the same basis as formalist theorists did personal letters or diary entries?[19] On the one hand, a conversation is a verbal text that used to be judged and valued as one might a literary work. "The pleasant conversational style [of Alessandro Manzoni] reminded me of Kapodistrias, who used to speak with logical precision, always curtly, yet with charming nonchalance and liveliness of spirit," Zhukovsky wrote in an 1838 letter to Ivan Kozlov. "The expressions Manzoni uses are, it seems to me, even more concise."[20] At the same time, conversations are, if we may say so, *performative* facts, with all the spontaneity and glitches peculiar to non-scripted spoken texts ("[Manzoni] has a slight stutter, but this shortcoming does not spoil anything, and he is not in the least ashamed of it"[21]) and, as such, are as evasive as anything about all performing arts: you have to be there to enjoy it. Histories of performance, unlike literary histories, must make do with facts in the murky mirror of opinion: "I do remember, in general, what Manzoni and I were talking about, but I am unable to commit it to paper. The only thing I know is that those few minutes brought me the same happiness as, in the old days, similar minutes spent with Karamzin, in whose presence my soul was always warmed, and understood more clearly why it was put on this earth."[22]

In an ideal world, literary history should have consisted of two tracks: a history of writing and a history of speaking.[23] Karamzin and Pushkin, as we have just heard, were blessed with a talent for both. But there were some, naturally, whose contribution to and influence upon the cultural life of their epoch was primarily conversational rather than written; sadly, we only know of *their* work from other people's tributes.[24] Consider, for instance, Petr Kozlovsky, a man of the world who found the very process of writing "burdensome and detestable," and declared "the living oral speech to be his direct vocation."[25] In an 1840 obituary that warrants quotation at length, Petr Viazemsky does all he can as a writer to keep Kozlovsky the talker alive in our memory.

> Partly in jest, but also with a firm conviction did [Kozlovsky] assert that Providence sent him to this earth with the mission to talk. Indeed, those blessed to have heard him speak, to have experienced the force, thrill, and charm of his conversations will agree—this was, indeed, his calling. In him, the gift for talking was as powerful a tool as is the poetic gift in a poet or the artistic gift in an artist. As an orator, he needed no platform, no prepared podium nor prepared public; he was not one of those orators who play a role or fulfill an obligation; he was an orator for every day and every minute, always ready, on an inner or outer impulse, to take the commanding hold over the attention of his interlocutors. Issues of history, modern politics, literature, social life, or ethics equally resonated with him, setting in vibration the fine and sensitive fibers [*fibry*] of his intellect to suddenly explode in bright and lively improvisations. Everything in him contributed to the life, power, and color of his words. His mind was insightful and perceptive. He could go deep into subjects or skirt lightly and pleasantly around their margin [*na opushke*]. His words had about them both the virtue of value and the beauty of polish, that is, carried both thought and expression. His auxiliary faculties were just as strong: erudition, acquaintance with the world's celebrities, and an astonishing memory. Add to this the courage of having an opinion: contrary to Talleyrand, who once said that words serve as masks for thoughts, [Kozlovsky's] words were like hot living imprints of his thought.[26]

If, indeed, the totality of literature can be imagined as written texts combined with texts orally performed, it becomes easier to see how, in the Golden Age, light or fugitive poems—as light and fugitive as spoken words—came to be seen as the closest written equivalent of oral speech. That, in Viazemsky's assessment, Kozlovsky—"an orator for every day and every minute"—saw no need of a podium or public squares well with the reorientation of poetry that, according to Tynianov, occurred on the cusp of the nineteenth century. Parlors, not palaces, were the shared habitat of poets and *parleurs*.

From the standpoint of its pragmatics, poetry, too, was stepping down from its time-honored podium—from, for instance, the domestic stages on which "noble amateurs" (*blagorodnye liubiteli*[27]) from the late eighteenth century on used to showcase their talent and knowledge of Russian and European poetry and drama. Two career trajectories are indicative of this shift in orientation. Vasily Pushkin, Karamzin's supporter and coeval (both were born in 1766), the best of whose poetry was too frivolous to see print, began his society career onstage. At eighteen, as Vigel' has it, Vasily Pushkin "used to recite, at soirees, lengthy tirades from Voltaire and Racine, acquainting the public with names as yet little known in Russia; at twenty, he played Orosmane in *Zaïre* at domestic theaters, and composed couplets in French. How little it took to become famous back then!"[28] The career of Ivan Dolgorukov, Vasily Pushkin's senior by two years, followed a similar curve. As a young man, Dolgorukov recalls, he aspired to act in (home) theaters; toward this end he worked on improving his French and "enriching the memory with many a verse—a resource that later helped win my way into society."[29] When, some thirty years later, the same Dolgorukov published the collection *The Being of My Heart* (*Bytie moego serdtsa*, 1817–18), he dismissed society's opinion of it with the same studied lightness we have seen in Batiushkov's attitude toward *his* creations: "Some liked it, others did not. . . . As I write my poems for women, not for scholastics, I remained indifferent. Having observed that my poems amused the finest individuals of the female sex, I was perfectly satisfied, as one who had attained his goal would be."[30] Light poetry had to be taken lightly.

Verses, Verses Everywhere: Poem as Postal Fact

Lightness, as understood in the Golden Age, was not a characteristic of pen alone; it also had to do with the philosophy of use. Earnest Plato had suggested banishing poetry from the ideal society; Golden Age poets would have rather banished earnest prose. Why can't poetry be the medium of daily life? Some uses of poetry seen in this period verge on conscious pragmatic experimentation in this plane. What things could be done with verse? Touching hearts, as Dolgorukov felt his poems had done, had been poetry's bailiwick since Sappho; what else could verse be good for? Could it work as a legal document? Dolgorukov, we recall, tested these waters when he used verse to compose his last will and testament. It is one thing to send a poem enclosed in a letter to a friend; but what did the carrier make of it when he saw the address of Viazemsky's intended recipient on the envelope written in metered rhyme?[31]

No genre of writing, it seems, was immune to poetry; postal and hand-to-hand correspondence was particularly afflicted. Writing to Viazemsky, Aleksandr Turgenev described the revival of Zhukovsky's genius thus: "He goes so far as to put his daily notes [*zapiski*] into verse, and is no longer capable of saying, in prose: 'Send me some ice cream and sugar-coated almonds.' He even uses verse to correspond on Senate matters."[32] In the Golden Age, a familiar letter was often a hybrid affair. Some letters were written entirely in verse; in others, a poem was attached to or interpolated (as a column or in line) into the letter's prose.[33] A postal poem could resemble a letter not only in function and theme but sometimes in form and formulae as well. Thus does Batiushkov begin an epistle to Nikolai Gnedich written in July 1808 and mailed from an army camp in Finland:

Прерву теперь молчанья узы
Для друга сердца моего.
Давно ты от ленивой Музы,
Давно не слышал ничего.[34]

[I will now break the bonds of silence / For the friend of my heart. / It is long since you have last heard / From my lazy Muse.]

As we can judge from the above, the postal poem of the Golden Age was a quaint mixture of the poetic and the postal. A conventional poetic epistle—one aimed at a wider readership than its nominal addressee—would have no need to open with a ritualistic apology of the kind still resorted to by anyone behind on their email. Only two persons, you and your pen friend, are likely to remember or care about the history of your mutual correspondence. For that matter, a muse does not typically write letters; she inspires her poet or lends a benevolent ear to their verse. At the same time, Batiushkov's chiding of his muse's laziness in no way demotes her to scribe status. A postal muse is still a muse. Embedded in a letter, a poem became its featured constituent, the verbal equivalent of a gift. A gift requires an equivalent gift in return. "I count on one little word, at least, from your Muse; shame on her if she fails: rhyming costs us nothing," Batiushkov notified Gnedich in a postscript (in prose) attached to his letter-poem from Finland.[35]

Some letters come with strange attachments. Virginia Jackson tells of the time Emily Dickinson enclosed in an envelope, along with a poem, a dead cricket.[36] When, in 1831, upon Zhukovsky's request, the poet and hussar Denis Davydov remitted the tip of his left moustache—a mock-heroic attribute hymned in Pushkin's and Davydov's own poetry—he both apologized for not supplying this gift with a dedicatory verse and warned the recipient not to use this fact as an excuse to reply in prose. "I am sending it enclosed with prose, not with verse as you demanded, because I only write in verse when the demon of poetry awakens in me, which did not occur on this occasion. Since, in you, this demon never sleeps, I ask you to repay my gift with at least a quatrain."[37]

Paradigms Lost: Private-cum-Public or Private versus Public?

In literary studies, conceptual clarity comes at the cost of historical fidelity. The very paradigms that make us aware of distinctions and oppositions easily blind us to connections and transitions. The paradigm *private versus public*, for instance, looks increasingly suspicious in the eyes of scholars of the Russian Golden Age.[38] On the one hand, it helps us distinguish literary texts—those intended for publication and circulation—from those designated for private communication, familiar or official. And when it comes to epistolary literature, including poetic epistles, the distinction between the private and public spheres remains helpful. Indeed, we would always do well not to conflate correspondence between fictional characters with actual letters written to actual people, epistles addressed to a social group (like Karamzin's "To Women") or a social type (like Pushkin's "Epistle to the Censor" ["Poslanie tsenzoru"]) with letters bearing specific names and addresses, and so on.

On the other hand, we should take care not to lock a literary fact or figure into one of these categories, whose main value, after all, is theoretical and pedagogical convenience. No private letter, let alone verse epistle, can ever be shown to be literarily innocent. Conversely, as Joe Peschio reminds us in his study of Arzamasian letters, for all their literary qualities, these letters were not literary affairs masquerading as epistolary; they were written and sent to geographically distant addressees, as all letters are.[39] True, a distance always exists between literary letters and those that people write to their relatives, but nothing compels us to dramatize this distance or treat it as a gap, as occurs in Virginia Jackson's study of Emily Dickinson. She presents the very fact of Dickinson's archival legacy, made public and categorized as lyric, not as a story of literary redemption but of alienation and betrayal.[40] The private and the public do not come as neatly delineated "spheres," or at least they never did in the Russian Golden Age. Rather, as Todd shows in his study of the familiar letter as a literary genre, private life and literature in such missives were like two handheld looking glasses facing and mirroring one another: "The familiar letter traditionally caters both to its immediate recipient and to [the] larger public. . . . Although they are composed to seem so, familiar letters are not a 'mirror' of an author's mind, as the nineteenth-century editors understood that metaphor. The author himself, limited in movement by epistolary tradition, decorum, knowledge, and range of vision, holds up and maneuvers the "mirror"—a framed, uneven surface—to capture certain objects, hastily pass others by, and leave still others utterly unreflected."[41] The continuum between private and public was flexible enough to be played with and manipulated at the writer's discretion.

Neither the public nor the private were, in those days, very private or very public. Poems, like letters, were balancing acts on the fickle and mutable line between the two. Del'vig's encomium "My Hut" was aimed at the larger public, including perhaps posterity, as were Batiushkov's and Viazemsky's homages to their paternal homes—the topos whose productivity for Russian poetry we have already observed. But the pun contained in the last line—the *pointe*—of Del'vig's "Hut" sounds much like an inside joke for an in-group of friends. My parental estate, Del'vig says in closing, may be too small to find on the map (*na landkarte*) next to Athens and Sparta. "But then, no one will take it away / by a lucky draw of the cards [*schastlivo vydernutoi kartoi*]."[42] This final verse could have been a tongue-in-cheek allusion to Viazemsky's ancestral Ostafievo, mortgaged to pay off its owner's gambling debt. That this debt was as enormous as the Ostafievo mansion itself was a running joke among friends, Viazemsky included. Transparent to the few, opaque to many, the last line of Del'vig's poem was a *sapienti-sat* coda, a joke he would hardly have allowed himself had he feared the larger public might get it.

That certain themes and subjects were more sensitive than others (in this period, one must not forget, a leak could spark a duel) does not entitle us to consider that Golden Age literature, as has been suggested, targeted "segregated audiences."[43] Pragmatic paradigms are more misleading than helpful. There were poems written for the public and poems sent privately to family or friends, but in the poetry of the Golden Age, this did not necessarily translate into *private versus public*. Nor did the distinction between the published and unpublished ever define what was known or remained unknown—given the extent to which poetry's circulation in early nineteenth-century Russia depended on social networking.[44] As such, this distinction was, too, not a dichotomy but a continuum. We recall how annoyed Viazemsky was that Zhukovsky's "Summer Evening" had been published in a widely read literary journal. What must be added here is that by that time Zhukovsky's poem had already been published in 1818 in *Dlia nemnogikh* (For the few), a six-volume not-for-sale Russian-German bilingual collection of Zhukovsky's poems and translations that had been made for his royal pupil, future empress Alexandra Fedorovna.[45] Printed in only a few dozen copies, *Dlia nemnogikh* was very well known in literary circles but not among the wider reading public. "Published" did not mean "public"; "private" did not mean "not for publication."

The story of Viazemsky's pie poem is a good example of the blurriness, in this time, of the borders between poems sent to a friend, made known to a group of friends, and published in a literary journal. In late December 1819 (old style) Viazemsky, then in Warsaw, shipped a sumptuous, "fat and fragrant" Perigord pie to Aleksandr Turgenev in St. Petersburg. The pie came accompanied by a poem ("Go forth, oh pie, onto Turgenev's table, / A gift that befits gluttony and friendship"), which decreed, with comic seriousness, which sort of guests should and should not be seated at the table when the pie was served. Your selection criterion, the author-cum-donor instructs the beneficiary of the gift, should be their table talk. Be wary of gossipy neighbors; "off with [*Net! Net!*] the high-flown style of well-born liars"; off with the knave with his "sugar-coated [*obsakharennyi*] style." As a token of gratitude to me, Viazemsky implores, let none but our mutual friends savor my pie, and let their "guileless banter" (*vzdor bez zatei*) rule at your table. The poem ends with this wishful vision: "Flying in my thoughts I traverse the distance, / And espy my plate among my friends,"—yet sadly, at this table, our poet is but an invisible guest. Comes the *pointe*, the last verse, the punchline of the poem: "O, my Turgenev, you'll eat for us both!"[46]

With Turgenev's name mentioned twice, in the beginning and closing, Viazemsky's pie poem seems like a regular verse letter whose only felicity is to please and amuse the gift's recipient. Yet, situation-bound as the piece may at first appear, its pragmatic potential went beyond that of its postal companion, the pie. If we grant, for interest's sake, that Turgenev, following Viazemsky's wishes, did invite their mutual friends to a pie party, we can safely assume that, before cutting up its subject, Turgenev read Viazemsky's poem aloud. This, to repeat, is no more than an assumption; what we do know for certain is that the recipient of poem and pie made sure the former would outlive the latter. Among Golden Age literati, Aleksandr Turgenev was as noteworthy for his gargantuan appetite as for his reluctance to write verse. So, instead of repaying the poem with a poem, he wrote back to Viazemsky, in prose: "Thank you for the pie, thank you for the poem! The one is worthy of the other— you can expect no greater praise from a glutton. . . . Your poem to me is now being printed, and will come out in *Syn otechestva* under the title 'Epistle to

Turgenev [Sent] with a Pie.'"[47] This was dual felicity in action: the *sapienti sated*, the reading public could now enjoy the poem on its own merit.

"Oral Literature": A Constructive Contradiction

Handwritten or printed, addressed to a friend or a circle of friends, or aimed at the broader public or posterity itself—salient as such distinctions may in theory appear, they were easily disregarded on the ground. So was the distinction between the written and the spoken, and even the seemingly unbridgeable gap between literature on the one hand and bureaucratic correspondence on the other. The element common to all of the above species was Russian, a language in the making, the shared environment on which all kinds of texts depended, and to whose ecology each kind was expected to contribute. Spoken or written, epistolary or familiar, official or private—whatever its medium or its pragmatic target, the utterance, in the Golden Age, was judged on the merit of what mattered most: mastery of expression. In his capacity as minister of justice (1810–14), the poet Ivan Dmitriev filled clerical vacancies with writers, not just to supplement their income but also to improve the quality of official prose.[48] Late in his career, Batiushkov, known as a poet and war veteran, sought a position in the diplomatic service. While many doubted that a poet could make a good diplomat,[49] Zhukovsky thought otherwise; as he put it in a postscript to his friend's petition: "A copy of Batiushkov's published writings should be handed to Kapodistrias [at the time minister of foreign affairs] to document his suitability not only for the military but also the civilian walk of life."[50] And when Dmitry Bludov, a professional diplomat and man of letters, was entrusted with the state-sponsored project of translating all diplomatic documents from 1814 on, it was Karamzin and Zhukovsky who helped him find (or coin) Russian equivalents for Francophone diplomatic language.[51] Engineering Russia's own beautiful and articulate officialese was not seen as a mission unworthy of a poet.

Nor was the distinction between the written and the spoken as clear-cut as is imagined in our scholarship today. Half a century of groundbreaking inquiry, from Milman Parry's to Walter Ong's, into the poetics and noetics of oral lore has primed us to associate the oral with the preliterate—so completely, that the very phrase "oral literature," a perfectly harmless catachresis, has come to sound like a "monstrous" theoretical oxymoron. "This strictly preposterous term remains in circulation today even among scholars now more and more acutely aware how embarrassingly it reveals our inability to represent to our own minds a heritage of verbally organized materials except as some variant of writing, even when they have nothing to do with writing at all," asserts Ong in his *Orality and Literacy*, the book whose typological clarity and intellectual brilliance derives from the two eponymous terms here uncompromisingly opposed.[52] And yet, oral literature was a real (if historically less tenacious) presence in the Golden Age, and not some pale variant of the written but an active co-ingredient thereof. It may be harder for us than it was for Pushkin's contemporaries and immediate descendants to assess the importance of the spoken and the written as literary components working in tandem with one another. Take Petr Bartenev, the pioneer of Pushkin studies, who, unlike his colleagues of later generations, had the opportunity to interview Pushkin's friends and acquaintances. It was this near-eyewitness perspective that enabled Bartenev, writing in 1862, to see Pushkin's oral environment as a powerful echo chamber of sorts, one feeding back on its source. In Bartenev's account of Pushkin's exile in the south of Russia, it is hard (and hardly necessary) to separate the writer from the talker: "An apt phrase, a witty epigram, a surprisingly fresh and novel verse—all that made Pushkin a most pleasant conversation companion—quickly spread over the capital and Russia at large. Nationwide approval lent wings to Pushkin, generating new pranks, new witticisms, and new forbidden poems."[53]

From Socrates and Plato to Ferdinand de Saussure and his recent skeptics, our philosophic imaginary returns to ponder what it posits as a split between the oral and the written. It must have been Socrates's argument from *Phaedrus* that Viazemsky was following when, in a letter to Turgenev, he observed that spoken words "cut themselves" (*vrezyvaiutsia*) into his memory, whereas things he read faded like pictures drawn on its surface.[54] Young Zhukovsky's distrust of books sounds no less Socratic: wisdom (*mudrost'*), his 1805 diary insists, is better espoused via conversations, by way of listening, looking, trying to answer, imitating. The Russian Golden Age's disparagement of the written may be summarized using Goethe's dictum from *Dichtung und Wahrheit*: "Writing is an abuse of language, reading silently to oneself is a pitiful substitute for speech."[55] So much for the awkwardness of the term "oral literature"—to hear Goethe tell it, literature had never been written.

Walter Ong, whose book sees orality and literacy as consecutive stages of literary development, presents the transition between the two as a point of no return: "Oral cultures indeed produce powerful and beautiful verbal performances of high artistic and human worth, which are no longer even possible once writing has taken possession of the psyche."[56] In Ong's strictly stadial perspective, early nineteenth-century literature in Russia, with its developed typo- and chirographic infrastructures, would have to be categorized as post-oral—which it decidedly was not.

Another (and better) way of understanding the Russian Golden Age would be to explore the oral as *embedded* in the culture of the written—not as a fossil or ghost from the forgotten past but as an inescapable point of reference, writing's ubiquitous and wakeful alter ego. How we speak has always been a touchstone for how we write—whether a given writer strives to stand at a remove from or, on the contrary, approximate the spoken. Should written texts replicate oral discourse, or dissociate themselves from it? Should they be spontaneous, performative, unordered—or stay aloof, ennobled by archaisms and faithful to their own, non-oral grammar? There was no lack in the Golden Age of proponents of either position: guardians of the "high style [*shtil'*]" campaigned against Gallicisms and conversational phrasing, while supporters of the "new style [*slog*]" promoted "free and pleasant" prose, banishing Slavonicisms, for instance, right down to the tiniest pronoun.[57]

Asked to explain the distinction between the literate and the oral, one is likely to think first of the material tools—stylus, pen, printing press—used (or not) to (re)produce a verbal message. This criterion makes perfect sense when our goal is to encompass, diachronically, the whole span of human history, and establish when and how forms of writing emerged to supplement oral culture. But if we shift the perspective from diachronic to synchronic, homing in on early nineteenth-century Russia, other criteria come to the fore. To supplement is not to supplant: people who can read and write typically remain quite capable of speaking. In addition, in the Russian Empire, which was predominantly illiterate and rural, oral lore remained at the back of every mind—and yard. Today, literacy is not perceived as a form of diglossia; in those years it could have been. Orality was alive and present, albeit culturally, stylistically, and linguistically interiorized and insulated; the written and the spoken cohabited, forming complex patterns. To get a better sense of these patterns, we need to leave behind us the time-honored criterion of the "techno-psychic," that is, the idea that the technical tools and skills humans devised to put facts and thoughts on paper somehow got ultimate hold of the human psyche and of those very thoughts, making us irredeemably literate. We would do better to interrogate the epoch itself: what criteria did people living in the Golden Age resort to when it came to the issue of writing versus speaking? This was, first of all, always a matter of choice. Being literate means being able to write *along with* (not instead of) being able to speak; speaking and writing thus became, for every literate person, a matter of speaking *or* writing, a choice of alternatives, a crossroads. Secondly (indeed, consequently), the criteria such a choice called for were topical and pragmatic. Russian as a literary language—which, taken broadly, encompassed Russian poetry and prose, official and postal Russian, the Russian spoken in countryside estates and city parlors—was considered to be in a nascent state. The Golden Age being an age of forking roads, the parting-of-the-ways posted SPOKEN OR WRITTEN was a nodal one. An important concern—not to say national anxiety—was how to make the Russian language work, and work in all its multiple facets and functions. The written as spoken; the written minus the spoken; the written plus the spoken—these were, far from being purely academic, all burning questions of pragmatics.

The Orality of the Written

How to write a proper letter? Practical manuals and guides informed their readers—potential letter writers—of the importance of balancing between the pragmatics of the oral and semiotics of the written. "The letter is a free imitation of a good conversation," *The Latest, Fullest, and Most Detailed Letter-Writing Manual*, published in St. Petersburg in 1822, instructed the beginner, because "letters are conversations between absentees."[58] Briefs like that, and the practices they instantiated, carved, within the very material of writing, a niche for oral—well, oral-like—behavior. Like a good actor, a good letter makes us forget it is a letter.

To achieve this effect, an appropriately composed letter had to meet certain felicity-conditions, four of which can be extracted from contemporary maxims and observations on the subject. Conditions one and two (both worded as a warning) are found in the above-cited *Manual*. Firstly, a felicitous letter, more than any other genre of writing, must be wary of too flamboyant a prose: "It has no use for rhetorical figures: plentiful exclamations, prosopopoeia, addresses; neither is it in need of lengthy clauses of the sort sometimes necessary in compositions of other kinds" (11). Secondly, letters must not sound too coherent or orderly: "An order that is artful and methodical, or parts composed too thoughtfully, are as inappropriate in letter-writing as they are when speaking. . . . In letters, no one attempts great consistency of components. A letter is a portrayal of a verbal conversation; therefore, a reasonable disorder befits a letter, particularly if it is on multiple matters" (4, 11).

While the first two felicity-conditions are stylistic, the other two might be called histrionic. Condition three has to do with what linguists call turn-taking—techniques that everyday speech shares with dialogue on the dramatic stage.[59] As Peschio argues, an orientation toward conversation did not mean that letters did in fact imitate any actual live speech patterns; what made the epistolary practice conversation-like was mainly turn-taking.[60] "I would be happier if I were getting your reply letters not in three weeks, but in at most a week's time. As it stands now, our letters to each other remind me of monologues," Del'vig wrote to Grigory Karelin.[61] Lastly, a felicitous letter was expected to have an individual "voice." This development may have been encouraged by the success of eighteenth-century epistolary novels, beginning with Samuel Richardson's *Clarissa, or, the History of a Young Lady*. A critical remark (found, incidentally, in a familiar letter) regarding Jean-Jacques Rousseau's *Julie, or the New Heloise* shows how high such expectations had been raised—at least when it came to fictional letters exchanged by fictional characters. In an 1831 letter to Ivan Kireevsky, Evgeny Baratynsky extols Rousseau "as a moralist, dialectician, and metaphysician, but . . . not at all as an author," on the grounds that *Julie* sounds to him more like a treatise on ethics than a novel. It may be true, Baratynsky admits, that Rousseau's novel is analytical, never claiming to faithfully depict characters or passions; but his novel is not just a novel, "it is a novel-in-letters; and in a letter, its writer's voice must be heard, since every letter is, sui generis, a conversation; note the superiority of the author of *Clarissa* over Rousseau."[62]

Writing in the 1860s, Viazemsky would sketch an evolution of Russian epistolary style as (to rephrase his observation in Tynianov's terms) a shift of orientation from written to oral speech:

> For a long time, letters in our country were written in a language that was either completely illiterate or bookish; letters written by many a statesmen serving in the time of Catherine [II] prove that. The pen was always approached with a sort of solemnity and circumspection. The language of letters, that is, epistolary language [*pis'mennyi, to est', epistoliarnyi iazyk*], came into use later, and was here to stay. It was then that the letter became a stenogram of thoughts and feelings put on paper in warm blood and without hesitation. Iv[an] Iv[anovich] Dmitriev, and also Neledinsky [-Meletsky] both adhered to the old style and

order of letter-writing. Karamzin's letters are already much simpler. In them, you can hear him speak, like in an oral conversation.[63]

Poetry was as protean as letters. Poems, as we saw earlier in this chapter, easily penetrated postal prose; conversations, from genteel ones to banter, did as well. Any letter, according to that 1822 *Manual*, is a conversation with those not present; in those days, the same thing could be said of a poem. In an 1811 letter to his friend Nikolai Gnedich, Konstantin Batiushkov, a great advocate of light poetry, declares: "Saint-Lambert is a kind man, fun to converse with."[64] The reference, of course, is to the French poet Jean-François de Saint-Lambert, at this point long since deceased.

More typically, however, a poem, or a line or maxim therefrom, would be used to correspond and converse among the living—regardless of whether the verse's author was still around, or even remembered by name. Poetry in this period was treated like public domain property. A line of poetry in the middle of a letter or in the middle of a walk with a young lady might derive from a poem of one's own, or by someone else, or by who knows whom—it hardly mattered, so long as it was cited apropos. A poem's felicity hinged less on the authority of its author than on its performative potential—how well its lines could be used to turn a phrase. Making your poem as conversation-friendly as possible was a pragmatic drive powerful enough to fuel aphoristic and modular tendencies within Golden Age poetry and poetics.

Pointing the Line, or How to Make Your Verse Remembered

Verbal culture is constantly in flux. What may look on the surface like separate pools of activity—oral conversations, postal correspondence, literary texts—functioned, in effect, as communicating vessels whose verbal material was always in circulation. We might envision two currents flowing in opposite directions. Poetics—formalist and structuralist poetics in particular—examines how, under the poet's pen, the language we use in practical life is transformed into the language of poetry. Running counter to this, from poetry to praxis, is poetry's verbal debris; this is the current to be examined by the pragmatics of poetry. What factors, for instance, saturated the language Russians still speak with little phrases broken off from Krylov's fables and Alexander Griboedov's verse comedy *Woe from Wit* (*Gore ot uma*)?

Several avenues are worth exploring in this regard. One has to do with a trade-off between idiomatics and thematics. Generically, comedies and fables alike gravitated toward topical satire, a fact that engendered two logical corollaries well expressed in Krylov's own tongue-in-cheek comment on his fugitive fables: "This genre is understood by everyone: servants and children read it . . . and tear up soon after."[65] Indeed, the topicality of Krylov's "Wolf in a Kennel" ("Volk na psarne") expired in 1812, but the felicitous line "*Ty ser, a ia, priatel', sed*" ("You are gray [skinned], but I, my friend, am gray-haired"), detached from its political context (abortive peace talks between Napoleon and Kutuzov), successfully fossilized into, if not an idiom, then a near-proverb. Another factor that eased the passage of such phrases from literature to life was their frequent status as direct speech, which is intrinsic to comedies by definition, and to fables by tendency. Chatsky's (the protagonist of *Woe from Wit*) defiant "*A sud'i kto?*" ("I wonder who the judges are!")—a phrase now hardly even considered a verse quotation—might not have proven so enduring without its pithy dialogical inversion. Metric choices were a factor as well: fables and verse comedies favored the so-called *vol'nyi* (free) iamb; syntax dictated line length, not the other way around. All this enabled the language of the literary work to grow back into the thicket of practical speech—which, of course, exists independently of the thematics of the spoken. "To create a cliché is genius. I must create a cliché," Charles Baudelaire would say later in the century.[66] In their way (and language), Krylov and Griboedov already had.

For a line of poetry to be assimilated into practical speech, it did not necessarily need to sound either colloquial or folksy. The main thing was to be memorable. Arguably, Krylov's *Ty ser / ia sed* is easy to remember because the narrative faceoff between hunter and wolf is replicated, in the paradigmatic plane, by the minimal phonological pair *r*/*d*; likewise, *s korablia na bal* ("from the boat to a ball," Pushkin's proverbial allusion to Griboedov's *Woe from Wit*)—is memorable because of the acoustic *ablianabal* that bridges the two narrative locations. To recur to models of language pragmatics, this is precisely how Jakobson defines the poetic function of language. Distinctions granted, it is also close to how Soviet psychologist Aleksandr Luria, in his study *The Mind of a Mnemonist*, describes the technique of memorizing.

Why certain verbal structures are easier to memorize than others, or whether the mind's storage capacity can be increased with training, are questions and problems for the psychology of reading to explore.[67] What interests us here is how these problems and questions were addressed in the period under discussion. The first logical item to examine would be doctrines and routines of education. The right way for a child to learn, it was firmly believed, was by rote, from the catechism to grammar to geography; great poems in various languages were, of course, included too. But among all things to be learned by heart, poems were found (by me as well) to be the easiest. No wonder, then, that special mnemonic poems used to be composed in seminaries and schools to help pupils memorize things other than verse. Goethe recalls the silly geographic doggerel, "Ober-Issel; viel Morast / Macht das gute Land verhaßt."[68] Russian schoolchildren, in order to memorize the six cases of Russian noun declension, still use an acrostic almost certainly traceable to nineteenth-century pedagogics: "Иван родил девчонку, / Велел тащить пеленку" ("Ivan sired a little girl / And ordered that a diaper be brought"). Were Jakobson's definition of poetry in need of further evidence, how might we better transpose the equivalence principle from the axis of selection to that of combination? "I like Ike," Jakobson's example of how the poetic function of language can be politically exploited, is also, in a sense, a mnemonic verse. "I support Dwight D. Eisenhower" would be less easy to learn by heart, not because it is overlong but because it is understructured.

Memory—memorability—was, in the Golden Age, a touchtone of poetry itself. Nowadays complimenting a poem as "memorable" or "unforgettable" has mainly to do with conventional forms of paying tribute; but back then, such a statement would typically be anchored in one's personal, not to say visceral experience. Let us recall Viazemsky's letter to Turgenev, in which spoken words, unlike written ones, are said to "cut themselves" into the reader's mind. One frequently sees the same word—*vrezyvat'sia*—used to characterize the effect of poetry as opposed to prose.[69] This is why, in the same Viazemsky's view, the fabulist Aleksandr Mazdorf did not merit the status of poet: "Some poems . . . cut into your memory; yet even I, a walking memorial to Russian scribblers [*zhivoi pamiatnik russkikh pisak*], cannot remember a single verse by Mazdorf."[70] And here is what Viazemsky wrote in a letter to Pushkin: "Your 'Sea' is delightful! I learned it by heart at once, which, for me, is the best proof."[71] Pushkin's apostrophe "To the Sea" ("K moriu") numbers sixty-three lines, no little amount to memorize—but a felicitous poem, maintains Viazemsky, makes you do so "at once."

There were people, besides Viazemsky, known for being able to memorize a poem of virtually any length, reputedly at a glance or a single hearing. Lev Pushkin was famous for such feats, to the occasional dismay of his brother who would, at times, prefer that fans *purchase* his works instead of hearing them from Lev for free. Generally, however, wholesale memorizing was not something poets expected or wanted the reader to do. Typically, a poem would include one line or quatrain more readily memorizable than others. This was a purposeful poetic technique that drew on European models. Stepan Shevyrev, writing on Lermontov in 1841, noted that some of the latter's poems are "sharpened [*zaostreny*] at the ends through the use of a thought or simile" in a manner recalling Baratynsky, "who, in many poems, conveys beautifully in our language something the French call *la pointe*."[72]

La pointe was, by design, the most memorable and citable, not to say the most "oral" segment of a poetic text. Consider two poems, both on the subject of transience: Baratynsky's "The Skull" ("Cherep," 1824/26); and "Triumph of the Victors" ("Torzhestvo pobeditelei," 1829), Zhukovsky's translation of Friedrich Schiller's 1803 "Das Siegesfest." Baratynsky's eight-stanza elegy is set in a cemetery, by an open grave; the poet addresses a skull, Hamlet-like, as his gleeful companions look on. The skull remains silent; the truth of the beyond is not for us mortals to know, the poet concludes. The two final lines of the last (eighth) stanza constitute *la pointe*:

Пусть радости живущим жизнь дарит,
А смерть сама их умереть научит.[73]

[Let life bestow its joys upon the living, / And death herself will teach them how to die.]

Zhukovsky, after Schiller (twenty-six stanzas), tells a rather different story, also capped with a two-line *pointe*. In the wake of the fall of Troy, the victorious Greeks return to their ships, reveling and toasting the living and the fallen, both their own and the unfortunates of Ilium. Look at the smoking city of Troy, the eternal gods whisper to Cassandra: mortal glory is but a wisp. Zhukovsky's *pointe*:

Спящий в гробе, мирно спи;
Жизнью пользуйся, живущий.[74]

[You who sleep in the coffin, sleep in peace; / Make use of life, you who live.]

Structurally, the two poems have more in common than may be apparent on the surface. Each begins with a narrative; each ends on an aphoristic *pointe*. Baratynsky replays a scene from Hamlet; Zhukovsky, after Schiller, conjures up an epilogue to Homer's story of the Trojan War. In both, the anecdote is but a pretext for a poetic speculation; their respective *pointes* take these speculations to a new level of abstraction. *La pointe* is, quintessentially, a thought; but it is also a poem within a poem. In both examples, it takes the form of an antithetical distich, with conjugate words consistently repeated within each verse: *zhivushchim-zhizn' / smert'-umeret'* in Baratynsky and *spiaishchii-spi / zhizniu-zhivushchii* in Zhukovsky—a device known in traditional rhetoric as paregmenon.[75]

Aphoristic, sententious, and terse, the *pointe* of a poem could serve two goals at once: it could be a part of the whole, and a whole in its own right, depending on usage. A memorable stanza or verse could easily be detached and repurposed for use in genteel conversation, in a letter or a book—in the new capacity of a maxim or an appropriate bon mot. It would be hard to overstate the importance of such uses. The smallest literary currency, the bon mots, were, in the Golden Age, collected and traded by many, from seasoned literati to young ladies preparing themselves for social success. "Ask the princess [*kniaginia*] to inquire Princess [*kniazhna*] Mary about the phrase Elim used on that occasion," Viazemsky wrote in a letter to Turgenev—by no means an unusual errand for a bon-mot hunter to entrust to a friend.[76] Iakov Galinkovsky's *Matinee for the Fair Sex, or Ladies' Calendar for Every Day* (1807) left blank pages to be filled by (1) visits to entertain, (2) balls to attend, (3) gambling wins and losses, (4) anecdotes heard, and (5) pointed words and mots.[77] Albums, too, as Larisa Petina shows in a detailed study of that genre, helped people piggy-bank and disburse micro-literary coinages, from poetry lines and stanzas to apothegms and gnomic sentences in prose.[78]

Rules for verse-pointing (*puantirovka*) were helpfully flexible and loose. The end of the poem was deemed the best but by no means the only place for the *pointe*; there could be more than one *pointe* per poem; a felicitous verse, not necessarily intended as a *pointe*, could easily become or be perceived as one. Pushkin was reportedly so enamored of one line in Kondraty Ryleev's *Voinarovsky* that he wrote on the margin next to it: "Sell me this verse!"[79]

There thus coexisted two perspectives on appraising a poem: a holistic one, in which lines and stanzas were assessed as constituents of the overall composition; and a modular one, for which a poem was an assembly of lines and stanzas, some happy, some less. "Her long poem lacks philosophy (while its subject is philosophical), lacks coherence in plan, lacks many things, but then, has beautiful verses," opines Batiushkov in an 1811 letter to Gnedich regarding Anna Bunina's didactic *On Happiness* (*O shchastii*, 1810).[80] In Batiushkov's frame of reference, such a judgment did not spell dispraise. A poem could fail as a whole and succeed as a collection of happy lines, or score in both games, which was seen as a double victory. "Your 'Winter' ["Zima"] . . . is good, and many verses [in it] are beautiful," Karamzin wrote Viazemsky. To us, the compliment may appear redundant; to Viazemsky, it made perfect sense.[81]

On the other hand, this trade-off between wholesale and retail, as it were, had its critics. Aleksandr Odoevsky—who, as Boris Eikhenbaum shows, perceived Baratynsky and Viazemsky as poets afflicted by a French penchant for the cerebral—suspected a double standard here: "In a poem, many look for remarkable verses, not poetry; they find it admirable when a poet sacrifices the harmony of the whole for an isolated thought, often brilliant on the mere strength of well-placed notions [*rasstanovka poniatii*] and pseudo-didacticism."[82] Apprehensions like Odoevsky's are understandable. Potentially (though it never actually transpired), ranking poems by verses, beautiful or not, promoted the disintegration of the poetic whole, hence the erosion of authorship. Indeed, in 1821, Ivan Georgievsky published the *Pocket Library of Aonides*—a twelve-poet anthology in which, alongside some sizable samples, we find "apothegms," that is, noteworthy *pointes* culled from the oeuvres of the Russian poets presented therein. Similar selections of particular, out-of-context lines of poetry, as Petina shows, used to appear in literary periodicals, mixed with sundry maxims in prose from the pen of European or Eastern thinkers.[83]

Textual Instability and Problems of Authorship

If this is the case, then who owns verses? Even with authors duly mentioned, a pocket library like Georgievsky's made punch lines easier to pocket. Though himself a futurist poet in his teens, Roman Jakobson was hardly the author of "I like Ike"—but do we know who was?[84] Nor do we ask who authored folk riddles and proverbs. Apparently, culture treats memorizing as a form of appropriation. "Congratulations, Messrs. Writers [*Pozdravliaiem Gg. sochinitelei*]," the *Moskovskii telegraf* (Moscow telegraph) in 1828 ridiculed some unfortunate contributors to a recent literary almanac. "And let us add but one request: would they, as they imitate well-known authors in thought and style, at least refrain from imitating their very words. . . . As you read some of our poets, you feel you can sort them out by familiar compartments, and bow, stanza by stanza, to your old acquaintances, much like Piron [in his *La*

Métromanie]: one verse you have read in Pushkin, another in Baratynsky, a third in Zhukovsky; the only credit our new authors deserve is for compilation [*chest' sostava*]."[85]

Critical arrows of this sort, of course, were targeted specifically at epigones; but the question of verses' ownership remains relevant even when we turn to such luminaries as Pushkin, Baratynsky, or Zhukovsky. So far as we can tell, two different standards of quality—two sets of felicity-conditions—applied, depending on whether a poem was taken as a whole, or a sum of more or less memorable and well-crafted verses. While the grand design, the overall plan of a poem was up to the poet and their muse, the little details—the how-to of this or that verse—were matters to be resolved between the poet and their peers. "Another poem I am sending you is a madrigal I composed in imitation of Voltaire," wrote Denis Davydov to Pushkin in 1836; "I can't stand [*mne protivny*] the first four verses of it; crunch them [*perelomai*] your own way, and publish it [in *Sovremennik* (The contemporary)] with or without my name, as you see fit."[86] If this sounds almost like an apprentice yielding to the judgment of a master, it is not (or not only) because Davydov, while a very fine poet, may have felt more confident about his moustache and saber than his muse; but rather because, as Viktor Shklovsky observes in the 1929 essay discussed above, in the age of Pushkin, poetry's modus operandi was quintessentially workshop-like.[87]

What rendered the Golden Age workshop period-specific was the peculiar dynamics between authorship and ownership. To author a poem was not, in this time, synonymous with owning it; rather, every new poem was seen—and assessed—as a potential contribution to Russian poetry writ large, whose future was strongly felt as a common cause. In this or that form, therefore, a new poem was supposed to go through a process we might nowadays call peer review. A poem presented at a sitting of a literary society would be approved for publication in the journal thereof so long as its author was ready to accept the corrections suggested by other members.[88] In less formal, familiar associations, a similar procedure would often be initiated by the author. We are not sure whether Viazemsky had plans to publish "To My Soulmate" (he ultimately did not), but, as soon as the poem was finished, he sent a handwritten copy to Batiushkov and Zhukovsky with the following cover note: "I ask that you read, reread, and mark everything that would appear to you as wanting correction. Tell me what you think of the ending. Can I end it like this, or should I return to the main point of the poem, from which I have digressed. In any case, I ended with an ending."[89] Batiushkov, having forcefully denounced (as we have seen) the string of epithets Viazemsky had used to celebrate his native roof, also suggested replacing "witches" with "fairies" (which Viazemsky did), but was otherwise much impressed by the ending that had Viazemsky so concerned. Zhukovsky, too, penciled in the ending as "beautiful," underscored a number of "excellent" verses, and suggested his own replacements for less felicitous ones, two of which Viazemsky would integrate when producing the fair copy of the poem.

Cross-correcting one another's verses was, indeed, a creative imperative, as we see formulated in Batiushkov's 1814 letter to Turgenev regarding the former's corrections to Zhukovsky's epistle to Emperor Alexander: "I adjure him in the name of both the Muses and common sense not to dilly-dally when it comes to making corrections—the only way to approach perfection."[90] Add here an ethical dimension: in the eye of the Golden Age, there was scarcely any distinction between the duty to perfect one's style and to perfect oneself. Form follows feelings. As Vasily Pushkin declared in his 1796 epistle to Ivan Dmitriev:

Не крючковата мысль творит прекрасным стих,
Но плавность, чистота души и сердца чувство:
Вот стихотворцев в чем прямое есть искусство![91]

[What makes verse beautiful is not some chicanerous [*kriuchkovata*, lit. "hooked"] thought, / But fluency, the purity of soul and the heart's feeling: / This is where the true [*priamoe*, lit. "straight," "direct"] art of poets resides!]

Such an attitude, at once caring and forthright, toward one another's verses (when it came to criticizing your peers' manuscripts, there was no place for seniority, and little for niceties) would prove a nightmare for post–Golden Age textology. Which Viazemsky is more "genuine"—the one before or after Zhukovsky's and Batiushkov's amendments? In the climate of constant mutual (and self-)correcting, all authorship was, in a sense, a blend, and any text a draft. Not even the final/posthumous autograph fair copy of a poem was sacrosanct and uncorrectable. Even after Pushkin's death, his posthumous publisher Zhukovsky continued revising his late friend's verses. Today, we are tempted to see this as disregard for Pushkin's genius and will (and/or Zhukovsky's nod to censorship); from the point of view of the epoch, this was a tribute, a participatory token, a communion of sorts. Counterfactual assumptions are scarcely allowed in a historical study, but even so, it is hard to imagine that Pushkin, looking on from Elysium, would mind Zhukovsky's every alteration.

Variability and mutability was, in Pushkin's day, a normal textual condition that did not cease either with the fairest of the fair copies nor, indeed, at the printing press itself. Before printing, publishers had to clear fair-copy manuscripts with the censor; when sending his poems (through Turgenev) to be printed at *Syn otechestva*, Viazemsky would preemptively enclose a number of plan-B verses to replace those most likely to elicit the censor's carping.[92] Or as occurred with less provident authors, an unscrupulous publisher would insert a stop-gap verse of their own in lieu of the censored one.

Not even the act of being published finally put the text to rest. Having passed the censor, unscathed or otherwise, the poem found itself in the hands of the reader. In not just the Golden but every age, readers butcher and garble verses. The most memorable lines—*les pointes*—are typically also those most at risk. The flip side of being memorable is being misremembered. Memory is self-serving, tending to simplify the texts it stores. Pushkin's chiastic verse "Чем меньше женщину мы любим, / Тем легче нравимся мы ей" (The less we love a woman / The easier it is to attract her) is often (mis) remembered by way of replacing *legche* ("easier") with *bol'she* ("more")—"the more she likes us"—a sacrifice of subtlety for the sake of a comfortable symmetry and contrast.

Our memory plays tricks of this sort on any writer, regardless of the period they lived in.[93] A problem specific to the Golden Age was not such honest mistakes, but instances of intentional abuse. This was a time when poems were not only read but used—as part of pragmatic strategizing. The culture of album inscriptions is a case in point. Anonymous album suitors would tamper with a recently published poem, adapting it entirely, or certain of its verses and stanzas, to serve their hidden (and obvious) agenda. Here, variability was rampant. Vladimir Gorchakov, Pushkin's Kishinev acquaintance, complained:

> More than once, in such albums, have I come across poems by Pushkin, often so monstrously deformed that it was hard to understand what they were about; but every such poem was invariably signed with his name. Thus, in 1821, in an album belonging to one poetry aficionada [*liubitel'nitsa*], I recognized [Pushkin's] poem "To Doris" ["Doride"] written in 1820, with the following modifications. First, [the title became] "To Her"; then: "I trust: I am loved, is it possible not to trust you; / You are kind, good-looking, thus how could you be beguiling; / Everything is unfeigned about you: the vernal glow of your cheeks, /

Charming shyness, priceless gift of the gods, / The lively snow-whiteness of your attire and shoulders / And the infantile tenderness of caressing names."[94]

Indeed, only the final verse in the album version quoted by Gorchakov is faithful to Pushkin's original. The changes in the other five are too consistent to attribute to a lapse in the inscriber's memory. Take Doris's pleasantly casual manner of speaking—*rechei nebrezhnost'*—transformed, in the album, into *plechei belosnezhnost'*, the near-homophonous but far more sensual "snow-whiteness of [your] shoulders." Unlike Pushkin, his album alter ego employs the poetic device known as *blason*, the listing of physical features comprising a woman's beauty, even though neither bared shoulders nor glowing cheeks are ascribed to Pushkin's original Doris. Even more telling is the pronominal slippage. Though titled "To Doris" Pushkin's poem speaks of the eponymous woman in the third person; the album version, for its part, uses the third-person pronoun in the title ("To Her"), while in the text proper, *ona* (she) becomes the second-person *vy* (you). Form follows function: in an album, you talk to the album owner—in this case, one can surmise, a lady known to wear white, open-shouldered dresses.

Undeniably, the era of literacy came after ages of orality, but we must not be too quick to bury the latter. In his pioneering study of album culture in the Golden Age, Vadim Vatsuro describes it as a secondary folklorization of literature.[95] Among the features that define "album folklore," notes Vatsuro, are migrating madrigals, mostly unsigned (even those previously published as Baratynsky's or Zhukovsky's) and often rehashed depending on the inscriber's versificatory skills and communicative needs. Another feature of this "folklorization" is the fragmentation of the literary whole: in albums, quotations and excerpts prevail over texts adduced in toto.

Vatsuro's point encourages us to revisit, and reconsider, the time-honored division of cultures into the written and the oral. The culture of album poetry abutted on both—and belonged to neither. While the album is, par excellence, a written—handwritten—medium, its modus operandi is bound to here and now. Before it became a fait accompli, an album inscription had to debut as an *act* of inscribing, typically in front of whoever happened to be around. Can we afford to ignore the performance factor when considering the verbal form of Golden Age album inscriptions? You are writing, after all, while she waits; she must not be allowed to grow impatient. In albums, the very size of the written text could be a function of a paralinguistic situation. Preposterous as it may seem from a purely theoretical standpoint, I cannot imagine how better to characterize album poetry than as "oral literature." Orality was, in those days, a vital part of poetry's infrastructure, a sine qua non of its functioning. The oral and the written is not a binary, it is a spectrum.

The task I set myself in this chapter was to conceive of Golden Age poetry in terms of a spectrum—to establish how this or that literary fact would look when mapped onto a scale between the written and spoken, public and private, loud and low, fugitive and lasting, partial and holistic, authored and owned, casual and formal. Up to now, I have mainly looked at these choices from the point of view of those who wrote poetry; in the chapter that follows, I will focus on poetry's readers.

The act of reading a poem was, in the Golden Age, intimately connected with memorizing and reproducing it. It has been argued more than once—years ago by Jacques Derrida, more recently by Jonathan Culler—that the very idiom "to learn by heart"—*d'apprendre par coeur*—points to the centrality of the heart-image in our understanding of what poetry is.[96] Unreliable as etymological evidence tends generally to be, it may be worth noting here that the Russian equivalent for "memorizing by heart" is not heart-related at all. Literally, the inner form of the Russian *vyuchit' naizust'* can be rendered as "to learn by-out-of-mouth." If indeed the process of learning a poem *by heart* can be construed as being a metaphor of internalization, learning it *naizust'* implies externalizing, transporting poetry from the realm of the written to that of the oral, eye to mouth, reading to performing. *Reading to performing* is thus the spectrum to be examined in chapter 3.

3
Situations and Occasions

In late October 1822, an elegy titled "Spring" ("Vesna") appeared in the journal *Novosti literatury* (The literary news) with the following editorial footnote appended to its heading: "(*) Regretfully, this beautiful poem *on spring* has been received by us in the middle of *autumn*; but, better late than never. *Ed.*"[1] There is nothing like a system malfunction to highlight how systems are supposed to work. This footnote is one such telltale breakdown of a literary system, or rather, a quick attempt to patch it up. To be fully functional, a Golden Age lyric poem needed to be situationally—in our example, seasonally—anchored. This rule applied to writing and reading alike. "*On spring*" (*na vesnu*)—the phrasing used in the footnote—means "written *on the occasion* of spring." The editor who wrote it (Aleksandr Voeikov or Vasily Kozlov) opted for this expression despite knowing that, in this particular poem, vernal images served to set off, by contrast, its hero's disconsolate longing for a deceased beloved. Pictures of nature, it was assumed, had to be written from nature. Likewise, it was unnatural, or so the editors felt, to read about the joys of spring as the chill of fall settles in outside one's window. For best results, the here and now of writing a lyric poem had to be synchronized with the here and now of reading it—forming, ideally, an illusory "here and now" shared, if only for a moment, by the writer and reader of the poem.

The magic of moments like this is well captured in a letter (dated 26 August 1808) Aleksandr Turgenev sent his brother Nikolai (at the time, studying in Göttingen). The missive is layered with poignant reminiscences. Earlier that summer, writes Aleksandr, he paid a visit to their ancestral village of Turgenevo, where the Turgenev brothers (the eldest of whom, Andrei, died in 1803) had spent their childhood: "I could not look at any object [in the old house] without experiencing some secret sadness, something that disquieted my soul; even the sight of our old furniture stirred me; but the strongest source of memories of our long-gone life here was the window view from the hall in which we used to have our lessons."[2] It is through this window that Aleksandr Turgenev, now twenty-four, describes himself as gazing upon a sunset while reciting a poem recently inscribed in his album by Zhukovsky. Fittingly, Zhukovsky's poem (twelve lines of which are cited in the letter) pays tribute to just such enchanting evenings: "Recall how often in the fields / did you and I see off the setting sun / . . . / O bygone time, o unforgotten time!" The synchronization was perfect, attests Turgenev, both visually and in terms of mood: "Almost every line made me pause, for what it was saying was happening that very moment in reality—both before my eyes and inside my soul."[3]

Atmospheric convergence was but a visible part of a larger emotional ensemble. In the eyes of Golden Age poets and readers, poetry's calling was to provoke a whole range of poet-cum-reader co-experiences—be they of nature, history, friendship, or love. It is such cases of emotional complicity between poems and readers that I am going to examine in this chapter. Traditionally, the privileged (if not the sole) object of literary history has been a figure holding a pen. It is only recently that students of literature have begun attending to the figure holding a book—a shadier and more elusive subject, not so much a picture of a reader as a silhouette. As often occurs in scholarship, the history of reading is rapidly growing into a discipline in its own right, with its own set of methodologies and compartments. As discussed in this book's introduction, this budding field has furnished literary historians with a wealth of valuable data. We have a better idea than we used to of *what* books were read in nineteenth-century Russia, and *who* it was that was reading those books.[4] What interests me here is *how*: what reading devices were used, and how these devices, in turn, engaged with devices of writing. In other words, rather than study reading as such, the object I examine is reading-cum-writing and reading-as-writing.

"*Rock*-solid knowledge"; "*crystal*-clear prose." Such geological metaphors abound in our ways of describing human affairs, but few have shaped our thinking more than the famous *iceberg* analogy, with its proverbial *tip*. It may seem tempting at first to imagine literary history as another iceberg. Indeed, literary histories do at times seem impressionistic, like a Marinist painting with majestic snow-white masterpieces gliding by. The moment we factor in what is unseen—the host of contemporary readers for whom those great books were written—the picture changes. Now, literature-as-writing, with all its shiny names and brilliant works, becomes just the tip of a murkier submerged mass that the explorer of reading must dive deep under the iceberg's waterline to study. But despite its heuristic appeal, the iceberg analogy is of little help to literary studies: it conjures a polarized literary system, the divorce of writing from reading—much as, when applied to the human mind or human culture, the iceberg-imago overdramatizes the split between conscious and unconscious processes and drives. In actual fact, as glaciology tells us, the real iceberg is not a bipolar paradigm but a solid homogenous lump of ice; its putative duality—the above and beneath the waterline—is the observer's problem, not the iceberg's. No glaciologist would ever study the structure and migration of an iceberg's bottom in isolation from its tip; likewise, the history of reading—Golden Age reading in particular—cannot be separated from its counterpart, the history of writing.

"This Is My Life": Reading as Relating, Participating, and Performing

Open a collection of elegies—for instance, Baratynsky's—to the table of contents, and you will notice how many titles in it constitute one-word nouns that tag, as if on a shelf of vials, this or that situation, predicament, or emotional state a potential reader might find themselves in. Assurance, Disillusionment, Restlessness, Hopelessness, Vindication, Confession, Separation—any reader, whether in love or out of it, was welcome to pick one and walk away reassured and duly equipped.

This functionality was not confined to elegies, of course; nor was the repertoire of familiar situations limited to amatory mishaps. As his diary attests, Andrei Turgenev (Aleksandr's elder brother) was in the habit, when attending church services, of muttering secular poems under his breath—works whose plea for universal tolerance was more in tune with his sense of piety than was the canonical liturgy:

> Today, standing closer to the choir section [*krylos*] in the church, I began reciting with great pleasure Karam[zin's] "Chant to Divinity." This chant always affects me, but here, when it came to "Love! ... and when, caught by meek surprise / At the peak of their glory and triumph" etc., particularly at the word "love," I felt a quiet trepidation. I grew ecstatic, and all engulfed in this blissful state, began blessing the Bard and Poetry. Thereafter I recited silently [Karamzin's] "To Mercy" and [Schiller's] "An die Freude."[5]

The art of writing a poem entails the ability to relate; the art of reading, the ability to take part. Thus does Aleksei Merzliakov explain the joint machinery of reading and writing lyric poetry, elegy in particular, in his 1822 *Brief Outline of Literary Theory*. Relatability and participation, the critic believed, were mutually dependent.

> The appeal [of an elegy] is stronger when its content relates to the reader, and it is this relatedness that defines the degree of the reader's *souchastie* [complicity, participation]. The latter is at its highest when the subject-matter of an elegy directly affects or concerns its reader, or when the situation in which the poem finds the reader is similar to the poet's own or that of the character depicted in it.[6]

The term *souchastie* used in Merzliakov's perceptive definition is broader than any equivalent I have been able to find in English. *Uchastie* in Russian covers everything from the "participation" used above to "sympathy," "involvement," and "partaking"; the prefix *so-* transforms it into a sort of co-partaking, literally "complicity." A more accurate translation of Merzliakov's definition would be: the power of elegy (or, for that matter, of lyric poetry in general) is proportionate to readers' involvement or complicity in it; and the degree of that complicity, in turn, depends on how close the reader's circumstances are to those referred to in the poem. "When alone, [Emilia] should check the silent musings and moods of her innocent soul against the beautiful work of the Poet who will expertly tell her what her heart feels but is unable to express," an observer of polite society types (of which "Emilia" is one) wrote in the journal *Moskovskii vestnik* (Moscow herald) in 1827.[7] Poetry was where readers *looked up* names for emotions, as we do words in a dictionary. With time, those names settled down to form the common pool for future readers and future poets to draw from—precisely as Joseph Brodsky has it in his 1961 "In Memory of E. A. Baratynsky" ("Pamiati E. A. Baratynskogo"):

> Ну, вот и кончились года,
> затем и прожитые вами,
> чтоб наши чувства иногда
> мы звали вашими словами.[8]

[So, the years have now passed / in which you lived precisely / so that we might sometimes name our feelings / using your words.]

True, Merzliakov's account of what readers relate to in lyric texts includes the "character [*litso*] depicted" by the poet. This term, however, does not refer to *he-or-she* characters of the sort we encounter in fiction. Merzliakov has in mind the *I*-characters or "speakers" of verse—a mythological or historical mask to which a poem attributes what it says. Poems of this subgenre (sometimes dubbed heroides after Ovid's book of the same name) were in vogue in European lyric poetry of the eighteenth century, before reappearing in the form of "dramatic monologue" in the English poetry of the nineteenth. Whether under the impetus of this fact or not, a school emerged in the framework of American New Criticism by which lyric was to be analyzed primarily by positing a "lyric speaker" hidden "behind" a poem's text, as if it were a matter of "tell me who is speaking, and I'll tell you what the poem is about."[9]

Unlike this quasi-thespian, Stanislavsky-like method of analysis, the pragmatic model I propose here does not posit the speaker behind the lyric text but *ahead* of it. Far from being predefined by who is speaking, the lyric poem undertakes a search for a reader-speaker willing (and prepared) to make the poem their own. In this perspective, such properties as relatability and performability come to the fore: how many different situations may a given poem be related to, and on how many different occasions could it be *performed*, in the broad sense of this word, that is, both enacted and applied. In the framework of the guess-who-is-speaking method, our every surmise inevitably limits the range of possible meanings. Attempting to determine the putative speaker's gender, for instance, curtails this field by half. The approach I propose takes this question off the table: even when grammatically marked, the speaker's gender is up to the user—the performer—to decide. Poets make poems that make meaning—as evidence shows, this was not quite how lyric poetry worked in the Golden Age. Here, poets made *templates* for meaning; it took a reader to make the meaning work.

Acts of speech imply an agency: a speaker. When it comes to poetry, questions as to the speaker inevitably arise, but crucial here is where we situate this speaker in mental space and time. It seems intuitive to conceive of a speaker as located *behind* the spoken, and the speech-act as having occurred *before* we read it. Axiomatic as such presumptions may appear in relation to everyday communication, they do not necessarily apply to the workings of lyric poetry. In lyric, the "speaker" is not reducible to a role, a speaker-in-the-text (whether a dramatic mask, the poet in person, or the poet's abstracted proxy—the "lyric hero"), but is more helpfully envisioned as a function, a movable agency or *speakership* that lyric poets delegate to their future readers.

Delegating a work to a performer did not amount to relegating it. Vladimir Gorchakov, we recall, once happened to stumble upon Pushkin's poem "To Doris" in someone's album, refashioned to fit the album holder's glowing cheeks and snow-white shoulders. Appalled as Pushkin's friend may have been by this appropriation, Pushkin himself would have seen it coming. His *Mozart and Salieri* (*Motsart i Sal'ieri*) includes a scene showing a blind old tavern fiddler perform an aria from Mozart's *Don Giovanni*, presumably out of tune. Salieri is outraged; Mozart finds it funny. Much like in music, in lyric poetry the very fact of having composed a work was tantamount to signing what may be called a "speakership disclaimer."

As speakership changed hands, so did the honor of being the speaker's treasured addressee. Mythic creatures like "Doris" or "Charis" (used to allegorize generic beauty, or to obscure reference to an actual one) were easy to highjack and reassign to a standby album-holder. But even when the real name of a person known to many happened to appear in the title or first line of a love poem—"O, you self-willed Sofia! . . ."—the verse could easily be repurposed. Poets, Pushkin included, had no qualms about resorting to this ruse. In 1821–22, Baratynsky, at the time in love with Sofia Ponomareva, wrote a number of poems to her; in 1823, his ardor cooled by Sofia's apparent inattention, Baratynsky readdressed two of them—"You are adored by far too many" ("Vy slishkom mnogimi liubimy") and "A blind devotee of beauty" ("Slepoi poklonnik krasoty")—to Annette Lutkovskaya, a niece of his regimental commander.[10] The second of these poems, now under the title "To L-ia," appeared in Baratynsky's 1827 collection of poetry, only to lose this title, in turn, in the 1835 edition. This disappearance was due, more likely than not, to the appearance of still another flame, this one contained in wedlock. After marrying Anastasia Engelgardt in 1826, that is, Baratynsky grew cagy about publishing his love poems, their dates and titles in particular. In the early nineteenth century, lyric poetry served as a form of relationship between people; as relationships thrived or soured, poems could textually change.

A common method of relating to a lyric text was simply to rewrite it. Rewriting, like reciting, was a form of *souchastie*, of becoming an "accomplice" or surrogate author of a lyric work. Traces of reading as rewriting are frequent in deposits of album lore, as we see in the case of an 1821 Pushkin elegy inscribed, in 1827, in an album (owner unknown):

Я пережил свои желанья,
Я разлюбил свои мечты;

Остались мне одни страданья—
Плоды сердечной пустоты.

Безмолвно жребию послушный—
Влачу страдальческий венец—
Живу печальный, равнодушный,
И жду: придет ли мой конец?

Так, поздним хладом пораженный,
Как ветров слышен зимний свист,
Один—на ветке обнаженной—
Трепещет запоздалый лист!¹¹

[I have outlasted my desires, / Have ceased to love my dreams; / What remains for me is only suffering, / The fruit of the heart's emptiness. // Silently obedient to my fate / I drag my martyr's crown, / I dwell, sorrowful and aloof / And wonder if my end will come. // Thus, stricken with a tardy chill / When winter's whistling winds are heard, / Alone on a bare bough / There trembles a belated leaf.]

Beneath the poem, in the same hand, is written "By Aleks[andr] Pushkin," and then "Written by [*pisala*] 6:2." To the left of the second stanza, behind a vertical stroke, is a note: "This is my life" (*Vot moia zhizn'*).¹²

As N. A. Tabakova suggests, the "6:2" inscriber was a woman with the initials E. B. (Е. Б., the sixth and second letters; signatures in such alphanumeric code were quite common). E. B.'s comment, in turn, lends room for speculation. As a remark, "This is my life" is unexceptional. That someone should find a doleful elegy (*unylaia elegiia*) well attuned to their melancholy mood—this fact in itself was nothing special.¹³ What *was* special was E. B.'s recording of her quasi-anonymous comment in an album—that is, making her reading experience quasi-*public*.

In the mind of the early nineteenth-century reader, writing and reading constituted one continuous, mutually segueing process. Reading begets writing: E. B., a model reader who knows Pushkin's elegy by heart (the few minor imprecisions would seem to rule out a printed source at hand), writes it out on the page of another person's album. Writing begets reading: now, the album's owner, and whoever else this person might show her album to, would become readers of Pushkin-plus—of Pushkin's elegy *plus* this particular reader-annotator. Placed back-to-back with Pushkin's line "I dwell, sorrowful and aloof," E. B.'s "This is my life" claims a role on Pushkin's stage. This is performing via writing.

We tend to picture reading as a passive activity, so to speak. Asked to situate reading in Michael Fried's famous *absorption* versus *theatricality* dichotomy, we would likely opt for absorption.[14] But the Golden Age was not as patient. Here, to read was to *act*—upon the thing you read, and upon its other readers. In this respect, not only writing a poem but also reading it was a performative act: *doing* things with verse. What can one do with verse? Sing it, cite, recite, rewrite, adjust it to your needs or apply it to your life.

Most such usages entailed approaching a poem not as a text set in stone, but a template for further use. Like many well-known poems of the period, "I have outlasted my desires" went on to an impressive career as a song (specifically, an "art song," *romans*). Beginning in 1831, no less than twenty composers are known to have set Pushkin's elegy to music. Through the eye of a performer—for instance, fin-de-siècle contralto Varia Panina—both Pushkin's poem and the musical score Mikhail Shishkin wrote for it in 1892 were but templates for Panina to vocalize on stage, much as, for the composer Shishkin, Pushkin's lyric was, first and foremost, a template for future lyrics. Writing "this is my life" on Pushkin's margin amounted to using his elegy as an expressive template.

In the world of letters as we are used to it today, reading and writing are two contrary, if interrelated, operations. Writers write; readers read. In our mind's eye, this is a diptych on which two profiled figures are shown facing each other: one with a pen, the other with a book. In Russia, this mental picture truly became incarnate in the 1830–40s—the epoch in which the developing book market progressively polarized writing and reading, casting writers as active producers and readers as passive consumers of literary works. But when thinking of the Golden Age, it would be more accurate to visualize the reader as a profile hunched over a book—but with a pen in her hand. In the case of E. B., this book is someone's album. For her, reading Pushkin's "I have outlasted my desires" entailed *rewriting* it for someone else to read, while at the same time using its textual margin as a proscenium on which to perform her own elegiac lament titled "This Is My Life."

Children of the Lyre: Poetry in Singing Situations

Early nineteenth-century poetry did not, as is sometimes believed, consist of easily identifiable occupations: those who wrote and those who read, with the printer and bookseller in the middle. Books did come out, and poems did appear in periodicals, but we must be careful not to limit poetry's habitat to printed matter. Much of it lived in regions that were less accessible—less convenient for observation. One of these, as we just saw, was what Simon Franklin calls nineteenth-century Russia's "graphosphere": the handwritten counterpart of print culture.[15] Albums constituted a sizable part but not the whole of it. Hand-copied poems (*spiski*, or *spisok* in the singular) filled many a reader's notebooks and self-bound books for a variety of reasons, most famously to circulate while bypassing the censor. Another reason had to do with the cost and availability of printed books. Not every country noble could easily get hold of a book everyone was raving about, or afford to buy it when they encountered it. A culture of sharing developed, especially among the provincial nobility: two or more country estates would put up money to subscribe to a journal or buy a book that would then barnstorm through a number of villages. It was cheaper for you to write out the poem(s) you liked (occasionally, one would hand-copy a whole novel!) than keep the book itself. Doing so likewise added a certain charge of creativity. A modern-day teenager, instead of buying an album of songs, would rather go online to compile their own playlists to be stored on a handheld device. Similarly, a custom-made handwritten selection of poetry or, say, favorite monologues from *Woe from Wit*, could be the pride of a reader's shelf.

In his memoir of his student days, the pedagogue and writer Nikolai Ivanitsky (1816–58) describes the (second-)hand reading habits of the typical provincial gymnasium pupil thus:

> Many of us developed a passion for reading poems. But, lacking the means to acquire any worthy author in full [*vpolne*], we used to obtain handwritten notebooks with odes by Lomonosov and Derzhavin, some of Pushkin's long poems, Dmitriev's tales, Zhukovsky's ballads and the like; all of this was diligently rewritten and most of it learned by heart. It still surprises me how, given the level of teaching at the time, such passion [for reading] could be born and developed![16]

Often, however, hand-copying what you had just read seems to have been motivated not so much by thriftiness or liberal ideas as by instinct or compulsion. We have witnessed this in the case of E. B., who no doubt felt strongly about the elegy she inscribed in the album. At times, having strong feelings *against* a poem would serve as just an effective impetus to copy it. The natural scientist and writer Andrei Bolotov, who spent most of his life on his parental estate in Tula province, kept a reading notebook titled "Magazine of Memorable and Curious Texts Circulating among the People [*nosivshikhsia v narode*]." One such text that had come to Bolotov's attention happened to be Denis Davydov's political fable "The Female Eagle, Ruff, and Blackcock" ("Orlitsa, turukhtan i teterev," 1804), which blatantly satirized the assassination of Paul I, the cruelty of his rule, and the miserliness of his successor Alexander I. Davydov's fable outraged Bolotov as "insolent, dripping with malice and venom, fit to be burned."[17] To his credit, rather that commit the darn thing to flames, our Tula Savonarola hand-copied Davydov's pasquinade into his "Magazine."

Poetry expanded, in particular, to three areas beyond the graphosphere itself. One was the art of conversation, discussed at some length in chapter 2. The tenet here was that poetic skill and the skill of conversation were two equally important manifestations of one and the same talent: the dexterous command of language. As Vera Bukharina-Annenkova tells it, Pushkin (by all accounts himself an accomplished conversationalist) could even find it unsettling when the two skill-levels did not happen to match: "I remember Pushkin's judgment regarding Countess Rostopchina. He paid tribute to her poetic talent, but also said that while she wrote very well, she spoke very poorly, growing intoxicated by her own discourse and giving the impression of a Pythia on her tripod discharging inconsistent thoughts, devoid of logic, solely for the pleasure of quarreling."[18]

The other two areas were singing and reciting. The best thing that could happen to one's lyric poem, claimed Ivan Dmitriev in his memoir *A Look at My Life* (1823–25), was to be set to music. As Dmitriev recalls, his own poetic success was owed to two factors. One was that his *Fashionable Wife* (*Modnaia zhena*, 1791)—a naughty narrative in verse involving a resourceful married woman, her cuckold husband, and her young lover—became popular among young men and poets in both capitals. The second factor—the one that interests us here—was that, turned by the composer Fedor Dubiansky into a song (*romans*), Dmitriev's "The Little Gray Dove Is Moaning" ("Stonet sizyi golubochek," 1792) "caught the fancy," as he put it, "of the fair sex."[19]

In Dmitriev's epoch, if you belonged to the fair sex and a song "caught your fancy," you needed, to indulge your affinity, a musical instrument, a songbook, and a score. Unlike the handheld and headset commonly used by music fans today, these antiquated pieces of equipment were designed to *make* music rather than consume it on the run. The eponymous noble maiden in Karamzin's sentimental tale "Evgenii and Iuliia" spends her summers contemplating nature and winters reading philosophy and rereading letters from her beloved who had been sent to study abroad. When Evgenii returns, he brings his Iuliia numerous books in French, Italian, and German, as well as volumes of printed music.

> She was most skilled at playing harpsichord and singing. Klopstock's "Willkommen, [o] silberner Mond" set to music by Ritter von Gluck was a song she particularly favored. Not once could she, without her heart melting, sing the last stanza, in which Gluck so skillfully attuned the tone of music to the great poet's feelings. You, mild and gentle souls! You and you alone are able to appreciate those virtuosos, and their immortal works are dedicated to you and you alone. A single tear you shed is their greatest reward.[20]

From the standpoint of narratology, Iuliia's song is a classic case of foreshadowing. As eighteenth-century readers would have remembered better than we might today, the title of Klopstock's elegy (which is never mentioned; Karamzin's subtle prose evades signposting) is "Early Graves"; and a few pages later in the book, young Evgenii indeed dies—on the eve of uniting his life with Iuliia's. This explains, of course, why Iuliia's heart melted precisely when she used to sing the last stanza—the one in which Klopstock's lyric speaker addresses the mossy graves of the untimely departed: "O, wie war glücklich ich, als ich noch mit euch / Sähe sich röthen den Tag, schimmern die Nacht" (O, how happy was I when, together with you, / I watched the day come and the night gleam!).

Iuliia, as Karamzin would have us see her, is both a sensitive soul and a sensitive reader. Not only does she brood over early graves, anticipating, perhaps, that she may before long find herself mourning over Evgenii's, but she cannot but weep, experiencing the beautiful encounter of great music with great verse; and, as if taking a curtain call, Klopstock and Gluck, as Karamzin imagines them, seem to come out and bow to Iuliia's tear. Singing was as highly valued a skill in a young woman as were conversing and dancing.

Lyric poetry of the Golden Age would hardly have become as popular in Russia as it was throughout the nineteenth century and beyond had it not been in collusion with Russian singers. Some poems, like Merzliakov's immensely popular "Amid the Level Vale" ("Sredi doliny rovnyia") had been custom-written as songs; others, like Baratynsky's "Dissuasion" ("Razuverenie"; to be analyzed later in this book), were set to music, with the lyrics' authors often forgotten in the process. The world of singing had its own hierarchy of hit titles independent of, but not unrelated to, their purely literary fame.[21] To get to the bottom of these dynamics, we would need to consider vocal culture in conjunction with its commercial offshoots like songbooks or popular prints (*lubok*), which, riding the wave of songs' popularity as songs, contributed to the popularity of their poetic prototypes. Along with novels and dream-dictionaries, songbooks were Golden Age best sellers. A truly comprehensive survey of poetry in the mirror of nineteenth-century opinion would have to examine not one reflection but three: a poem's prestige among its author's peers (the small mirror, as it were); its rating among composers and singers; and its post-vocal success—the printed spinoff of its career as a song. When one of Pushkin's 1814 juvenilia, titled "Song (One Rainy Autumn Evening)" ("Romans [Pod vecher, osen'iu nenastnoi]"), appeared in print in 1827, it did not outshine any of Pushkin's mature, peer-acknowledged masterpieces (nor did the publisher expect it to). But once in print, "One Rainy Autumn Evening" "took off" as a song (or more precisely, several songs, considering the number of composers it attracted); suddenly the market was awash in illustrated *lubok* editions, many not even crediting the famous author. As Oleg Proskurin maintains, in the course of the nineteenth century, "One Rainy Autumn Evening" grew to be Pushkin's most popular poem—if we factor in readers from *all* social strata.[22]

In 1796 Dmitriev published (anonymously) a songbook furnished with this epigraph from Antoine Houdar de La Motte: "Les vers sont enfants de la lyre, / Il faut les chanter, non les lire" ("Verses are the children of the lyre, / They are supposed to be sung, not read").[23] Taken broadly, de La Motte's motto applies to Golden Age poetry at large. Here, a lyric poem was both a performative act and a performable script. Performance, in other words, was prewired; whether euphonic or cacophonic, a poem's phonic form dictated the manner in which it was to be pronounced.

As Tynianov showed in his study "The Ode as an Oratorical Genre," reliance on pronunciation took root in eighteenth-century poetics. The ode was thought of, in Tynianov's phrasing, as an utterable genre (*myslilas' proiznosimoi*), hence its literal and figurative loudness.[24] For example, Derzhavin's "The echo rumbles across hills / Like thunder thundering upon thunders" (Грохочет эхо по горам, / Как гром гремящий по громам) with its fivefold recurring *gro-gor-gre*'s, five *m*'s and two *kho*'s, is not only magnificently onomatopoeic but also majestically hyperbolic, for here the sight and sound of a geographically specific natural site—the Kivach Waterfall on the Suna River—

carry the extra load of allegorizing the exploits of two historically specific Russian military leaders: one recently deceased, the other still alive when Derzhavin's "Waterfall" ("Vodopad") was written. Thundering is as much in the nature of the ode as in that of waterfalls. It is hard to recite Derzhavin sotto voce.

Tynianov is surely cogent in pointing to the importance of the oral factor in the poetics of the ode but less so in downplaying this factor when it comes to the rest of lyric poetry. There is nothing restricting oral delivery to oration; many poems were not just read but sung, and more were also recited. When a poem like "One Rainy Autumn Evening" becomes an actual song (*romans*), we cannot, contrary to what Tynianov suggests, dismiss it as something that has gone over to music and is no longer poetry; we should instead incorporate music into the study of poetry's pragmatics. Doing so, and adding various styles and schools of poetry recitation, we soon discover that in the Golden Age, poetry was as acutely attuned to the perspective of being voiced and listened to as its eighteenth-century odic incarnation had been. Writing your poem so that it reads well aloud, that is, was never the sole prerogative of the age of odes.

Neither is reading aloud the same thing as reading loudly. The master of thunderous onomatopoeia, Derzhavin was no less mindful of the softer end of the scale. "Poetry and music," he speculates in his "Discourse on Lyric Poetry" (1811–15), "make our hearts resonate to their gentle strings."[25] According to Derzhavin's treatise, a good judge of either of these two arts will always know whether,

> for instance, the articulation of a verse or a tone in music becomes whistle-like when it comes to depicting a whistling and hissing snake; whether a thunderclap thunders, a water-spring murmurs, a forest bellows, a grove smiles in the verse describing the crash of the first of these; the quietly prattling [*tikho-bormochushchego*] current of the second; the gloomily doleful [*mrachno-unylogo*] howling of the third; and cheerful aftersounds of the fourth—in other words, whether every thought, every feeling, every word is clad in a corresponding sound; whether these sounds reach our hearts; whether we recognize in each of these the action or image of nature [*deistvie ili obraz estestva*].[26]

The notion that lyric poems—infants of the lyre—wanted and needed to be listened to, not read, was sometimes bolstered by the mythopoetic—and metapoetic—image of the foundational poet. Derzhavin's "Discourse" conjures two of these: the Greek bard (with a lyre) whose cultivated and euphonious language made listeners think their soul was in their ears, and Northern skalds whose sense of hearing was said to be so refined that it could capture pictures made of living light—an ability never achieved by either ancient or modern Southern peoples. "As I understand it," Derzhavin remarks somewhat self-servingly, "[these skalds] were past masters of onomatopoeic verse."[27] Poetry, like music, is the art of sound: "Therefore a poet must always be mindful that his style is clear and fluent, easily pronounceable and suitable to be set to music. The slightest roughness, the slightest murkiness burdens attention and dispels thoughts."[28]

Poet, Player, Priest:
Poetry in Recital Situations

In January 1820, Evgeny Baratynsky, along with his regiment, was transferred from St. Petersburg to Finland. Here he devoted the elegy "Finland" ("Finliandiia") to what was then believed to be the glorious past of this imposing and desolate terrain: "So this is the homeland of Odin's sons, who once / struck fear in the hearts of distant peoples."[29] Strolling among "the crevices of granite rocks eternal," the poet contemplates the oblivion that would betide his poems as it once had the skaldic songs:

> Умолк призывный щит, не слышен Скальда глас,
>   Воспламененный дуб угас,
> Развеял буйный ветер торжественные клики;
> Сыны не ведают о подвигах отцов;
>   И в дольном прахе их богов
>   Лежат низверженные лики![30]

[Soundless now is the shield of summons, the skaldic voice / unheard, the blazing oak tree cold, / the raging winds have carried off the solemn cries— / the sons know nothing of the fathers' valiant deeds, / and the countenance of their gods / lie overthrown in the dust of the earth!]

As luck would have it, Baratynsky's commander in Finland, Staff Captain Nikolai Konshin, turned out to be a devotee of poetry who would leave us his reminiscences on Baratynsky. It is here we learn of an early (if not the first) recital of Baratynsky's "Finland" in front of company officers, which Konshin paints in glaring colors inspired, of course, by Baratynsky's "Finland."

> I remember one winter evening. There was a storm outside. Attentive silence surrounded our Skald when he, enraptured, read to us in a solemn singsong voice, in a manner learned from Gnedich, taken from the Greeks, accepted by Pushkin and all the famous poets of that time—when he sang to us his *hymn to Finland*. . . . [This was a memorable hour.] One of us then remarked that the shades of Odin and his heroes had flown down to listen to this hymn and were [blizzard-]knocking [*stuchali metel'iu*] on our windows in greeting to the poet.[31]

Its flamboyant atmospherics aside, Konshin's account is a useful portrayal of a nineteenth-century recital. Despite misnaming Baratynsky's elegy a "hymn" and summoning Viking ghosts to cheer "our Skald," he does perceptively link the poet's manner of reciting to that of Pushkin, and through him, that of Nikolai Gnedich, a man of theater, translator of French tragedies, and someone who had devoted years to rendering *The Iliad* in Russian, inventing, in the process, a Russian counterpart of Homeric prosody and its supposed enunciation.

Nowadays, we read poems more often than we hear them; in the Golden Age, this was not necessarily the case. Recitations took place anywhere: at dedicated venues like Moscow University's Society of Lovers of Russian Literature and its multiple lookalikes in both capitals and other towns of Russia; in less formal gatherings like literary salons (for example, at the Olenins', where Gnedich was a permanent star), friendly drinking bouts, and household parties; in improvised locations like that remote infantry garrison in Finland, or the fortress cell (*kazemat*) in which exiled Decembrists were housed when arriving at Petrovsky Zavod, Siberia. When the exiles' wives came in their wake, for the time being "they settled with their husbands in our communal barrack, inspiriting with their presence our monotonous captivity," reports Mikhail Bestuzhev. "It became our habit, when getting together in tight circles formed around every married couple, to read aloud literary works on less than serious subjects; this was the epoch in which poems, tales, short stories and memoirs flourished."[32] Recitals were thus heard in dungeons; at a dinner table or society event; on official academic and literary occasions; and, we must not forget, most public literary readings of this kind used to occur on a regular basis, weekly or monthly.

The importance of audial delivery comes to the fore if we consider poetry—or for that matter, literature in general—not as a stand-alone formation but as part of a larger verbal landscape. Within this landscape, poetry found itself flanked by two performative institutions fully dependent on oral delivery as a means to affect their respective attendees. One of these was dramatic theater, most of which in this period was in verse; the other, Russian Orthodox churches, with their extraordinary reliance on audial ambiance and vocal elocution.

The theater was not simply a place for poets to frequent as spectators; sooner or later, a poet of note would try their hand at dramatic composition themselves. The same is true of theater as a performing art. Acting in the Golden Age was not confined to the imperial theaters. Noble amateurs would showcase their thespian skills on home stages. Good acting in this period was largely about poetic diction. Schools of expressive recitation competed: Fedor Kokoshkin was known for asserting the classicist manner on professional and amateur stages in Moscow; in Petersburg, Pavel Katenin and his pupil, the actress Aleksandra Kolosova, vied with tragedienne Ekaterina Semenova, a pupil of Nikolai Gnedich.

Recalling the recital of "Finland" in Finland, Konshin traced Baratynsky's style of reciting to Gnedich. Known to have coached poets and actors in declamation, Gnedich was an effusive *chtets* (elocutionist) himself. Skeptics characterized Gnedich's "frenzied [*neistovyi*] recitals" as "chant-like, clamorous, screamy—but passionate and in accord with the meaning of the verse, which on the other hand was not something he was always able to bring out in his pupil [Ekaterina Semenova]."[33] Others sensed a method in Gnedich's reportedly vehement presentations. Thus, Petr Pletnev attributed their power to his volume control:

> Willing to make his recitals artistically expressive, Gnedich used to adjust the raising or lowering of his voice to suit the dimensions of the room he was reciting in. He also used to pre-rehearse his gestures so that they matched the meaning of a verse. Some verses were uttered in a slow singsong voice, others were barely audible. Credit where it is due: Gnedich usually attained the effect he was aiming for. Often, as you heard him recite, especially Homer's hexameters, something began moving within you involuntarily, and your blood circulation changed.[34]

The perceived importance of an effective recitation—or, for that matter, its sheer loudness—is well exemplified by the advice the clever but cynical professor of rhetoric Aleksei Merzliakov once gave his eager but talentless student

Stepan Zhikharev, who had hoped to gain entrée into St. Petersburg's literary circles with his tragedy *Artaban*. On 27 October 1806, Zhikharev's diary records, he showed the manuscript of *Artaban* to Merzliakov, his mentor. "'Galimatias, my dear man!' [Merzliakov] said bluntly. 'But then, so what? Go ahead and read it to Petersburg literati. Recite it yourself, loudly, split their ears, and you'll be a success.'" At first, Zhikharev's ego was wounded, but when, half a year later, he had occasion to hear Gnedich recite his translation of book 8 of *The Iliad* "with extraordinary ardor and in strident voice," he made the following entry: "[Merzliakov] may have had a point there. Now I think a poem can benefit from being read loudly; it was not for nothing that Gnedich was overstraining his chest over *The Iliad*."[35]

The other performative institution in poetry's vicinity was, as mentioned, the church, with its rigorous calendar of observances and wide repertoire of chants and liturgies conducted in Church Slavonic. While it was inconceivable for a churchgoer to critique these texts as texts (suggesting, say, improvements to the Lord's Prayer), there was nothing untoward about discussing how well this or that text was sung or read at this or that church or mass. "Use feeling, logic, pauses as you read, / Do not read like a deacon at an ambo," the character Famusov from Griboedov's comedy instructs a servant whose duties include reading aloud a to-do list for the week. Uttered on a theater stage, a line like this must have sounded like an in-joke, hinting at the Orthodox Church's open hostility toward theatrical forms of entertainment. At the same time, as one reads Stepan Zhikharev's diary of 1806–7, one is surprised to discover how often and readily this young theater buff attended religious services in order to experience what we would identify today—and Zhikharev himself comes close to identifying—as purely theatrical enjoyment. The diary records his frequent church visits, on weekdays, too.

> Thursday, December 6 [1806]. Listened to a mass [*obednia*] in the St. Nicholas the Mariner Church, it's their temple holy day today. . . . Court Archdeacon Aleksei Grigor'evich Vorzhsky, invited to serve on the occasion of the holy day, astounded me. What an unimaginable voice, and what mastery of elocution! Exact, lucid, clear; every word rolls out as a pearl, but what astonished me even more was the proper intonation he abided by as he read from the New Testament, emphasizing such words as would be better understood thereby; lowering and raising his voice in accord with the meaning of what was being said. He ranks number five at the court church, but in terms of quality he must be the

first. Senior Archdeacon Ivan Aleksandrovich has a stronger but less cultivated voice; he is as tall as Vorzhsky and even portlier than he, but his deportment is less noble, and he lacks Vorzhsky's extraordinary mastery of reading.[36]

If we replace, in the above, the words "church" and "archdeacon" with "stage" and "bass," Zhikharev's diary entry could easily pass as an opera review.

However, poetic recitals differed decidedly from ecclesiastic ones in a key respect: the allocation of authority. Whether you were a gifted presenter like Vorzhsky or a second-rate one like the honorary Ivan Aleksandrovich, (divine) authority was vested not in you but the Holy Writ—*the* book. Conversely, poetic authority lay with a poem performed, not penned. "I do not know if you are going to like my poor verses, which shall reach you unnamed (I truly could not think of a fitting title), in so ugly a copy, and without its author present," Konstantin Aksakov wrote from Moscow to his beloved cousin in Petersburg. "I wish this great distance that separates us were not so: I would have recited the poem for you using my face and voice to complement things unexpressed."[37]

Konstantin Aksakov, indeed, is better known as an essayist than a poet, but then, even a virtuoso versifier like Vasily Zhukovsky used to trust his ear more than he would his eye. "I always liked him," Zhukovsky wrote to Petr Viazemsky from Bad Ems, where he happened to run into Aleksei Khomiakov. "But this time, I bit into him like a hungry spider into a fly. I threw my verses at him so that he'd read them out before me. Thus am I able to detect my poems' covert flaws; when it comes to the overt ones, those I can notice and deal with on my own."[38] Performability is the name of the game: for Zhukovsky, any poem was presumed imperfect until proven perfect in performance.

In a recital situation, poetry became a theater-in-miniature. Sometimes, as in the case of Gnedich's recitals or Baratynsky's reading of "Finland" to infantry officers in Finland, the theater was composed of a single poet reciting to a group. Sometimes, a group of poets took turns reading to each other. Sometimes, when poems were recited face to face or heart to heart, this was the theater of two; and sometimes recitals took the form of what twentieth-century playwright Nikolai Evreinov would call *teatr dlia sebia* ("theater for oneself")—the kernel and ultimate form of theatricality. When in 1836 Sergei Aksakov decided to take his twenty-year-old son Konstantin from Petersburg back to Moscow, the latter lost the best listener he had: his beloved cousin

Maria Kartashevskaya. For want of his only gentle reader, Konstantin was left with no better option than to recite his favorite poems to himself. As we learn from a letter he sent to Maria from the road, young Aksakov found in himself an appreciative listener:

> Any verse line that I uttered I experienced tenfold; any verse that was even slightly sad or melodious filled my eyes with tears. When we arrived in Novgorod this agitated state reached its apex. I attended the evening mass: the tolling bells, chanting, and simple magnificence of the cathedral made a greater impact on me than I had ever experienced in a church; never had my soul felt tenderer and more sympathetic. After dinner, alone in the hotel when my father decided for some reason to pay a visit to a pub [*otesinka vyshel zachem-to k traktirshchiku*], I felt like reciting from Derzhavin, and this was when I really burst into tears.[39]

Productive Reading

In 1810 the sentimental tale "Modest and Sofia" ("Modest i Sofiia") appeared in the St. Petersburg magazine *Tsvetnik* (The flower garden). Having lived through a series of romantic upsets, young Modest is restored to happiness at a mansion of the country squire Priamodushin and his daughter, Sofia. Every night after their joyful rustic chores, Sofia, her father, and her future soulmate Modest "would gather round the fireplace and read the best among novels, laugh and cry over them, voice admiration and exchange feelings and thoughts."[40]

This evening idyll was meant to tutor the reader of "Modest and Sofia" in how to read. First, to "laugh and cry" together over a novel was, as Andrei Zorin has shown, a form of emotive and cultural co-tuning. In the age of sensibility in Russia, reading was seen as a form of cross-cultural appropriation: "Reading together and co-experiencing the same works of literature secured the spread of unified emotional models across national barriers and state borders."[41] Secondly, the fact that only "the best among novels"—presumably, *Julie, or the New Heloise*, or *Clarissa*—would be admitted into homes like kindhearted Priamodushin's sent an ethical signal. Reading solely for pleasure was considered suspicious: fiction was, indeed, only warranted by the lessons you could draw from it. Thirdly, the fact that Modest, Sofia, and her father "exchanged feelings and thoughts" about these novels tells us that proper reading was to be interventionist and dialogical.

The last of these requirements merits additional comment. Why would the author of a tale like "Modest and Sofia" encourage readers to distract themselves from the plot and engage in dialogue with each other? A plausible answer to this is found in the time-tested tradition of didactic discourse. Lessons, religious or moral, are commonly couched in dialogic terms. Questions and answers form the rhetorical backbone of any catechism—"You might ask" (*Voprosish*) and "I answer" (*Otvechaiu*). Explicitly or not, most didactic discourses engrain two agencies: the one who knows and the one who learns. Such dialogues were hardly native to religious treatises alone. The one-who-knows of Bernard Le Bovier de Fontenelle's seventeenth-century best-seller *Conversations on the Plurality of Worlds* educates Marchioness de G—the book's smart, fair-haired one-who-learns—about the celestial bodies above her nighttime garden, in which these conversations take place. "Like Fontenelle, he builds little dramas in which a problem, political or moral, is resolved," Konstantin Batiushkov wrote about Mikhail Murav'ev, who, inspired by de Fontenelle's 1683 *Dialogues of the Dead*—a series of transhistorical debates between ancients and moderns—came up with his own *Conversations of the Dead* (*Razgovory mertvykh*, 1790), adding a bunch of late discussants from Russia to the panel.[42] In the seventeenth and eighteenth centuries, dialogical (proto-dramatic) form was seen as a perfect match for the doctrine of *dulce et utile*, according to which entertainment had to be edifying and edification entertaining. "Truth and fiction are in some measure blended," writes de Fontenelle in his dedication of *Conversations on the Plurality of Worlds*, and "the union of philosophy and amusement is the chief aim of this work."[43]

As a literary convention, didactic dialogues à la Lucian and de Fontenelle did not survive the eighteenth century, but the practice of enlightened conversations—now staged *about* and *between* rather than *within* literary texts—remained in vogue throughout the Golden Age. Works of literature were debated at sittings of literary societies of every sort, and also—importantly for rural areas—at after-dark family gatherings like Priamodushin's. Reading a book you liked could feel like talking to its author, as Batiushkov said of the late French poet Saint-Lambert—"a kind man, fun to converse with."[44] Reading took readers beyond reading, beyond the graphosphere, as it were, into the semblance of live communication in absentia.

The question J. L. Austin poses in his book on language and pragmatics is how to do things with words. No less pressing a question is what things can be done with what we read. Golden Age reading practices were active, performative, and productive. The quintessential product of what I propose to call "productive reading" was always a new text—more words to read. In some cases, these were mediated applications: thoughts about, with regards to, or in the wake of what you read; in others, productive reading resulted in a straight reproduction—a new copy (usually, a copy of a copy, etc.) of what has been read or of a fragment thereof. But what entitles us to speak of these instances as one group is that, even in the case of copying, there is always a reason, a goal, and an attitude behind the act, a pledge of readerly solidarity or even an emotional expropriation or claim ("This is *my* life"). Productive reading, if only by virtue of generating texts upon texts, included more and more readers in the network. Being alone with a book was a waste of time—and of the book.

There is no better way of formulating the Golden Age philosophy of productive reading than citing a lifelong adherent and practitioner. One such exemplar would be Andrei Chikhachev, a country gentleman from Vladimir province who, together with his wife, Natal'ia, and her brother, Iakov Chernavin (whose estate was in a neighboring village), formed a three-person reading circle, complete with a handwritten daily, which T. N. Golovina appropriately terms "*domashniaia gazeta*" (domestic gazette)—part diary, part reading journal—to which each of the trio contributed in turn.[45] An avid reader, Chikhachev's rule was to keep a copy of anything that came his way. When a handwritten copy (of a copy of a copy . . .) of Woe from Wit landed on this village squire's desk, his immediate instinct was to write out Griboedov's masterwork in toto. He soon realized this would be impossible: the play was long, and the manuscript had to be returned to its lender in the morning. Chikhachev was up until the early hours, copying the monologues he liked best, and, as the deadline neared, the aphorisms one could scarcely let slip away.[46] It was Chikhachev, that inveterate reader and compulsive copier, who in their "domestic gazette" proclaimed what can be seen, in retrospect, as the ethical and philosophical platform underpinning productive reading. "To have read a beautifully written passage, to have enjoyed it and failed to write it out is the same as having had pleasure once and then forgetting all about it. There is something perverse and unholy about such behavior."[47] Copying out the thing you loved was a form of espousing it, making it your own; at the same time, it was a way of making it everyone's. It was this dual drive, I believe—appropriation and dissemination—that moved E. B. to inscribe "I have outlasted my desires" into an album, a medium accessible to others, while also rebranding Pushkin's elegy as hers: "This is *my* life."

Blue Notebooks

In the first third of the nineteenth century, then, Russian readers did not content themselves with the role of passive recipient. Reading, as we have seen, was merely the first step in dealing with a written text. Readers' main urge was to write. The written products of reading varied in subject and form. These could be underscorings and marginalia; notes to oneself, messages to others, or comments addressed to the author; or excerpts copied into a private notebook, a specialized album, or a handwritten tome intended for other readers. This last category, what we might call handicraft readership, was seen as the next best thing to creative writing. For instance, Aleksandr Turgenev replied thus to Viazemsky's exhortation to write:

> Just before I received your letter advising me to take up the pen, Zhukovsky... suggested that I begin writing down [my] "Thoughts" followed by "Notes."... I cannot commit myself to pen because to do so I need to have clarity of mind and silence in my heart.... I content myself with copying excerpts in a two-year album, which I am going to bring to you to read.[48]

Neither Zhukovsky nor Viazemsky would have been surprised to hear this. In this age long before it was possible for a book or poem to be a click away, a catalog (often, a catalogue raisonné) of excerpts from what one read (in Turgenev's case, in the course of two years) made a welcome and useful digest to share with family and friends. Aside from its practical convenience, moreover, sharing readership was regarded as a spiritually uplifting activity. As Zorin observes of Europe at the turn of the eighteenth to nineteenth centuries: "The epoch's most frequently read works functioned as tuning forks that readers used to listen to and check if their hearts felt in unison with others";[49] this felicitous metaphor is fully applicable to the social and cultural ensemble of the Russian Golden Age. The reading-in-forum performed in "Modest and Sofia," the reading-in-network engaged in by Chikhachev and his kin in the rural province of Vladimir—these were nothing less than forms of self-perfection.

This creed is splendidly exemplified by a series of notes jotted down by Vasily Zhukovsky in 1814. These have to do with an unusual undertaking that was at the time preoccupying Zhukovsky's mind. A believer in moral education and self-perfection, he held that common happiness could be attained—indeed, engineered—by a concerted effort on the part of community members. For Zhukovsky, community meant, first and foremost, the people he lived among—for significant stretches of time at the country mansion of Muratovo and later, for several months in 1815, in the university town of Dorpat (Tartu)—and whom he called his closest family: his half-sister Ekaterina Protasova, her daughters Masha and Sasha, and the resident family friend (eventually, Sasha's husband) Aleksandr Voeikov. "The masterplot of [Zhukovsky's] biographical myth is the search for the ideal familial unity," Ilya Vinitsky observes in his monograph on Zhukovsky and the emotional history of nineteenth-century Russia. "The members of such an ideal family would be bound together not only by the bonds of blood, but by a spiritual affection that enables an almost wordless understanding between them."[50] It was with an eye to attaining such affection and unity that Zhukovsky devised a project for what a recent commentator has dubbed "a spiritual ensemble," and which Zhukovsky himself used to call his "plan for happiness" (*plan shchast'ia*).[51]

The aspect of Zhukovsky's "plan for happiness" most significant for this discussion is the place it assigns to reading. Reading, like more or less everything in this ideal community, had to range from individual to public (to the extent "public" applies to a community of four), without ever remaining individual for long. Most evenings, Zhukovsky, Masha, Sasha, and Voeikov were to convene in the living room relating or reading out their daily reading to the group, in excerpts or in toto. This would inevitably generate an exchange of thoughts (otherwise, what was reading for?). Here is how Zhukovsky masterminds such an exchange in one of his diary entries:

> To figure out how to keep us from getting bored. Subjects for conversations must be prepared beforehand. Who will read what. In a word, we will have to think each minute through, for this is when everyone wants to relax after a busy day, when everyone must rejoice. To pose questions to be resolved in conversation. To read aloud everyone's favorite fragments. Games and anecdotes should emerge as if inadvertently. To have a plan for every evening. Voeikov and I [must take care of this].[52]

As envisioned by Zhukovsky, these lively group discussions would be interposed with reading separately, each reader engaged in a silent conversation with what was read. Zhukovsky would be the one to suggest the books to read, at least insofar as Masha (aged twenty-one) and Sasha (nineteen) were concerned, as Zhukovsky served as tutor to both. Reading had to be productive, with a pen and pencil in hand. Zhukovsky specifies: "*For Masha*: Read.

Use a special sign to mark in books the passages that are your friends. Copy out the best passages. Keep your own [reading] journal."[53] Along with a personal reading journal, everyone was expected to keep a circulating notebook with excerpts and comments of potential interest to others. "A journal for everyone and notes on others' journals, so that everyone might know what the others think of them and suggest what the others should read."[54] Capping this veritable pagoda of paper was yet another, shared journal to which all would contribute their thoughts. "The journal of our life [*zhurnal nashei zhizni*]; entrust Masha with [administering] it."[55]

In the small world of Zhukovsky's domestic utopia, there is no such thing as a finite or isolated act. Thoughts beget thoughts; writing grows out of reading as naturally as reading follows writing. Zhukovsky even came up with a horticultural metaphor for this—*grafting*. You were to sprout your own thoughts by reading the thoughts of others—much like a scion belonging to one plant shoots from the rootstock of another. "*Reading the moralists*," notes Zhukovsky in his diary of September 1814. "I am definitely going to *make my engraftments* [*privivki*] on them, that is, select a good thought that is not mine and engraft on it several thoughts that will be mine, and so every day. Will make a collection of these thoughts for you. Every day must be marked by its own thought."[56]

Making *privivki* (literally, "tie-ons") was Zhukovsky's way of maintaining literary and intellectual continuity over epochs and across languages and cultures—in this particular entry, with French encyclopedists and German moral philosophers like Christian Garve. In this respect, the peer-to-peer network of reading Zhukovsky envisaged for his happiness project can be seen as an attempt to, as it were, modernize domestic gardening via the grafting technique. The blue-bound notebooks Zhukovsky himself kept in 1814–15, known in the family as little blue books (*sinen'kie knizhki*), appear custom-made for this. In the *"reading the moralists"* entry just cited, having set himself a reading agenda (read to think) and a timeline (a thought per day), Zhukovsky projects an outcome: a collection of thoughts, now all his own. Peculiar to these blue notebooks was that they purported to constitute a collection "for you." Zhukovsky, the reader of moralists, wrote this note for Masha Protasova to read, copy, and make her own engraftments on Zhukovsky's. Blue-bound notebooks were an affair for two; in 1815 Zhukovsky instructed Masha: "I ask you to copy all this in the way the previous blue-bound notebook was copied: one page is yours, the next is mine."[57]

This textual proximity meant more than an exchange of moral thoughts. For years, the two had been in love, weighing with hope and trepidation how her mother (his half sister) would react to the possibility of their marriage. Time and again, motives of *personal* happiness steal into Zhukovsky's plan for happiness for *all*. While the blue notebooks were, at least in principle, open to everyone in the family, cryptic signals could be exchanged between the two in the know. Thus, in notes for his own reading journal, Zhukovsky pledges that whatever he writes in verse from that moment on shall be (mentally, spiritually) devoted to Masha (*stikhi—slava ei*).[58]

One hardly needs to compose "a plan for happiness" if one has happy plans. The reason why Zhukovsky made his was the elder Protasova's decision not to give him Masha's hand, taken in early 1814. Yet at one point after that she did consent to having Zhukovsky live under the same roof with them but strictly as a relative. It was for this new prospect (which proved to be short-lived and profoundly unhappy) that Zhukovsky resolved to think their life through in order to make it as happy as possible under the circumstances. The happiness plan was penned in late 1814; earlier that year, after the two lost the hope of becoming a married couple (save for a miracle they dreamed of until the last moment), Masha received two blue notebooks. One is blank, apart from a few excerpts from the New Testament, five mirthless maxims, and a dry flower inserted between empty pages.[59] The other, filled with text, begins with Zhukovsky's comment on the first.

> *June 21. Monday.* I return May to you; it is completely *empty*. What could I write in it? What need to express to my friend a state of mind [*dushi*] unworthy of her? Emptiness of heart, lack of attachment to life, a sense of fatigue—that's all. Could I have written about that? My hand refused to take a pen. In a word, a life like that was death alive.[60]

But then, Zhukovsky continues, a sudden thought illumed his heart: can a love like theirs perish from the mere fact of them living apart? "We cannot be together. But living under the same sky—is it not like living under the same roof! *The main thing, our heart*—who is able to change it?"[61] The impossibility of their marrying could only empower their love, Zhukovsky fancies; it would refashion their relationship in medieval—chivalric, spiritual, disembodied—terms: "Away from you I am more with you."[62] For want of the same roof, the space of their new togetherness will be the graphosphere, the cosmos of reading and writing. Several pages into the June notebook, Zhukovsky remembers he has a blank space ready, and makes the following irrationally strange request:

I added *the entire empty May*. I ask you to copy all this onto its pages, word by word, and add your own reply. This notebook will be my law. And I will rewrite for you what you will have written to me. I promise to you that all my life will be devoted to the fulfilment of these good intentions, or (to draw a bottom line) *of my love for you*.[63]

Zhukovsky's proposal is not an easy one to figure out. A mentor by nature, and Masha's former tutor, Zhukovsky may have believed in the didactic power of recopying, but there is clearly more than pedagogy to his plan. Here we might recall what Andrei Chikhachev—that avid and very productive reader from Vladimir province—claimed in his homespun "*gazette*." To him, as to many in the Golden Age, there existed an ethical dimension to copying. Reading a book you liked without committing the passages you liked to paper was, Chikhachev believed, "perverse and unholy." Zhukovsky's strange proposal must have been driven by a kindred impulse. Asking Masha to rewrite by *her* hand *his* new plan for *their* future life and his new vision of their union was not, of course, a mere exercise in penmanship. It sounds more like Zhukovsky saw it as a ritual, a vow, almost a substitute for exchanging rings in church.

Chaque texte n'est qu'un prétexte: any text is but a pretext. Attributed to French actor Jean Mounet-Sully and deployed by stage director Vsevolod Meyerhold in his struggle against the dictate of written plays, this slogan remains apt for our study of pragmatics. Here, as on a stage, what a line says hinges on who says it and to whom. Whether two identical texts will sound identical is always contingent on a situation, its participants and performers. When Zhukovsky tells Masha to hand-copy—word by word—into the May notebook what he had written to her in the June one, or when he says he would rewrite for her what she will have written to him in the May notebook—we are faced with something more than just redundant reduplication. These were not identical documents: they were texts in two different handwritings and, behind identical words, two different voices. In Zhukovsky's fancy, the May notebook—the space of conjoined reading and writing—was to become his and Masha's shared refuge in the face of impending separation.

For a given situation's participants, situational meanings override textual ones. The amatory cryptography fairly widespread in the gallant Golden Age is a helpful (if crude) example. Anna Kern and her bon ami in the Pskov garrison used to correspond by underscoring passages in books the two exchanged;[64] likewise, when in the autumn of 1814, Zhukovsky left the Protasov household to stay in Dolbino with Masha's cousin Avdotia ("Duniasha") Elagina (then Kireevskaya), who sympathized with their love, he, as usual, left Masha a detailed instruction, capped with his stated intention to use a practice right out of spycraft:

> Make a notebook for writing out the best passages from the Holy Scripture and spiritual authors. Add your comments. Another notebook for writing down the best thoughts from all [other] books and your comments on those too. Finally, use ten lines per day in the journal (the blue book) to [summarize] all this for me. This journal will be a replacement for letters. Use occasions to take it to the post office, which should be easy. I should be cautious of writing to you specifically. But everything underlined in Duniasha's letters to you will be from me.[65]

The copresence of the plain and the cryptic; public and private; spiritual and anecdotal make Zhukovsky's blue notebooks hard to disambiguate. Now they sound like a reading journal, now like a confessional diary; now it is a letter to Masha, now a letter from Masha to Zhukovsky. Such elusiveness might have easily caused later commentators great headache but thankfully did not: to accommodate the blue notebooks' dual identity, the first editor (1907) of this particular part of Zhukovsky's domestic legacy, Pavel Simoni, came up with a tandem term: "letter-diaries" (*pis'ma-dnevniki*).[66] Simoni's coinage is remarkably accurate: it preserves the dynamics of the phenomenon it names. Our reflexive generic matrix tells us that diaries and letters are different animals: it is either one or the other. While diaries pivot around the pronoun *I*, letters are typically addressed to someone's *you*. The idea of a diary for *you* sounds as preposterous as that of a letter written to oneself. Simoni's "letter-diary" is as adequate a name for blue notebooks as "pushmi-pullyu" is for that palindromic artiodactyl from Doctor Dolittle's animal clinic. Such creatures are impossible, it is true. Yet it was precisely the energy of the impossible that made Zhukovsky's plan for happiness unique. The blue notebooks he and Masha filled in 1814 and 1815 (plus the one left poignantly unfilled) are, in a sense, two-headed creatures. When the heads of a pushmi-pullyu talk to one another, how can we tell the "you" from the "I"?

Projections

The blend of genres represented by Zhukovsky's notebooks might seem unusual, but in the Golden Age such mixtures were not uncommon. In this epoch, a personal diary, for instance, could easily function as a letter and be sent to a specific postal address—a practice employed by Zhikharev, Aleksandr Turgenev, and Anna Kern. Or a personal diary would all of a sudden assume the tone and syntax of a printed book—shifting from the first-person "I" to a novelistic-sounding "she," as Anna Olenina does in her diary, or morphing into moralistic philosophical reasoning, as Zhukovsky's diaries were so prone to do. A typical diary could readily embrace a text by someone else—an overheard verse or an excerpt from a recently read book—which made a diary border on an album. The boundaries between private genres—diaries, letters, albums, and notebooks—were as porous and diffused as the line between private writings on the one hand and public literature on the other. Thus, Batiushkov, in lieu of starting a diary, kept a notebook titled "What's Not Mine: My Treasure" ("Chuzhoe—moe sokrovishche"), a mixture of diary notes, personal reminiscences, excerpts from poetry and prose—all this preceded by a list of potential subjects for literary works he himself might compose.

The instability of intraliterary boundaries raises the question of how strict the *outer* boundaries of literature are—between the perceived realities of life and the perceived conventionality of art. As literary scholars, we are rightly cautioned not to conflate literary texts and biographical evidence. That Pushkin, as we happen to know from his letters, was in love with Anna Kern is not insignificant per se, but how does this pertain to our understanding of "I still recall the wondrous moment" (*Ia pomniu chudnoe mgnoven'e*)?[67] Poems are part of literature; love affairs, military service, or gambling debts—of the life of their authors. The boundary seems too self-evident to even discuss, but it is exactly here that we must watch our step. Much of what we recognize as "facts of life" are deduced from this or that written document, and any written document is, in turn, prone to become a *literary* fact. Documents like these constitute what Tynianov proposed to call a "set" of works that "neighbor" literature (*sosednii riad*) and may cross the line and become literature. Correspondence between friends, as Tynianov noted in "On Literary Fact" and Todd has shown in great detail in *The Familiar Letter as a Literary Genre in the Age of Pushkin*, was largely predicated on playing with, balancing on, and challenging that boundary; as were the poetic epistles, album verses, and elegies on the other side of it. "In the early nineteenth century," Vadim Vatsuro remarks apropos Zhukovsky and Andrei Turgenev, "an elegy, a letter, and a diary were seen as kindred forms of self-expression."[68] The internal affinity between technically literary and technically extraliterary forms comes to the fore when writings by figures like Zhukovsky and Andrei Turgenev are explored against the background of the emotive history of Russia—as has been done in two recent monographs, by Ilya Vinitsky and Andrei Zorin respectively.

Here we might again cite Simon Franklin's notion of the graphosphere. This theoretical construct is not divided into two hemispheres called "literature" and "other stuff"; it is, rather, an irregular array consisting of numerous and crisscrossed constellations and galaxies. On this map, Pushkin's letters to Kern will not appear as belonging to some faraway galaxy called "biographical documents"; while none of these letters claim literary laurels, they all belong in the same tightly grouped constellation as does Pushkin's lyric masterpiece "I still recall the wondrous moment"—not only thematically but also because Pushkin's letters, like poems, were composed in line with established verbal and, yes, also literary models.[69] Ambiguity rises when it comes to scattered written debris. Several documents in French that have been preserved in Pushkin's archive remain unattributed to this day.[70] Does this or that sheet represent a draft letter to a lady Pushkin knew, or an excerpt from an unidentified epistolary novel? Any text pivoting around the pronouns "I" and/or "you" could have been an honest letter, a fragment of epistolary prose, a poem, or a diary entry. But they belong to a single graphospheric subsystem, in the sense that each can be seen in two perspectives: private and public, human and literary, as a communicative or an expressive act.

Both naïve biographism and, if one may say so, naïve bio-skepticism—the two extremes justly critiqued by Jakobson in 1937 and Bakhtin in 1973—treat biographical facts as a given: as a hardcore, preliterary and extraliterary formation.[71] Formalist theorists, most of whom were also experts in nineteenth-century Russian literature, would have dismissed the assumption as simplistic, pointing to many biographies that, much like literary works, were handmade according to a plan. As Boris Tomashevsky observes in his "Literature and Biography," nineteenth-century writers strove "to create for themselves an artificial legendary biography composed of intentionally selected real and imaginary events."[72] Various amalgamations of literary and biographical legend constituted what Tynianov termed a "literary persona" (*literaturnaia lichnost'*). Such were Davydov, the poet-hussar, and Kozlov, the poet-sufferer; recall early Iazykov, a poet and hard-partying student, or early Baratynsky, a Nordic outcast. And, as Yuri Lotman has shown, in the Golden Age some literary biographies were tailored to live up to literary standards.[73]

Making literature of biography was always a combination of chance and choice. A poet would normally have no say in where they would serve, or be exiled, but, as Stephanie Sandler demonstrates in *Distant Pleasures: Alexander Pushkin and the Writing of Exile*, it was up to the poet whether to turn a given fact of life into a literary fact. Baratynsky's journey to the north and Pushkin's to the south readily lent themselves to such refashioning. Following Batiushkov, who had served there ten years earlier, Baratynsky fancied Finland as a homeland of savage warriors and skalds. Exiled to Bessarabia in 1820, Pushkin found himself in the land to which Ovid had (reputedly) been exiled; as he was preparing to leave Odessa in 1824, Pushkin dedicated a poem to the sea immediately separating him from the graves of Napoleon and Byron.[74] It was his southern exile that mandated that Pushkin should write a long poem about a young Circassian woman in love with a captive Russian; Baratynsky, for his part, when sent to Finland embarked on a long poem about a young northern beauty ("her eyes pale-blue like the Finnish sky") seduced by a Russian hussar.

It was a common belief that "poetic inspiration" derived from the current situation of the poet. Inspiration, in this philosophy, depended on *where* a poet landed, not least on the historic geography of the place. Having helped to arrange Pushkin's transfer from Kishinev to Odessa, Aleksandr Turgenev sent Viazemsky the following account of his conversation with Count Mikhail Vorontsov, the Odessa-based governor of Russia's southern provinces who was at first willing to act as Pushkin's patron: "I explained to [Vorontsov] what Pushkin is, and what is needed to save him. As it appears, the matter will take a favorable turn. A patron, the climate, the sea and historical memories—all of this is present [in Odessa]; talent will not be long in coming."[75] When, after over a year in Odessa, Pushkin was restricted to living in his ancestral Mikhailovskoe, he wrote desperate letters, wanted out—but never vested the place with quite the same literary significance as he did his southern exile.

When poets owed a poem to a genius loci, they would normally repay the debt by indicating, beneath the text, the place of the poem's birth. "Unknowingly, I found myself living in the times of chivalry, whose breath is present in everything here," wrote Anton Del'vig to Baratynsky from Revel' (Tallinn), where he and his wife, Sofia, were traveling in 1827. "If I don't start speaking in verse now—then I am not a poet."[76] Del'vig's self-test must have put his friends on guard. "Has chivalrous Revel' awoken your sleepy muse yet?" Pushkin asks considerately in a letter to Del'vig from Mikhailovskoe.[77] The result was not long in coming. That summer, Del'vig wrote a sonnet, with the date and place of its production duly marked: "Revel', in July 1827."[78] Dates and toponyms were not just the "birth certificate data" of a poem. These were instant bio-poetic projections, cherished moments when life and poetry crossed paths.

The greatest evidence of the power of bio-poetic projections is the attempt of some poets to suppress them. As mentioned earlier in this chapter, Baratynsky used to alter the names in the "dedication field" of his love lyric depending on whom he was currently addressing. Nor was he above tampering with dates. Lev Pushkin was appalled when he learned of Baratynsky's plan to marry. "[Baratynsky] is dead for poetry," he wrote Sergei Sobolevsky. "His genre, namely, erotic poetry, is unbecoming to a husband. This is why he has jettisoned the best verses from his collection about to come out. Eliminating Baratynsky from poetry is a Herostratic joke [*shutka Erostrata*]."[79] Lev Pushkin's misgivings, while not unfounded, overstated the case. To keep his new verses from being read as biographical clues, Baratynsky would resort to what D. S. Mirsky, writing in 1936, called "camouflage dating" (*maskirovochnaia datirovka*).[80] A good example of this is the date we find under Baratynsky's "The Fairy" ("Feia"), published in 1830 and written, as most commentators agree, in 1828 or 1829. The poem, a lyric meditation on human reveries, tells of an obliging yet wicked "fairy" (Agrafena Zakrevskaya) from a recurrent dream. A letter survives addressed by Baratynsky to the publisher Nikolai Konshin (that same staff captain) that says: "I am sending you, dear Konshin, the poems I promised . . . Under my 'Fairy' is a year: don't forget to print it in your almanac—I need it."[81] The date found in Konshin's almanac situates "Fairy" in 1824, that is, in a year not only from Baratynsky's bachelorhood but, importantly, before he had even met his future wife.

Whether a lyric poem was an authentic projection of the poet's personal situation played a role in its critical assessment, as if the literary value of a work depended on its merit as a documentary, as it were. A lyric poem is a vehicle for emotions; readers and critics thus felt entitled to demand that these emotions be genuine. Poets, like actors, would be reproached for being cold, histrionic, or derivative. Adhering to what M. H. Abrams has termed the "expressive theory of poetry," Viazemsky in his epistle to Ivan Dmitriev (1819) portrayed a prototypical ham poet:

Иль, и того смешней, любовник краснощёкой,
Бледнеет на стихах в элегии: К жестокой!
Кривляется без слёз, вздыхает невпопад
И чувства по рукам сбирает напрокат;

Он на чужом огне любовь разогревает
И верно с подлинным грустит и умирает.⁸²

[Or, even funnier, a red-cheeked lover / Blanches over verses for his elegy "To the Cruel One!" / Makes faces without tears, sighs at the wrong moments, / And rents his feelings from anyone at hand; / Warms up his love on others' fire / And *certified true copy* grieves and dies.]

Certified true copy—the rather performative statement on a notary's stamp—was not enough for a verse to become a lyric poem. Lyric feelings could not be borrowed; they had to come guaranteed by facts (or myths) from the poet's life. Hence the pun in the last line of the quoted stanza, which can also be read as a candle-and-moth ending: "And when he encounters a genuine [fire], he grieves and dies."

The ad hominem criticism sounded especially germane when it came to war poems. "Can I really be moved by a description of a battle written by a professor of versification?" asks Andrei Raevsky in his 1822 *Memoirs of the 1813–14 Campaigns*. Consider, he continues, the difference between Zhukovsky's "The Bard's Song at the Tomb of Victorious Slavs" ("Pesn' barda nad grobom slavian-pobeditelei," 1806) and "The Bard in the Camp of Russian Warriors," written in 1812 by Zhukovsky, then serving in the Patriotic War:

> The reedpipe of [young Zhukovsky's] bard may charm me, but it cannot fill me with that ambrosial involuntary rapture that envelopes my soul as I harken the sweet voice of [Zhukovsky the] warrior who, under the walls of the destroyed capital, to the crackling of falling cities, amid the fiery glow of battles, paints for his jubilant brethren, ready to gain victory or die, what is revealed to his sight or imprinted on his heart, as the cup is passed round.⁸³

Raevsky here foregrounds the importance of experience and participation, true, but we should be wary of misconstruing these as hoped-for *prerequisites* for writing poems about war. Raevsky's point is subtler: it is less about Zhukovsky as poet and more about himself as reader, and others like him. Unlike the readers of war memoirs, for instance, readers of war lyrics were primarily interested in what they already knew. What mattered most was relatability to—in this case, recognition of—"the pictures imprinted on [Zhukovsky's] heart." For readers like Raevsky, having participated in the anti-Napoleon campaign meant being in "complicity" (*souchastie*, to recall Merzliakov's term) with the poet, an ideal condition for co- (and re-)experiencing it—as it is for those imagined warriors that sit at Zhukovsky's imaginary table listening to their bard.

Needless to say, we must be careful not to nail the literary legacies of Golden Age poets to their biographical reputations. True, Zhukovsky did find sudden fame with his patriotic "Bard in the Camp of Russian Warriors," and the reputation of Denis Davydov's poetry spread along with his renown as a war hero, but neither confined his literary activity to servicing his biographical legend. For all this period's tendency to personalize poetry, generic versatility (as literary historians note with a shade of surprise) remains a distinctive feature of the Russian Golden Age. Apart from hussar drinking songs, Davydov wrote passionate love elegies, epistles, fables, epigrams, imitations of Horace, and more. Zhukovsky's public image as bard of war was crowded out by his numerous other identities: Zhukovsky the balladist, Zhukovsky the elegist, Zhukovsky the translator. Serious as it was about history, tragedy, and fate, Golden Age poetry was also a comedy of masks. Unlike Raevsky's heroic projection of Zhukovsky, Davydov's biographical self-projection verged on self-parody. In true hussar fashion, Davydov never took his hussarship too seriously. His moustache, the left half of which, we recall, he mailed in a letter to Zhukovsky, gained fame as a mock relic: "Let my moustache, / That beauty of nature, / That black-brown curly thing, / Be frayed to shreds [*issechetsia*] while it is young / And vanish as the dust."[84]

Counterintuitively perhaps, the diversity of genres and forms that surprises us when we examine the corpus of writings by individual poets could itself result from what we have discussed here as a mutual projection of texts and conduct. "Poets must pour their soul into manifold vessels," wrote Viazemsky as he complained about what he perceived as the unwelcome monotony of Zhukovsky's poetic output. "There was a time when [Zhukovsky] hit upon the idea of death and would end every poem with his own funeral. The premonition of death is only striking if it breaks out; but when we see someone waiting for death every day and yet remaining in good health, his foreboding is bound to grow ludicrous."[85] At work here is that same life-to-line presumption: when poets say "death," they should mean it. That poetry in Viazemsky's view was not one but a whole collection of "vessels" meant that it was to store and convey a range of different, short-lived, and constantly changing emotions, rather than, say, melancholy every time. Poetry is thus a kaleidoscopic projection of the emotional self.

When a poem can be seen as a literary text and at the same time a projection of someone's personal situation, one side of this dual existence becomes temptingly easy to ignore. Some too-credulous readers, and some professionally suspicious censors, did precisely that. As the writer Aleksandra Zrazhevskaya once explained, her sisters of the quill found publication problematic: "What [kind of story] can a young woman create? What passion should she describe? Anyone will point a finger at her and say: she must have not just imagined, but experienced it."[86] An anecdote coming from somewhere deep in Ukraine, as conveyed in a letter Grigory Sokolov wrote to Mikhail Pogodin in 1829, justifies, if indirectly, such misgivings.

> We have a wonderful old lady in the neighborhood, a classic Ukrainian gentry woman. As is usual with this sort of lady, she has raised half a dozen young wards, all crazy about modern writings, especially Pushkin's. In the wake of their ceaseless conversations about current literature, the old dame (imagine!) took to literature too, so she had them read to her any new thing that would come out. When it came to Tatiana's letter, her injured sense of propriety exclaimed in sincere outrage: *Eka prokliata divka! Nekhai sibi pisala, da v svit by ne vydavala* [Such a darned girl! Write what you want, but don't put it out there.].[87]

The old lady's verdict, rendered by Sokolov in Ukrainian, stems from a twofold projection. Pushkin's Tatiana, in her mind's eye, is not only a real person like Pushkin but also a writer like him, who dares to print her shameless letter to Onegin.

Another story, documented in Viazemsky's notebooks as exemplifying the idiocy and pharisaism of Russian censorship, makes a perfect companion piece to Sokolov's. In 1823 the censor Aleksandr Krasovsky banned Valerian Olin's "Stanzas to Eliza" ("Stansy k Elize"). Having underlined a number of words and lines in Olin's manuscript, Krasovsky penned on it nine cavils so absurd that Olin felt obliged to appeal, adding a fairly acrimonious "clarification" addressed to the St. Petersburg Censorship Committee. The ban quickly became a cause célèbre; handwritten copies of Olin's poem, complete with Krasovsky's comments and Olin's retort, circulated among liberal literati; one such copy found its way into Viazemsky's notebook. Summarizing his conference with the censors, Olin wrote:

> In conclusion, Messrs. censors, having characterized my work as sinful and seductive, asked to whom precisely it was addressed. To a woman or maiden; a

stranger, or a relative of mine? They said they needed to know this because, judging by many verses, it transpired that I was in a rather close relationship with this person. I told them that I would begin fasting and confessing next week, and repent my sins to a priest; but that, since censorship is not a confessional, and censors are not priests, I felt no need to deliberate with them on such matters.[88]

Censorship Committee members made no distinction between literary works and human documents. There is no smoke without fire; in the censor's eye, there had to be a real flame behind Olin's stanzas to Eliza—a consideration that hardly differs from scolding Tatiana for publishing her letter to Onegin. Casuistically, in their written response to Olin's tongue-in-cheek clarification, the Committee interpreted his witty repartee—when I decide to confess, I'll talk to my priest—as an admission of guilt: "As can be sufficiently concluded from [Olin's] interesting footnote, he himself acknowledges his 'Stanzas to Eliza' to be indecent reading matter. . . . We need not comment on the propriety of his remarks on [the sacrament of] confession."[89]

Reading-cum-Writing Spaces

No censorship, however draconian, could do much in the way of affecting literature—other than change its configuration in the graphosphere. "Never have [writers] been so repressed as now," Pushkin wrote to Denis Davydov in 1836, "not even in the final five years of the late emperor's reign, when thanks to Krasovsky and Birukov, literature became handwritten."[90] Being banned from print never meant being silenced. Rather, the opposite was true, as we know from the fate of *Boris Godunov* or *Woe from Wit*. Olin's perfectly unremarkable "Stanzas to Eliza" would likely have gone unnoticed had Krasovsky greenlighted it for print. Recopying a work by hand was part of an unofficial yet wide—countrywide—preservation and dissemination effort. Readers and writers alike took part in and took care of the constantly expanding network of *spiski*—handwritten copies of literary musts. "My [satirical] 'In Luck' ['Vezet'] was never published," recalls Ivan Dolgorukov, "but copies of it circulated in every town. Many knew some of its stanzas by heart. People would borrow [the original] from me to make *spiski*, and thus did my 'In Luck' fly to army quarters in Orenburg, to Odessa and Petersburg."[91] The fair copy of Dolgorukov's comedy *Durylom* went round and round until it wore out; "I had to have a 'second edition' hand-copied [*vtorym izdaniem perepisyvat'*]."[92]

Productive reading was thus a form of reproduction. While it is true that person-to-person handwritten circulation came to be widely used in Russia because it allowed literary works to fly under the radar of censorship, we should take care not to gauge the then relations between the forbidden and the unpublished by the standards established much later during the age of samizdat. Unlike the nameless, as-if-nonexistent Soviet censors, their fully credited imperial predecessors would ordinarily train their sights on particular lines or stanzas instead of banning the whole work; it was up to the author to decide whether to soften the objectionable passage, strike it entirely, or—as Pushkin used to do—replace it with a line (or whole stanza) of telltale dots. This was where rewriting and memorizing would come in. Dolgorukov's memoir was not quite accurate in depicting the fate of his satirical verse: at one point, "In Luck" *was* published, but with the omission of one (anticlerical) stanza, which, to be sure, was precisely the stanza that many knew by heart and constituted the gem of every *spisok*.[93] Compared to manuscripts, books were valued for their durability, but were not necessarily very reliable as a source, or convenient as a vehicle of circulation. By the time the handwritten copy of *Woe from Wit* reached Chikhachev's countryside estate in 1836, a stand-alone edition of the play (1833) had already been published. However, the printed and hard-bound *Woe from Wit* was known to have been heavily censored, which made it likelier to sit on your bookshelf while handwritten versions of the play continued to circulate. What to choose—a nice gold-lettered but censored volume, or a plain but authentic handwritten script—must have been a dilemma familiar to many a Golden Age reader. Nikolai Iazykov, for one, devised an ingenious solution. Having learned that one of his brothers had just acquired Pushkin's freshly published *Boris Godunov*, he proposed in a letter (11 February 1831): "You have already bought *Godunov*. Here is what I am going to do. I will hand-copy the passages omitted in the printed version and bind these together with the printed text, exactly where each of them belongs. This way our library shall be adorned with the complete *Godunov*."[94]

Today, a complete, printed-plus-handwritten edition of Pushkin's *Godunov* may seem like a freak of a book, something in the nature of a centaur. But this polygraphic monstrosity was, in a sense, part and parcel of its age. We tend to paint readers and writers as two different animals, and printing and writing as two different ways of committing words to paper. Ink marks on the margins of library books make us wince. But in fact, margins were originally meant to be marked up. In the Iazykov-ian idea of the complete *Godunov*, as in the eyes of Golden Age culture at large, reading and writing, the written and the printed, are inalienable parts of the same literary organism. When Iazykov the reader (himself an extraordinary poet) picks up a pen to restore the printed version of Pushkin's tragedy to its original completeness, he is no longer acting as "mere" reader—in this period, anyway, the concept of such "mereness" is scarcely admitted—but rather as a coproducer of the book; as did Pushkin when, having acquired a copy of *The Lay of Igor's Campaign* (*Slovo o polku Igoreve*), he inter-leaved its printed pages with blanks for making notes.[95] In each case, we witness productive reading at work.

Together with typeset pages, blank sheets sewn thus in between can be subsumed under a category that might be called *reading-cum-writing spaces*, the material base for participatory reading. Uses of such spaces could range from practical and ceremonial to imaginative. When Pushkin interleaved his *Igor* with empty pages, it was to prepare a commentated edition. Alternatively, a hybrid between a book and a notebook could serve as a platform for an emotional and intellectual exchange between writers with their characters on the one hand, and readers with their sorrows on the other. Andrei Turgenev's diary, parts of which have come into scholarly use thanks to Andrei Zorin's recent study of the emotional culture of the Golden Age, gives a rare inside glimpse at such reading practices. In 1801, not long before his untimely death, Turgenev conceived of a plan, in collaboration with Zhukovsky and Merzliakov (two other members of the Friendly Literary Society), to produce a Russian translation of Goethe's *The Sorrows of Young Werther*. As we learn from his diary, he had two copies of *Werther*. While one of these may have served him as a source, the other, dissected and combined with spaces for writing, became a vehicle for imaginary communication between Turgenev, Goethe, and his Werther; add here Turgenev's flame Anna Sokovnina, yearnings and pinings for whom, as Zorin observes, inevitably steered Turgenev's thoughts toward Werther's letters.

It is from Andrei Turgenev's diary that we learn how a reader of considerable talent could conflate their personal world with the intellectual and emotional diegesis of a book. To believe the diary, Turgenev's first instinct was to expand the book he loved to make room in it for himself. "With no far-reaching aims, I had [*Werther*] rebound so that every other page was a blank insert. I was not sure what I might need it for," the diary admits.[96] This need, in fact, was prompted by Goethe's novel:

A quick thought crossed my mind. Werther says somewhere: *So eine wahre, warme Freude ist nicht in der Welt, als eine große Seele zu sehen, die sich gegen einen öffnet.* [It is the greatest and most genuine of pleasures to observe a great mind in sympathy with our own.⁹⁷] . . . Recalling this passage from *Werther*, I said to myself: in my *Werther* book I will be checking my feelings against his, making notes each time I felt as he had felt. As I thought of this I jumped out of my chair, rushed to my room and instantly wrote down the present lines.⁹⁸

Andrei Turgenev's project sounds similar to what his friend Zhukovsky would a few years later call "engrafting." Indeed, Turgenev used his blank pages to harvest thoughts and emotions grown out of Werther's—much like a garden for growing plants from other plants. That Werther's remark about mutual empathy of minds (or souls, as any Russian would have translated Goethe's *Seele*) could have sent young Turgenev out of his reading chair to his writing desk is proof enough of the efficacy of productive reading. Underlying Zhukovsky's grafting metaphor and Andrei Turgenev's planned intervention into Goethe's *Werther* was a sense of performative empathy, as it were. Good readers, like good performers, grow into the book they read and the thoughts they find therein. You not only enact what you read, you let it *become* you.

The ideology of *literary becoming* also explains the Golden Age's sweeping devotion to poetic translations. Unlike translations of prose—mostly novels and nonfiction published widely with an eye toward commercial success—translations of poetry were mainly intended for poetry lovers, which in practice meant that most, if not all, of those willing to read Thomas Gray, Évariste de Parny, or Gottfried August Bürger in Russian translation were equally (if not better) equipped to read these authors in the original, or in already-existing translations into languages they knew (usually French). Nonetheless, poetic translations not only proliferated but were also debated as seriously as were poems written in Russian. One reason for this was that poetic translations were vested with an ethos and mission uniquely theirs. As Tomashevsky says in his *Pushkin and France*: "Their aim was not to render the original precisely, but to enrich Russian poetry with the forms that existed in a foreign language."⁹⁹ And, one might add, to advance Russian as a language—its stylistic repertoire and expressive tool kit.

Translating from European poetry was a way of making it one's own. After Pavel Katenin's translations from Torquato Tasso and Ludovico Ariosto, his friend Nikolai Bakhtin could write: "As some of Katenin's experiments have proven, Italian octaves can be appropriated [*prisvoeny*] by Russian versifiers."¹⁰⁰ The connotations of *prisvoeny* may verge on the downright military ("seized," "grabbed"), and the latter sense was occasionally made explicit by valiant translators. Batiushkov, much of whose time was spent on military campaigns, wrote in a letter to Gnedich: "Find enclosed, my dear friend, a little piece of poetry [*p'ieska*] that I have taken, that is, conquered [*zavoeval*] from Parny."[101]

Normally, conquests of this kind would be printed on the same footing with the poet's original works, sometimes marked as "translation" or "imitation," sometimes not. Poetic translation was the ultimate form of productive reading, a way of conversing, across languages, with the author of the original work. A German, English, or French poem in Russian translation was seen as a reincarnation, not a replica. This attitude made poetic translations easy to transplant. When Thomas Gray's "Elegy Written in a Country Churchyard" (1751) became well known, so did the eponymous English graveyard. By the same token, the hill in the Mishenskoe village on which Zhukovsky had reportedly been strolling while composing his first (1802) reincarnation of Gray's elegy became locally known as "Greieva elegiia."[102] When, many years later, Zhukovsky visited England, he made certain to stop at the churchyard in Stoke Poges where Gray supposedly wrote his elegy and where Gray himself was definitely buried. The visit and, in all likelihood, the lines from the churchyard elegy chiseled on Gray's tomb moved Zhukovsky to retranslate—this time in Homeric hexameters—Gray's poem, which now, in Zhukovsky's long memory, became associated with a whole cluster of literary facts, including the long-ago premature demise of his poet-friend Andrei Turgenev. So that readers would be aware of every text, event, and person looming behind the new translation, Zhukovsky furnished it with a moving footnote that deserves to be quoted in full:

> Gray's elegy, which I translated in 1802, was printed in *Vestnik Evropy* [Herald of Europe] when it was published by Karamzin in 1802 and 1803. That was my *first published* poem. That one was dedicated to Andrei Ivanovich Turgenev. Passing Windsor in May 1839, I paid a visit to the graveyard in Stoke Poges nearby, the one that gave Gray the idea for his elegy; there I reread Gray's beautiful poem and decided to translate it again, as close to the original as possible. It is this second translation, made almost forty years after the first one, that I dedicate to Aleksandr Ivanovich Turgenev as a sign of our mutual friendship that has lasted since then, and to the memory of his brother.[103]

Note that Zhukovsky refers to the 1802 "Graveyard" as a translation and as *his* poem—both in the same breath. For him the difference hardly mattered. The possible titles Zhukovsky played with in a number of early manuscripts range from "Elegy" to "An Elegy Written at a Country Graveyard. From Gray [*Iz Graia*]." This *iz*—literally, "out of," a habitual way of attributing a translation in those days—posits the parent poem as a source, a root rather than a prototype of Zhukovsky's elegy.[104]

The ideology of conquest renders the *whose* question irrelevant. As Zhukovsky explains in a remarkably perceptive introspection we find in an 1847 letter to Nikolai Gogol:

> I often notice that most of my brightest thoughts are improvised when I have to express or supplement the thoughts of others. My mind, like a fire steel, must be stricken by a flint for a spark to jump off. This, in general, is characteristic of my authorial self: almost everything I create is someone else's, or apropos of something said by someone else—and, at the same time, all this is fully mine.[105]

Chronotopes

In the footnote appended to the second translation of Gray's "Churchyard," Zhukovsky informs his readers of several things they ought to know about his present effort. First, the footnote alludes to the translation made almost forty years before; secondly, it links two dedications: that of the 1839 version to Aleksandr Turgenev, and that of the 1802 version, which Zhukovsky had dedicated to Aleksandr's elder brother Andrei. Thirdly, the footnote offers a testimonial regarding the poem's genesis, namely that the idea of writing it occurred to Zhukovsky during his visit to the very churchyard that, almost a century before, inspired Thomas Gray to write his poem.

A peculiar trait of such testimonials is the attention they pay to the chronotopography of the lyric. The when and where of a poem—written one quiet evening in a cemetery, on a summer day in Revel, or while treading the grounds trod of old by Pushkin's cheerless Ovid or Baratynsky's Nordic skalds, in other words, the moments when poetry interlocked with one's existential situation—were seen as meaningful not only for a poem's author but also for its listeners and readers. Not that these poems had to be written or even composed *en plein air*—standing by the sea or walking amid graves, but it was important that a poem's coming into being be associated with its author's *being there*. Nor were its readers or listeners expected to travel to St. Giles's Church in Stoke Poges in order to enjoy reading Zhukovsky's "Second Translation out of Gray," or climb "Gray Elegy" Hill in Mishenskoe to savor the first one—though we do recall how thrilling Staff Captain Konshin found the Finnish blizzard raging outside the window as Baratynsky recited "Finland." But on the other hand, it is easy to imagine someone transformed, by the mere fact of finding themselves in a graveyard or caught in a snowstorm, into a vocal performer of lines "out of" Pushkin or Zhukovsky. A tree is a tree and a grave is a grave: cultural landscapes are poetically isomorphic. In actual fact, outdoor or onsite reading/reciting of descriptive poetry was a consciously cultivated practice, and it easily spread to lyric poems. As Zorin summarizes the back-and-forth between reading and life-shaping: "The European public learned to love à la *The New Heloise* and *The Sorrows of Young Werther*, enjoy nature à la Rousseau, visit graveyards à la [Edward] Young and Gray, and seclude oneself from the world à la [Johann Georg von] Zimmerman."[106]

What was true of topography was also true of the four seasons, the three divisions of the day, and every type of weather. Thus, in the already-cited letter to his brother Nikolai from their parental estate, Aleksandr Turgenev nostalgically recounts how he spent the previous evening observing a sunset from that wide-windowed room in which the Turgenev brothers used to have classes as boys; here, Turgenev recited a doleful description of a sunset from a Zhukovsky poem that suited the beautiful view and the meditative mood that view induced. Or take that editorial footnote we recall from the beginning of this chapter, in which an editor of *Novosti literatury* apologized to subscribers for printing a poem titled "Spring" in the October issue. We might think of seasonal dishes in a menu. Indeed, why publish "Spring" at all, when verses titled "Autumn" were proliferating like mushrooms in this period: at least fifty of them, in Natalia Mazur's estimate (not counting those printed in newspapers), appeared in the first half of the nineteenth century alone.[107]

Poetry takes nature personally, and so must its readers. A lyric description of a season (or tempest, sunset, waterfall) was seldom, if ever, an honest rendering of a natural phenomenon but rather a seasonality matching or contrasting whatever human emotion a poet purported to impart to their readers, and so an out-of-season poem interfered with the cardinal tenet of the age: in order to succeed, a poem must be relatable, applicable, and performance-friendly. In a word, it must be *complicit* with the reader's cast (and state) of mind.

The when and where of the verse depended, in part, on its place in the system of lyric genres. This makes Bakhtin's notion of literary chronotope, originally devised to handle novelistic plots, instrumental for poetry as well. Typically, the chronos ($\chi\rho\acute{o}\nu o\varsigma$) of a lyric poem came in tandem with its topos (τόπος). Thus, the choice of autumn (rural rather than urban, and arboreal rather than campestral) as your χρόνος situated your poem in the generic range somewhere between doleful elegy and philosophic ode. The action of such an autumnal poem was, as a rule, a solitary ramble set in a natural landscape (Zhukovsky: "I am alone on the shore . . . All around me is silent") attended by musings suited to the occasion ("Everything here involuntarily steers us toward contemplation").[108]

Conversely, a lyric τόπος could prompt the choice of a fitting χρόνος. Take, for instance, Baratynsky's elegy "Desolation" ("Zapustenie"), in which the nature and destination of a trip dictates—or so the poet claims—the one and only time to take it. "Desolation" was written in the wake of Baratynsky's return to Mara, the paternal mansion whose once lovingly groomed garden had fallen into neglect after the death of his father, when he was only ten. Now in his thirties, the poet revisits Mara in search of lost time, but everywhere he looks, he finds but tokens of desolation: the lanes, now overgrown; the cascade, dry; the grotto and footbridge, dilapidated. Baratynsky's elegy opens with an apostrophe addressed to the garden of his boyhood; here the poet explains why he chose this season to return:

Я посетил тебя, пленительная сень,
Не в дни весёлые живительного Мая,
Когда, зелёными ветвями помавая,
Манишь ты путника в свою густую тень;

[I paid my visit to you, captivating bower, / not in the joyful days of life-restoring Maytide, / when, beckoning with verdant branches / you lure the wanderer into your leafy shade.[109]]

"Yet springtime garb was not what I was seeking here," the poet postulates, "but memories from a time gone by." This was why Baratynsky "delayed [his] return" (*zamedlil vozvratom*) until "the trees were standing in autumnal nakedness, / their aspect dark and uninviting."

Upon first encounter with Golden Age poetry en masse, the tenacity of situational chronotopes may appear inexplicable. Here are a bunch of smart and creative poets, none of whom, however, appears to have had any qualms about writing, again and again, poems about autumns and waterfalls, loves and friendships, the vagaries of fortune, and sad or happy returns to ancestral homes. As to the possible strategy behind such recurrences and repetitions, two historical explanations present themselves. The customary explanation traces this propensity to repeat to pre-romantic rhetorical culture, which privileged imitation over innovation. Writing poetry, in this framework, was understood as learning from tradition; learning, in turn, equaled matching an established model. "Describe a tempest for me; compose a eulogy to modesty; retell the fight between the Horatii and Curiatii" was how Vladimir Pecherin recalled a university exam he took (ca. late 1820s–31) in French.[110] Or consider the more adventurous task Nikolai Ozeretskovsky, professor of Russian at the Cadets Corps, assigned his students in 1795: compose a letter a wounded son might send his father from the battlefield.[111] This pedagogy might remind us more of exercises assigned in an acting studio than foreign language tests (to say nothing of a writing test in one's mother tongue). Foreign or native, languages and literatures were not thinkable or teachable apart. Language proficiency was measured less by your ability to chat on daily topics than to write a literary text that would live up to ancient examples.

This explanation may seem satisfactory, but it fails to account for precisely the aspects of Golden Age poetry I foreground in this book: its uncommon, one-off, or personalized poetic practices. How personal and familial semantics dovetailed with the commitment to the canon will be easier to fathom if, following Yuri Lotman, we factor in the unusual role of performance in this period's everyday life and culture.[112] Recall how quickly and readily people memorized and recited verses to each other. Society ladies sang and played music; ambitious young men made reputations declaiming monologues, in French or German, on domestic stages. This was a participatory culture, or, to deploy Merzliakov's definition of the lyric, a culture of complicity, *souchastie*. Whether you act as a reader, write a letter, or embroider a tea cloth, you reproduce a preexisting model—but you also *appropriate* this model, make it your own. When a lady, alone in her room or in a social situation, took up her needle and embroidery hoop, she normally followed a pre-traced design; still, the choice of hues, of stitches to use, and, of course, of the design itself were all hers. Choosing the right design for your needlework was as creative an act as a poetic translator like Zhukovsky's choice of poem to translate. For a true translator, as for a true embroiderer, genuinely yours did not mean originally yours. When having received a postal reproof from his father for this or that act of debauchery, a young man reached for the *Newest Complete Letter-Writing Manual, or Everyone's Secretary for 1810* to copy model letter number forty-four, titled "A Reply to His Father by a Repentant Son,"[113] the resulting letter—even if rewritten verbatim—was genuinely his. What made a letter or a piece of embroidery your own was not the design but the hand; not the pattern but the performance.

"Any text is but a pretext"—this may sound arrogant to those who would equate theater with the *written* drama, but from the standpoint of a performer, the French actor's mot becomes a self-evident truth. In the eye of the player, performing means giving life to abstract signs, be it a string of notes on a piano score or a chain of words in a play script. Mutatis mutandis, Mounet-Sully's maxim can be applied to literature as well—especially when literary texts are viewed from the standpoint of their readers. When Pushkin wrote his "I have outlasted my desires," he initially planned to put these words into the mouth of the Russian prisoner of the Caucasus as this character tells the Circassian maiden about himself. When, on second thought, Pushkin decided to publish his verse as a stand-alone elegy, the text underwent a change of implied performer. Elegy readers tend to project the words they read onto the poet with whom, as Merzliakov had it, they willingly enter into complicity. "This is my life"—when the unknown woman with the initials "E. B." wrote this on her self-made copy of Pushkin's elegy, this was equivalent to signing a pact of complicity with the poem. Uses of poetry, like poetry itself, allow for multiple interpretations, none of which exclude any other. E. B.'s inscription next to Pushkin's elegy can be understood as a public lament using Pushkin's words, or as using his words as a secret confession; but we could also interpret the phrase "this is my life" as a performative act, the act of giving life to Pushkin's verbal score—much as a piano player gives life to Mozart's written music, an unskilled correspondent lends their handwriting (and perhaps even their voice) to a template found in a letter-writing manual, or a skilled embroiderer follows a preprinted imitation pattern to create an inimitable headdress.

At the same time, we should not lose sight of the poetics of the commonplace. The Golden Age could only be the age of the performative because it was also the age of stable scripts and proven patterns. These were not, as we have just seen, set pieces from which to construct an indifferently beautiful literary work. The lyric scripts and patterns that poets and readers used and recognized were grounded in very specific, carefully compartmented, reality-related situations. In this respect the poetics of the commonplace was, quite literally, the poetics of common places and common times.

In this chapter I have spoken of lyric chronotopes and cases of mutual projection—of writing upon reading and reading upon writing; I have also explored ways in which reading and writing projected upon living, and the other way round. My attention has been on performance; now it is time to focus on the scripts. In the two chapters that follow, I will examine lyric scripts vis-à-vis their uses, actual or potential, in three different communicative settings: alone with oneself, alone with one's love interest, and in company with one's peers. The reason I refer to these as "scripts" remains the same throughout the book: our interest will be in how verbal patterns coined by lyric poets were used by lovers of lyric as currency in corresponding life-related circumstances.

PART II

One, Two, Many
To Whom Poems Speak

WHAT CONSTITUTES A LYRIC POEM? This question has been raised more than once in period poetics and modern literary theory.[1] The standard way of answering it has long been to produce a list of traits—formal, stylistic, and thematic—that distinguish lyric poetry from its epic, dramatic, and other counterparts. Most lyric poems (by no means all) tend to be relatively short; rather than tell a story, they convey the speaker's emotions, and while often prompted by past events, the place and time of these emotions is the here and now. Another oft-noted peculiarity of lyric is that, grammatically, lyric poems tend to pivot on first- and second-person pronouns. Such, in a nutshell, is the descriptive anatomy of lyric—undoubtedly helpful, because it teaches us to know a lyric poem when we see one. It tells us nothing, however, of the internal dynamics of the lyric or of its *functional* anatomy, as it were. What forces and factors, beside sheer tradition, account for the modest length of your typical love elegy compared, for instance, to Pushkin's sizeable "Ode to Liberty" ("Vol'nost'")? What changes as the pronominal axis of lyric address shifts from *me speaking to you* to *me speaking to us* to *me addressing me*? And the like.

It was with an eye to examining literature in terms of its dynamics that Yuri Tynianov proposed a relational rather than taxonomic approach to lyric genre(s).[2] Elements of a lyric system define (and redefine) themselves against each other and in relation to the extraliterary communicative environment. The latter kind of relatedness is what Tynianov terms "orientation" (*ustanovka*). In the course of Russian literary evolution, ode as a lyric genre remained primarily related to oratory as a speech genre, while the lyric genre of elegy became increasingly oriented toward personal (conversational, melodious) genres of speech. Resonant halls were the communicative environment endemic to odes; elegies, for their part, were better suited to intimate, sotto voce, or even whispered parlor conversations. If earlier on the notions of "ode" and "elegy" were mainly used to pigeonhole definite types of verse, under Tynianov's pen, they came to signify the poles of a bipolar, internally conflictual system—the system of lyric, of poetry, or of late eighteenth- to early nineteenth-century literature at large. A reallocation of literary value from the odic to the elegiac pole was part of the emergence of Golden Age poetry as we know it.

If, indeed, literature is a dynamic system, we could hardly do better in exploring its elements and genres than to relate them to each other. In this sense, my approach to lyric genres in this chapter is going to be relational as well. Our historical understanding of poetry can only benefit from a more detailed map of poetry's adjacencies to speech. That Golden Age poetry was oriented toward non-oratorical, unaffected conversational speech should not make us think invariably of albums and salons, diaries and alcoves. There were more speech genres and genres of lyric to the epoch than the dichotomies of private versus public, conversational versus oratorical, and quiet versus sonorous would suggest. True enough, lyric poetry in the Golden Age typically implied what Tynianov calls the "live address," but there is no reason to narrow the speech repertoire of this implied addressee to pleasant parlor conversations. People toasted and prayed, speechified and lectured to each other. If indeed, as Tynianov has shown, Golden Age poetry is oriented toward live speech, the next logical question should concern the range of speech-involving circumstances this poetry arose in relation to.

Not that the back-and-forth between poetry and its verbal vicinities remains completely unexplored. "Poetry has many family resemblances with its near verbal relatives," states Jahan Ramazani in his recent study of modernist and postmodernist Anglophone literature, *Poetry and Its Others*.[3] Drawing theoretically on Jakobson and Bakhtin (Tynianov's model, while closest to Ramazani's, has slipped the latter's attention), the book deals precisely with poetry's entanglement with adjoining speech genres. As Ramazani shows, the three significant others of modern Anglophone poetry are news, prayer, and song. For us, Ramazani's triad is instructive vis-à-vis both its overlap with and divergence from the verbal environs of Russian poetry. Thus, in the Golden Age, prayer as a speech genre appears as productive for poetry as Ramazani finds it in the modern Anglophone world; on the other hand, in early nineteenth-century Russia, songs were seen as *part of* poetry rather than its extraliterary other.

And—unsurprising for a culture as steeped in poetry as Russia was in the period—here the repertoire of interactions between poetic and non-poetic speech genres was broader and more varied. Cataloging these interactions would be a daunting task, but there is a work-around. If we agree to foreground lyric, as I plan to in this part of the book, this plentiful repertoire can be usefully categorized according to three operative options, or modes of address, endemic to the genre. Consider the centrality of personal pronouns for the lyric. Approached from the standpoint of stylistics and thematics, the predilection for *I*, *you*, and *us* may be explained as a way of personalizing emotions, such that the feeling you express sounds authentically yours. My aim here is to explore what lyric is—*was*—from the viewpoint of historical pragmatics. If lyric poets preferred to write in the first and second person, singular or plural, what did this fact entail for lyric's readers?

The question will be easier to address if we recall that, by *persona*, the Greek and Roman grammarians meant "role," a term they likely derived from the vocabulary of drama. As Katie Wales says in her study of personal pronouns, "The pronouns therefore invoke, as it were, a mini-drama, with 'participants.'"[4] Indeed, from the standpoint of language philosophy, personal pronouns are but "participatory roles." Whom "I" or "you" refers to in a sentence is only known when we know who is speaking, and to whom. Lyric poems, too, offer readers participatory roles to jump into. The situational pragmatics of a love elegy in action, as I am going to show in chapter 5, changes depending on which of the two actants, at this or that specific moment in a dialogue, takes up the "I," leaving the "you" for his or her counterpart to impersonate.

That the present part of this study is titled "One, Two, Many: To Whom Poems Speak" is because here the lyric poetry of the Golden Age is viewed in three communicative perspectives: *Me to myself*; *Me to you*; and *Me to us*. Each perspective, I posit, led to a set of specific genres, verbal and lyric. Addressing oneself in a poem rendered such a work the literary counterpart of a diary entry, or a prayer; the lyric chronotope ("written when and where") of such a poem is, typically, a secluded place (as in Zhukovsky's "Country Graveyard") or a private hour (as in Pushkin's "Lines Composed at Night during Insomnia" ["Stikhi, sochinennye noch'iu vo vremia bessonnitsy"]); its master mood is quietude (as in Tiutchev's "Silentium"); its stock setting, surrounding nature, with an occasional deity hiding in the foliage.

The opposite perspective was, by contrast, full of people. In the Golden Age, the main function of the us-centered discourse and corresponding lyric poems was community-building: from toasting and drinking songs (tableside solos, often with a refrain sung or recited by a table-chorus) to regimental and national solidarity marches. An epistle in verse or simply a friend's letter to a friend—read or shown, as a rule, to a group of other mutual friends—was a powerful tool of informal community-building in the Golden Age, the literary epoch of familial associations.[5] None of these genres was isolated from another. Thus, Zhukovsky, in his instantly famous 1812 "A Bard in the Camp of Russian Warriors," made use of the drinking-song format to celebrate the Russian military campaign against Napoleon; in 1813, Batiushkov resorted to the same format and formulae, now familiar from Zhukovsky's heroic "Bard," in a spoof aimed at his (and Zhukovsky's) literary enemies titled "A Bard in the Colloquium of Friends of Russian Letters." Here, the heroic comically interferes with the hedonic: in their zeal to make poetry as great as it had been at the time of Vasily Trediakovsky and Mikhail Lomonosov, the present-day advocates of the Slavonic sublime pledge to drink Lomonosov himself under the table: "Let's hit the booze to please the Muse / As our granddads used to do!"[6] *I to us* is thus the communicative axis of the lyric that I explore in chapter 4, "The Extended Self: 'I' to 'I' and 'I' to 'We.'"

Of the three communicative perspectives sketched above, *Me to you* was, in the Golden Age, the most productive and ubiquitous. Anything phrased in a love letter or an album, during a mazurka chat or moonlight tryst, could be, or at least could be interpreted as, a speech act. Central among the lyric speech acts I will attend to in chapter 5 ("You and I: Love Elegy and How to Use It") is Baratynsky's famous "Dissuasion" ("Razuverenie") and its uses as a speech act in an 1828 love affair as recorded in the diary of one of the participants. My task in this case study is twofold. On the one hand, it is the study of uses—how a love elegy, in full or in excerpts, used to be doctored and customized to match a given situation; on the other, it asks what performative opportunities and participatory roles are implicit in the equivocal vocabulary and grammatical ambiguity of Baratynsky's text.

4

The Extended Self

"I" to "I" and "I" to "We"

IN 1824 OR 1825, Kondraty Ryleev asked his friend and coconspirator Nikolai Bestuzhev for advice. A beautiful young woman was showing signs of affection toward him, and Ryleev, to his embarrassment, found himself reciprocating her feelings. What to do? Bestuzhev was skeptical: "All this sounds very strange to me—precisely because this is happening to you. You are neither handsome nor polished, nor are you gallant with women. Your poetic gift is insufficient for a woman to fall in love with you." We learn of this from Bestuzhev's "Reminiscence of Ryleev," written after the Decembrist Bestuzhev was sent to Siberia and the Decembrist Ryleev executed. A few pages down, Bestuzhev extols Ryleev's poetry for having struck the chord of freedom innate in the hearts of his oppressed compatriots, and exclaims: "What else is poetry for, if not for making our heart resonate to it?"[1]

While the two assessments of Ryleev's poetic gift differ, the criterion for both remains the same: your poetry is only as good as its effect on the intended reader. In this respect, Bestuzhev's judgment aligned with those eighteenth-century theories of poetry that M. H. Abrams calls "pragmatic."[2] The verbal impact on the reader, such theories decreed, was the ultimate measure of success.

The impacts a poet might seek vary, but lyric ones are typically emotional. A lyric poem was supposed to resound in our hearts—with earthly love or righteous indignation. If not, "what else is poetry for," to use Bestuzhev's words? For generations now, readers have been taught that the main thing about poems is meaning—what poems say. The primary critical procedure, in this view, is to interpret. But for a Golden Age critic, the main question was not what a poem says but what it does. If your poem is about this or that emotion, your task as a poet is not to describe, but to induce it. Heart, and its various strings, was a catchword in critics' and readers' responses to poetry. Thus, in Konstantin Aksakov's view, "Le Désespoir" by that "watery poet" Alphonse de Lamartine "leaves no *désespoir* [despair] in our hearts."[3] Conversely, too fiery a poem could set your heart on fire. Such, for instance, was Pushkin's *Ruslan and Liudmila* in the eye of the critic Nikolai Kutuzov. Perhaps inspired by Dante's depiction of two all-too-passionate readers in *Inferno*, Kutuzov conjured up this cautionary scene of moral melting:

> Behold: an ardent youth and a young maiden are running hungrily through [*Ruslan and Liudmila*]. . . . They sink into ambrosial slumber; their eyes are ablaze with flame. . . . Fire fills the former's veins; the latter's heart starts languidly beating, then halts. . . . Heated imagination will banish quiet, placid life and immerse their hearts into a sea of desires, perhaps also an ocean of predicaments.[4]

In each critical assessment of this type, poetry is judged on its power to transform—in the above examples, a love interest, society, or the readers' code of conduct. Less evident, but no less important, was poetry's power to transform the lyric self. Such was also the aim of those lyric speech acts whose sole participant is the lyric "I."

AUTO-COMMUNICATIONS

Pronominal explorations of Russian lyric poetry go back to the heyday of structuralist poetics—the school of thought that encouraged studying literary works from the linguistic point of view. We use pronouns like *I* and *you* when we address someone or someones—and so do lyric speakers in lyric poems. Poems are thus akin to the acts of communication we perform on a daily basis. In a number of other aspects, however, lyric speech differs from ordinary speaking. One such aspect is the gravity of auto-communicative acts in the pronominal universe of lyric—cases in which lyric speakers appear to be conversing with themselves. In the early 1970s, the propensity of lyric poetry to think aloud instead of engaging in "straight talk" was discussed in two studies: Yuri Levin's "Lyric from the Communicative Standpoint" (1971, published in 1973) and Yuri Lotman's 1973 "Auto-Communication: 'I' and 'Other' as Addressees (On Two Models of Communication within the System of Culture)."[5] While the questions posed in these studies are of the same nature, the theories Levin and Lotman propose to tackle them differ. Where do we draw the line between communication and auto-communication? Between the lyric utterance and the act of practical speech? Between the lyric self and the self in the existential sense? These questions will loom large in this chapter, and so here we might examine them through the bifocal lens of Levin's and Lotman's structuralist accounts.

Levin's account presents the self-centeredness of the lyric as a poetic anomaly—a feature that distinguishes communicative acts as modeled in lyric texts from the way we communicate in real life. If an act of communication sensu stricto requires at least two agents—a sender and a receiver, both of whom share a common code—then lyric communications, according to Levin, are first and foremost from *I* to *I*; except when the pronoun *you* is manifested in the text. The absence of an explicit address does not deprive a poem of its communicative status; such cases constitute acts of auto-communication—when "a poem posits itself as a meditation, a self-addressed memo, a conversation with itself."[6] Auto-communicative poems function by triggering auto-communication in their readers. "The act of auto-communication that led to the creation of a poem (a poet's conversation with him- or herself) projects upon the act of the poem's perception, turning the act of reading into the reader's conversation with him- or herself."[7] Life teaches us to talk to others; poetry, to ourselves.

Lotman's theory proceeds from a different premise. The fact that auto-communication plays an exceptional role in lyric poetry, per Lotman, does not mean that lyric poetry constitutes an exception from a rule; rather, this fact lays bare the ambivalence inherent in communicative mechanisms at large. Communication, as we observe it in human culture(s), is a dynamic system whose functioning involves incomprehension as much as comprehension, switching between languages no less than exchanging messages, and talking to oneself, not solely to others.

What would be the point of communicating with myself if anything I can say to myself is (as common sense would have it) already known to me? Lotman's answer to this may appear somewhat paradoxical at first: if not informative, auto-communication is *self*-formative. The role of auto-communication in culture is not unlike that of echolocation in nature. To navigate, bats and dolphins emit ultrasound signals that bounce back, transformed, from surrounding objects. Auto-communicative acts do not take place in empty space or in an airtight retort: the signal sent to oneself travels through what Lotman in his later studies would call the "semiosphere"—it gets encoded, recoded, and re-recoded via multiple languages of culture—to return transformed and, in turn, affect and change the sender's mind. Auto-communication results in self-impact: talking to myself restructures what I am.

For the purpose of this study, Lotman's model is more suitable than Levin's: it foregrounds a continuity rather than a distinction between auto-communication as a poetic and everyday practice. Whether, at nighttime, we are one on one with our diary or evening prayer, walking amid tombstones like Zhukovsky's lyric speaker in "Country Graveyard," or talking ourselves to sleep like Pushkin in "Verses Written at Night during Insomnia"—our self-addressed messages never travel naked. Rather, they walk clad in appropriate cultural codes: confessional, pious, or poetic. Widespread in the nineteenth century, for instance, were self-critical diaries, in which one's daily deeds and thoughts would be submitted to a nightly moral scrutiny—a textbook example of auto-communication used as a vehicle of self-transformation (specifically, self-improvement). In self-centered lyric poems a metric code, of course, is layered on top of the verbal one—be it Zhukovsky's slow-paced iambic hexameter, or Pushkin's wakeful four-foot trochee.

Lotman's idea of auto-communication opens a new perspective on the roles personal pronouns enact in lyric poetry. A theory I intend to test and explore in this chapter has to do with pronominal boundaries in lyric texts vis-à-vis everyday usage. When I say "I," I tacitly define it as non-you, non-we, non-them, and so on. Wherever I go, my pronominal self travels with me, as it were. Roughly speaking, the boundary of the first-person singular pronoun as I use it outside any lyric context coincides with the bubble of my body and mind. Not so—not always so—in lyric poetry. Here, the lyric "I" (also known, in different scholarly traditions, as the "lyric hero" or "lyric speaker") is less constrained, if at all, by the boundaries of the author as a physical person. Lyric pronouns are simply more mobile, malleable, and mutually exchangeable.

Zhukovsky, for instance, was a past master of pronominal games. His "Country Graveyard"—a poetic translation of Thomas Gray's "Elegy Written in a Country Churchyard" and a Russian meditative elegy in its own right—is, in essence, its lyric speaker's long conversation with himself. Yet, as many have observed, not one of its thirty-five stanzas contains a single instance of a first-person singular pronoun—whether lexically manifested or grammatically implied.[8] This absence of an easily identifiable subject position was a carefully calculated gambit. As Tatiana Fraiman's study shows, across the long history of its making, the configuration of "Graveyard's" pronouns kept changing from version to version; Zhukovsky experimented with these quite a bit.⁹ The lyric "I" is not *absent* from the pronominal architecture of the elegy; rather, it is made invisible and elusive, hiding now behind the second-person singular, now within the first-person plural. Now the poem evokes "our graves," implying, as Catherine Ciepiela reads it, that "the speaker includes himself among the dead";¹⁰ now the speaker calls himself *ty* ("And you, friend of the deceased . . . / Your hour, too, shall toll"); now cites the inscription "he was mild of heart and sensitive of soul," engraved on his own, the speaker's, imaginary tombstone. Now you see "me," now you don't, is the game Zhukovsky's lyric poem plays with me, its reader. Rather than point to the subject of the speech act, the lyric "I" is a mere pragmatic opportunity, a lacuna for me, a reader, to fill; a role to jump into.

Zhukovsky's "Graveyard" pertains to a well-established tradition of nocturnal poetry that poses great existential questions about time, fate, mortality, or the meaning of life. As a rule, such nocturnal reflections eventually provide sensible and intelligible answers to these questions, mainly in religious terms. Auto-communication in this context amounts to self-consolation or perhaps self-preparation for the worst. Exceptions do occur, however; Pushkin's "Insomnia" is one of these. Here, the questions are asked to no avail—as happens, for instance, when a phone connection is lost and we go on shouting "hello" to silence or a dial tone.

This is how Pushkin sets the scene:

Мне не спится, нет огня;
Всюду мрак и сон докучный.
Ход часов лишь однозвучный
Раздаётся близ меня.¹¹

[I cannot fall asleep, there is no light; / Everywhere is gloom and tedious sleep. / Only the monotone running of the clock / Is heard near me.]

In three subsequent lines, the soundscape expands in three different dimensions.

Парки бабье лепетанье,
Спящей ночи трепетанье,
Жизни мышья беготня

[Womanish prattling of a Parca, / Quivering of the sleeping night, / The mouse-scurrying of life]

Various interpretations of this sonic catalog have been proposed, each to this or that extent sanctioned by Pushkin's remarkably polysemic poem. These include allusions to ancient mythology and literature—for instance, the metaphor of scurrying mice from the *Meditations* of Marcus Aurelius, as Natalia Mazur has suggested.[12] Plentiful evidence can be found in Pushkin to support such philosophical readings. The early draft, for instance, characterizes the Parcae as "horrible" (*uzhasnye*) and speaks, metaphysically, of "the immortal quivering of eternity" instead of the earthbound "quivering of the sleeping night" of the final version. On the other hand, we would do well to balance this evidence with the obvious observation that mice as mice, not only mice as a philosophical allegory for human life, were a quite familiar feature of Russian countryside households; Michael Wachtel is right to have categorized the mice as "the 'realia' of the poem."[13] We may even go one further and suggest that Pushkin's Parca, her antique ancestry notwithstanding, is grounded in Pushkin by the vernacular "womanish" (*bab'e*) appended to her "prattling" (itself a hardly classically solemn way to refer to prophesying). The sound of spinning wheels worked by a team of peasant maidens (*devki*) and women (*baby*) was as much a part of the familiar soundscape of a Russian country estate as the underground bustling of mice. (In Pushkin's ancestral estate of Mikhailovskoe, the spin-house was installed in the manor-house—which, granted, could hardly have been the case in cholera-ridden Boldino where his "Verses Written at Night during Insomnia" were composed.)

The question is: are these different sounds, or one and the same differently described? A. D. Grigor'eva has a point when she proposes in a 1974 essay that the above-quoted lines be read as three successive attempts to interpret and render the kernel sound, the tick-tock of the clock.[14] The Parca's prattling? Life scurrying like mice? Read this way, "Insomnia" becomes a poem about (to apply to the Golden Age a phrase coined in the Silver one) the "noise of time."

The kind of mutual projection of the sublime and the quotidian employed by Pushkin in "Insomnia" is likewise characteristic of Zhukovsky's "Country Graveyard," but the way it occurs in Pushkin is different. At the core of nocturnal meditations like Zhukovsky's and Gray's are the length, gradualness, and difficulty of the ascension. The way from rustic landscapes to rural graves and on to the metaphysics of life and death must be a process, a pilgrim's progress, whereas all Pushkin needs for these extremes to meet is a single line. The difference is not in tempo but in the character of movement: where Zhukovsky builds a trajectory, Pushkin shuttles to and fro. The three lines cited, for instance, are variations of the same basic structure: a disyllabic noun in the genitive case with a disyllabic adjective attached (after/before/after) followed by a polysyllabic (therefore pyrrhic) noun. Three trials, each starting anew. Pushkin's clock is ticking yet does not lead anywhere, only back and forth. Three consecutive attempts to translate this ticking into familiar symbols (a Parca? the night? rodent activity?) yield nothing intelligible. Pushkin takes three bites into the available tradition of nocturnal meditative poetry—from ancient mythology to the "quivering" night of natural philosophy—and, after the third bite, casts it away.

That this is a matter of periphrastic decoding, an intense interrogation, a frenetic attempt to understand the transrational language of the night, becomes clearer in the second half of "Insomnia," whose seven lines include five questions and a final ellipsis:

Что ты значишь, скучный шопот?
Укоризна, или ропот
Мной утраченного дня?
От меня чего ты хочешь?
Ты зовёшь или пророчишь?
Я понять тебя хочу,
Смысла я в тебе ищу . . .

What is your meaning, boring whisper? / Is it a reproach, or the grievance / Of my lost day? / What is it you want from me? / Are you calling or prophesying? / I want to understand you, / I seek sense in you . . .]

Clocks tick; spinning wheels spin, droning as they do; mice, too, make their presence heard. None of these sonic trivia points to anything other than their physical source—or so it would seem. Yet the insomniac keeps asking about their meaning and intentions. Whisper, reproach, grievance, calling, and prophesying—all these are words pertaining to human speech rather than nature's noises.

Where there is speech, there must be a speaker. In his analysis of "Insomnia," Michael Wachtel indicates what precisely makes the poem teasingly enigmatic. The devil is in the second person pronoun. Wachtel calls it "a mysterious 'ty'" that comes in mid-poem (in line 8) to remain center stage to the very end: "Until this point, the poem was focused on the 'I,' and there was no reason to expect a 'ty.' The 'ty' appears to be a conflation of all the previous impressions, and the poet's turn to it an attempt to make sense of the world beyond."[15] Only no such comprehension is forthcoming. The poem becomes a monologue despite itself, a failed dialogue with someone who never answers questions.

This nowhere-leading conversation sits strangely with Roman Jakobson's pragmatic model of language, Jonathan Culler's theory of the lyric, and Yuri Lotman's idea of auto-communication. Of Jakobson's six functions, it never gets past the phatic one. On the surface, "Insomnia's" lyric address would seem to jibe with Culler's claim that apostrophe—the convention that sanctions a lyric poem to speak to absent inanimate or nonhuman addressees—is at the core of any lyric act, but Pushkin's apostrophe is anomalous in that, unlike Shelley's west wind, William Blake's sick rose, or John Keats's nightingale, here, the ticking clock is not a "gentle listener" but an incessant speaker whose gibberish (or is it something else?) the sleepless "I" seeks to decipher. While every reader of "Insomnia" understands from the outset that a mock interview between a human being and a mechanical clock can only be a cover-up for an act of auto-communication, the latter, pace Lotman, results not in self-enrichment but rather in self-frustration. Self ends up not being self's best collocutor.

The term I use in the title of this chapter, "The Extended Self," is borrowed from a relatively recent (1998) and increasingly influential study in the philosophy of mind coauthored by Andy Clark and David Chalmers. Titled "The Extended Mind," the study posits a model of cognitive activity that is not confined by the "skin/skull boundary."[16] Rather, taken together, the human mind and the external world form what Clark and Chalmers term a "coupled system." We think both inside and outside our heads, looping back and forth between the environment and mind. "What, finally, of the self? Does the extended mind imply an extended self? It seems so," Clark and Chalmers assume toward the end of their study.[17] If further evidence were needed to demonstrate the existence of the extended self, Russian lyric of the Golden Age would be exhibit A. The lyric self respects no bounds, least of all the bounds of skull and skin. The "I" of Pushkin's "Insomnia" is straining to decode what its lyric double, "you," is straining to communicate, using the nonsensical tongue of environmental noises. Zhukovsky's lyric "I" melts into the big lyric "us": us, the deceased; us, their sensitive friends; us, Zhukovsky's gentle readers. This lyric "I," per Lotman's theory of "auto-communication," is but an epitome of how culture at large shapes and reshapes our self-perception and thereby our self. We change ourselves by sending out signals—dynamic loops—that return translated into the language of mice, verse, diaries, and prayers. Golden Age culture is, in more than one sense, a paragon of Clark and Chalmers's "coupled system." Its literary system is hardly thinkable decoupled—from Golden Age readers with their daily and nightly verbal acts, from toasting and boasting to journaling and praying.

Poetry, Diary, and Prayer: Auto-communication in a Pragmatic Perspective

Talking to others and talking to oneself are different yet not alternative choices. Communication and auto-communication are two ends of a continuous spectrum. Every "dear diary" contains a modicum of "urbi et orbi"— and vice versa. Prayers generally address a divinity but can also work as self-confessions. We know of diaries meant to be delivered to others, and, inversely, of epistles addressed to others but never intended to be sent. Zhukovsky's letter-diaries (quoted at some length in chapter 3) stubbornly refuse to make a distinction between auto- and allo-communication. While the communicative spectrum of this period's literature indeed ranged from stone-deaf, John-Stuart-Millian introspections to open, extrovert "live addresses"—I and others, I and you, or I and us—we must be wary of taking any such communicative position at face value, or overly relying on every declared boundary between them. The line separating the two is fluid and culturally conditioned, and must be examined in a historical perspective.

The same should be said about the line between lyric and extra-poetic genres of auto-communicative speech. We will not get far in studying auto-communicative lyric without collating it with other auto-communicative verbal practices such as diaries and prayers—not solely as texts but also as performative events with their established rituals and routines. An important aspect of praying, for instance, was the cyclical character of the procedure. Praying was tied to mornings and evenings. One's morning and evening prayer thus used to bracket one's day and night—each opened with an act of self-communication. It was this discursive two-act structure of everyone's every day that Lomonosov made use of in the mid-eighteenth century in his paired scientific/spiritual odes—"Evening Reflection on God's Majesty" ("Vechernee razmyshlenie o bozhiem velichestve") and its companion piece,

"Morning Reflection on God's Majesty" ("Utrennee razmyshlenie o bozhiem velichestve") on the same subject—which combined physical explanations of the universe with the glorification of the universal. In Zhukovsky's "Country Graveyard," the internal affinity with evening prayers is manifested in the commanding role allotted to retrospection: set at the end of the day, and heading into night, the elegy first looks back at our dead. In Pushkin's "Insomnia," the retrospective urge is condensed into two lines: "Is it a reproach, or grievance / Of my lost day?" As Natalia Mazur convincingly demonstrates, this distich from Pushkin's "Insomnia" belongs to the tradition of "nocturnal confessional self-accounts"—speech acts that stem from antiquity and that, in later times, took the form of evening prayers (and, arguably, bedtime diary entries).[18]

Keeping a diary, too, was seen as a daily chore, if less frequent and less rigorous than praying. A diary closed your day, thus serving as the secular counterpart of evening prayer. In Russia, a diary entry tended to complement, rather than duplicate, one's evening prayer: the latter, pronounced predominantly in Church Slavonic, functioned more as a ritual than as living speech. Diaries have received considerable attention in recent scholarship on the Russian nineteenth century; this has revealed, among other things, the multiplicity of diary types.[19] There were diaries that merely chronicled the day's events; these were, in effect, diary-clad records that people like Aleksandr Turgenev or Stepan Zhikharev used to keep in order to share (and actually mail) to other people. Such diaries can hardly be called genuine acts of auto-communication. On the other hand, there existed diaries of both the intimate (genuinely private) and "confessional" type (written to enable a particular, often religious, group to judge the moral progress of its writer). And as is so often the case with genres generally, diary genres would frequently segue into one other. Thus, Andrei Zorin's recent study of Andrei Turgenev's diaries kept between 1799 and 1803 examines these as a variety of transitional forms between the "confessional" (specifically, Masonic) and intimate genre of diary writing.[20]

Confessional diaries "went with" evening prayers—functionally as well as in temporal terms. The purpose of evening diaries was not merely to record but to draw a line under the day's events, assess one's behavior during the day, and balance sinful and virtuous deeds. "Nine o'clock: diary and prayer; half past nine to half past five: sweet dreams," prescribed a daily timetable by which the heir to the Russian throne and his fellow pupils lived in the 1820s.[21] The liminal time slot typically allotted to diary writing—after the day is done, and before the night sets in—made it easier to look at one's day not merely with an outer eye but also from a higher point of view, be it God's or the standpoint of a moral ideal. After the diurnal pursuit of worldly rewards, a diary was supposed to furnish a spiritual stocktaking.

The high point of the genre were the so-called "(Benjamin) Franklin virtue charts" that enabled diary authors to check which virtue they had or had not exercised that day. Zhukovsky from time to time kept his diary in the Franklin style, a fact shedding additional light on his lyric poems.²² In the space of a given poet's oeuvre, the self of ego-documents is quite liable to spill over or blend into the lyrical self of their verse, Vadim Vatsuro's study shows: "The lyric 'I' of Andrei Turgenev's and Zhukovsky's elegies is very close to the authorial 'I' in their letters and diaries; lyric incorporates the experience of self-observation and emotional response to reality that is registered in [their] prose."²³ This can also be true of prose fiction: as has been suggested by Boris Eikhenbaum (and much discussed to the present day), a powerful resource for Lev Tolstoy's psychological prose was his Franklin-style diary—a day-by-day catalog of daily sins requiring a day-to-day auto-confession.²⁴

Another usual preoccupation of diary writers is the passage of time as such, both from the moral and spiritual standpoint, and in terms of practical scheduling, that is, writing and checking to-do lists. As Irina Paperno observes: "An account of the present as much as a plan for the future, [the young Tolstoy's] diary combines the prescriptive and the descriptive."²⁵ The same can be said of the young Zhukovsky's diaries, written almost half a century before Tolstoy's. The diary, then, was a tool, not just for accounting for time past but also for saving time, or at least avoiding losing it, both in the ethical and practical sense.

This brings us back to the question raised above: are cases of what we, following Lotman and Levin, tend to identify as auto-communication truly about "auto-"; and is "communication" the best common denominator for these cases to be reduced to? Prayers, at least linguistically, are appellations. While diaries could also be addressed to particular readers, they usually were not; but the logic (and long-standing practice) of self-perfection ruled out the sealing of confessional diaries. If the young heir to the Russian throne was required to write a diary entry (each equipped with a biblical quote) every night before prayers, we can be reasonably sure the educational regimen required him to show the diary to his tutors. The same is true of moral self-perfection. In his novel *The Kholmsky Family: Some Traits of Mores and Lifestyle of the Russian Nobility, Married and Single* (*Semeistvo Kholmskikh: Nekotorye cherty nravov i obraza zhizni, semeinoi i odinokoi, russkikh dvorian*, 1832), Dmitry Begichev recommends (through a "voice of wisdom" character) that newlyweds keep a Franklin diary together—and in it "confess to each other not just their deeds, but also thoughts and feelings."[26]

One cannot but agree with Lotman's observation that texts addressed from "me" to "me" (except, of course, purely informational self-reminders or to-do lists, addressed from "me today" to "me tomorrow") are intended to self-transform, to restructure the very sender of the message. But it is precisely because of this restructuring that the term "auto-*communication*" looks like a misnomer. We have already spoken of the notion of verbal impact (effect or "aim") current in the pragmatic poetics of the epoch. This impact was understood, no doubt, as a rhetorical virtue of poetry, but nothing prevents us from extending it to poetry's immediate neighborhood: solitary speech acts like diaries and prayers. In other words, the pragmatics of one's evening diary and nightly prayer had to do with sustained and regular self-impact more than it did with self-informing.

Writing a poem to be circulated; writing a letter to be posted—these were rational, motivated forms of writing. Writing for no reason and to no one in particular raised writing to the rank of self-sufficient activity—the favorite pastime of graphomaniacs on the one hand and perfectionists on the other. The latter group included not only zealots for moral self-improvement but also believers in the daily chore of diary-keeping as a useful exercise or mental workout. Take Stepan Zhikharev's detailed—predominantly chronographic—diary (1805 through 1819), cherished by every historian studying the life and culture of this period. The idea—indeed the ideology—of keeping a diary like this was given to Zhikharev by one Fedor Kartsev (a drama translator whose name we remember mainly thanks to Zhikharev), who said, "Your diary [*zhurnal*] is a wonderful undertaking: it accustoms you to work and keeps you aware of our own thoughts, feelings, and actions. Keep keeping it, always: with time, you'll come to love it [*sliubitsia*]."[27]

The value of a diary, per Kartsev (and Zhikharev, who not only registered Kartsev's advice but also followed it day in, day out for many years), lies not in particular thoughts or observations per se but in the continuous process of thinking and observing. Diaries are continuous affairs. The succession of diary days, the chain of diurnal events and train of thoughts these leave on a diary page, are primarily available to the one doing the writing; hence, the longer the diary lasts, the more it becomes part of its writer. This must be what Kartsev meant by falling in love with your diary *with time*, and this is also what I mean by the self-impact produced by diary-keeping.

Writing as exercising, writing out of the pure love of writing, as a way of engaging in dialogue with oneself—these facets of diary ideology bordered on the conceptions of poetry cherished by many in the Golden Age. Earlier in this book, I quoted Prince Dolgorukov on poetry-writing as no more, for him, than a pleasant princely pastime. But even Kartsev, that translator from Zhikharev's diary, claimed that the pleasure of poetry was in writing it, not in its being noticed and noted by others. Thus does Zhikharev render another conversation with his diary guru:

> "Do you ever read your poems to anyone?"—"Yes," he says, "I have to my wife and, in parts, to Prince Gorchakov and Karin."—"Yet you never intended, and still don't, to publish those?"—"Why would I, my dear fellow? I write and translate for myself, because I love this work. As if there were no other reasons for writing poems than becoming renowned!"—"True; but renown serves to encourage talent."—"This, my dear fellow, is something only idle people believe, people who do not understand the joy ingrained in the very process of working."[28]

Several elements of this dialogue may aid our understanding of self-addressed poetry and its peculiar ideology. Unlike Prince Dolgorukov, Kartsev (whose very obscurity as a literary figure was part, it turns out, of a purposeful literary program) posited poetry-writing not as an idle hobby but as joyful work (*trud*, the same word he uses in explaining the joy of diary-keeping). Of particular significance for us is that, alongside diaries, Kartsev included poetry in his philosophy of self-writing.

The Narrow We

Lyric meditations, one-on-one with oneself, are less monologic than their settings would seem to suggest. In Pushkin's "Insomnia" the lyric subject clamors for an interlocutor. One hears this yearning, indeed, not just in particular poems but also in statements *about* poetry. Asked if he writes poetry, the first-person observer in Karamzin's *Letters of a Russian Traveler* (*Pis'ma russkogo puteshestvennika*) gives a characteristic answer: "[Yes,] for those who love me."[29] To Karamzin (and Karamzinians), poetry was, first of all, a love-bound community of minds, at times understood in concrete, neighborhood terms. On 21 June 1818, Vasily Pushkin complained in a letter to Viazemsky: "I no longer write poetry, and do nothing at all. You are not here [in Moscow]. Zhukovsky and Batiushkov have vanished as well. Without you, my dear friends, I am good for nothing, my talent is mute, and my Muse is mute."[30] This is not a complaint about boredom but has rather to do with poetry's intrinsic orientation toward dialogue, communication, and cocreation (which explains why so many modern selections of works by major Golden Age poets include a subsection titled "The Collective").

Familiar associations were at the ideological core of Golden Age poetry. Poetic tributes to the like-minded, to one's cohort, comrades-in-arms, or companions-in-arts, were typically arranged around what we have singled out as the pronominal configuration of "I to us," whose semantic ambivalence—the subject "I" that addresses the object "us" is, at the same time, a constituent of the latter—served as an infinite source of pragmatic ambiguity. Who is speaking to whom? On one level, a poet addresses a set of others, be they a tiny group or a larger crowd; in this respect, this is a regular act of communication. On another, by virtue of referencing "us," the lyric speaker includes him- or herself in this set. The meaning becomes unstable: the poem is both an act of communication and (as the reading flips) of auto-communication.

Among lyric speech acts, such poems may be categorized as community-building texts; this was their aim (built-in function, projected impact), regardless of whether their "I's" or "us's" were textually manifested or implied. In the world of familiar circles and literary associations, this rubric would include friendly epistles in verse (addressed, as a rule, to someone, yet also to someone as privy to the group)—a genre that stood remarkably high in the hierarchy of the lyric, and tended to proliferate, insofar as every epistle was expected to be reciprocated. Less explored, but no less important in terms of community-building, were drinking songs, school anthems (of these, the lyceum anthem and lyceum anniversary songs constitute a subset important in Pushkin studies), and military songs (and other soldierly lore). Written to be sung in chorus, these latter downplayed the "I" in favor of the "us" (as in ecclesiastical rites, in which community-building is pursued through communion with God). Embedded as they were in everyday routines, these lyric forms proved poetically productive and tenacious—productive enough to engender verse as inspired and inspiring as Zhukovsky's "Bard in the Camp of Russian Warriors" proved during the 1812 campaign, and tenacious enough to have resurfaced in Bulat Okudzhava's 1967 "Let's Join Hands, My Friends"

("Vozmemsia za ruki, druz'ia") or Viktor Tsoi's 1986 "We Await Changes" ("My zhdem peremen").

From today's standpoint, Golden Age poetry's self-confinement to narrow circles is easy to mistake for a form of aristocratic elitism. From the period point of view, the picture was more complex, in some respects even the opposite. In the eyes of their ideologists, literary coteries existed in defiance of, not compliance with, the overcodified rules of conduct accepted in the *svet*—that is, the aristocratic milieu. In the just-mentioned *Letters*, published in 1791–92, at the dawn of the Golden Age, Karamzin branded high-society gatherings a "bad comedy called restraint," with no room for human contact (*obshchenie*), for one to make an argument, tell a story, or express an emotion. "All one is permitted is to utter a remark en passant and slip away, letting someone else take center stage; everyone is afraid of giving themselves away, of showing their ignorance of bon ton."[31] As for human contact, the uninhibited outpouring of feelings, or genuine exchange of thoughts and observations, continues Karamzin, "we only enjoy these things in close dealings with friends [*v korotkom obkhozhdenii s druz'iami*]."[32] Karamzin's "we" is a telltale pronoun. Some thirty years later, when Ivan Kireevsky avowed to Baratynsky his "societal cretinism" (*v obshchestve tupoumie*), the latter reassuringly diagnosed this as a syndrome endemic to the unspecified community of "we": "While we do drop in on high-society gatherings, we are not high-society people [*my ne svetskie liudi*]. Our mind is of a different cast, it has different habits. Small talk for us is a science to be studied, a dramatic creation, for we are foreign to the real life, real passions of high society."[33]

An invisible intellectual thread leads from contemporary introspections like Karamzin's and Baratynsky's to Eikhenbaum's 1929 essay "Literary Domesticity" (a study that clarifies, among other phenomena that may appear curious today, why poets like Batiushkov or Iazykov invested more energy in sending their works to lists of their friends than in getting them published), whose theses were further elaborated that same year in *Literary Circles and Salons* by Mark Aronson and Solomon Reiser, and on to the most recent explorations into the literary habitats of the Golden Age, like Joe Peschio's *The Poetics of Impudence and Intimacy in the Age of Pushkin* (2012).[34] Peschio approaches the collective "we" of two of the most prominent informal literary circles—Arzamas and the Green Lamp—from the standpoint of the linguistic strategies formative to each. As Peschio shows, the literary trend that Eikhenbaum identifies with the cozy, homey term "domesticity" takes the form of rudeness in the speech practice of Arzamas and sexual banter in the

Green Lamp—in both cases, as opposed to the politeness of salons and the bureaucratic officialese of state institutions.

As Peschio's study reminds us, it is important to distinguish friendly circles from such other forms of the literary everyday as salons and state-recognized literary societies. Unlike the latter associations, circles were unofficial on principle, lacking structure; they tended to eschew documentation or even mocked it in parodic minutes—as taken, for example, at Arzamas meetings or annual lyceum celebrations. This was also what made such circles different from salons: while a typical literary salon was, like a circle, an unofficial assembly, its attendees obeyed (unwritten) rules of conduct and had, conspicuously or otherwise, to comply with the tastes and interests of its hostess or host.

To be sure, all these organizational forms coexisted; many literati would frequent several salons each, serve as members in different literary societies, and attend more than one literary circle. The main distinction between a literary salon and a literary circle lay in the degree of productivity. As Aronson observes, a salon (and, one should add, a regular literary society) was a site of reception and assessment of literary texts, whereas familiar circles were where such texts were not only received but also produced.[35]

What cemented literary circles was not social elitism but its members' closeness to one another (granted, an intimacy at times artificially exaggerated, as Peschio observes[36]). Karamzin views personal closeness through the lens of literary ideology and ethics, another closeness factor being the physical (not always willing) proximity of students under the dormitory roof of this or that educational institution. That our mental picture of literary life in the first half of the nineteenth century tends to foreground the role of literary salons is due, primarily, to our comparatively solid knowledge of them. But in fact, literary circles nesting in various educational institutions, from the Cadets Corps to provincial gymnasiums (including, for instance, in Vologda or Riazan), with their own (typically, handwritten) literary journals, were, as a form of the literary everyday, more widespread and more productive than salons.[37] Most writers we deal with in the epoch under consideration emerged from a circle of this sort; for many (for example, Pushkin and Zhukovsky), the friendly bonds established in their student years defined subsequent literary relationships and alliances. While the latter would grow, accruing friends of friends, colleagues, and so on, the main thing about such familiar circles was that they were shaped not according to birth status (except of course for the general belonging to a socioeconomically diverse nobility), but (as such things happen in any society) at the crossroads of manifold personal affiliations—familial, familiar, office, Masonic, or even (particularly when living in the countryside) vicinal.

A circle is, in principle, a non-hierarchical association. It has no need for infrastructure, and may conjoin persons geographically far-flung. Unstructuredness, the absence of hierarchy, and the ability to be there without being there enabled the horizontally unifying "we" to function in a vertically hyper-structured empire.[38] Geographic dispersion often serves to strengthen the sense of belonging together. Being apart is compensated by exchanging letters, which in turn become a pledge of togetherness no matter what. Togetherness may be easier to maintain on paper than in real life. Thus, as Lotman observes, "when, after years of tender correspondence, Karamzin and Dmitriev finally met, talking to one another proved more difficult than writing."[39]

The lyceum alumni made 19 October the day of their ritualized reunion, for which the poets among them (Pushkin, Del'vig, Küchelbecker, Aleksey Illichevsky) wrote verses designed, as a rule, to be sung together. The more broadly their "we" dispersed in space (and over time), the stronger became the need to invigorate the narrative of that "we" whose magic appeared to bind them. What was in 1811 a purely incidental grouping of some thirty-odd adolescents under one roof fused into what Pushkin would refer to as his "holy brotherhood." It is not by chance that the poem that includes this phrase is titled "Parting" ("Razluka"). Parting in space is made a constructive factor in pledging a union in words.

Without delving too much into the notion of friendship as understood and practiced in the early nineteenth century, we should keep in mind that the friendly circle was conceptualized not just as a company of friends but rather something like a spiritual community.[40] Friendship meant mental and spiritual affinity between selected kindred souls, the highest form of sensitivity, and was therefore understood as a virtue. Hence the exceptionally sentimental vocabulary used in correspondences between friends in this milieu. "I love you as I do my soul" surfaces in correspondence between members of Arzamas with the regularity of a refrain. In one Baratynsky letter to Kireevsky, the language of friendship could easily be confused with that of romantic love: "I am glad . . . that you, whose sensitivity is ardent and varied, came to love [*poliubil*] me, and not someone else."[41]

In the Golden Age, the word "friend" sounded almost sacred. Aleksandr Bestuzhev, age ten, sermonized to one of his four little brothers: "Anyone can be a brother; being a friend is different."[42] In one 1805 diary entry, Zhukovsky included the following analysis of his relationships with "K . . ." (apparently, Ivan Kireevsky's father Vasily):

> Friendship results from a peculiar disposition of mind [in common], from a similarity if not in every feeling then at least in the way both feel. I never assured him of my cordial friendship; but I did say to him that I loved him. What I said was true, but only in part. That is, I love him as one can love a straightforward honest man, an honorable man, incapable of meanness, but also incapable of friendship, or at least of making friends with me.[43]

I love him, but he is not my friend: to the modern ear, Zhukovsky's statement sounds like a paradox. In *our* language of feelings, the phrase would make more sense with the assertion and negation reversed. The same could be said of the maxim coined by the ten-year-old homilist Bestuzhev.

In 1826 Petr Viazemsky asked Pushkin to take a critical look at his essay on the life and works of Vladislav Ozerov (a playwright whose talent was a matter of controversy between the two friends). In Viazemsky's portrayal, "the main quality of [Ozerov's] heart was love for his friends; he would often act as his friends' captive, feeling through them, seeing with their eyes; he would get angry at the least indelicacy on their part, but at the same time could not but succumb to the slightest sign of their love"—at which point, Pushkin comments in the margin: "Love for one's friends is called friendship [*druzhba*] in Russian. . . . All this is inconsistent: you speak of his love . . . then of friendship, then again of love, again of his touchiness [*shchekotlivost'*], again of love. Be more methodical and clear."[44]

Pushkin's suggestions are of a conceptual, not merely a lexical, nature. What he objects to here is the cult of sensitivity he had been growing increasingly skeptical about since the early 1820s. At the core of this cult was precisely its refusal to draw a distinction between friendship and platonic love, a belief that, on Russian soil, had its roots in Schiller and the Schillerians on the one hand, and Masonic ideals on the other.[45] According to this mind-set, both love and friendship are manifestations of divine harmony and unity. An assessment of Schiller published in a Russian journal in 1820 put it thus: "He would lovingly open his meek and noble soul to a worthy friend to double his being in the exchange of kindred feelings."[46] This sounds quite similar to the definition of friendship from Zhukovsky's diary. Friendship is more than mere mutual affection: for it to arise, the two must discover a common disposition of minds; kindred feelings must be exchanged, being must be "doubled." It was hardly by chance that Schiller's "Ode to Joy," with its embrace of millions, garnered quite a number of Russian translations, rendered by such luminaries as Karamzin and Tiutchev (and certainly not by chance that, with Beethoven's score attached, Schiller's hymn to human unity is now the official anthem of the European Union).

Skhodnyi (similar) and *srodnyi* (kindred) are the two keywords most likely to surface in contemporary definitions of friendship and familiar circles. The discontent with high society voiced in Karamzin and Baratynsky's judgments cited above rests upon the character of mutual communication. Baratynsky calls high-society talk a "dramatic creation," Karamzin, a "bad comedy," whose choreography—shoot a remark and slip away—he refuses to recognize as human contact (*obshchenie*). What both find satisfying about a conversation among friends is not just its unstarched ease but mainly the preestablished similarity—if not identity, then kinship—between the ways people feel.

Kinship (*rodstvo*) was another password granting entrée to the holy land of friendship. In 1817 the German thinker and statesman Friedrich Ancillon defined the secret of a friendly conversation thus: "The inalienable ability of a true friend is to understand the thoughts of the one you love as if these were words, and to keep their words as secret as if these were thoughts."[47] Zhukovsky was familiar with Ancillon's works before he had a chance to meet the man in person.[48] One entry in Zhukovsky's Berlin diary (1820) states: "Dinner at Princess Alexandrine's. Sat next to Ancillon, with whom I got acquainted. Literature is kinship."[49] Who says there is no kinship at first sight?

Conversations between friends whose kindred feelings double, as in a mirror, their being thus constitute a special kind of communication. Here, language is used indirectly, if at all. Among friends, words serve not to channel verbal information, but to reach beyond the verbally expressible, to communicate soul to soul. Charged with so serious a task, the language of a friendly conversation is expected to live up to poetry—poetry as understood, of course, by believers in sensitivity like Karamzin or Zhukovsky. In their view, the indirect use of language wedded poetry, friendship, and religion. "Every beautiful feeling animates everything in your soul," wrote Zhukovsky, "friendship, poetry; and all this melds into one: God."[50]

Ordinary speech, which Zhukovsky's essay "On Friendship and Friends" labels "cold," is a hindrance (*pomeshatel'stvo*) when it comes to conversations between sensitive hearts. What *does* work instead? One option Zhukovsky explores is the language of silence, enhanced by nonverbal means of communication (a handshake, a glance, a sigh, the squeeze of a hug). Another is to resort to what we might call "extraordinary speech"—the speech genres marked by pragmatic, linguistic, and sonic otherness, like lullaby and prayer. This line of reasoning brings together two alternatives to ordinary speech: the sub-language of silence and super-language of poetry. No wonder that silence, the inexpressible, and other forms of what Sofya Khagi terms "verbal skepticism" became a productive subject in Russian poetry, from Zhukovsky and Tiutchev to Mandel'shtam and Brodsky.[51]

In this frame of reference, human contact within a friendly circle entailed a special, uncommon use of language—of the kind Shklovsky terms "allo-speaking" (*inakogovorenie*). Shklovsky's term could also be used to refer to conversations with oneself—the domain of lyric meditations. Talking to oneself and talking among friends—diametric as these two speech situations may appear, in the context of lyric poetry they often lead to similar results. Auto-communication, as we have seen in "Country Graveyard" and "Insomnia," cannot go far without a *ty*; it always finds (or seeks in vain) its double being. Conversely, your close friend is like your "double-I," talking to whom is like talking to oneself. "How few of us know the sweetness of silence, pensiveness, tranquility; of carefree meditation by oneself in the presence of a dear friend!"[52]

Likewise (and mirror-wise), one can speak (mentally) with friends in their absence. Thus, in its Germany section, young Küchelbecker's epistolary travelogue (inspired by Karamzin's) stages a conversation in absentia, using a network of loose associations.

> The green waters of the river Rhine were murmuring at our feet; the morning was clear, warm and quiet; Batiushkov's beautiful poem on Russian troops crossing the Rhine resonated in my soul. Del'vig had asked me to remember him on the banks of the Rhine; with Del'vig, all [our] friends appeared in my imagination. I remembered our nice evening gatherings at F. N. G[linka's] place, where, in the course of silent and dreamy, deeply felt conversations over Rhine wine, our hearts flew out and fused in a language [*vyrazheniia*] understood only within our circle, in our dear family of friends and confreres.[53]

While Küchelbecker's train of thought uses different tracks, the destination remains his friends at home. The Rhine at his feet becomes the Rhine of Batiushkov's poetry, from the river Rhine to Rhine as wine, and from there to conversations spirited by it. It should not surprise us that Küchelbecker wants friendly conversations over Rhine wine to be "understood only within [their] circle": insider parlance—the galimatias of Arzamas, the sensitivity-language of the turn-of-the-century Schillerians of the Friendly Literary Society, or the bawdy banter customary within the Green Lamp—put a face on a literary circle.

The Rheinwein theme logically segues into a toast—the genre of speech endemic to many "evening gatherings" as well as to many poems addressed from "I" to "us." While not included in the travelogue, Küchelbecker's toast poem ("To Friends, on the Rhine" ["K druz'iam, na Reine"]; published posthumously) proposes a long-distance toast:

Други! я в мечтаньях с вами;
Братия! я вижу вас!
Вам сей кубок, отягченный
Влагой чистой и златой;
Пью за наш союз священный,
Пью за русский край родной![54]

[Friends! I am with you in my dreams; / Brotherhood! I see you! / For you this chalice, heavy / With a clear, golden liquid; / I drink to our sacred union, / I drink to the native Russian land!]

Küchelbecker's poem unfolds in two planes, diegetic and imaginary. Diegetically, its lyric "I" is said to be crossing the Rhine river in a boat, presumably alone. While doing so, this "I" conjures up the image of his narrow "us"—Küchelbecker's friends—a vision followed by "I drink to," the traditional opening of a toast. No friendship will fall apart as long as there remains at least an imaginary table.

Symposia: One Too Many

In the second chapter of this book, we had more than one occasion to encounter a tableful of guests—in the epistle appended to the pie that Viazemsky once sent to Aleksandr Turgenev, in Del'vig's poetic tribute to his eponymous hut, and, prototypically, in Batiushkov's "My Penates." In a series of studies devoted to epistolary symposia of poets, Savely Senderovich has traced this running metaphor from "My Penates" to Zhukovsky, Viazemsky, and on to Vasily and Aleksandr Pushkin. This uniquely tenacious and open poetic dialogue on the nature and ethics of poetry predetermined for decades (if not centuries) the mythology of poethood in Russia. Describing the recurrent feast-image, Senderovich emphasizes its indirect, metaphorical meaning, which echoed Plato's symposium. Thus, Senderovich writes of "My Penates": "All this, of course, takes place in the imagination: Batiushkov's world is an ideal one. All great poets, from Pindar to Batiushkov's elder contemporaries, were invited to the feast."[55]

Senderovich is right to stress the discursive nature of these (and similar) feasts, but to call them purely metaphorical seems somewhat unspecific. The genre of speech (or more broadly, the type of intercommunication) toward which these epistles were oriented was something particular; it obeyed different rules than the sober pragmatics dictated by poetic dialogues. A philosophical dialogue (like Pushkin's between a bookseller and a poet) included taking turns in listening and speaking, agreeing or disagreeing with an interlocutor. But the format of table camaraderie is the unfocused white noise of conversations punctuated by toasts and clinking goblets. A stanza from Pushkin's draft of "19 October 1825" captures well the swift transition from discordant table talk to the consonant toast-in-verse, here sung in chorus: "They will come! Will seat themselves / Before idle silverware, / Will foam their glasses, / Their conversations will meld into discordant [*nestroinyi*] chorus, / And our merry paean will resound."[56]

To varying degrees, latently or manifestly, this speech genre inhabited every friendly epistle of the 1810s (their peak decade). While normally addressed to someone specific, all these verse epistles (and their speech prototype, the toast) were about the "we" in whose name and to whom the speaker speaks—a "we" that, by the very act of being spoken of, is being consolidated.

Вооружись фиалом,
Шампанского напень,
И стукнем в чашу чашей
И выпьем все до дна:
Будь верной Музе нашей
Дань первого вина.[57]

[Arm yourself with a wineglass, / Foam it up with champagne, / And we will clink our chalices / And drain them to the bottom: / Be a tribute to our faithful Muse / You, the first glass of wine.]

Addressed to Batiushkov in response to his "Penates," Zhukovsky's 1812 toast is raised to poetry—the muse that unites them all. When in 1817, Griboedov and Katenin included a parody of it (and, by extension, of the entire literary movement associated with Batiushkov, Zhukovsky, and the like-minded) in their comedy *The Student* (*Student*), the only word they altered in the line given to the naïve young poet Benevolsky was "Muse"—she was replaced by "friendship." Parody works by baring the principle: poetry and friendship, to which the first toast is raised, are synonymous.

Epistolary feasting was a solitary game—of dreaming up presence in absentia, as Küchelbecker did in the middle of the Rhine. The intended effect was the sense of being there. Before publishing their reciprocal epistles in verse, Viazemsky and Vasily Pushkin sent them to Zhukovsky for critical comments. Zhukovsky responded with a detailed stylistic analysis—in verse. One thing he liked about a make-believe feast described by Pushkin was precisely its liveliness:

Воображение мое он так кольнул,
Что я, перед собой уж всех вас видя в сборе,
Разинул рот, чтобы в гремящем вашем хоре
Веселию кричать: ура! и протянул
Уж руку, не найду ль волшебного бокала.[58]

[It so prodded my imagination / That, seeing you all together before me, / I opened my mouth in order to shout hurrah / To merriment, with your resounding chorus; and stretched / My hand in search of the magic goblet.]

What made those magic goblets and silverware feel particularly palpable was the attention to detail in their broader settings. Around the invariable table, we typically find other pieces of furniture. True, the conceptual significance of household descriptions goes back to the foundational text for Russian imaginary symposia—Batiushkov's "My Penates," whose very title deifies domesticity—but we should not forget that the tradition wends its way back to actual, not virtual, verse "Invitations," like Derzhavin's 1795 "Invitation to Dinner" or Denis Davydov's 1804 "A Call to Punch" ("Prizyvanie na punsh") addressed to fellow-hussar Aleksei Burtsov.[59] As discussed in chapter 2, the constant property of a lyric invitation is a figure of modesty. The domestic setting—factual or fictional—for a friendly drink is always homey, even sometimes homely. Derzhavin describes his house as "unadorned" by "engraving, gold, or silver"; Davydov describes his as a soldier's wretched shack, with a sack of oats for a sofa, and a wall-hung saber for a mirror, just to adjust his "beloved moustache."[60]

When it came to describing food and drink, there was less emphasis on moderation and humility. All the gold and glitter Derzhavin spared on interior decoration went into portraying the treats:

Шекснинска стерлядь золотая,
Каймак и борщ уже стоят;
В графинах вина, пунш, блистая
То льдом, то искрами, манят.[61]

[Golden sterlet from Sheksna, / Kaimak and borsch have been served; / Wines are in decanters; punch beckons / Glittering now like ice, now like sparkles.]

All Davydov promises is punch poured into "ugly" (*uzhasnye*) tumblers. Each is said to be full of "heavenly heat" (*nebesnyi zhar*), and all (a total of five) are for Burtsov to drain dry. ("Prove you are a hussar" [*Dokazhi, chto ty gusar*], dares the punchline.)

An abundance of food and excess of drink were not, however, a defining feature of Russian table epistles. Poetic meals (that is, meals *as* meals) varied from opulent to frugal, depending on what ethical doctrine the author was espousing at the moment of composing their contribution to the ongoing exchange of imaginary treats. Each in their own way, Davydov and Zhukovsky adhered to the principle that Batiushkov, writing in 1817, summarized by the term "poetic dietetics" (*piiticheskaia dietika*): "Write as you live and live as you write."[62] Indeed, if the early Davydov drew his poetic material from the meagerness and roughing-it of bivouacs and winter quarters, then Zhukovsky wanted poets to live by the laws of what Senderovich calls "ascetic idealism."[63] In the above-cited opening to his epistolary response to Batiushkov's "My Penates," Zhukovsky does propose to foam his friends' glasses with champagne and drink to their mutual muse; but in the rest of the poem (some 650 lines), the theme of drinking vanishes into the thin air of allegorical and mythological homilies. No trace of food remains, except of the spiritual variety.

In June 1812, Batiushkov, at the time in Petersburg, sent an epistolary reply to Zhukovsky, then residing near his native Mishenskoe, where, in Batiushkov's ironic vision, Zhukovsky's dietetics was less than austere—unlike Batiushkov's own.

И роскошь золотая
. . . .
Тебе подносит вины
И портер выписной,
И сочны апельсины,
И с трюфлями пирог.⁶⁴

[And golden luxury / . . . / Serves you wines / And imported porter, / And juicy oranges, / And a truffle pie.]

That fantasy menus like Batiushkov's foreshadow the sumptuous dinner dishes from chapter 1 of *Eugene Onegin*—replete with truffles, snipes, and pies—is a sign of literary succession, not a mere coincidence in taste.⁶⁵ It was not only the hybrid of poetry and novel that defined *Onegin*'s stylistic amalgam; part of the latter comes from epistles in verse. Oriented toward free-floating table conversations, such epistles could be (or had to be) as unfocused and thematically omnivorous as their real-life prototype. The pragmatics of table talk is that topics change. From allegories of innocence to erotic fantasies, from the lyre to a balalaika, from a parody of elegy to a translation from Schiller, from geese to muses—anything goes, provided nothing goes on for too long. "A novel calls for chatter," as Pushkin, writing in the 1820s, defined the advantage of the genre; *his* verse novel is as chatty as epistolary table talks in verse—a genre that Pushkin, too, helped develop.⁶⁶

And, like table talks, their epistolary simulations had to be stylistically brilliant. This would explain why these were passed around—and not just as finished products, as one might pass on a joke one liked, but also in the process of their making. Insofar as an epistolary poem always featured, aside from the author's name, that of others as well, these works had to go through peer review—more so than any other genre. In sending "My Penates" to Zhukovsky and Viazemsky (whose initials are included both as the epistle's addressees, and within its text), Batiushkov was not asking for opinions—he was calling for amendments and corrections. Addressees were expected to participate in the text; poetic dialogues on the nature of poetry thus used to occur not only among poets and their respective texts, and not only among poets within the given text ("To visit my little house—/ To argue and drink a bit," Batiushkov inveigles), but also between poets *about* this particular text.

This "we" tends to engulf not only the addresser and their addressee(s) but other members of the literary circle as well. Zhukovsky's review in verse (quoted earlier) of Viazemsky's and Vasily Pushkin's reciprocal verse epistles was just one of three texts the former produced apropos the latter two. All three were in verse: one, composed in iambic tetrameter, appeared in the journal *Rossiiskii muzeum* (Russian museum); the second constituted a more detailed critique of both, composed in free iambus; the third, Zhukovsky's free-iambus self-redaction of the first—tetrametric—review. The latter two were sent to Vasily Pushkin and Viazemsky by mail. By way of correcting your peer's poem, you were recruited into its authorship. Potentially, the lyric "I" expands to the size of the lyric "we," in which case we are back to the effect of auto-communication.

Where there is a "we," there is a "they." A number of table poems quoted in chapter 2—Viazemsky's verse attached to Turgenev's pie, his "To My Soulmate," and, prototypically, Batiushkov's "My Penates"—list the kinds of people *not* to be invited to the imaginary feast. In his reply-epistle to Batiushkov, Zhukovsky also blacklists seven allegorical vices; in *his* reply-epistle "To Zhukovsky," Batiushkov complains of Petersburg, where his poetic diet is restricted to poems by Khvostov and Khvostov's literary allies: "They read and read to me, / And, murderers, / They will read me to death [*do smerti menia . . . zachitaiut*]!" By the late 1810s, epistles in verse had become the spearhead genre of literary struggle.

And yet, the practice of apophatic listing does not mean that familiar circles posited themselves as some exclusive clubs. The mutual work on cross-correction and editing each other's epistles took these texts in the opposite direction. In the Karamzinian circle, a poem would not be released to press until, owing to the members' collective efforts, it was clear and transparent to everyone, not only those in the know. This choice—the utmost purity (*chistota*) of style—was seen as an ethical one, something that reflected the impeccability of the poet's household, mind-set, very soul. The artless domesticity, unpretentiousness, and table-side pragmatics of these epistles promoted community-building—not so much among poets themselves as between those who wrote and those who read. As Peschio notes, one of the goals the Karamzinians set themselves "was to expand the boundaries of the domestic sphere by projecting ever-broader sections of the readership as part of the writer's intimate circle. By and large, Karamzinians like Zhukovskii, Batiushkov, Viazemskii, and Pushkin chose [to make] their readers into domestic intimates, in part, by bringing domestic genres and themes into the fold of public literature."[67] As the reader of an epistle of this sort, you found yourself at the table of the verse.

Bards and Warriors

The transparency rule does not always apply to Denis Davydov's hussar-to-hussar epistles in verse addressed to Davydov's comrade-in-arms Burtsov. One needed to have been in light-cavalry skirmishes in order to get a full sense of the line "If we should ever expose / Our left side while flanking [*flankirovka*]." Yet the narrow target also explains why Davydov's verses to Burtsov, written in 1804, continued to be sung at army binges well into the 1830s, long after Burtsov's death. This popularity was owed, of course, to the lapidary quality of Davydov's verse, but not to that only. Pragmatically, Davydov's poetry was oriented toward martial table talk, with, on the one hand, its demarcation between "us" and "them" and, on the other, its welcoming, into the communion of "us," the rest of *pravoslavnye* (literally, the true-believers), hence the daring vision of the Savior in a bowl of booze and the daring metaphor of baptism applied to a routine garrison carousal:

В дымном поле, на биваке
У пылающих огней,
В благодетельном араке
Зрю спасителя людей.
Собирайся вкруговую,
Православный весь причёт!
Подавай лохань златую,
Где веселие живёт![68]

[At a bivouac, in a smoky field / By blazing bonfires, / In beneficent arak / I see the savior of people. / Gather round, / You, the whole Orthodox parish! / Bring on the golden tub, / In which merriment lives.]

This was how Davydov's epistles entered literature—not through the front door of literary journals but over a tankard of bivouac lore. As Vatsuro perceptively observes, Davydov's epistles to Burtsov gained fame retrospectively, after Davydov became famous as a war hero.[69] The war of 1812–15, with its standing demand for hymns, oratories, and songs for the unending series of feasts and festivities accompanying its course, from the liberation of Moscow through the whole foreign campaign to the taking of Paris, turned out to be a pivotal event in the history of Russian poetry.[70] Alongside Denis Davydov, Vasily Zhukovsky woke up famous—after his "Bard in the Camp of Russian

Warriors" came out. It was "Bard" that brought Zhukovsky nationwide acclaim and also (after victory was announced) a pension from the court—not a monarch's finger ring but an unheard-of act of recognition on the part of the state, a breakthrough in poetry's social status. The 4,000 rubles per year, as the emperor's cover letter specified, were to provide Staff Captain Zhukovsky "the financial independence needed for his occupation."[71]

The commentary included in the latest collection of Zhukovsky's works stresses the generic instability of "Bard," whose tone oscillates "from that of cantatas and laudatory odes to notes characteristic of long poems, ballads, and elegies."[72] Echoes of all these poetic genres do, indeed, resound across the seven hundred lines of "Bard," but its dominant orientation is clearly toward drinking song (or, to be more precise, the German genre of *Tafellied*; in Russian, *zastol'naia pesnia*). Pushkin identified the latter as a "paean"—the generic tag he used for his own table addresses timed to the lyceum anniversaries.[73]

Structurally, "Bard" consists of a series of toasts of varying length, each proposed by the bard; the toasts are punctuated by a refrain, which the present warriors sing in chorus. In most cases (though not invariably), the four lines of a refrain echo the four final lines of the toast, resulting in a dialogue whose "I" is thus echoed and multiplied in "we." The pragmatics of camaraderie is laid bare: the word "we" and its derivatives (especially "our") occurs, on average, roughly once every ten lines. War splits the world into "us" and "them"; the more patriotic the subject matter, the stronger the drive to speak in chorus.

Odes on victorious events are typically ascending in their address: Pindar hymning the winner of an Olympic race, or a bard praising a Suvorov, usually address a hero higher up. Zhukovsky's "Bard" is not a case in point. Here, the address is as horizontal as only a flat tabletop can be. The poem was not composed in the flush of victory—quite the opposite, it was written (and is set) after Moscow was abandoned to Napoleon, when the outcome of the war was far from certain. "Bard" does not celebrate a victory; the bard calls his brethren into battle. But in doing so, Zhukovsky expands the thematic range beyond the bounds of the current war. The first toast is to the warlords of ancient times, beginning with Sviatoslav; then, the entire army leadership, including the emperor, is toasted; vengeance, friendship, love, poetry, and God follow suit; finally, one for the road, wherever it leads each of us:

Друзья, прощанью кубок сей!
И смело в бой кровавый

Под вихорь стрел, на ряд мечей,
За смертью иль за славой...[74]

[Friends, this cup is to farewell! / Go bravely into the bloody battle / Under the whirlwind of arrows, up against the line of swords, / For death or for glory...]

What concerns us here is the continuity and change between two kinds of "us": the martial and the poetic. Significantly, the wave of reciprocal epistles triggered by Batiushkov's "My Penates" (1811–12; answered by Zhukovsky in spring 1812) and the appearance of "Bard" (autumn 1812) overlapped in time and, in important ways, in terms of pragmatic impact. In a number of respects, the great wartime "we" and the narrow "we" of a familiar circle of poets were isomorphic; sacrosanct values like friendship, love, or poetry took root in both. On the other hand, the "we" of "Bard" and "Bard"-like round-the-table songs formed not so much a circle as a rippling-out effect. The inner "we" shared by the bard and his echoing chorus ripples out to encompass everyone under arms, with the cult of friendship scaled accordingly:

Святому братству сей фиал
От верных братий круга!
. . . .
О! будь же, други, святость уз
Закон наш под шатрами;
Написан кровью наш союз:
И жить и пасть друзьями.[75]

[This goblet is to our holy brotherhood / From the faithful brethren of the circle! / . . . / Oh! Friends, let the sanctity of bonds / Be our law in these tents; / Our union is signed with blood: / To live and fall as friends.]

Toasting the muses, Zhukovsky's bard extols them for filling warriors' hearts with ardor for glory (*slavy zhar*) and thirst for battle (*zhazhda boia*)—lauds them, that is, for something that also constitutes the function of the very poem we are reading, and of the very toasts its lyric speaker raises. Yet, alongside weaponizing the lyre, Zhukovsky smuggles into the toast to poetry in wartime the time-honored motif of "the death of a poet," except that, naturally, unlike that wistful poet from the 1802 "Country Graveyard" who dies from yearning, the bard of 1812 imagines himself struck by an arrow, to which the solidary chorus of warriors responds:

Хвала возвышенным певцам!
Их песни—жизнь победам;
И внуки, внемля их струнам,
В слезах дивятся дедам.[76]

[Praised be the lofty bards! / Their songs give life to victories; / Our grandchildren, heeding their chords, / Marvel in tears at their granddads.]

In this refrain, the common "we" of bards and warriors ripples over a generational divide to harbor hypothetical, as-yet-unborn keepers of the flame. An indirect yet traceable path winds from here to a Baratynsky poem of 1828, whose threefold "us-ness" would include the poet, their contemporary friend, and their future descendant.

The Pragmatics of Proxemics

The meaning of "we" is entirely contextual. In political talk, "we" can stand for one person ("We . . . Emperor and Autocrat of all the Russias") or encompass a population ("We, the people"). In everyday usage (the same goes for political discourses), we know the precise or approximate value of a "we." The language of poetry releases us from this knowledge—poems can afford to not be context-bound. The "we" of Zhukovsky's "Bard" refers at the same time to the reveling cohort at the table, the warring army of which they are a part, and, as easily, all Russia, past, present, and future. A poem addressed to a group of "us" also includes the less visible but no less influential "us" who are reading it.

In early 1815, Batiushkov sent to Bludov a bound copy of a handwritten collection of his poems, the fact of which Batiushkov would invariably remind his friends in letters to them. The notebook opens with the dedicatory poem "To Friends" ("K druz'iam"), which specifies the chirographic nature of this edition, and the makeup of its potential readership: "Here is a fair copy of my poems / Which may be precious to my friends."[77] Two years later, Batiushkov used the same poem to open the poetry section of his book *Essays in Poetry and Prose* (*Opyty v stikhakh i proze*)—a typographic venture with the considerable run of 1,200 copies. Apparently, in Batiushkov's view, the new bottle did not spoil the old wine. What earlier had served as an epistolary dedication to a finite handful of specific friends functioned just as well as a poetic address to countless nameless readers. Unlike in social situations, in a poetic context people you did not know counted as your friends. Intimacy as a literary category projects onto a readership of any size. For Batiushkov, size only mattered when it came to the dimensions of the folio: "No large formats, God forbid!" he wrote Gnedich in 1816 when the edition was still in the planning stage. "It must look like a *lady's* book, on the smaller and thicker side."[78] Even if printed in sizeable numbers, a book to "friends" ought to be of an intimate size. Perhaps counterintuitively, the reading public was expected to perceive a book of poetry addressed to a small circle of friends as something inclusive and inviting. It enabled them to talk to the poet as a friend—much as Batiushkov, as mentioned in chapter 2, felt he could "converse" with Jean François de Saint-Lambert by opening one of his books.

Proxemics as part of literary pragmatics—unlike spatial-cultural proxemics as analyzed, for instance, by Edward Hall[79]—is a dynamic rather than taxonomic category. Inclusion in or exclusion from a poet's inner circle (or world) is not measured by social or spatial proximity, or by one's being in the know. This makes it hard to agree with the theory that attributes to Pushkin, Baratynsky, or Del'vig the intent to "segregate" their readership into those few who were equipped, and the rest who were not, to read the veiled references and in-jokes planted in their literary works.[80] Indeed, only those in the know would easily guess the identity of the "D." of Pushkin's simile "like drunken D[el'vig] at a feast." This, however, does not imply that those who knew the ways of their inebriated friend were thought of as Pushkin's privileged readers—in contrast to the informationally challenged majority. Rather, the opposite is true. The pragmatics—indeed, dialectics—of leaking and withholding worked to implicate and initiate the uninitiated. No wonder there were readers and critics that routinely accused Pushkin and his friends of impertinence; too *much* information was dumped onto the reader.

In other words, what mattered was not so much the withholding of Del'vig's name (a code, arguably, not hard to crack for those who followed Golden Age literary debates), but the apparently uncalled-for details of a poet's freewheeling behavior within the circle. To share such details was tantamount to flouting the rules of propriety, or, in more modern terms, violating the boundaries of the reader's space. Worse, by letting us readers into their reveries and revelries, critics suspected, the "union of poets" (a phrase from Küchelbecker's 1820 poem dedicated to Del'vig, Baratynsky, and Pushkin) was spoiling their readers. *Vestnik Evropy* pounced on Pushkin and Baratynsky: "[Their] easy and tripping philosophy squares with every pleasure of life, every disposition or fancy we may have, depending on the influence of the weather on readers' mores," adducing italicized quotations and near-quotations as exhibits of the baleful hedonism their poetry supposedly inculcated. "At times it says: *rejoice! Rejoice! The present is yours!* At times it remembers *the past [byloe]* and longs for the *forgotten sound of cups*, until the moment the bard hears the current sound of goblets—and it is this philosophy that makes the *breezy sage* sing a *prayer to joy*."[81] The "prayer to joy" comes from an early version of Baratynsky's long poem "Feasts" ("Piry"), as does the "breezy sage" (*vetrenyi mudrets*), Baratynsky's reference to Pushkin. Reminiscent or not of Schiller's ode, Pushkin's prayer to joy is doubtless a paraphrase for a drinking song.

We have grounds to suspect that unwarranted familiarity with the reader was a pragmatic strategy on the part of Pushkin and his ilk. I have my doubts regarding "segregation of audiences" as the most fitting characterization of this strategy, but Igor' Pil'shchikov's other statement is undoubtedly true: "It was as important for Baratynsky [as it was for Pushkin in *Eugene Onegin*] to mark the presence of friends in a poetic-communicative situation."[82] It was this textual copresence of extra-textual friends that rendered Pushkin and Baratynsky's poetries uniquely bifocal. What Tynianov calls the "live address" of a lyric text lived both inside and outside this text, turning a verse novel like *Eugene Onegin* into a literary semblance of a Moebius strip—into a work in which pragmatics and semantics are as hard to tell apart as the paper's outer surface is from its inner. The text exists at the cross-point of two (or more) perspectives. On the one hand, it is addressed to a friend at hand and is, quite often, about "us," a group of friends at hand; on the other, it targets a larger, unknown, distant community of people that, against all odds, Pushkin or Baratynsky insist on treating as friends, the friends out there. The pragmatics of poetry like theirs pivots on a refusal to distinguish between the polarities of distance and proximity. A poem is never exclusively for either the inner or the outer "us"; its power derives from inclusion, short-circuiting the distinction.

Baratynsky's famous self-reflective poem from 1828 offers this credo of poetry's proxemics:

Мой дар убог и голос мой не громок,
Но я живу, и на земли мое
Кому-нибудь любезно бытие:
Его найдет далекий мой потомок

В моих стихах: как знать? душа моя
Окажется с душой его в сношеньи,
И как нашел я друга в поколеньи,
Читателя найду в потомстве я.[83]

[My gift is meager and my voice not loud, / but I'm alive, and my existence is / beloved to somebody on the earth: / my descendant will find it years from now / in my poems. Who knows? His soul and mine / may prove to be in intimate relation, / and as I found a friend in my generation, / a reader in posterity I'll find.[84]]

The act of self-abasement the poem opens with is both functional and formulaic. As a formula, it echoes Batiushkov's defiantly modest self-definition as a "minor talent," poetry's "little bee" (*pchelka*; only, in Baratynsky, a similar exercise in humility is clad in dignified iambic pentameter). Functionally, by deprecating his poetic self (and voice), Baratynsky was bringing to the fore the figure of his pragmatic other. Or, rather, others: a nearby "friend in my generation" and a far-flung "reader in posterity." The relationship between the two is through verse, soul to soul, bypassing discursive language: precisely the Golden Age idea of poetry and friendship. For soul to soul, distance is no matter.

The secret of the sudden—frighteningly so—intimacy between me, the reader, and him, the author of Baratynsky's poem, is in its uncanonical use of personal pronouns. The author/speaker's self-identification as "I" is unsurprising; such was, and still remains, the reigning convention of lyric verse. But we as readers are more used to being addressed as *you*, which is not the case in Baratynsky's little poem. Baratynsky does not, in fact, address anyone: his present friend and future reader are referred to in the third-person singular. Rather than *addressing* a presumed reader or friend, as a lyric poem like this typically would, Baratynsky's poem *seeks* a reader. I, someone who is reading the poem in real time, only realize in the last line that the reader the author is looking for is me.

Baratynsky's "My gift is meager . . . ," with its unusual pronominal configuration and its bold and somewhat enigmatic equation between an unnamed coeval friend and a tentative (*kak znat'*, "who knows?") reader in posterity, attracted attention among contemporaries and, yes, descendants. In the wake of Baratynsky's death, Ivan Kireevsky, most likely the "friend" mentioned in the penultimate line, interpreted Baratynsky's terse verse in this rather wordy piece of prose:

> Born to spend his life in a sincere circle of family and friends, unusually sensitive to people compassionate to him, Baratynsky spoke willingly and profoundly in quiet, friendly conversations, thus silencing in him the urge to speak before the public. Once a thought that preoccupied his soul was vented in friendly conversation—conversation lively and varied, endlessly captivating, warm and tasteful, witty when appropriate, farsighted and subtle, original and enlivened by inner poetry—Baratynsky was often content with the vivid response on the part of his close circle, and cared less about possible distant readers.[85]

By "distant readers" Kireevsky means, of course, the broader public, not the future readers evoked in Baratynsky's "My gift is meager . . ."; still, Kireevsky's theory of who was and who was not the prime target of Baratynsky's verbal art is of interest for Baratynsky scholarship, precisely because Kireevsky mentions the variable missing in this poem's pragmatic equation. In Baratynsky, that is, we find a friend of today and a reader in the future—but what about the distant readers of today?

A poem is not a checklist, to be sure; still, there may have been a reason both for this omission and Kireevsky's observation regarding Baratynsky's non-engagement with the reading public. Baratynsky's first collection of poems, eagerly awaited and in the works as early as 1823, came out only in late 1827, and was lukewarmly received by critics—which was particularly painful when these critics turned out to be young literati with whom Baratynsky had grown close since his relocation to Moscow.

Unkind criticism has always been a fact of life, particularly in times of literary struggle. How to react in the face of possible derision—this topic formed a separate rubric in the familiar epistles of the mid-1810s. In his attitude to criticism, Baratynsky largely followed the guidelines Zhukovsky had laid out in an earlier epistle to Viazemsky and Vasily Pushkin. Rule number one was stoic scorn: "Let us abandon to contempt / The crown given *to all* by society; / A different glory is our object, / The bard hopes for a different reward." Secondly, "Let us transfer / Our hopes to the world of posterity." And lastly, do not forget that we don't sing for the critics; "We sing for the muses, for joy, / For the faithful heart of our friends."[86]

To follow this philosophy, Baratynsky was left with two groups of addressees out of three: his friends, with whom he shared the past; and the descendants with whom he planned on sharing the future. The unmentioned group—Baratynsky's contemporary readers—were too distant and not distant enough;

too far in space to talk soul to soul with, as one does with close friends, and too close in time to pick up the signal as future readers would—or so the poet hoped. To avoid mentioning this third group in a poem about a poet and his readers was tantamount, to borrow Zhukovsky's wording, to abandoning them to contempt.

Baratynsky was right about the future. In 1913 Osip Mandel'shtam picked up the signal ("What reader of Baratynsky's poem would not shiver with joy or feel that twinge of excitement experienced sometimes when you are unexpectedly hailed by name"[87]) and wrote a brief essay on what I call here literary proxemics: the tacit balance of intimacy and distance a poem allows between the lyric "I" and its addressee, an agency Mandel'shtam aptly calls the poet's "interlocutor" (*sobesednik*).[88] Konstantin Bal'mont disinvites interlocutors from the world of his poems; his *ty*s are too outright and harsh to "find an addressee," as Mandel'shtam puts it.[89] "What a contrast . . . to the deep and modest dignity of Baratynsky's poem."

> Baratynsky's piercing eye darts beyond his generation (yet in his generation he has friends) only to pause in front of an as yet unknown, but definite "reader." And anyone who happens across Baratynsky's poems feels himself to be that "reader," the chosen one, the one who is hailed by name . . . Why then should there not be a concrete, living addressee, a "representative of the age," why not a "friend in this generation"? I answer: appealing to a concrete addressee dismembers poetry, plucks its wings, deprives it of air, of the freedom of flight. The fresh air of poetry is the element of surprise. In addressing someone known, we can speak only of what is already known.[90]

This is how Mandel'shtam, writing in 1913, reads Baratynsky's logic of 1828. To find a friend in your own generation, no poetry is needed. Being among friends is self-sufficient. It takes a poem to talk across time. The Batiushkov of 1815 and Karamzin of 1792 (to stage a debate across epochs) would disagree; poetry, both claimed, was primarily for friends, "for those who loved you," and only by extension for the rest. To venture another guess, the Mandel'shtam of later, less optimistic years than 1913 would probably agree with Batiushkov; as an acquaintance of Mandel'shtam recalls, the poet claimed to have wished he had written Batiushkov's "To a Friend" ("K drugu").[91]

Nadezhda Mandel'shtam, speaking of how important for Mandel'shtam was the "we" of the circle of his poet-friends, adduced this truly remarkable piece of reasoning: "I am quite convinced that without such a 'we,' there can be no proper fulfillment of even the most ordinary 'I,' that is, of the personality. To find its fulfillment, the 'I' needs at least two complementary dimensions: 'we' and—if it is fortunate—'you.'"[92] Devised to account for Mandelstam's poetic personality, the pronominal triad "I-us-you" appears instrumental for our understanding of poetry's pragmatics on a larger scale. Chapter 4 of this book has focused on "me and us"; chapter 5 will discuss "you" and "me."

5

You and I

Love Elegy and How to Use It

IN 1960, AT THE First International Conference of Poetics in Warsaw, Roman Jakobson presented a paper titled "Poetry of Grammar and Grammar of Poetry," whose principal thesis sounded almost iconoclastic; if we reduce poetics to essentials, the paper claims, we will see that poetry is not speech dressed up in periphrastic images and tropes but a naked geometry of grammar.[1] One of the examples Jakobson gives to illustrate his point is Pushkin's "imageless poem" "I loved you" ("Ia vas liubil"). In 1970, in his book *Bowstring* (*Tetiva*), Viktor Shklovsky questioned Jakobson's theory—both the entire idea of grammar being central to poetics and the specific use of "I loved you" to support this argument. Both as a theorist and as someone who had once, in his capacity as prose writer, published a collection of love letters titled *Zoo* and subtitled *Letters Not about Love* (*Zoo, ili Pis'ma ne o liubvi*, 1923), Shklovsky held that doublespeak was endemic to love lyric—which was precisely why he disagreed with Jakobson's disregard for tropes: "When in love, we are frequently compelled to speak of love indirectly. Love lyric—all of it—is, if not a trope, then allo-speaking [*inakogovorenie*]."[2] Importantly for this chapter, Shklovsky's objection leans upon poetry's pragmatics. Love poetry is a form of speech peculiar to love. When in love, we often resort to equivocations, and equivocation, insists Shklovsky, is what love lyric is all about.

This definition of love poetry could use a historical footnote. Shklovsky's "we" here is that of the twentieth century. In the first third of the nineteenth century, speaking of love directly was not just "frequently" out of place—it was downright forbidden, except among the officially engaged or married. If still among the "eligible," your rights were circumscribed; you could mention love as if just wondering out loud, sing about it, underline love-related wording in a book—do pretty much anything but talk about *your* love directly. An actual love message needed to be depersonalized, estranged. However genuine, your love had to be enacted, not stated. Or stated, but in a love poem—love talk in love poetry was as inoffensive as nudity in a park statue.

In this sense, Shklovsky is right: love poetry *was* a form of allo-speaking. Whether bursting with tropes, or as trope-deficient as Pushkin's "I loved you" or Baratynsky's "Dissuasion," a love elegy afforded the chance to talk of your love without talking of *your* love, or of love at all. As Shklovsky wrote in his 1923 preface to his book of "love letters not about love," when in love, anything goes: "All the descriptions [of Russian Berlin] thus came out as metaphors for love."[3]

Amorous Scripts

"When, in the language of love, / Shall *no* be *no*, and *yes* be *yes* / . . . ? / When? When?" asks Viazemsky among a number of other "when, when?" questions in an 1815 poem that longs for a more truthful world.[4] Indeed, love talk—a whole large class of speech events—proceeded, if not literally by contraries, then on the principle of mandatory disparity between the saying and the said. The "language of love" was more game than language. It is hardly by chance that a trivial parlor game or a domestic theater production, rather than a face-to-face conversation, served as the vehicle and medium of love. As Aleksei Galakhov recalls, a Christmastide parlor game called *fanty* was popular among Moscow students in the 1820s precisely because of the romantic capability built into it:

> We loved to play it: it gave those young people who were mutually inclined a legitimate license to go beyond what was allowed in common communication. When drawing your *fant* [role to play] . . . the particularly exciting part to draw was that of a confessor, particularly for a young lady; in this case she would be seated in an armchair, her head covered with a shawl. The confessant, a young man, would kneel before her, putting his head under the shawl. Confessing his sins made it easy for him to confess his love.[5]

Home theatricals offered as many romantic opportunities as parlor games, particularly for someone cast as leading man. Thus, a character in *The Kholmsky Family* had this advice to offer a friend in love: "If only you could . . . convince her to take a part in some comedy, and play along, this would be the best way of opening your heart. At rehearsal you would be free to talk, with no one noticing; playing a fervent lover, you should be able to set her heart on fire."[6] A play, like the *fanty* game, served as a tool of self-estrangement; once on stage or under a shawl, you become, in a sense, your own surrogate who speaks your heart.

While lyric poetry readily lent itself to amatory stratagems like this, we ought to be wary of reducing its pragmatics to disguising or laundering immodest advances. Poetry—and this includes love lyric—always aims at *dual* felicity, not solely at being felicitous as (in this case) a back channel for love messages. In a poem from 1828 addressed (but not sent) to Anna Olenina, Pushkin is remarkably clear on why poetry makes a better love-medium than postal prose:

Тебя страшит любви признанье,
Письмо любви ты разорвешь,
Но стихотворное посланье
С улыбкой нежною прочтешь.[7]

[A confession of love scares you, / You will tear up a love letter, / But will read with a gentle smile / An epistle in verse.]

For a society maiden like Olenina, tearing up a love letter was a prescribed act of behavior, a gesture as codified as the phrase "how dare you!" that it stood for. Failing to meet such a letter with a resounding rebuff could be read as a sign of improper complicity with the sender. Conversely, no young lady would tear up a poem, especially not a poem by Pushkin, and especially not one addressed to her. Pushkin's poem just cited, then, is not only about a love poem's felicity as a messenger of love but also its felicity as a poem. That Pushkin imagines Olenina's "gentle smile" as she reads his love poem is both (he hopes) because she accepts his love and because (he knows) she finds poems fun, while, as he also knows, she is easily bored by "languid" (*neradivaia*) prose. Poetry is licensed to say things prose is not. It is this differential treatment of poetry and prose that decades later would be parodied in Dostoevsky's novel *Demons* (*Besy*)—when the pathetic and comic rhymester Captain Lebiadkin appends this note to his latest verse opus addressed to a young lady: "Consider it as verse and no more, for verse is nonsense after all and justifies what is considered boldness in prose."[8]

Poetry's role and license in matters of love was frequently treated as licentiousness and a menace to chastity. As the writer Nadezhda Sokhanskaya complained in a letter to Petr Pletnev, at the institute she had attended as a young lady, "poetry... was considered a crime, a depravity.... There was not even a single Krylov [fable] in the entire institute."⁹ The same Galakhov who told us of the romantic potential of the *fanty* game speaks with irony of the amatory practices of the 1820s, and of the part played therein by poetry:

> The time we wasted on philandering of a distinctly sentimental-romantic character! An educated young man at that time was, we must not forget, under the double influence of Karamzin and Zhukovsky. The latter's works affected us more strongly; having familiarized ourselves with them, we acquired a taste for ideal love in its entire sequence: exposition, peripeteias, and catastrophe.... Mutual feelings had to be platonic.... There were different [invisible] means to express love: glances (mostly doleful), sighs, silences—etc., etc.—everything prescribed by Zhukovsky's ballads. Love acquired its visible and vocal expression in album poems; hence, albums became the most interesting of all gifts that a young lady could be given—complete with golden edges, of course, and with poems of all kinds: elegies, songs, sonnets, and acrostics.¹⁰

Sighs, silences, and furtive sightings—to believe Galakhov, a young man in love would rather delegate anything verbal to poetry's domestic graphosphere, not counting, of course, a parlor game on holidays. This graphosphere, with its gold-rimmed pages, had its own rules of allo-speaking. Galakhov alludes to the warm, high-minded Zhukovskian sensibilities that provided guidelines for amatory behavior, but another contemporary source (albeit one hardly less subjective than Galakhov's memoir sounds) points in a different direction. In 1823 Aleksandr Bestuzhev, then twenty-six, published a rather short *Novel in Seven Letters* (*Roman v semi pis'makh*), judging by which this epoch's album culture—or more specifically, its practice of album-based flirting—was rooted in eighteenth-century habits of gallantry, and inherited the cool (at times, chilling) air characteristic of them. In love with young Adele, Bestuzhev's main character (a young man like him) is confronted with the problem of her album. "What shall I inscribe in her album? What can I write?" he complains to his friend, the poet and hussar George, whose help he counts on. "An unkind spirit must have whispered in her ear [that is, prompting her to ask that he make an inscription in her album]. When I asked her 'In what language,' she answered: 'In the language of truth.' The language of truth! I could have spoken it as easily as she asked, but is society tolerant of truth, and do I dare to say, 'Adele, I love you?'"[11] Denied the possibility of directly saying what he wants, Bestuzhev's hero weighs (and discards) two other options. One is to inscribe a readymade love madrigal, no matter whose. "But I detest peacocking with others people's feelings [*pavlinit'sia chuzhimi chuvstvami*]."[12] Another is to *compose* something nice and gallant, but "I hate all these airy compliments kneaded in rose oil, all these transitory traces of human worthlessness."[13] In addition, the language question, which Adele evaded slyly, remains unresolved: "I was not schooled to speak finely in Russian, and I am too proud to be expressing myself in an alien tongue; moreover, Adele loves our homeland too much to approve of this."[14] The plea for George's advice ends on this desperate summary of the lover's dilemma: "I cannot write afresh, I don't want to scribble rubbish, and I am not allowed to tell the truth!!"[15]

The identity crisis into which Adele's routine request plunges Bestuzhev's epistolary hero lays bare the complexity of having to talk about love only periphrastically: the mass of cultural conventions you had to know, the skills you had to cultivate. One requirement was, indeed, command of Russian, the ability to feel the emotional temperature of its terms of endearment and diminutives, and be on top of Russian pronominal proxemics—for instance, the precise distance between the polite *vy* and the intimate *ty* accepted between close friends and spouses. When Anna Olenina once misspoke (one hopes, intentionally) and said *ty* to Pushkin, he devoted a whole love poem to her slip, "Thou and You" ("Ty i vy")—a brief course in the linguistics of courtesy and love:

Пустое *вы* сердечным *ты*
Она обмолвясь заменила,
И все счастливые мечты
В душе влюбленной возбудила.
Пред ней задумчиво стою,
Свести очей с нее нет силы;
И говорю ей: как *вы* милы!
И мыслю: как *тебя* люблю![16]

[The empty *you* by the warm *thou* / She by a slip of the tongue replaced / And all happy daydreams / Stirred up in the soul in love. / Before her pensively I stand, / To take my eyes off her I have not the strength; / And I tell her: how lovely *you* are! / And think: how I love *thee*![17]]

Secondly, for love to survive in the polite environment of the Golden Age, it had to rely upon the conventional. Incapable of coming up with his own "fiery idiom" (*ognennoe narechie*) of love, Bestuzhev's young man is also unwilling to entrust it to a madrigal. A feeling like love was *shaped* by literature, not just *expressed* through it. Like no other speech genre in the epoch, the language of love and courtship depended on literary fashions—as did the concomitant emotions. "I have a great occasion to write a madrigal for you," wrote Pushkin (in French) in an innocuously flirtatious letter to Vera Viazemskaya in 1826; "but both [gallant] madrigals and ["sincere"] feelings have become equally ridiculous."[18]

In the early nineteenth century, the range of amatory behaviors included—aside from the coquetry affiliated with the genre of madrigal ("I am always glad to prefer coquetry to love," as Viazemsky says in a madrigal inscribed on Anna Olenina's fan in 1828), calculated libertinage, platonic sensitivity, "forbidden passion," and the like. One could choose one of these—or two, as did the sensitive Andrei Turgenev when involved in two parallel affairs of the heart: one, platonic, cerebral, and bookish, with Katerina Sokovnina; the other, more carnal, with a married woman in Vienna nicknamed in Turgenev's diary "the Tyrolean woman" (*Tirol'sha*). As V. M. Istrin observes, Turgenev preferred to keep his affairs in two separate mailboxes, as it were; Zhukovsky was privy to Turgenev's soulful torments as concerned Sokovnina, but was never updated on the Tyrolean woman; Petr Kaisarov, on the contrary, was kept apprised of Turgenev's fleshly Vienna adventure but not his spiritual Moscow one.[19] What Turgenev enacts are two amatory scripts, one à la Pierre Choderlos de Laclos, the other after Schiller and Goethe, reporting the unfolding of each to a postal correspondent sympathetic to this particular type of plot.[20]

Other than serving as love strategy guides, literary models furnished ready-made lines and phrases, which, endowed with one's uncommon voice and feeling, could be enacted in amatory situations, particularly since so many love-related plots, in novels Western and Russian alike (including Bestuzhev's *Novel in Seven Letters*), took the form of epistolary dialogues. As Robert Darnton's analysis of readerly reception of *La Nouvelle Héloïse* has shown, fictional correspondence (more readily than fictional narration) lent itself to readers' comparison with their own emotional life, and with experiences they may have had with the emotions of other—living, nonfictional—people.[21] One may even take a further step and say that some of these readers helped themselves to some of these letters with some very simple aims in mind. As we learn from Ivan Dolgorukov's autobiography, one of his victories in love as a young man was owed to his good memory of epistolary prose. "Having caught her alone for a brief moment, I poured out the best confessions of love that I could remember from *Héloïse* and other novels, and opened my heart to her."[22] If Louis Sullivan's artistic program "form follows function" applies to literary works, it does so first and foremost to literary letters. Or, to look at it from a pragmatic—for instance, Dolgorukov's—point of view, function follows form.

Sofia and Vul′f, or How to Use Novels and Elegies in Courtship

Despite all dissimilarities in literary form, a love elegy in verse and a letter from an epistolary novel had one pragmatic trait in common: both are addressed from "I" to "you," which makes them easy to steal and use in a romantic situation. To apply a term from Roland Barthes, in cases like these we are dealing not with love stories but with available "fragments of a lover's discourse."[23] And, as is evident from Barthes's fragmentary treatise, the pragmatics of a lover's discourse is not confined to confessions of love—the discursive problem wrestled with by the flesh-and-blood Dolgorukov and the fictional hero of Bestuzhev's *Novel in Seven Letters* alike. The catalog of love elegies available to a Russian Golden Age lover included the elegy of jealousy, that of swelling passion begging to be shared, of longing in separation, of gratitude for mutual happiness, and more. On the darker side of love, there were elegies of infidelity rebuked, and of breach, of never again, or those advising the once-loved to find another lover. As we will see shortly, one and the same elegy, doctored or intact, could cater to various, often quite dissimilar amatory situations.

Fragments, by their name and nature, are but debris of a former whole—which makes them prone to being reassembled. Elegy was not necessarily perceived as a stand-alone, self-sufficient genre, nor as a genre standing on the same footing with tragedy or novel; rather, like debris, elegies gravitated to and orbited round their larger literary neighbors. In France, it was habitual to liken Racine's monologues to elegies (was this also why domestic stages were seen as a safe haven for aspiring lovers?);[24] the Vicomte de Valmont, the libertine hero of Pierre Choderlos de Laclos's epistolary novel *Dangerous Liaisons* (and libertine-in-chief for its many Russian emulators) uses "elegy" as a term to characterize a confession in postal prose sent to his beloved.[25] Or a series of elegies presented as fragments of a lover's discourse would be so sequenced as to coalesce into a complete love story with a beginning, middle, and end—as occurs in collections of elegies by Évariste de Parny greatly admired by Russian poets and readers. Or else, put in the mouth of one character (or more), a quintessential elegy sneaks into a verse narrative—a trick Pushkin used, as Oleg Proskurin shows, quite often, particularly in the "southern" poems.[26]

In other words, an elegy was two things at once: an emotional address in which "I" and "you" were spaces for a user to fill in, like blanks in letter-writing manuals; and a line from a preexisting dramatic dialogue, in which the speaker represented a specific, recognizable type of amatory behavior, whether of a young idealist like Werther or a hard-headed libertine like Valmont, to speak of males alone. Nor were elegy's identities mutually exclusive. The blanks for "I" and "you" were both blanks and masks. Even filled in with specific names and faces, an elegy in use remained a game, a complex product of cultural coding and role-playing.[27]

For a more detailed picture of this dynamic, we might turn to a personal diary that chronicles an actual love affair that took place in Petersburg in 1828. One of its two participants was Sofia Del'vig, wife of the prominent poet, and close friend of Aleksandr Pushkin and Evgeny Baratynsky, Anton Del'vig. The other was Pushkin's countryside neighbor and casual acquaintance Aleksei Vul'f, from whose diary we learn how his affair with Sofia unfolded and, most importantly, about the role in it of Baratynsky's love elegy "Dissuasion" (1821)—in part thanks to Glinka's music, one of the most popular Russian poems of the whole nineteenth century.

Не искушай меня без нужды
Возвратом нежности твоей:
Разочарованному чужды
Все обольщенья прежних дней!
Уж я не верю увереньям,
Уж я не верую в любовь
И не могу предаться вновь
Раз изменившим сновиденьям!
Слепой тоски моей не множь,
Не заводи о прежнем слова
И, друг заботливый, больного
В его дремоте не тревожь!
Я сплю, мне сладко усыпленье;

Забудь бывалые мечты:
В душе моей одно волненье,
А не любовь пробудишь ты.²⁸

[Don't try to tempt me by restoring / your tenderness—there is no point: / all the enticements of the past are / strange to the disenchanted man. / No more do I trust assurances, / no more do I believe in love, / nor am I able to succumb / to dreams that once were traitorous. / My pain is blind—do not augment it, / say not a word about the past, / and, solicitous friend, do not / disturb the sick man when he's dozing. / I sleep—and I find slumber pleasant; / forget the dreams that are no more, / for in my soul you will awaken / mere agitation, but not love.²⁹]

What will interest us in this story is the role Baratynsky's elegy played in Sofia's love game with or at times *against* her suitor; which lyric and, more generally, literary templates shaped and steered this affair, helping our lovers stage their own feelings and affect those of the other.

Some such templates were supplied by libertine novels. Two eighteenth-century European epistolary novels of this kind appear to have been particularly productive in Russia. One, as already noted, was Laclos's *Dangerous Liaisons*, with the calculating seducer the Vicomte de Valmont at its center; the other was Samuel Richardson's *Clarissa, or, the History of a Young Lady* (mostly read in Russia in French translations) with its no less proverbial villain Lovelace. These characters constituted two masks readily donned by well-read men in boastful epistolary banter. Thus Pushkin, when in Tver, added the following jotted greeting to a letter to Vul'f from the latter's sister: "The Lovelace of Tver wishes health and good luck to the Valmont of St. Petersburg."³⁰ As Vul'f infers in his diary upon receiving the letter, Pushkin's telltale alias may have been part of a love game or flirtation (a reasonable assumption, given the letter's composition under *at least* four eyes): "He must have been in a really good mood, exchanging pleasantries with local beauties, and, to poke fun at them, wrote this to me."³¹

Vul'f's diary describes the outset of his affair with Sofia Del'vig as follows. Soon after graduating from Dorpat University, Vul'f arrives in Petersburg, where he makes the acquaintance of Sofia Del'vig, who, he discovers, is well disposed to flirt: "From the very first day of our acquaintance, I felt I was in her good graces, which flattered me a lot because, not counting my first cousins, she was the first woman to show coquetry toward me."³² Albeit conscious of being more of a callow youth than a seasoned libertine, Vul'f reasons and behaves as would the latter. He initiates a relationship, not because he has fallen in love but because he senses the opportunity, and his first step toward this end represents a methodical calculation regarding his prospects.

> Having assumed ... that her principles cannot be too strict, that a liaison with a married woman gives you a better advantage than an affair with a maiden [*s devushkoi*], I decided to give my preference to her, all the more so since, having skipped the stage of preliminary niceties, I had a quicker chance to reach the essentials. I was not wrong in my calculations; all that remained for me to do was to await an opportunity.[33]

After so hopeful an exposition, there follows, as in a well-crafted drama, a complication: "But suddenly things went awry. Her husband, moved by jealousy, and not toward me alone, ... took my fair beauty away."[34] When, nine months later, Del'vig and his wife return to St. Petersburg, the affair, which had seemed over before actually commencing, begins anew. This time, however, as follows from the diary, Vul'f becomes hesitant about the whole plan—because of his friend Del'vig. "Sofia's tenderness toward me has grown, which makes me feel confused and awkward—I don't like the idea of having a good time at his expense [*na ego schet guliat'*]."[35]

Be that as it may, the next step Vul'f undertakes is to cover Sofia's hand with kisses and whisper to her of his present happiness—the same happiness, he emphasizes, he felt upon kissing this hand for the first time. Reading Vul'f's diary further, one senses a certain ambivalence in this episode. When Vul'f confides to Sofia the joy kissing her hand affords him, he is not lying; the diary, indeed, states, with a touch of surprise, "it is a long time since a trifle like this could make me feel so happy."[36] In the same breath, however, Vul'f's diary makes it clear that he is not in love with Sofia. This push-and-pull may conceal a specifically literary motivation: in their respective novels, Valmont and Lovelace only flourish in their chosen occupation until the moment they fall in love with their respective targets. The true—that is, conventional—libertine must never fall in love.

It must be said, however, that in our love story it is not Vul'f alone but also Sofia who plays a double game. She appears to welcome Vul'f's advances but is wary of showing it. As we have seen, the love culture of the Golden Age was not short of ways of saying without saying and showing without showing. We learn of two of these from Vul'f's diary. Device number one is this: Sofia suddenly bursts into tears and, full of remorse, confides to Vul'f her "former sins" (*prezhnie grekhi*). Vul'f sounds perplexed: "It put me in a strange position, to be alone with a woman, with whom I was supposed to be in love, as she bewailed her former sins."[37] A more experienced "Valmont of St. Petersburg" would have shown a greater savvy; here, as elsewhere in her dialogues with Vul'f, Sofia Del'vig acts by contraries. The signal she sends her suitor by crying is intentionally mixed. That Sofia repents her sins tells him of her virtue; that she *has* sinned tells him that this virtue is not entirely impregnable.

Upon the cessation of Sofia's tears, continues Vul'f, "she asked me to change the way I was behaving toward her: I must not pretend to be in love if I am not in love. This would make things easier for us both, [she said,] we would feel less constrained. She wants me to be with her as a friend."[38]

This offer of friendship is Sofia's other love device, a cleverly arranged mousetrap. Sofia could hardly have hoped that Vul'f would accept it; rather, her offer pushes him into a corner. Indeed, Vul'f's reaction is telling: "Deep inside, I liked the idea of remaining friends, and was ready to agree, but it was impossible to say so to her. I continued to insist that I loved her, that my desire for her was genuine and natural, but that of course I would consent to be less insistent in the future."[39]

The "let's-be-friends" trick was scarcely invented by Sofia herself. A love trap of this sort, and with the same outcome, had been staged, for instance, by the experienced coquette the marquise de Lursay from Claude Prosper Jolyot de Crébillon's *Strayings of the Heart and Mind* (*Les Égarements du cœur et de l'esprit*), one of the first masterpieces of libertine literature. Are we not friends, says the experienced marquise to her callow mark—and he feels compelled to say he loves her. There was no template in the culture of the time that would allow him to consent to mere friendship.

This Crébillon-inspired conversation between Sofia and Vul'f took place on the morning of 18 October 1828. It was at this point that Baratynsky's elegy "Dissuasion" was brought into the game. That evening, Vul'f visits the Del'vigs again, this time with an eye to launching a more vigorous attack.

> Wasting no time, I declared to her that what she had said that morning was unfair, for it was founded on the false premise that I did not love her. In response, she wrote down a poem by Baratynsky and showed it to me: Do not seduce [*ne soblazniai*] me, I cannot love, you only excite the blood in me. I then complained that in reproaching me, she was laying her own guilt on me. She offered me her friendship; I said there can be no friendship between a man and a woman. . . . I paused, not having the nerve to say, "I love you." Then, "c'est

l'amour" broke from my lips. She rebuked me: I was just repeating myself, she said.⁴⁰

On this indefinite note, the 18 October conversation was over. Within a few days, to believe Vul'f's diary, Sofia gave in, declaring that there was no longer any room for friendship between them. The 7 November entry includes this description of the amatory mise-en-scene: "I spent all that evening sitting on the floor at Sofia's feet; she was quite tender to me, and kept singing: 'Don't try to tempt me by restoring your tenderness,' etc."⁴¹ There was more singing on 24 November, with the mise-en-scène adjusted, to Vul'f's advantage: "She was sitting at her piano, and, standing on one knee by her side, with her arm around my neck, it was convenient for me to embrace her."⁴² Then,

> she reproached me for my tenderness toward her, and was herself tenderer toward me than she ever had been. The sweetness of her kisses was not diminished by the garlic smell of her breath (she and her husband had eaten a lot of garlic three days prior). . . . After each kiss, she would cover her face with her hands and suffer, both because she had allowed herself to do it and because she wanted to do it again.⁴³

The entry ends with Vul'f's account of his own reaction to this new stage of his and Sofia's rapprochement. Notably, two of the terms he uses in his diary stem from Baratynsky's elegy: "I was silent; I would not dare console or dissuade her [*razuveriat'*], I could not speak at all; from time to time I would let go of her and stride back and forth across the room. We should cease thoughtlessly enjoying one another, cease tempting ourselves in vain [*ne iskushat' sebia naprasno*] altogether."⁴⁴

The culmination of Vul'f and Sofia's love affair took place in an unusual setting, or so his diary pictures it. At one point that winter, it was decided to go for a sleigh ride. Vul'f found himself in the same sleigh as Sofia. There was also a third person in the sleigh, the writer and editor Orest Somov.

> Sofia's and my secret desire was fulfilled: I was seated next to her, Somov was the third, but one could not wish for a better and more harmless companion than Somov. He went on describing the various summer-houses we were passing (quickly, too quickly); he aimed to entertain us, which was handy because talking was something I was not in the mood to do. The wind and wet snow made

us bundle up rather than look around. I availed myself of this opportunity to cover my beautiful seatmate with my large bearskin sleigh-robe, so that my hands were all around her. But this alone did not satisfy me. I had to take full advantage of this happy circumstance. . . . If only respectable Orest Mikhailovich knew what was going on, and how we listened to his descriptions of the gardens that kept flashing by as we rode.[45]

Persuasive Dissuasions: Was Baratynsky Falsified?

Let us close Aleksei Vul'f's private diary on this triumphant scene straight out of a libertine novel (plus the snow and the bearskin), and take another look at Baratynsky's elegy, which our lovers evoked more than once in the course of their affair. Here my concern is the particular leverage between poetics and pragmatics; should we disregard variant uses by various readers of the same love elegy as arbitrary misreadings, or regard them, rather, as sanctioned by the poem's text? The latter seems more plausible. Love elegies like Baratynsky's were read, used, and performed the way they were because their authors *made* them so. Love elegies had to be doubly felicitous: to be enjoyed as pieces of pure poetry, and weaponized in the course of amatory contests and conquests. Both kinds of use grow out of Baratynsky's poem.

In the case of Sofia Del'vig and Aleksei Vul'f, the key issue is one of textual versus *con*textual semantics. When Sofia wrote out "Dissuasion" on a piece of paper for Vul'f to read, what lines and words, in particular, did she hope would catch his eye? And how did Vul'f, for his part, interpret the message Sofia was sending to him through Baratynsky's "Dissuasion" as quoted (in part, misquoted) in his diary? And were Sofia's contextualization and Vul'f's recontextualization of the elegy semantically warranted by its text?

On the face of it, the love situation "Dissuasion" speaks of hardly dovetails with that of Sofia and Vul'f. "Dissuasion" is a post-love elegy—the poem's "I" asks the once-loved "you" not to fan the former flame in vain. Sofia and Vul'f, by contrast, are just embarking on a relationship. At the same time, however, Sofia's affair with Vul'f had its own "before and after"—before and after her husband precipitated her months-long absence. It makes no matter that this "before" boils down to a verbal flirtation and (admittedly unforgettable) hand-kissing. The important thing is that there is a "past"; so Baratynsky's opening line, "Don't try to tempt me by restoring / your tenderness—there is no point," could be used to invoke the possibility of a tender tomorrow, for, as Viazemsky reminds us, in the language of highly ritualized love, a "do not tempt" might translate as "do." All it took to deploy a love poem in a love situation was to disambiguate it.

It was precisely the unstable semantics of lovers' yeses and noes that gave love games an inexhaustible opportunity to play with the notions of believability and credence. Sofia, we recall, repeatedly asked Vul'f not to pretend he was in love with her, warning him she would not believe him anyway. Baratynsky's lines, "No more do I trust assurances, / no more do I believe in love" are easily understood, if needed, as "I do not trust *you* when *you* try to assure me; I do not believe in *your* love." Very likely, this was Sofia's appropriation of these lines. Likewise, the lines "and, solicitous friend, do not / disturb the sick [one] when [they're] dozing" readily echoed Sofia's recurrent, if not very credible, plea of "let us be friends, do not claim my love."

Of course, any analysis of Sofia's interpretation of Baratynsky remains conjectural. We are on surer footing with Vul'f, whose diary serves as a piece of hard, noncircumstantial evidence of how he understood Baratynsky's words and, through their lens, Sofia's message. Made from memory, Vul'f's diary digest of Sofia's rendition of "Dissuasion" contains a few deviations. Baratynsky's "don't try to tempt me" (*ne iskushai*) has turned into Vul'f's "do not seduce [*ne soblazniai*] me"; the former's "no more do I believe in love," into the latter's "I cannot love"; and the elegy's famous *pointe*—"for in my soul you will awaken / mere agitation, but not love"—has been paraphrased as "you only excite the blood in me."

To repeat the earlier question: do these deviations distort Baratynsky's elegy? Textually, they do, yet from the standpoint of semantics, Vul'f's changes would seem sanctioned, if not provoked, by Baratynsky himself, whose "no more do I believe in love" offers two roles to its users. One role is hopeful and hesitant: "I do not trust your love," as Sofia Del'vig had wanted it to convey; the other, cynical, is the role of the philosophically minded libertine: "I do not believe in love as such." Even if Vul'f misinterpreted Sofia's message, he has not distorted Baratynsky's meaning, but merely revealed the poem's potential to mean different things to different readers.

Indeed, the two interpretive roles are not only implicit in Baratynsky's very text, but alluded to therein, albeit hintingly. Everything depends on how we connect the dots. Linked to the line that precedes it—"No more do I trust assurances"—the line "no more do I believe in love" seems to mean what Sofia wants it to: "I do not believe you when you try to assure me of your love." Vul'f's philosophical reading, in turn, derives from connecting "no more do I believe in love" to the epithet "disenchanted" (*razocharovannyi*), as Baratynsky calls his lyric speaker; the meaning this particular new word-montage will foreground is something like: "Disenchanted as I am, I do not believe any more in the existence of love." Baratynsky's elegy is like a magic crystal that changes what it says at the slightest turn.

Or take, "Do not seduce [*ne soblazniai*] me," that other misquote of Baratynsky in Vul'f's diary. The Russian verbs for "seduce" (*soblazniat'*) and "tempt" (*iskushat'*) both entered the language of gallantry from the Bible, where they refer to things satanic, but "to tempt" remains more firmly rooted in religious, rather than erotic, discourse.[46] By replacing "tempting" with "seducing," Vul'f narrows down the context. Equally, then, was Baratynsky's elegy instrumentally suited to Sofia's intricate and evasive love game, and to the one-dimensional chess of her homespun Valmont.

The pliability of Baratynsky's elegy is largely due to his particular method of choosing words. Rather than hunt for the one and only word to fit his meaning, Baratynsky plants his words in clusters. Consider two lines already quoted: "No more do I trust assurances, / no more do I believe in love." In the original, the lexical backbone of this distich is *figura etymologica*, the rhetorical device that clusters different words with kindred roots: *Uzh ia ne **veriu** uveren'iam, / Uzh ia ne **veruiu** v liubov'*. These *ver-ver-ver* vertebrae (which also echo the eponymous *razuverenie*) are nonsynonymously, while of course etymologically, related to one another, and also to the semantics of *verity* crucial both to the world of love and the world of faith. Especially Baratynskian here is the pairing of *veriu* and *veruiu*. Both translate as "I believe," but stylistically the two words belong to different fields. The former of the two is quotidian and secular; the latter is only used in religious contexts. *Ne veruiu v liubov'* sounds philosophical and disenchanted, and very Vul'f-like; *ne veriu uveren'iam* sounds so Sofia. Choose one.

On the other hand, Vul'f's reading of Baratynsky is consistently erotic: consistent both with Vul'f's self-image as a seasoned seducer and with the elegy itself—which, to repeat, is pregnant with quite a number of potential meanings, including this one. The last two lines of the elegy read: "for in my soul you will awaken / mere agitation, but not love." Much in agreement with his other misquotations, Vul'f replaces Baratynsky's "soul" with "blood." Indeed, Baratynsky's word, *volnen'e* ("agitation"), can be read both as "unrest" and as "arousal." Vul'f is, of course, decidedly for the latter. When he misspeaks, saying "you only excite the blood in me," the meaning he attributes to Baratynsky's phrase is exclusively erotic (and virtually physiological).

Still, Vul'f's reading hardly runs counter to Baratynsky's poetic vocabulary itself. One of the tropes the latter used to characterize the heroine of his long poem *The Ball* (*Bal*)—which, as we learn from Vul'f's diary, had at this time been recently brought from Moscow, and was much read and discussed at the Del'vigs'[47]—likewise approaches the physiological: "She has the glow of a drunken Bacchante, / The glow of fever, not the glow of love."[48] What changes is the generic perspective. In Vul'f's reading, the lyric plot of "Dissuasion" shifts away from the genre of doleful (*unylaia*) elegy associated in Russian literature with the ethics of sensitivity. From his perspective, "Dissuasion" is no longer a renunciation of love on the part of a disenchanted speaker (habitually, such disenchantments in love elegies are motivated by a lover's infidelity) but a declaration of physical desire. In Vul'f's and Sofia's hands, "Dissuasion" is transformed into persuasion; it assumes an air of erotic and ethical liberty alien to doleful elegies, compatible with other literary genres, gallant and libertine novels primarily but also erotic poems, including Baratynsky's own. Vul'f-as-Valmont votes for a cool, controlled affair; no wonder each time he feels he is losing his head, he jumps up from his kneeling position, strides across the room, and tells himself it is going too far. Sofia, as she hammers "Dissuasion" into Vul'f, now in written, now in musical form, wants Baratynsky to tell Vul'f: if you are cold, call it friendship and call it a day. She is not unwilling to give vent to sensuality; she had sinned before but is not willing to play the prey of a libertine. This is the condition she puts into "don't try to tempt, there is no point." The original of the latter clause, *bez nuzhdy*, can also mean "without a need." In other words, temptation *would* be justified—by the "need" of love.

Indeed, Baratynsky's elegy is an object that looks different when viewed from different angles. The poem does not belong to the genre of erotic literature, but some aspect of it allowed Vul'f to see it this way. Nor does Baratynsky's love elegy belong to the genre of aphoristic philosophy, yet its last two lines, its *pointe*—"for in my soul you will awaken / mere agitation, but not love"—could be read as a rational maxim of the sort beloved by the cynical heroes of libertine novels. And it *has* been used this way. "For in my soul you will awaken / mere agitation, but not love," was how Aleksandr Mukhanov—yet another lady-killer and a good acquaintance of Baratynsky and Del'vig—justified (in a letter to his brother) walking out on his relationship with Vera Viazemskaya.[49] And, of course, one did not have to be a libertine to avail oneself of Baratynsky's punchline. Our own Sofia, some four years before she met Vul'f, and before she even married Del'vig, had been romantically involved with the future Decembrist Petr Kakhovsky; when the relationship ended, she wrote a friend: "Nothing could serve me better to counter his pursuit, which has tired me out, than Baratynsky's elegy."[50] It was, to be sure, the same "Dissuasion" that Sofia would later sing to Vul'f—but in Kakhovsky's case, it was love's epitaph, not its epigraph.

You and I: Pushkin and Baratynsky

"Dissuasion" as a poem and a sentimental ballad (*romans*) has an impressive history of uses—not only in boudoirs and on parlor floors but also outside the medium of poetry. We find it sung, for instance, in Aleksandr Ostrovsky's 1878 drama *Without a Dowry* (*Bespridannitsa*); in Andrei Bely's 1913 novel *Petersburg* and Marina Tsvetaeva's 1937 *Tale of Sonechka* (*Povest' o Sonechke*); and we hear it from the stage in Vsevolod Meyerhold's 1924 production of Ostrovsky's *The Forest* (*Les*). Nor is it solely in the verbal sphere that one stumbles upon Baratynsky's "Dissuasion." One of the earliest instances of a line from this elegy being reshaped to fit another work comes from the pen of Pushkin—and in this case, the work is a drawing (figure 1).

Drawn in 1829 in a young lady's private album, Pushkin's caricature features his own head in profile with the monastic head-covering known as the *klobuk*. Facing Pushkin's profile from the left is the horned profile of an imp (in Russian: *bes*), shown teasing the monk-Pushkin by sticking out its tongue. The caption, in Pushkin's hand, reads: *Ne iskushai (sai) menia bez nuzhdy*. This, needless to say, is the famous opening of "Dissuasion" ("do not tempt me . . . there is no point"), except that Baratynsky's verb "do not tempt" is followed by Pushkin's tongue-in-cheek alternate ending (in parentheses), which turns *ne iskushai* into *ne iskusai*, literally, "don't bite me all over."

Pushkin's pun on Baratynsky's use of "tempt" is both verbal and visual. As noted, *iskushat'* can, depending on the context, be understood in either the erotic or religious sense. Tempting is what devils do to people, and especially (according to tradition) to clerics. Pushkin's caricature foregrounds the latter, religious meaning of the word, the one that, in Baratynsky's actual line, is merely lurking in the background. Here, as elsewhere, the (graphic) reading of "Dissuasion" reveals, rather than distorts, the elegy's second—dormant—self. Yet, in addition to that, and to its being a tribute to trivial album flirtation, Pushkin's pictorial pun hints at another, more risqué poem by Baratynsky and, to put it in a lengthier temporal perspective, constitutes a line in the two poets' extended dialogue.

FIGURE 1. Pushkin's self-portrait as a monk tempted by an imp. The caption reads: "Не искушай (сай) меня без нужды."

In the autumn of 1828—while the romance of Sofia Del'vig and Aleksei Vul'f was underway in St. Petersburg—Baron Del'vig and Pushkin were busy putting together an issue of *Severnye tsvety*. While he and Sofia were visiting Moscow, Del'vig landed a sizable contribution of poems from Baratynsky, two of which, however, their author would subsequently insist not be published. One of these, as Mikhail Stroganov suggests, must have been "With the tender tongue of heart" ("Serdechnym nezhnym iazykom"), whose central *figura etymologica*—tongue as language and tongue as tongue—may have indeed appeared immodest.[51]

Сердечным нежным языком
Я искушал её сначала:
Она словам моим внимала
С тупым, бессмысленным лицом.
В ней разбудить огонь желаний
Ещё надежду я хранил
И сладострастных осязаний
Язык живой употребил . . .
Она глядела так же тупо,
Потом разгневалася глупо . . .
Беги за нею, модный свет,
Пленяйся девой идеальной!
Владею тайной я печальной:
Ни сердца в ней, ни пола нет.[52]

[With the tender tongue of heart / I was tempting her at first: / She listened to my words / With a dull, vacant face. / Keeping the hope / To awaken the flame of desire in her / I used the vital tongue / Of voluptuous tactility . . . / She looked at me as dully / And then became stupidly angry . . . / Go chase after her, you fashionable world, / Be captivated by an ideal maiden! / I know her sad secret: / She has neither heart, nor sex.]

A libertine loser's reprimand of virtue (or indifference) was, indeed, a dubious point of view to advertise, even under the auspices of poetic license. Unsurprisingly, Baratynsky's poem was read and talked about regardless, first of all at the Del'vigs'. We know of this from Vul'f's diary; specifically, in 1830, when his and Sofia's affair was long since over, Vul'f recapped some of their erotic activities using Baratynsky's image: "the vital/fiery tongue/language [*iazyk*] of voluptuous tactility."⁵³ The poison of Baratynsky's pun is subtler in the original than may be conveyed in English: the Russian word *iazyk* is the primary, denotative form used to refer either to a language or a tongue. When "With the tender tongue of heart" was eventually published seven years later, its censor found the line "the vital tongue of voluptuous tactility" *too* tactile, and (rather foolishly) replaced "tactility" (*osiazanii*) with "kisses" (*lobyzanii*).⁵⁴ In the kissing context, the word "tongue" lost the precarious semantic balance between linguistics and anatomy, conveying the proverbial "too much information."

On the other hand, even in the first two lines, which clearly allude to the language of lyric poetry—"With the tender tongue of heart / I was tempting her at first"—the carnal meaning of "tempting with the tongue" hovers dangerously close. The erotic pragmatics of love elegies, if only in the fantasy of their male fashioners, must bring palpable (so to speak) results. To believe Vul'f's diary—and on this, there seems no reason to mistrust it—it was Pushkin who gave Vul'f lessons in how to do things with words: "Occupy her imagination with voluptuous pictures; having once bitten into this seductive fruit, women succumb to the power of the one who is able to nourish them with it; after the language [*iazyk*] of sensuousness, everything else appears to them listless and banal."⁵⁵

A tongue that tempts—this job description was emblematic enough of a lyric poet for Pushkin to add a teasing tongue to the imp profile in his drawing. Depicted here is a situation of temptation, which may also account for the *klobuk* Pushkin the draughtsman mounted upon the head of Pushkin the poet and Pushkin the mock monk. The canonical symbolism of the *klobuk* is that of a protective (or salvific) helmet; wearing it was believed to shield monks from temptation.

The apparition of an imp next to the line from Baratynsky is probably explained by the following episode in the course of Baratynsky and Del'vig's correspondence apropos Del'vig and Pushkin's work on the forthcoming issue of *Severnye tsvety*. In a follow-up letter from Moscow to Petersburg, Baratynsky, as we recall, asked Del'vig not to include two poems in the planned publication, promising to send a new one, titled "The Little Imp" ("Besenok"): "Please me, my angel, by eliminating those two poems. Next week I will send you a new poem instead, called 'The Little Imp': if the piece itself is not too fanciful [*ne zateilivo tvorenie*], its title is perky [*zadorno*]."⁵⁶ The imp in Pushkin's 1829 cartoon may be imping Baratynsky's imp of 1828, or even Baratynsky himself, given that the "gentle little imp"—the miraculous maker of poetry and childhood dreams—is introduced in the poem as Baratynsky's mascot, and, by implication, his second self.

If so, this would explain the vis-à-vis composition of the two profiles, and also the perky teasing tongue of Pushkin's imp. For years, Pushkin and Baratynsky were linked by an intense mutual interest tinged with friendly rivalry. As I show elsewhere, Baratynsky's "Little Imp" itself contained a covert response to the second edition of Pushkin's *Ruslan and Liudmila*.[57] And, as Samuil Shvartsband has demonstrated in a recent book, Pushkin's avidity for Baratynsky's poetic output goes back to the early 1820s, and was initially connected with love poetry.[58] Indeed, in the spring of 1821, Pushkin opens the tenth issue of *Syn otechestva* and marks in his diary: "Baratynsky is a gem (*prelest'*)."[59] This praise, as it sounds in Russian, connotes elegance and grace, and seems clearly aimed at Baratynsky's gallant "To Lida," rather than his imitation of plaintive folk songs titled "Russian Song" ("Russkaia pesnia") printed alongside it.

"To Lida" triggered a series of efforts on Pushkin's part to out-Baratynsky Baratynsky. Much of what constitutes the grace and elegance of Baratynsky's "To Lida" has to do with the poem's pragmatic self-denial. In a sense, what we are dealing with is a lyric equivalent of the proverbial inscription "This is not a pipe" under the image of a pipe in René Magritte's 1929 painting *The Treachery of Images*. The poem addressed to a young lady named Lida, all of its thirty-five lines, presents a rhetorical argument to the effect that Lida should wish for no such poem from Baratynsky ("Your childish challenge pleases me, / But, do not crave my verses"), and that he himself has no cause to address a poem (*this* poem) to Lida, as opposed to writing verse for himself and his muse. When in our academic writings we say, "needless to say" and then say the needless, we perform more or less the same trick as Baratynsky's.

That same year, in August, Pushkin wrote a love elegy that, albeit different from "To Lida" in terms of lyric plot, employs a similar method of addressing its unnamed female addressee. Here as there, the lyric speaker advises the lyric listener against listening to what the poet has to say. In both, the imagined listener is a young woman, too young to be prepared to hear what the speaker has to say. The difference lies in what motivates the putative refusal. Baratynsky blames the "light-minded" listener: "The language of poetry and the gods / Is only accessible to the chosen few." Pushkin reverses the blame: for his *ty*, her mind's lightness is a blessing, and ought to be shielded from burdensome knowledge of the speaker's past:

Мой друг, забыты мной следы минувших лет
И младости моей мятежное теченье.
Не спрашивай меня о том, чего уж нет,
Что было мне дано в печаль и в наслажденье,
    Что я любил, что изменило мне.
Пускай я радости вкушаю не в полне;
Но ты, невинная! ты рождена для счастья.
Беспечно верь ему, летучий миг лови:
Душа твоя жива для дружбы, для любви,
    Для поцелуев сладострастья;
Душа твоя чиста; унынье чуждо ей;
Светла, как ясный день, младенческая совесть.
К чему тебе внимать безумства и страстей
    Не занимательную повесть?
Она твой тихий ум невольно возмутит;
Ты слезы будешь лить, ты сердцем содрогнешься;
Доверчивой души беспечность улетит,
И ты моей любви . . . быть может ужаснешься.
Быть может, навсегда . . . Нет, милая моя,
Лишиться я боюсь последних наслаждений.
Не требуй от меня опасных откровений:
Сегодня я люблю, сегодня счастлив я.[60]

[My friend, I have forgotten the traces of my bygone years / And the riotous flow of my youth. / Do not ask me about what is already gone, / What was given to me for sorrow and delight, / What I have loved and what betrayed me. / Let it be me who does not savor joys; / But you, the innocent one! You were born for happiness. / Trust it, carefree, and catch the volatile instant: / Your soul is alive for friendship, for love, / For voluptuous kisses; / Your soul is pure; gloom is unknown to it; / Your infant conscience is bright as a clear day. / Why should you listen / To the uninteresting tale / Of madness and passions? / It will disturb your calm mind; / You will shed tears, your heart will be shaken; / The carefreeness of a trusting soul will fly away, / And my love . . . may horrify you. / Maybe, forever . . . No, my dear, / I am afraid to lose my final joy. / Do not demand dangerous revelations from me: / Today I am in love, today I am happy.]

In Pushkin studies, this poem has been approached primarily from the standpoint of factual pragmatics: who could have been the prototype of

Pushkin's nameless addressee—a question particularly burning in the context of the grand debate about "Pushkin's secret love."[61] It might be more productive, however, to interrogate the *lyric* pragmatics of Pushkin's love epistle in verse. The card it plays is simple, and hardly unknown among "players" like Lovelace and Valmont. The more one "attempts" to persuade the object of one's love interest not to be interested in the (oxymoronically) "uninteresting tale / Of madness and passions," the more ardently, wagers Pushkin, will she (and, hopes the poet, his readers at large) be interested in it. Planting telltale hints (like "what I have loved and what betrayed me"), the poem elaborates, if obscurely, on what it says it is reluctant to bring up. The projected emotional affect caused in the listener by the speaker's "dangerous revelations" (*opasnykh otkrovenii*) is inferred and verbalized in the penultimate quatrain: "You will shed tears, your heart will be shaken." Yet the most daring stunt of amatory doublespeak is performed when, in conclusion, the lyric "I" shares his "fear" that the ghost of his past loves might frighten off the love of his lyric *ty*, even as, by this point, we readers are quite certain that all this "past" talk is but bait to attract her. Telling a prospective lover of one's former loves was a time-tested libertine gambit. Recall Sofia hiding her face as she confided to Vul'f that she had sinned before; and two years later, Vul'f, as an officer in a far-off Bessarabian garrison, would likewise strategize another love conquest: "Must start with the story of my love adventures."[62] One wonders if these included Sofia Del'vig.

To return to the story of Pushkin and Baratynsky: Pushkin's competitive spirit had been especially fired up in November 1821 when Baratynsky's "Dissuasion" came out—the same "Dissuasion," of course, that, seven years later, Sofia would sing for the kneeling Vul'f, and which eight years later Pushkin would hang a pun on in that droll drawing penned in a young lady's album. In a January 1822 letter to Viazemsky, Pushkin, himself at the time known as an unsurpassed master of love poetry, exclaims: "What a devil [*no kakov*] Baratynsky is! You must admit, he will surpass both Parny and Batiushkov if he strides on as he has so far, and, lucky one, he is only twenty-three! Let us cede the erotic field to him, and run every which way, or no one will be safe."[63] The run-for-your-life signal was clearly a joke, but Viazemsky was concerned, less for himself than for Pushkin; as late as 1825, Viazemsky would still return to the subject of the Baratynsky scare: "You seem," he wrote Pushkin, "to take me for an opponent of his, but I don't know why. I fully respect his gift. The only thing I ever disagreed with was your humility—when you told me you wouldn't be writing any more elegies."[64]

Pushkin did not, of course, give up this form, but from 1821 on he would indeed consider love elegy the lot staked out by Baratynsky. In winter 1822, Pushkin sketched two brief epistles to Baratynsky, one referring to him as Ovid, the other as a troubadour. From "Ovid" to "troubadour"—the two aliases marked the entire spectrum of what love poetry could be, from seductive to chivalrous. Pushkin conceived of Baratynsky's love poetry as managing to be both: remaining suggestive even while keeping up a chaste and saintly countenance. When, in a sanctimonious epistle to his admirer and commander Staff Captain Konshin, twenty-one-year-old Baratynsky pledged to "Leave blind thirst for lusty passions / To the naughty young," in favor of finding, instead, "a trusty love" and "gentle soulmate," Pushkin found this highly unconvincing. In an epistle of his own to Nikolai Alekseev, he called Baratynsky, oxymoronically, "my pensive prankster," appending a sober one-line epilogue to Baratynsky's aspiration:

Как мой задумчивый проказник,
Как Баратынский, я твержу:
"Нельзя ль найти подруги нежной?
Нельзя ль найти любви надежной?"
И ничего не нахожу.[65]

[Like my pensive prankster, / Like Baratynsky do I say: / "Cannot one find a gentle soulmate? / Cannot one find a trusty love?" / And find nothing.]

Two years later, in 1823, Pushkin wrote to Del'vig: "I share your hope regarding Iazykov and your longtime love for Baratynsky's immaculate Muse."[66] "Immaculate" here is an ironic antiphrasis. What Pushkin valued in Baratynsky's love poetry was its cloven tongue, the play between the pensive what-it-says and the prankish what-it-does.

Loveless Elegies

Another of Pushkin's admiring remarks on Baratynsky, followed by another symbolic abjuration of love poetry, comes in early 1824, after the latter's "Confession" ("Priznanie") came out in *Poliarnaia zvezda na 1824 god* (The polar star for 1824). "Baratynsky is a gem and a miracle [*prelest' i chudo*]," Pushkin writes in January to Aleksandr Bestuzhev. "'Confession' is perfection. After him, I will never again publish my elegies."⁶⁷ We find the same assessment and the same gesture repeated in a letter Pushkin sent Bestuzhev a month later: "Baratynsky is a miracle, my pieces [*piesy*] are bad. This is all I can tell you about *Poliarnaia* [*zvezda*]."⁶⁸

Adduced below is the entire text—all forty lines—of an early version of Baratynsky's elegy "Confession" as it appeared in the Bestuzhev-coedited almanac *Poliarnaia zvezda* in December 1823.

Притворной нежности не требуй от меня;
Я сердца моего не скрою хлад печальный:
Ты права, в нём уж нет прекрасного огня
    Моей любви первоначальной.
Напрасно я себе на память приводил
И милый образ твой и прежних лет мечтанье;
    Безжизненны мои воспоминанья!
Я клятвы дал, но дал их выше сил.

    Спокойна будь: я не пленён другою;
Душой моей досель владела ты одна;
Но тенью лёгкою прошла моя весна:
Под бременем забот я изнемог душою,
    Утихнуло волнение страстей,
Промчались дни; без пищи сам собою
    Огонь любви погас в душе моей.
Верь, беден я один: любви я знаю цену,
    Но сердцем жить не буду вновь,
Вновь не забудусь я! Изменой за измену
    Мстит оскорбленная любовь.

    Предательства верней узнав науку,
Служа приличию, Фортуне иль судьбе,
Подругу некогда я выберу себе,
    И без любви решусь отдать ей руку.
В сияющий и полный ликов храм,
    Обычаю бесчувственно послушный,
    Введу её, и деве простодушной
Я клятву жалкую во мнимой страсти дам . . .

И весть к тебе придёт; но не завидуй нам;
Не насладимся мы взаимностью отрадной,
Сердечной прихоти мы воли не дадим,
    Мы не сердца Гимена связью хладной—
    Мы жребий свой один соединим.

Прости, забудь меня; мы вместе шли доныне;
Путь новый избрал я, путь новый избери,
Печаль бесплодную рассудком усмири,
Как я безропотно покорствуя судьбине.
    Не властны мы в самих себе,
    И слишком ветрено в младые наши леты
        Даём нескромные обеты,
    Смешные, может быть, всевидящей судьбе![69]

[Do not demand of me pretended tenderness: / the mournful coldness of my heart I won't conceal. / You're right—it burns no longer with the beautiful / blaze of my initial love. / In vain I've tried to summon into memory / your darling image and the things we once imagined— / but lifeless now are all my recollections; I did make vows, but proved unequal to them. // Don't worry, I'm not in thrall to any other beauty— / You alone to this day possessed my soul, / but my springtime has passed like a light shadow: / my soul is exhausted under the burden of cares, / agitation of passions has calmed down, / days flashed by; untended, all by itself / the blaze of love went out in my soul. / Believe me, I'm the wretched one. I know the value of love, / but my heart won't live again, / I won't be lost again! Love, once offended, takes revenge: / betrayal for betrayal. // Having learned the lesson of perfidy, / paying my dues to propriety, Fortune or destiny, / one day I will choose a companion / and, without love, choose to offer her my hand. / Senselessly submissive to custom, / I will lead her into a glowing church, replete with icons, / and to the naïve maiden / will give a miserable oath of false desire . . . / And you will hear the news, but do not envy us: / we will never delight in mutual joys, / we'll never give vent to our hearts' vagaries, / for what we join by Hymen's cold bond / won't be our hearts—only our destinies. // Farewell, forget me; till now, we walked our road together. / A new path I have chosen; a new path you should choose. / Your fruitless sorrow let your reason soothe, / submit to destiny like I do, without complaint. / We have no power over ourselves, / And too giddily in our youthful years we utter / bigheaded promises, / ridiculous perhaps to all-seeing fate.[70]]

As critics and scholars have frequently noted, the theme of lovelessness is paradoxically prominent in Baratynsky's love lyric. This applies to the above "Confession," the elegy Pushkin called "perfection."[71] Why should the waning of love have loomed so large in Baratynsky's oeuvre? A number of explanations have been proposed. Parallels have been suggested between the cold lyric speakers in Baratynsky and disillusioned heroes from nineteenth-century poetry and prose, most prominently Benjamin Constant's *Adolphe*.[72] Or has the denial of love to do with Baratynsky's increasing interest in poetic meditation, as Sergei Bocharov seems to suggest when, analyzing "Dissuasion," he postulates the existence of a special "lyrico-philosophical state?"[73]

Underpinning such accounts is a tacit assumption that Baratynsky's lyric speaker speaks his heart. The resigned mood of loveless elegies, and all the post-love rationale their lyric "I" typically adduces to justify lovelessness, are usually taken at face value. But should they be? Do Baratynsky's "Dissuasions" and "Confessions," that is, actually constitute dissuasions and confessions? Not if we read Baratynsky through the lens of a diary of someone as predatory as Vul'f. From the viewpoint of pragmatics, a poem is like a silent movie. Listen not to what Baratynsky's loveless poems say; follow what they do. As we saw earlier in this chapter, an elegy that sounded serenely withdrawn from desires could easily become passionate, even dangerously so, in action. In the hands of a skilled love gamer like Sofia or Vul'f, a strategically chosen quote from "Dissuasion" could serve as both sheep's clothing and wolf's bite. As Pushkin's doodle reminds us, the Russian for "tempt," *iskushat'*, might easily be converted into *iskusat'*, to bite all over.

The performative possibilities that loveless elegies opened for their potential users shed additional light on their literary kinship. Undoubtedly, contemporaries like Adolphe have much to do with "Dissuasion" and "Confession" and their disillusioned speakers. But a more complete picture would include predecessors. As we know, certain habits distinctive to Russian literary heroes and, by extension, of the modus vivendi accepted in literary spheres, had been borrowed from French libertine novels. Pushkin's Onegin, in the novel's first chapter, acts according to libertine rules, and so does Lermontov's Pechorin in "Princess Mary."[74] Love elegies—the loveless ones in particular—did as well.

A recognizable trait of the true libertine was coldness.[75] Passion is boring, Vul'f's diary proclaims.[76] Anna Kern, whose relationship with Pushkin was very much constructed on the libertine model, reminisced on his aloof demeanor: "As to [Pushkin], he almost never shared his feelings; he seemed to be ashamed of them and was in this sense a son of his century, in which, as he himself wrote, 'feeling was weird and ridiculous.' A witticism, a quip—*la repartie vive*—was what pleased him endlessly."[77] No doubt, this cult of coldness did its part to fashion the lyric mask of Baratynsky's loveless speaker.

Another libertine requisite was the hero's invariable (so to speak) inconstancy. Lasting love was deemed preposterous and tedious. The idea of love boils down to love as a conquest. The love story of your average Vul'f was thus always a modular narrative, each of the modules shaped by the same emotional ebb and flow. After a victory, the libertine feels cloyed. This is how Pushkin's Faust feels after seducing Gretchen, as mirrored in Mephistopheles's lines: "Having slaked my thirst for enjoyment, / I look upon the victim of my whim / With an overwhelming aversion."[78] While it is true that regret, rather than aversion, is the thematic dominant of Baratynsky's loveless elegies, their coordinates on the emotional curve of an exemplary libertine are unmistakably post-conquest.

The title of Baratynsky's "Confession" comprises a trick—and a surprise. In Russian (as in English), *priznanie* can mean two things: a confession, as when a criminal confesses a crime or a sinner a sin; on a brighter note, when someone declares their love, this act is also called *priznanie*, literally, "a confession of love." Arguably (or perhaps inarguably), when one opens an elegy titled "Priznanie," one expects to find a declaration of love; instead, Baratynsky declares non-love, farewell, the parting of ways. At the same time, the title "Confession" gestures toward libertinage—specifically, toward a tiny subgenre nesting within the larger pool of traditional libertine themes. When Onegin, in his role of a magnanimous libertine, calls his coldly sympathetic reproof of Tatiana's letter a "confession" (*priznanie*, and, in the next line, *ispoved'*), he taps precisely into the literary paradigm trademarked by Duclos's *Confessions of comte de ****, to some extent the *Confessions* of Rousseau, and Karamzin's anti-Rousseauian *My Confession* (*Moia ispoved'*).

Not unlike Onegin's, Baratynsky's "Confession" plays two tunes at once, counterpointing *what* is said to *how* it is said. In the plane of *how*, the poem intones precisely as doleful elegies were expected to. Baratynsky's melancholy metrics (some of whose free-iambic patterns, particularly in the first stanza, are reminiscent of Zhukovsky) sounds impeccably tender; its message, implacably cruel. To the sound of the lulling, even caressing, music of his words, Baratynsky's lyric speaker informs his lyric *ty* of the fact that his heart is cold, his vows are void, and even his recollections grow lifeless with the passing of time.

The notion of time is pivotal to this confession. The elegy shifts the blame for the loss of love from human agency to the factor of time: "Days flashed by;

untended, all by itself / the blaze of love went out in my soul"—a move that earned Baratynsky his critical repute of subtle psychologist. The time-blaming argument is, in fact, not psychological but rhetorical, and comes straight from the Vicomte de Valmont's cruel breakup letter to Madame de Tourvel in *Dangerous Liaisons*: "One tires of everything, my angel, it is a law of nature, it is not my fault. If, then, I am tired today of an adventure which has occupied me exclusively for four mortal months, it is not my fault."[79] The justification of vow-breaking in Baratynsky has the same precedent: "I am very sensible that here is a fine opportunity to call me perjured: but, if nature has only gifted men with constancy, whilst it has given women obstinacy, it is not my fault."[80]

Valmont's letter, while calling its addressee "my angel," is dry and rational; the refrain "it is not my fault" makes its argument almost legalistic. Compared to Valmont's, Baratynsky's breakup note—for this is what "Confession" pragmatically is—sounds like an affecting, grievous farewell. *Prosti, zabud' menia*, for instance, can be read both as "farewell, forget me" and "forgive me and forget." This is *how* the elegy says it; yet *what* it says, and, by implication, what it *does* to its lyric address is precisely what Valmont says and does, including the final advice his letter gives to Madame de Tourvel: "Believe me, take another lover, as I have taken another mistress. This advice is good, very good; if you think it bad, it is not my fault."[81]

Advice like Valmont's is included in Baratynsky's elegy as well, though here the pill is philosophically sugar-coated. In "Confession," the lyric speaker assures his former lover that, having fallen out of love with her, he also fell out of grace with love as such: "Love, once offended, takes revenge." Love's revenge, to believe the lyric speaker, precludes him from ever falling in love again, not even with the "naïve maiden" he plans on marrying one day. "We have no power over ourselves"; "submit to destiny like I, without complaint"; and then, suddenly, in the thick of his elevated soliloquy, Baratynsky's lyric "I" throws in a perfectly libertine one-liner straight out of Valmont: "A new path I have chosen; a new path you should choose." He even repeats the verb that Valmont used in the original French—"choose:" "choisis un autre amant, comme j'ai fait une autre maîtresse" (take—choose—another lover, as I have taken—chosen—another mistress). Mythopoetic or philosophic as this confession of lovelessness may sound, in the final—pragmatic—analysis it boils down to the "law of nature" (of predatory nature, one must specify) formulated by Valmont: "One tires of everything, my angel."

Perhaps the best-known and most often quoted among Pushkin's pronouncements on Baratynsky's poetry is this: "Baratynsky is unique among our poets, because he thinks" (*Baratynsky u nas originalen, ibo myslit*).[82] This also happens to be a phrase frequently quoted out of context—not out of the context of its immediate textual surroundings but rather unrelated to contemporaneous notions of what distinguishes poetry from prose, and neglecting the literary-historical context of the word "thinks." When we read of a lyric poem endowed with the gift of thinking (*myslit'*), we almost instinctively imagine a poet-thinker, their mind immersed in what Bocharov calls the "lyrico-philosophical state." In Pushkin's frame of reference, however, thinking is a specific type of literary practice rather than a speculative activity. In the view then prevalent, lyric poetry, elegies especially, was the realm of feeling; thinking—conceived of as cold reasoning, deep insight, or swift esprit—was considered the property of prose (which term, at the time, comprised more than fiction, to include, for instance, letters and critical essays). In an 1824 letter to Viazemsky, Pushkin dismissed the former's new poem for being too intelligent, "whereas poetry, God forgive me, should be a little silly."[83] As to Viazemsky's prose, Pushkin wrote: "Fortunately, he thinks, which is fairly rare among us."[84] Pushkin's opinion of Viazemsky's prose was transferred almost verbatim into his assessment of Baratynsky's poetry.

While an exceptionally profound thinker in his poetry, Baratynsky had little use for nineteenth-century philosophy as a system of thought. Rather than intending to extol Baratynsky as a unique philosopher among Russian poets, Pushkin's remark points to an outlying peculiarity of Baratynsky's poetry: its paradoxical orientation toward prose, its beginnings in the libertine novel, and its adherence to the stylistic devices characteristic thereof—specifically, to cold and clear, pointed or generalizing thoughts often meant to sound aphoristic.[85] Hence, too, the cruel "laws of nature" that Baratynsky's "Confession" inherited from Valmont—and that Valmont, or, rather, his creator Laclos received from nature's earlier lawmakers—the French old masters of aphoristic prose.

It is no news that much of the wit or wisdom that eighteenth-century novelists like Richardson or Laclos put into the mouths of their Lovelaces and Valmonts comes from the pool of moralistic maxims.[86] As Denis Diderot observed in 1762 in his "Eulogy of Richardson," "what Montaigne, Charron, La Rochefoucauld, and Nicole had put into maxims, Richardson puts into action."[87] Of a number of maxims that enlightened their readers as to nature's laws of loveless loving, let me single out two that, in hindsight, appear particularly relevant to Pushkin on the one hand and Baratynsky on the other. One, written by Jean de La Bruyère, could serve as an epigraph to Baratynsky's loveless elegy "Confession": "It is no more in our power to love always than it was not to love at all."⁸⁸ The other, a chiasmus by Nicolas Chamfort—"A lover who is loved too much by his mistress seems to love her less, and *vice versa*"⁸⁹—changed into Pushkin's lines: "Чем меньше женщину мы любим, / Тем легче нравимся мы ей" (The less we love a woman / The easier it is to attract her). Both French catchphrases quoted above belong to the genre known as *pensées*; both Pushkin's punchline and Baratynsky's elegy belong to the strange genre of poetry that *thinks*.

Elegy in Narrative Dialogues

Baratynsky's attentiveness to Pushkin's work was as acute as Pushkin's was to his. A stark testimony to this was *Eda* (1824; published in 1826), a narrative poem composed in intense dialogue with Pushkin's *The Prisoner of the Caucasus* (*Kavkazskii plennik*, 1820–21; published in 1822). Both poems perfectly exemplify the tendency by which, as noted in chapter 3, Golden Age poets—in this case, Pushkin and Baratynsky—would convert their personal geopolitical circumstance into the lyric chronotope of their work. This applied to verse narratives as well. Pushkin's *Prisoner* is a southern poem in two senses: as a poem written during Pushkin's southern exile, and as one that tells of an outlying "Oriental" village beyond the southern frontier of the Russian Empire. Likewise, Baratynsky took advantage of his regiment's transfer to Finland to set his *Eda* in the North. Both *Eda* and *Prisoner* are love stories; in both, love flares between an innocent local maiden—in Baratynsky, the blue-eyed Finnish peasant girl Eda, in Pushkin, the black-haired "mountain girl" (*deva gor*) referred to by the ethnonym "Circassian" (*cherkeshenka*)—and a Russian man who has wound up in their respective villages not of his own accord. In both, the man survives, while the non-Russian girl perishes, with a hint in each case that the cause of death is suicide.

For all the success of Pushkin's *Prisoner*, many critics found its hero unconvincing; his manner of acting and speaking, complained Petr Pletnev in 1822, felt out of place amid the mountains of the Caucasus, and incongruous with their "daughter's" gentle simplicity and untamed temper alike: "[The Prisoner's] words, like 'I am not worthy of your admiration,' or 'The victim of [my forlorn] passions, void of desire, I wither,' kill any sympathy we might have for him."⁹⁰ In a critical essay of 1824, Aleksandr Voeikov seconds Pletnev, adducing another quotation from the prisoner's reply to his enamored Circassian:

Другого юношу зови.
. . . .
Не долго женскую любовь
Печалит хладная разлука:
Пройдет любовь, настанет скука,
Красавица полюбит вновь.

[Call some other young man. / . . . / Women's love is not / Saddened for long / By cold separation: / Love will pass, ennui will come, / [And] a beauty will fall in love once more.]

When we read this, writes Voeikov, "[our] heart feels outrage toward the prisoner. This is the sort of thing he could have said to some high-society coquette [*svetskaia prelestnitsa*] who had cheated on him, but not to a virtuous village maiden aflame with incurable passion, a passion that could only be extinguished together with her life."[91]

"Call some other young man. . . . Fall in love once more"—no doubt Voeikov sensed Valmont's *choisis un autre amant* behind these words. We may not quite hear it today, but the tone and diction of the prisoner's rejection come from the joint thesaurus of loveless elegies and their predecessors, libertine novels.

How such cold gallant formulae found their way into a work as exotic as Pushkin's *Prisoner* is partly explained by its very structure. Pushkin's long poem, that is, combined a number of easily detectable (and detachable) literary modules: landscapes of the Caucasus; ethnographic descriptions of Circassian customs; the prisoner's backstory; his life in captivity; and even, under a separate heading, a Circassian song. In addition, its text included an epistle dedicatory, an epilogue, and footnotes, which, in turn, featured longish inserts of preexisting verse descriptions of the Caucasus and its nature. As part of this complex genre structure, Proskurin shows, Pushkin used lyric—mostly, elegiac—insertions in the dialogues and descriptions of both protagonists.[92]

The implied speaker of a lyric poem was as prone to materialize as someone's narrative "I" as it was to be interpreted as the poet's real "I" or the alter ego of a reader. When, as we saw in chapter 3, the reader half-hidden under the initials E. B. inscribed a provincial album with Pushkin's poem "I have outlasted my desires," adding beneath it, "This is my life," she, of course, was unaware that originally, the poem had been written as part of a soliloquy addressed by a captive Russian to a Circassian woman from the mountain village in which he lived enslaved.[93] But had she known this, it would hardly have mattered. To turn a would-be monologue from *The Prisoner of the Caucasus* into a stand-alone elegy, all Pushkin had to do was remove the quotation marks.

To judge by Pletnev's and Voeikov's reactions to the libertine overtones of the prisoner's words and conduct, transposition in the opposite direction was trickier. Stitches remained. Viazemsky called the prisoner a "son of a bitch" for not mourning the Circassian properly. Pushkin himself was not quite pleased with how his prisoner turned out, but in a letter to Viazemsky he at least attempts to defend his conduct: "[Some] deplore that he never jumps into the river to pull my Circassian out. Try and jump—I have swum in Caucasian rivers, you'll drown before you find anything. My prisoner is a judicious and clever person, he is not in love with the Circassian—he was right not to have gotten himself drowned."[94]

As a story, Baratynsky's *Eda* is deliberately simple—simpler than *The Prisoner of the Caucasus* and even their shared plot-deficient prototype, Karamzin's *Poor Liza*. Quartered with troops in Finland, a Russian hussar seduces a naïve, innocent girl. He leaves, she dies. Pushkin was intrigued by the closeness of this plot to his own in *Prisoner* (save for a great leap to the north), suspecting this to be a literary gauntlet. "Pray, send me a copy of Baratynsky's *Eda*," he wrote his brother Lev. "That wretched Finn [*chukhonets*]! If she is prettier than my Circassian I will hang myself near two pine trees and will never speak to him again."[95]

It may well have been that in Pushkin's judgment, it was Eda who won the contest—if not of beauty then of love. He describes her infantile credulity: "She loves like a child, accepts his presents with delight, gambols with him, becomes freely accustomed to his caresses."[96] Important as the Circassian maiden's love is to *The Prisoner of the Caucasus*, in the poem's complex structure her story is but a part: Pushkin assigns fewer than half the work's lines (not counting extra-diegetic parts of the poem) to this subject. *Eda*, by contrast, is all about Eda, aside from scant descriptions of northern landscapes and a section introducing the hussar (removed in the second edition). Naming the poem for her was, moreover, a highly unusual move on Baratynsky's part. It was Pushkin, again, who, in an essay on Baratynsky drafted in 1828, summed up *Eda* as a deeply emotional tale of female love. Pushkin barely mentions the male—or, rather, brilliantly dismisses him as an "enterprising [*predpriimchivyi*] seducer."[97]

Baratynsky's cunning design was to use the hussar figure for a contrast—as a painter might a complementary color. A walking parody of a libertine hero, the "sly dog" (*khitrets*) of a hussar acts by the book: to extort a kiss, he bemoans his loneliness; he gains the "desired victory" by threatening a separation. His little speeches look like elegiac inserts from Pushkin's *Prisoner*; but, unlike Pushkin, Baratynsky continuously emphasizes their cynical pragmatics. The clearer we, readers, see through the hussar's love game, the more we empathize with Eda, to whom it would never occur to treat love as a game. "Serene merriment was shining / In her infant [*mladencheskie*] eyes"[98]—every act of guile on the part of the hussar reveals, by contrast, the guilelessness of Eda's artless soul.

Baratynsky was of three minds as to which way to steer the hussar's behavior after his "conquest." One scenario (the 1826 edition) was to turn him into the type of the "sinner reformed by love." Compelled by his memories of her, the hussar returns to Eda ("What were his intentions? / God knows," the author wonders) only to find her dying.[99] In another (the 1835 edition), the hussar grows tired of Eda and, glad at heart, departs forever when his regiment is transferred.[100] In 1825 Baratynsky circulated (though never published) an ending that sounds more cruel and libertine than the other two. After the hussar is sent off with his troops into what we are given to understand will be a combat, Eda receives his farewell letter.

On the face of it, the letter (twenty-four lines in iambic tetrameter) looks like a faceless variation of a separation elegy, replete with generic formulae of the sort found in *The Prisoner of the Caucasus* or Baratynsky's own "Confession." Had he met her before, explains Pushkin's prisoner in his lyric monologue to the "mountain girl" by way of justifying his coldness, he would have fallen in love with her, "but now, it is too late: I am dead for happiness."[101] Baratynsky's hussar tries the same move with Eda: he would have lived happily with her, his exit letter explains, "were I able to believe in happiness [*kogda b umel ia v schast'e verit'*]."[102]

Further into the letter, the hussar offers Eda the standard gift of promiscuous generosity:

Забудь меня; в душе своей
Любовь другую возлелей.
Всяк будет пленником послушным
Твоей цветущей красоты.[103]

[Forget me; in your soul / Foster another love. / Anyone will be a submissive prisoner / Of your blossoming beauty.]

The hussar's stanza-opening appeal, "Forget me," is a third-generation verbal resonance. It echoes, "Farewell, forget me" from Baratynsky's "Confession," which, in turn, echoes, "Forget me: I am not worthy / Of your love and admiration"—the words Pushkin gave his prisoner (whose sobriquet [*plennik*] also reverberates in the hypothetical "submissive prisoner" of Eda's love conjured by the hussar—who never materializes). The main thing, of course, is not the word, but the message: find yourself someone, *choisis un autre amant*, have fun. The dreadful irony of it, by no means lost on Baratynsky and his readers, is that these words are addressed not to a "high-society coquette who had cheated on him" (to quote Voeikov) but to the bright-eyed Eda. Who is going to die.

Despite swarming with elegiac clichés, or, rather, because it swarms with them so densely, the hussar's letter is not a mere lyric insert into a narrative whole, as the direct speech of Pushkin's prisoner is. What Baratynsky's hussar says or writes is part and parcel of what he is as a literary character. "What a gem this *Eda* is!" Pushkin exclaimed when he finally procured a copy: "Our critics won't appreciate the originality of the story. But how diverse it is! The hussar, Eda, and the poet himself—each speaks their own way."[104]

Pushkin had good reason to admire *Eda*, particularly the polyphony in it that he notes here. What Baratynsky had hit upon was precisely what Pushkin missed in *Prisoner*. Both prisoner and Circassian, as well as "the poet himself" (the narrator as he is describing them) speak the same language, the language of elegy. This was exactly the problem Pletnev and Voeikov sensed: the elegiac "I" and "you" had to be transformed to work within the narrative. This was what Baratynsky did in *Eda*.

In particular, he endowed his hussar with the distinctive feature of speaking in featureless clichés, whether extempore or in his letter. As Baratynsky pictures him, the hussar is not a thoroughbred libertine like Valmont, nor is he a genuine Byronic type, as Pushkin's prisoner was supposed to be. Baratynsky's hussar is a poser—pragmatics personified. What he says works for what he wants, having little bearing on anything meaningful, least of all (most poignantly) Eda's feelings. All we know about Eda is her unalloyed sincerity. Meanwhile the hussar, having seduced her, asks himself (in a letter to her) whether her caresses were genuine or fake ("[Whether] in your love to me you were, / Not [merely] appeared truly tender"), because, as every misogynist is quick to reason, "your sex is good at being twofaced!"[105]

We also know, deep down, that poor Eda is going to die, for this is how innocent maidens in literary works used to redeem the sin of succumbing to seduction. All the more incongruous, then, is the note of self-pity we hear in the hussar's letter.

> Меня зовет кровавый бой;
> Не знаю сам, куда судьбой
> Я увлечен отселе буду;
> . . . .
> . . . но если из очей
> Слезу уронишь в самом деле
> Ты на листок заветный сей,
> Утешься: жребий мой тяжеле
> Судьбины бедственной твоей.[106]

[A bloody combat calls me; / I don't know myself where my destiny / Will lead me from here; / . . . / . . . But if indeed a tear / Drops from your eyes / Onto this cherished sheet, / Be consoled: my lot is harder, / Than is your unfortunate destiny.]

The hussar's letter to Eda, a potpourri of elegiac motifs, constitutes a false elegy, a pastiche. Disguised as a fictional utterance, Pushkin's elegy works better as a lyric poem, and feels almost like a digression from the narrative: take it out of *Prisoner* or put it back again, the framing action will not substantially change. *Eda* is different. Eda's actions arise directly from her collocutor's speech acts, from the hussar's proficiency with a handful of lyric clichés.

Earlier in this book I spoke of the dual felicity of lyric. A good love elegy had to be of use in love—as Baratynsky's "Dissuasion" was in Sofia's game with Vul'f, *and vice versa*. To be a successful love elegist meant, in the Golden Age, to be a supplier of arms, mostly tender, at times deadly. In *Eda*, Baratynsky masterfully reduced this premise to absurdity. His hussar, a joke of a lyric speaker, cares chiefly about the combat capacity of the lyric speeches Baratynsky provides him with; his Eda, a child of nature, takes them at face value, and pays for her credulity. Where poetry recedes, pragmatics advances.

Pushkin's dialogue with Baratynsky continues in *Eugene Onegin*, with varying degrees of explicitness. Two of several textual references to Baratynsky in the novel are traceable to *Eda*. One can be inferred from a rhetorical gesture toward the Finland-locked Baratynsky in chapter 3, which was written after Pushkin had heard of *Eda* yet before he could actually read it. Faced with the difficult task of translating Tatiana's letter into Russian, the author of *Eugene Onegin* invokes the absent master of *Eda*, whom, if present, he would trouble

> Чтоб на волшебные напевы
> Переложил ты страстной девы
> Иноплеменные слова.
> Где ты? приди: свои права
> Передаю тебе с поклоном...¹⁰⁷

[To convert / The foreign words / Of the enamored maiden / Into enchanted melodies. / Where are you? Come: / I transfer my rights / To you with a bow ...¹⁰⁸]

The other trace of *Eda* is found in the opening stanzas of chapter 5, written in 1826, by which time Pushkin had already read the poem. Pushkin begins with a superb depiction of a first snowfall, then slyly yields to Baratynsky, singer of the Finnish winter: "But I do not intend to contend / . . . with you, / The bard of the young Finnish maid."¹⁰⁹

The concluding chapter of this book will discuss lyric layers in *Eugene Onegin*, but here I would comment on the one pertaining to Baratynsky. Even as he abjures any intention of "contending with" Baratynsky, Pushkin slips in the caveat "not yet" (*pokamest*). Of course even the most chivalrous of literary dialogues is but a form of literary contest, often more productive than outright literary struggle. As Pushkin scholars agree, Onegin's "confession" (chapter 4) in response to Tatiana's letter was to a large degree Pushkin's response to Baratynsky's "Confession" and other love elegies.¹¹⁰ Neither should we leave unattended the amazing back-and-forth between Pushkin's matching of elegiac components to the polyphonic narrative of his verse novel, on the one hand, and Baratynsky's method of doing this in *Eda* on the other. To what extent Pushkin was familiar with *Eda* when composing the beginning of chapter 4 remains an open question.¹¹¹ But even if he was not—or was not firsthand or in toto—the larger historical question remains, not dissipating in mere coincidence.

The overarching story of *Eugene Onegin* famously pivots on four fragments of love discourse in verse: two love letters—Tatiana's to Onegin in chapter 4 and Onegin's to Tat'iana in chapter 8—and two spoken rejections thereof. Each of the four is both a fictional utterance in a narrative context and, at the same time, an autonomous lyric poem. Onegin's response to Tatiana's letter belongs to loveless elegies, with themes and motifs characteristic of this genre. I am unworthy of you; I am unable to love; you will fall in love with another before long—Onegin's confession to Tatiana echoes both Baratynsky's "Confession" and Pushkin's own prisoner's loveless rejection of the Circassian's love.

At first it might appear that, in making Onegin stick to the libertine rhetoric typical of a loveless elegy, Pushkin was ignoring Pletnev, Voeikov, and other critics who took the prisoner of the Caucasus to task for speaking this way to a virtuous "mountain girl." Tatiana is, after all, a virtuous rural maiden too, and likewise no deceitful "high-society coquette"—was Pushkin doubling down on his reluctance to reframe Onegin's elegiac confession to fit the narrative situation? But Pushkin's plan is more complex than that, and so is Onegin as a character. After passionate nightly trysts, the prisoner says what he says to the Circassian and they part; in an act of self-sacrifice, the Circassian sets him free; the prisoner crosses the river and disappears from our view. For Onegin, by contrast, chapter 4 is merely a beginning. Rather untypically for a loveless speaker from a doleful elegy, he makes his cold confession not *after* a nocturnal tryst with Tatiana (as would a true Lovelace) but *instead* of one. This pragmatic turn gives a new meaning to Onegin's words, or, to use today's fashionable term, reframes them.

As if to stress the ironic contradiction between the questionable overtones of Onegin's speech and his apparently righteous intentions, Pushkin slyly sums it up in his address to an imaginary reader:

Вы согласитесь, мой читатель,
Что очень мило поступил
С печальной Таней наш приятель;
Не в первый раз он тут явил
Души прямое благородство.[112]

[You will agree, my reader, / That our friend acted toward / Sad Tania very kindly; / Not for the first time did he reveal here / True nobility of soul.]

On the face of it, this sounds like a vindication, but, to repeat, Pushkin's game as an author is infinitely more complex than his presentation as narrator. Onegin the character, as Nabokov the *Onegin* scholar warns, cannot be pinned down to a reading or a type.[113]

Indeed, Onegin's "confession" from chapter 4 is preceded by four stanzas that prompt a different framing of what follows. In the first two, ruinous promiscuity—pleasure sans loving, once lauded as the "art of love"—is dismissed as the tedious game of old monkeys whose fame has faded away with their vaunted times. *Eugene Onegin*, however, is anything but a cautionary tale. While the opening as a whole represents a derisive epitaph to libertinism, its initial distich sounds like advice from a libertine's guidebook: "The less we love a woman / The easier it is to attract her." Whether owing to its foremost position or its aphoristic form, this phrase became proverbial—more so than its cautionary conclusion: "And thus more surely do we destroy her / Amid webs of seduction."[114]

As occurs more than once in *Eugene Onegin*, what we initially take for *authorial* reflections—a whole stream of them—turn out (in stanza IX) to be those of Pushkin's title *character*.[115] He too, we learn, devoted the best eight years of his life to womanizing. This led to the atrophy of feeling:

В красавиц он уж не влюблялся,
А волочился как-нибудь;
Откажут—мигом утешался;
Изменят—рад был отдохнуть.[116]

[With belles no longer did he fall in love, / But dangled after them just anyhow; / When they refused, he solaced in a twinkle; / When they betrayed, was glad to rest.]

Was Onegin's rejection of Tatiana's love an act of kindness on the part of a truly noble soul? Onegin's backstory as a seasoned libertine undermines this reading—but does not rule it out. Or, was Onegin displacing his post-love ennui onto the innocent creature offering him her love? This version, in turn, is undermined by the sudden wave of tenderness Onegin is said to have experienced on receiving Tatiana's letter: "Perhaps an ancient glow of feelings / Possessed him for a minute." This glow cooled—because, we are told, Onegin did not wish to deceive her trustful soul. Or was it, as Olga Peters Hasty suggests, Tatiana's naïveté, rather than Onegin's "nobility of soul," that saved her from the potential downfall their rendezvous would have resulted in, had Tatiana been versed enough in the language of amatory games?[117]

Onegin's confession was Pushkin's probe into elegy's narrative pragmatics. Here, Pushkin stages a collision of two logics—a narrative and elegiac one.

From a narrative perspective, Onegin behaves like a responsible older person, admonishing an idealistic maiden for an ill-advised act. In this sense, he does no harm. But the elegiac template Onegin recurs to in his speech casts Tatiana in the role of his abandoned lover—for this is the "you" loveless elegies are addressed to. What the story does, the elegy undoes—and instead of exclaiming, with the censorious old lady from Sokolov's anecdote cited in chapter 3, "such a darned girl!," we pity Tatiana as a victim of Onegin's lovelessness. The libertine semantics of Onegin's confession run almost comically counter to its fictional pragmatics. Despite the current of narration, elegy remained standing.

While most loveless elegies are doleful, not every separation was: some turned out bitter and vengeful. There were elegies for these moods as well. One way of hurting one's ex-lover was, paradoxically, to confess one's love to her or him. The trick here was in the choice of tense. "I love you" remains a nice thing to say and hear, even after you two have parted ways; "I loved you" hurts; the past tense translates love into loss, and shifts the blame onto the other's shoulders. Baratynsky's 1823 elegy "A Falling Out" ("Razmolvka") is custom-made for this:

> Кого жалеть? Печальней доля чья?
> Кто отягчён утратою прямою?—
> Легко решить: любимым не был я;
> Ты, может быть, была любима мною.[118]

[Whom to pity? Whose lot is sadder? / Who is burdened with an outright loss? / Easy to tell: I was not loved by you; / You, perhaps, were loved by me.]

Loveless echoes of Baratynsky's "A Falling Out" and, more broadly, of a host of post-love and falling-out elegies like it, can be heard, paradoxically, in Pushkin's perhaps most famous lyric poem—the one we often find to be his gentlest.

> Я вас любил: любовь еще, быть может,
> В душе моей угасла не совсем;
> Но пусть она вас больше не тревожит;
> Я не хочу печалить вас ничем.

Я вас любил безмолвно, безнадежно,
То робостью, то ревностью томим;
Я вас любил так искренно, так нежно,
Как дай вам бог любимой быть другим.[119]

[I loved you: the love, maybe, / Has not wholly expired in my heart; / But let it not bother you anymore; / I do not want to sadden you with anything. / I loved you wordlessly and hopelessly, / Anguished now by timidity, now by jealousy; / I loved you as sincerely and gently / As God grant you to be loved by another.]

No autograph copy of this poem survives, but from Pushkin's list of titles to be published, it follows that it was written in 1829.[120] A long-standing attribution links the poem to Anna Olenina, Pushkin's would-be fiancée, who eventually declined his courtship in late summer 1828.[121] While clearly a farewell elegy, Pushkin's "I loved you," much like Baratynsky's "Dissuasion," was put to sentimental music, which made it an incredibly popular sentimental ballad (*romans*) about everlasting, undying, selfless love. Even Shklovsky, in his polemics with Jakobson, labeled "Ia vas liubil" a love poem. And yet, if we turn down the music, and listen only to the motifs and grammar, we might hear another, dispassionate voice registering his "not wholly expired" love even as he relegates it to the past tense—three times in eight lines. And ending it with that famous libertine punchline: God grant that another man love you as strongly as I did. *Did*, not do. The pronoun "you" (*vas*) tells the same tale. Earlier on Pushkin, as we recall, wrote to Anna Olenina the touching poem "Thou and You," in which *ty* was the covert pronoun of his hopeful thoughts as he used the polite *vy* in spoken space. The same phenomenon is at work here, albeit now without any hopefulness in sight: the distant *vas*, that is, combines best with the *past* tense of *liubil*.

I am not saying the poem must be interpreted *this* way, only that it can be interpreted *both* ways. Pushkin, like Baratynsky, knew how to engineer ambiguity. One little clue from the immense pool of anecdotal facts amassed in Pushkin lore, in any event, does seem to sanction the loveless, post-love reading of "I loved you" alongside emotional ones. This clue is Pushkin's own one-word post-analysis of the poem. To believe Anna Olenina's granddaughter, in 1833, that is, years after Pushkin's intent to marry Olenina misfired, he made a new inscription in her album under his earlier autograph of "I loved you."[122] It consisted of a single word: *plusqueparfait*, followed by the date. This sounds like a pun: the word can be read as a self-compliment, "more than perfect," and as a grammatical category, *plus quam perfectum*, or past perfect—the tense for things buried in the distant past. In this case, the message Pushkin was sending to his former flame was "you are history." I would not be surprised if it was this grammatical aside by Pushkin that moved Roman Jakobson to make "I loved you" the star example of his essay "Poetry of Grammar and Grammar of Poetry."

The Art of Epilogue
Critique of the Golden Age in Eugene Onegin

THE BEST WAY TO ASCERTAIN what lies at the core of a literary phenomenon—a genre, a style, an author—is to see it parodied. A parody both summarizes the key features of the phenomenon and highlights its inner vulnerabilities, providing a critique of and propelling changes in a literary system. Yuri Tynianov was first to recognize the evolutionary role of parody:

> The baring of convention and the unmasking of speech behavior and speech poses are part of the enormous evolutionary work done by parody. The process of mastering any literary phenomenon is the process of mastering it as a structure, as a system connected and interrelated with the social structure. This process of mastering hastens the evolutionary succession of aesthetic movements.[1]

Throughout this book, I have described and analyzed Russian poetry of the early nineteenth century as a system. It so happened that this system received its most powerful critique in the same year—1824—as the critic Petr Pletnev pronounced it "the Golden Age of Russian literature." The critique, of which more later, came from the pen of Wilhelm Küchelbecker, in his essay "On the Direction of Our Poetry, Especially Lyric, in the Past Decade." The essay inspired Pushkin to offer his own critique of the Golden Age— ironically, within the work that became one of the most brilliant achievements of said age (and of Russian literature overall): *Eugene Onegin* (hereafter *EO*). Here, the critique takes the form of a parody condensed in the figure of a fictional poet, Vladimir Lensky. My task in this final chapter is to expose the lines of Pushkin's parody and critique of the Golden Age as the latter has been portrayed in this book: as a system of relationships between poets, poems, and readers. To do so, we must first take a step back to the beginning—both of Pushkin's poetry and Pushkin's problems.

Two "Liberties" in One

Since adolescence, Pushkin, along with those he had mingled with—largely, though not exclusively, elder-generation Karamzinians—had nurtured an aspiration that was at odds with the program they avowed. What they said, and how they wrote, all went to espouse "light poetry" with its "live address," the cult of minor forms, user-friendliness, an almost amateur attitude toward poetry. Yet, at the same time, Pushkin and his elder poet-friends harbored a more serious ambition: to surprise the world with a king-size work of a major genre. This dream was a little embarrassing; after all, a majestic achievement of this kind was precisely the cause openly venerated by their opponents—the "archaist" literary group. Yet it was Batiushkov who plugged away at translating Tasso's magnum opus, and it was Zhukovsky who attempted (if unsuccessfully) to write an epic poem (to be called *Vladimir*). Only a few succeeded in what would count as a major life achievement, and each of these came at a price. Gnedich's translation of *The Iliad* pushed everything else he wrote to the brink of oblivion; most radically, Karamzin renounced verse entirely, and chose history as his sole field of endeavor.

The war called (then as now) "Patriotic," and German influences in literature and philosophy, intensified the search for a national core: the sought-after major form would also be a national one. One easy solution was generic compromise—the devising, that is, of surrogates for this major form: for instance, Zhukovsky's "Twelve Sleeping Maidens" ("Dvenadtsat' spiashchikh dev"), "Bard in the Camp of Russian Warriors," and "Epistle to Voeikov" are large in size but oriented toward the chamber genres of the ballad, the drinking song, and the epistle, respectively.

Pushkin's toying with national epic in *Ruslan and Liudmila*, which appeared in 1820, could be seen, against this backdrop, as a parody of the very demand for a national epic. A young man of twenty had, with seeming effortlessness, composed what was considered to be the crowning achievement of a poet's career, a guarantee of poetic immortality, and the Mount Olympus of the genre system. As Oleg Proskurin has shown in his recent commentary to *Ruslan and Liudmila*, Pushkin drew more upon comic than on serious epic models—as often happens in the history of literature, a lacuna was filled, but not in the box where the check was expected.[2] By making a shift of a single degree, from the heroic to the heroi-comic, the work simultaneously solves the problem and obviates it with a demonstration of its inadequacy. Shifting is precisely how the demand for a national epic would be met later as well: first, through a shift into another artistic medium (*A Life for the Tsar* [*Zhizn' za tsaria*] by Egor Rozen and Mikhail Glinka); then, through a shift from poetry to prose (*War and Peace* [*Voina i mir*]).

Ruslan and Liudmila brought Pushkin success (Zhukovsky rather slyly recognized him as his "conquering pupil"), but for him, (mock) national epic represented little more than an impasse: the form had been used to full capacity.[3] Meanwhile, Pushkin immersed himself in lyric of every possible genre, and it is precisely within the lyric that he began to sense, paradoxically, a new constructive principle for a major verse form: the free montage (that is, one not welded seamlessly but held together purely by contiguity) of lyrical (and other poetic) genres. The overall form that grew out of this principle of loose connectedness would be united (if you will) by its unboundedness—the free play between elements and parts, that is, constitutes its primary structural material.

I will cite an example that demonstrates how this principle works in its most embryonic state. Apparently in late 1817 or 1818 (the date remains a matter of debate), Pushkin wrote his famous ode "Liberty" ("Vol'nost'"), a long philosophico-political oratory (of almost one hundred lines) in sublime style.[4] It begins thus:

Беги, сокройся от очей,
Цитеры слабая царица!
Где ты, где ты, гроза царей,
Свободы гордая певица?
Приди, сорви с меня венок,
Разбей изнеженную лиру—
Хочу воспеть Свободу миру,
На тронах поразить порок.[5]

[Flee, vanish from my eyes, / Cythera's feeble princess! / Where art thou, where art thou, bane of kings, / Freedom's proud singer? / Come, tear from me the wreath, / Smash the effeminate lyre ... / I want to sing [of] Freedom for the world, / Strike at vice upon thrones.[6]]

This is a traditional move of invoking the muse, in this case through opposition: the odic muse is summoned; the erotic one (Aphrodite, "Cythera's feeble princess") is banished.

Pushkin's "Liberty" was not published during the poet's lifetime. The following manuscript versions are considered the most authoritative: (1) an authorial fair copy (*belovoi avtograf*)—as the commentators in the most recent Pushkin academic edition put it, a "show" (*paradnyi*) copy—from the archive of the Turgenev brothers (who in many ways inspired this effort by Pushkin); (2) twenty lines written by Pushkin "in a careless hand" on a manuscript in the same archive, on which Aleksandr Turgenev recorded several more lines of "Liberty," although the first half of the text is missing entirely; and (3) an authorized copy in the Ostafievo archive of the princes Viazemsky.[7] The first and third of these primary sources contain what are conventionally called the early and late versions of the text, respectively.

Following the text of "Liberty," both manuscripts contain another poem in the author's hand (now published separately), written in a genre directly opposed to the ode. This is the madrigal "To Princess Golitsyna. Sending Her the Ode 'Liberty'" ("Kniagine G[olitsyn]oi. Posylaia ei odu 'Vol'nost'"):

> Простой воспитанник природы,
> Так я, бывало, воспевал
> Мечту прекрасную свободы
> И ею сладостно дышал.
> Но вас я вижу, вам внимаю,
> И что же?... слабый человек!...
> Свободу потеряв навек,
> Неволю сердцем обожаю.[8]

[A simple pupil of nature, / Thus I used to sing of / The splendid dream of Freedom / And breathed it sweetly. / But then I see you, hear you, / And so?... man is weak! / Losing freedom for ever, / I adore captivity with my heart.[9]]

As Vadim Parsamov (one of the few scholars to have written about this poem and analyze the playful juxtaposition these two texts constitute) observes, the madrigal for Golitsyna "entirely undermines the proud pathos of political freethinking [in 'Liberty']."[10] I view it, however, as more of a dialogue between different lyric voices treating the problem of freedom from two perspectives—the political and the amatory, the serious and the gallant—not so much canceling each other out as complicating one another.

What Parsamov calls "pathos" is not undermined—such a sabotage would be hard to substantiate, considering how widely "Liberty" has been regarded as precisely a political text—so much as defamiliarized by the introduction of another perspective, specifically, the author's perspective on his own "Liberty" ("Thus I used to sing"). As a result, the ode is suddenly displaced into the past; the "voice" of the ode is no longer equated with the author's; the foundational lyric convention of the "here and now" is broken; the juxtaposition of past and present lyric voices begins to function as an edit. A simple contrasting collocation becomes an interaction—as in Sergei Eisenstein's montage theory, from the collision of two, a third is born.

Such a plot twist has an illustrious precedent in Horace's second epode ("Blessed is he . . ." ["Beatus ille . . ."]), an emotional panegyric to rural life, modesty, and domesticity. As we are surprised to learn in the last lines of the text, the speaker is not a virtuous tiller of the soil but a predatory moneylender, who has never entertained any ideas of "downshifting" to a rural lifestyle. Many translators preferred to discard the text's defamiliarizing ending; the formula *Beatus ille* remains a label of rural modesty.[11] As mentioned earlier in this book, the afterlife of poetic texts often simplifies and flattens their semantic structures in the pursuit of plain morals and convenient one-liners. Returning to *EO*, this is precisely what has happened with Pushkin's own take on "Beatus ille . . . ," the tenth stanza of chapter 8:

Блажен, кто смолоду был молод,
Блажен, кто вовремя созрел,
Кто постепенно жизни холод
С летами вытерпеть умел;
Кто странным снам не предавался,
Кто черни светской не чуждался,
Кто в двадцать лет был франт иль хват,
А в тридцать выгодно женат;
Кто в пятьдесят освободился
От частных и других долгов,
Кто славы, денег и чинов
Спокойно в очередь добился,
О ком твердили целый век:
N. N. прекрасный человек.[12]

[Blessed is he who was young in his youth, / Blessed is he who matured in time, / Who gradually learned with the years / How to endure life's coldness; / Who didn't give himself to strange dreams, / Who didn't keep aloof from the high-society mob, / Who was a dandy or a fop when he was twenty, / Married with fortune at thirty; / Who, at fifty, was free from private and other debts, / Who achieved fame, money, and ranks / Calmly, in his turn, / About whom people always said: / N. N. is a fine man.[13]

The line "Blessed is he who was young in his youth" ("Блажен, кто смолоду был молод]") has become an oft-cited piece of "folk wisdom," even though the life trajectory described in the stanza as a whole is treated with ironic contempt. In *EO*, such shifts occur all the time. In fact, the novel's narration opens this way, with the turn between stanzas I and II replicating Horace's trick in the second epode: what we took for authorial voice in the first stanza turns out in the second to have been *Onegin's* thoughts. The unfolding of *EO* is retroactive rather than cumulative: every new stanza can change the meaning of the previous one(s).

Pushkin had experimented with this trick earlier, in "Liberty," whose "bifurcated" text—an ode-cum-madrigal—is arguably Pushkin's first attempt at joining two dissonant lyrical texts into a single poetic whole by means of montage. I would even go so far as to claim that Pushkin, intending this dissonant effect, saw the "Liberty" ode and the madrigal to Golitsyna as a unified text, and that, indeed, they should be published and analyzed as such.[14] Here is why. Of the three authoritative manuscript sources of "Liberty," two consist of both the ode and the madrigal to Golitsyna (and the third, lacking the first half of the ode, is obviously incomplete). Indeed, the Ostafievo archive manuscript includes the ode's text faithfully copied out, and Pushkin nevertheless considered it necessary to write the text of the madrigal himself—a clear sign of authorial intent.[15] In the authorial fair copy in the Turgenev archive, Pushkin's signature and the date are found not directly under the text of the ode, but under the added madrigal, as if signaling Pushkin's finalization of them thus as a unified text.[16] Moreover, the madrigal is written in a nearly identical stanzaic form: aBaBcDDc for the ode, AbAbCddC for the madrigal. This is the same eight-line stanza with alternating rhymes in one quatrain and a ring rhyme in the other, except with masculine and feminine rhymes consistently switched.

There is one other decisive factor indicating that the madrigal belongs to the text of "Liberty," a factor related directly to poetic pragmatics. In the extraordinarily vast literature on the "Liberty" ode, including on its versions and dating, one simple question has not yet been posed: why did the madrigal to Golitsyna appear in the autograph kept by the Turgenevs and in Viazemsky's authorized copy in the first place? If Pushkin had seen this poem as a typical gallant madrigal meant to accompany a missive, he would have sent or given it directly to Princess Golitsyna along with a copy of the ode, and the story would have ended there. Instead, Pushkin included it in both the Turgenevs' authorial manuscript and Viazemsky's copy. Considering the Turgenevs' and Viazemsky's tendency to disseminate manuscripts on a virtually industrial scale, this was effectively a sanction for "manuscript publication" (and this is exactly what happened with both the copies of the "Liberty" ode in question, from which all the numerous extant copies of the ode derive).[17] The only scholar to come close to posing this question was Iulian Oksman, who reckoned that the fair autograph in the Turgenev archive had actually been intended for Golitsyna but was for some reason left by Pushkin to be relayed to the princess through the Turgenevs, who failed him in this mission.[18] Unfortunately, this hypothesis rests on two unknowns, and in any case does nothing to explain why Pushkin inscribed the madrigal into Viazemsky's copy as well.

Including the madrigal in the text of "Liberty" (as a coda or epilogue) changes this text's composition, lending it, specifically, a circular structure; now we have a work that begins with the banishment of the amatory (Aphrodite) and ends with the amatory coming back to reclaim the poet. This is not incidental. The versions of the ode conventionally labeled "first" and "second" (from the authorial fair copy in the Turgenevs' archive and Viazemsky's copy, respectively) differ substantially only with regard to their endings. The first ends with a depiction of Paul I being murdered and the line "The crowned villain is no more." The final stanza in the authorial fair copy, the "moral" that concludes the ode ("And now, learn your lesson, tsars"), is written in Aleksandr Turgenev's hand, whereas in the second copy it is included in the main text. The Turgenev brothers' role in the creation of "Liberty" is well known—especially the role played by Nikolai Turgenev, a liberal economist with serious political ambitions, who would later be convicted in absentia among the Decembrists.[19] In the latter half of the 1810s, he was busy forming a political movement with a liberal agenda on the basis of the Arzamas literary society, among others, as Maria Maiofis has recently shown.[20] The political program of the "Liberty" ode, to be sure, is closely related to that of Turgenev, if not directly derived from it. (It is no surprise that the eighteen-year-old Pushkin would fall under the influence of the charismatic Turgenev.) There is reason to think that the appearance of the last stanza as a conclusion and moral to the ode was also suggested by Nikolai Turgenev, who was prone to moralizing—this stanza summarizes his political platform, and could almost be his battle cry—or perhaps by both Turgenev brothers.

Despite Turgenev's intellectual influence, however, Pushkin was not at this point (or ever) about to become the mouthpiece of someone else's political program, nor play the role of mentee to even his most well-meaning older friends. After graduating from the lyceum in June 1817 and freeing himself from its fairly barracks-like court regime, he entered into political conversations with the Turgenevs, chased beautiful actresses, fell in love with high-society belles, played cards, visited bordellos, and wrote *Ruslan and Liudmila*—without particularly prioritizing any one of these activities. The older members of Arzamas, including the Turgenev brothers, chided him for his laziness and loose conduct. Pushkin laughed this off. In November 1817, he wrote an epistle to Aleksandr Turgenev, responding to the latter's reproaches. I cite the final stanza:

> Не вызывай меня ты боле
> К навек оставленным трудам,
> Ни к поэтической неволе,
> Ни к обработанным стихам.
> Что нужды, если и с ошибкой
> И слабо иногда пою?
> Пускай Нинета лишь улыбкой
> Любовь беспечную мою
> Воспламенит и успокоит!
> А труд и холоден и пуст;
> Поэма никогда не стоит
> Улыбки сладострастных уст.[21]

[Do not call me anymore / To the labors forever left behind, / Nor to poetic captivity, / Nor to refined verses. / So what, if I sing sometimes erroneously / And weakly? / Only let Nineta's smile / Ignite and calm / My careless love! / But labor is cold and vain; / A [long] poem is never worth / The smile of voluptuous lips.]

Passing the epistle along to Zhukovsky, Turgenev made the following comment: "I send you an epistle written to me by Pushkin, [nicknamed] Cricket, whom I rebuke daily for his idleness and neglect of his studies. To this [conduct] are added vulgar philandering and the equally vulgar freethinking of the eighteenth century. Where is the sustenance for a poet? Meanwhile, he wastes his talent on trifles. Give him a talking to."²²

Pushkin's epistle comes across as yet another pledge of loyalty to light verse, provoked, in this case, by Turgenev's summons to "labor," by which he apparently meant work on *Ruslan*. For our purposes, the most important lines of Pushkin's epistle are "Do not call me anymore / To labors, forever left behind, / Nor to poetic captivity." Here, Pushkin equates Turgenev's "labors" with "captivity." Poetic commitment (to a major form, in the vein of *Ruslan*, demanding effort and an integral vision) means "captivity" for Pushkin, the loss of the poet's freedom to write whatever he wants—especially when this commitment is demanded by another person.

The word "captivity" in the epistle to Turgenev sheds light on the semantics of Pushkin's verbal play with "freedom" and "captivity" in the "Liberty" ode and madrigal to Golitsyna. Although inspired by Turgenev's political agenda, Pushkin nevertheless refuses the role of bard of Russian constitutionalism—not because he was uncomfortable with constitutionalism per se, but because he saw *any* role as too constricting a commitment, as a captivity. This is why he insisted on including the madrigal to Golitsyna at the end of the "Liberty" text; it allowed him to slip out of that role, to escape from "poetic captivity."

The Turgenevs expected a moralizing ending from Pushkin, and he indeed produced a final stanza with a "lesson for tsars." The authorized copy from the Ostafievo archive establishes the text of the ode in its finished form, including the moralizing ending. Yet Pushkin insists on *his own* ending and adds the madrigal, as if deliberately informing his mentors that the end of *his* "Liberty" will be not a finalizing moral for the ode but instead a way out. The ode remains an ode, its political pathos none the weaker, but the poet—like the gingerbread man or a snake that sheds its skin—ensures himself an exit strategy.

The lyric genre of the ode—even one to "Liberty"—harbors the same threat of "captivity" as an epic labor on a large scale. This is not the "captivity" of labor but the "captivity" of a performative speech act, of one who says "yes" before an altar or under oath. Pushkin was prepared to "sing of Freedom" but as a poet was unprepared to pledge allegiance to constitutionalism, or to the Turgenevs, or the odic genre, or the national epic. To this end, he needed to include another voice (also his own!) at the end of "Liberty." Behind the juxtaposition of two "liberties"—the ode and the madrigal, the political principle and the gallant flirt—stands a third "liberty," for Pushkin, the highest type:

the freedom of the poet. This is where we first begin to sense the form of the "free novel" (as Pushkin called *EO*), with its present but evasive author, built upon the discord among lyric tones, and striving for an open ending.[23]

Author versus Hero versus Poet

The action of *EO* begins with a departure from Petersburg. In his notebook, Pushkin recorded the date he began work on the text as 28 May 1823. A little farther up on the same page, he wrote another date: 9 May. Seven years later, when he summed up his work on *EO*, he started counting the time spent on this work from the same date: 9 May 1823. As Sergei Fomichev convincingly argues, Pushkin most likely did begin working on the first stanza of chapter 1 on 28 May but chose to date this commencement (and thereby the departure of his protagonist) as 9 May—the third anniversary of the author's own departure from Petersburg. This departure—caused, among other politically risky actions, by the "Liberty" ode—was a symbolic landmark in Pushkin's biography.[24]

Such a deliberate alignment with the protagonist seems strange for an author who also claimed to be "always glad to emphasize the difference / Between Onegin and myself" ("Всегда я рад заметить разность / Между Онегиным и мной"). Nonetheless, the remove between author and protagonist in *EO* is not constant; indeed, what Pushkin does by constantly modulating this distance is to turn this complex curve of approaches and withdrawals into a subplot of sorts, a separate intrigue.[25]

That who is speaking to us at each moment in *EO* is remarkably elusive and mobile goes back to Pushkin's earlier experiments in the southern poems and beyond—to supra-lyrical entities like "Liberty." While in "Liberty" Pushkin tried to transcend the limits of the lyric "I" simply by tacking on another lyric "I" and marking the temporal distance between the two, in the southern poems—*The Prisoner of the Caucasus*, *The Fountain of Bakhchisarai* (*Bakhchisaraiskii Fontan*), and *The Gypsies* (*Tsygany*)—the correlation between the lyric and the narrative is more intricate than that.

In the early nineteenth century, lyric poetry was generally understood as non-narrative. This understanding does not mean, however, that lyric and narrative genres lived apart. As we saw earlier in this book, fictional characters in *Prisoner* and *Eda* speak in elegiac inserts, as does Onegin in the fourth chapter of *EO*. In Pushkin's southern poems, the interaction between the lyric and the narrative is not confined to direct speech. Take the authorial voice.

Unlike in *Ruslan and Liudmila*, in which the "author" playfully interferes in the action, no overt interventions of the authorial "I" are found in the narrative segments of Pushkin's southern poems—or, none are found, unless we dig deeper and look for lyric (that is, typically "authorial") traces hidden within characters' lines and so on. Conversely, the authorial presence is stressed in non-narrative, extra-diegetic parts of the southern poems, such as dedications and epilogues. Here, this presence is markedly lyric. The lyric, then, is present in the southern poems on two different planes, and has a different function on each plane. In the narrative parts, the lyric serves as verse material; in non-narrative ones, it functions as wrapping material, as it were. Flanked by the dedication, epilogue, and other non-narrative parts, the narrative found itself snugly "wrapped" in lyric, in the author's lyric persona—turning what appeared, on the face of it, a self-sufficient piece of storytelling into an authorial tale.

Pushkin began work on *EO* while still in the south, and by all appearances it was also supposed to become a southern poem of sorts (minus the exoticism); at the very least, Pushkin was planning to send Onegin to the Caucasus and Odessa. Onegin's journey never entered the main text, but Pushkin included "fragments" from the journey as an appendix to the novel in the first full edition of 1833. Thus, as Tynianov has correctly remarked, the text concludes not with the protagonist's love fiasco but with the final line from the "Fragments from Onegin's Journey": "And so, I was living at the time in Odessa..." ("Итак, я жил тогда в Одессе...").[26] The composition took on a circular form, though this circle was closed with events not from the life of the protagonist but of the author: it was Pushkin who lived in Odessa when the novel was begun.

The complex proxemics between author and protagonist, the poet and Onegin, began with a blatant misdirection. Even before the first chapter of *EO* appeared in print, Pushkin submitted part of the second chapter to *Severnye tsvety na 1825 god* under the title "Excerpts from *Eugene Onegin, a Narrative Poem by A. Pushkin*." This publication consisted of stanzas VII through X, containing a portrait of Lensky, in abridged form. As scholars have noted, the published fragment, with abridgements made exclusively at the ends of stanzas, leaves the author's irony toward his character to some extent muted. For instance, the lines "He sang of life's faded bloom / At not quite eighteen years of age" ("Он пел поблекший жизни цвет / Без малого в осмнадцать лет") were omitted.[27] Here, the character comes across as a bit naïve, but a poet-hero nonetheless, and an appropriate subject for a bildungsroman. What has remained unnoted is that Lensky's name does not appear in the published excerpts, and so readers would have ended up with the impression that the poet-hero being described was, in fact, Eugene Onegin (duly mentioned in the title of the publication). After getting their hands on the first and then second chapter of *EO*, readers would have realized that they had been doubly deceived: Lensky turns out to be less than a hero; Onegin, to be no poet.

We now return to the "difference" the author of *EO* insists on at the end of the first chapter (stanzas LV–LX).[28] The reason for this "difference" is trifling: Onegin is bored living in the countryside, while the author enjoys village life: "Flowers, love, countryside, leisure, / Fields! I am devoted to you with all my soul" ("Цветы, любовь, деревня, праздность, / Поля! я предан вам душой"). These stanzas were written in the autumn of 1823, in Odessa, and the praise of rural life in stanza LV, just like Horace's "Beatus ille...," amounts to little more than wishful thinking. After unsuccessfully requesting leave, Pushkin was obliged, unlike his characters, to keep serving (that is, at the very least, to physically remain in his place of service), and his Horatian leisure, which seems to be conveyed deliberately in the quasi-autobiographical present tense ("Each morning I wake up / For sweet bliss and freedom: / I read a little, sleep a lot"), remains an ironic projection of the common image of a poet—a downgraded version of what Batiushkov, as described in chapter 4, called "poetic dietetics."

This oversold "difference" is entirely contrived—Pushkin himself betrays the true purpose of this maneuver: to mark his difference not from Onegin, but from Byron:

Всегда я рад заметить разность
Между Онегиным и мной,
Чтобы насмешливый читатель
Или какой-нибудь издатель
Замысловатой клеветы,
Сличая здесь мои черты,
Не повторял потом безбожно,
Что намарал я свой портрет,
Как Байрон, гордости поэт,
Как будто нам уж невозможно
Писать поэмы о другом,
Как только о себе самом.[29]

[I'm always glad to emphasize the difference / Between Onegin and me, / So that a sarcastic reader / Or some publisher / Of a sophisticated slander, / Looking for my traits here, / Won't mercilessly repeat later, / That I drew my own portrait, / As did Byron, the poet of pride, / As if we were unable / To write long poems about anything else / Other than ourselves.]

It is not by chance that this disclaimer and the name Byron appear toward the end of the first chapter. Its action begins with a departure from Petersburg and ends with an arrival in the countryside. Byron's narrative poems *Don Juan* and *Childe Harold* are essentially travelogues; the autobiographical *Childe Harold*, like *EO*, begins with a departure caused by boredom. But, instead of the adventures and hotspots through which Byron guides his heroes and readers, in the first chapter Pushkin brings his protagonist to the final destination, a boring countryside locale, where he soon grows bored again. In contrast to Byron's plots, the hero's journey does not advance the narrative at all; the action has not yet begun. At this point of deceleration in the story (a dead end, even), Pushkin makes the last "digression" of the chapter—not a lyrical digression but a meta-lyrical one.

After stressing the difference first between himself and Onegin, and then between himself and Byron, Pushkin proceeds to the next negative comparison, perhaps the most important to him of all—nothing less than a contrast between himself and "all poets":

LVII.

Замечу кстати: все поэты—
Любви мечтательной друзья.
Бывало, милые предметы
Мне снились, и душа моя
Их образ тайный сохранила;
Их после муза оживила:
Так я, беспечен, воспевал
И деву гор, мой идеал,
И пленниц берегов Салгира.
Теперь от вас, мои друзья,
Вопрос нередко слышу я:
"О ком твоя вздыхает лира?
Кому, в толпе ревнивых дев,
Ты посвятил ее напев?"[30]

[In this connection, I would emphasize [that] all poets [are] / Friends of dreamy love. / It used to be that dear subjects / Appeared in my dreams, and my soul / Kept their secret image; / Later, the muse brought them to life: / Carefree, thus I used to sing of / The mountain maiden, my ideal, / And the captives of the banks of the Salgir. / Now, my friends, I often hear from you / The question: / "Whom is your lyre sighing about? / To whom, among the jealous maidens, / Do you dedicate its melody?"]

The answer is: no one. The two subsequent stanzas provide, back-to-back, two single-line aphorisms about poetry-making vis-à-vis the poet's current feelings: "But, while in love, I was dumb and mute" ("Но я, любя, был глуп и нем") and "Once love had passed, the Muse appeared" ("Прошла любовь, явилась муза"). Both aphorisms insist on distancing, on mutual autonomy in relationships between poetry and feelings. The Golden Age, by default, expected a lyric poem to be felicitous both on paper and in love, that is, to succeed poetically and pragmatically. Pushkin disputes this default setting, claiming his independence as a poet. The most hackneyed of all possible clichés is "a poet in love." Pushkin's ideal is "a poet out of love":

"Чей взор, волнуя вдохновенье,
Умильной лаской наградил
Твое задумчивое пенье?
Кого твой стих боготворил?"
И, други, никого, ей-богу!

["Whose inspiring glance / Rewarded with a sweet caress / Your pensive singing? / Whom did your verse worship?" / Nay, no one, my friends, I swear to God!]

The above principle of distancing reaches back as far as Pushkin's epilogue to "Liberty," his madrigal to Golitsyna. Attesting to this lineage, for instance, is stanza LVII's seventh line ("Carefree, thus I used to sing" ["Так я, беспечен, воспевал"]), which repeats almost verbatim the line "Thus I used to sing" ("Так я, бывало, воспевал") from the beginning of the madrigal. As Pushkin discovered, the freedom from pragmatics such distancing provides works both ways: whether the epilogue catapults you from the political to the amatory (as in "Liberty") or away from the amatory, as it occurs in the above-quoted stanza.

The flurry of "differences" (from Onegin, from Byron, from "all poets") will be taken to its logical conclusion in the second chapter of *EO*. Here, "all poets" crystallize in one—the love-struck poet par excellence: Vladimir Lensky.³¹ It is to Lensky that Pushkin delegates the clichéd role of poet in love. Thus, in *EO* Pushkin liberates himself from the role of poet; the correlation of protagonist and author now plays out not on the straight axis of their mutual proxemics but along a triangle: author, hero, poet.

Two Lenskys in One, or the Power of Codas

Like everything else in *EO*, the figure of Lensky is not uniform but changes from chapter to chapter depending on immediate literary and historical context (the chapters involving Lensky, the second through the sixth, were written between 1823 and 1826). Of all the characters in *EO*, however, no other underwent so profound an evolution from draft to print version as Lensky—an evolution that forced Pushkin to rewrite certain lines entirely.

In the scholarly literature, discussions of Lensky have primarily concerned the stylistic and generic dimensions of his poetry, which have, in their turn, given rise to political questions. Tynianov was the first to point to an inconsistency in the character's poetic affiliation: Lensky is presented at one moment as the modest author of elegies in ladies' albums; at another, as a solemn poet, even a satirist à la Juvenal (in draft versions: "But more often it was with an angry satire / That his verse was animated" ["Но чаще гневною сатирой / Одушевлялся стих его"], "injustice and oppression ... stirred his blood from early on" ["несправедливость, угнетение ... в нем рано волновали кровь"]; in the published text: "indignation and compassion" ["Негодованье, сожаленье"]). But according to Tynianov, Pushkin never strove for definiteness in his characters; quite the opposite, "in the depiction of Lensky, the basis of the 'characters' of *Eugene Onegin* ... becomes evident—their traits are important to Pushkin not in themselves, not in their typicality, but as giving occasion for digression; Lensky is a composite [*kombinirovannyi*] 'poet,' a solemn elegist."³² Vladimir Nabokov put it this way: "Pushkin wavered between making Lenski [sic] a feeble elegiac minstrel and having him be a violent political poet."³³ Lotman examined in detail the heightened, "civic" plane in Lensky's depiction, including drafts, and came to the conclusion that the "original version of his characterization defined the political orientation of Lensky's poetry significantly more sharply, aligning it with the positions that

Pushkin's Decembrist friends in Petersburg and Kishinev insistently tried to inculcate in him," but Pushkin "in the finished text of the second chapter removed this complicated literary polemic, insofar as it had lost its relevance since the completion of the chapter's initial draft."[34] Proskurin rejects the solemn component in Lensky's depiction entirely: "Lensky is a pure elegiac poet.... This is very far from the 'Decembrist' ideal of true poetry."[35]

This conundrum is worth figuring out. The initial portrait of Lensky, occupying stanzas VI through X of chapter 2 in the final text, was written in the autumn of 1823, in Odessa. It is a few stanzas longer than in the published version and contains no trace of equivocation; here, Lensky is conveyed with palpable albeit subtle irony (no stronger than the irony of the description of Onegin in chapter 1) as someone given to sentimental enthusiasm.[36] Vadim Vatsuro justly links the image of Lensky to the Schillerian version of the early nineteenth-century cult of sensibility (which, in the Russian context, reigned first and foremost among the Friendly Literary Society; as we recall, this included such figures as Andrei Turgenev and Zhukovsky).[37] In the draft version, Lensky shows none of the "compositeness" Tynianov describes—this is, rather, a totally integrated complex of values, which includes a striving for virtue, seriousness and purity of intentions, sensibility and empathy (to victims of injustice, among others), the cult of friendship as a fraternity of souls, and exalted love in a neo-Platonic key.[38]

For Pushkin, the primary published source for knowledge on this subject was Madame de Staël's *On Germany*; among his nearest personal acquaintances, the adepts of this ethical philosophy were the Turgenev brothers.[39] The three that Pushkin personally knew all studied in Göttingen. As has been noted, Pushkin must have had the Turgenevs in mind when he characterized Lensky with the line "His soul is straight from Göttingen" ("С душою прямо Геттингенской"). He rewrote the line several times, invariably preserving the word "Göttingen" in the rhyming position (*Lenskoi / Gettingenskoi*). To keep it there, he was even obliged to change his character's surname (the draft originally had the name "Vladimir Kholmskoi").[40]

As Lotman aptly puts it, this ethical ideal was "insistently inculcated" in Pushkin in Petersburg, but Lotman certainly exaggerates its "Decembrist" orientation. Even the most politically active of the Turgenevs, Nikolai, scolded Pushkin for writing anti-government epigrams; to the Turgenevs, these were "trifles," in the same category as his "vulgar philandering," his "idleness and neglectfulness"—things unworthy of the high calling of a poet. The matter under discussion is clearly ethics, not politics. The Turgenevs' concerns were shared by their mutual friends, who complained about Pushkin in similar fashion. In a letter to Aleksandr Turgenev, Batiushkov proposed a solution: "It would be no bad thing to lock [Pushkin] up in Göttingen and feed him milk soup and logic for three years or so . . . However great the Cricket's [Pushkin's] talent may be, he will waste it if . . . but may the muses and our prayers save him!"[41] (Turgenev may have shown this letter to Pushkin for "pedagogical" purposes.)

Thus, the Lensky of the first draft was no "feeble elegiac minstrel," nor was he a "violent political poet"; he embodied, rather, the ideal of the sensitive and sublime poet imposed on Pushkin since the Lyceum by his older friends. Within the plot structure of *EO*, Lensky is conceived as Onegin's primary antagonist. When beginning work on chapter 2, Pushkin did not yet have the novel's intrigue entirely thought out, but three main characters were already in place. The triangle is made up of a heroine (Ol'ga) and two contrasting heroes: a "sensitive" one and a "cold" one.[42]

The "wavering" that Nabokov describes came later, after Pushkin edited the Lensky-portrait stanzas in the first fair copy of chapter 2.[43] Here they are still fairly close to the draft versions.[44] Then, in September 1824, Pushkin sat down to work on them again, preparing to send four stanzas, from VII to X, to Del'vig, who had requested "about twenty lines" from *EO* for his *Severnye tsvety*.[45] The fragment published in Del'vig's almanac, with (as mentioned above) the endings missing in three of four stanzas, attests to Pushkin's vacillations. He had already rejected the first, mildly ironic versions of the three stanzas' endings but had not yet written new ones, so Del'vig received them as they were, with omissions.

In the spring of 1825, Pushkin began work on the second fair copy, which he would send to Viazemsky in late April. Its text was similar to the final version; this was where the openly mocking stanza endings finally appeared. These new endings turned Lensky into an almost comic figure—in stanzas VII and X, for instance: "To him, the purpose of our life / Was an enticing riddle; / He racked his brains over it / And suspected marvels" ("Цель жизни нашей для него / Была заманчивой загадкой / Над ней он голову ломал / И чудеса подозревал") and, "He sang of life's faded bloom / At not quite eighteen years of age" ("Он пел поблеклый жизни цвет, / Без малого в осьмнадцать лет").[46] As Lev Sidiakov has established, the second fair copy was preceded by a rough draft of endings to stanzas VI, VII, VIII, and X written on the same pages in the notebook (no. 835) in which Pushkin was writing the middle of the fourth chapter.[47]

Thus, in the autumn of 1823, Pushkin depicted Lensky as a perfectly likable young enthusiast, in September 1824 he began to reconsider this depiction, and in the spring of 1825, he added overtly comic characteristics, downgrading Lensky as a hero. This turnaround may have had at least two motivations. First, the plan for the novel's plot had changed: in the second part of chapter 2 (after Lensky), Tatiana appears, and the existing triangle is canceled out as a result; in chapter 3, the plot takes off in the direction of Tatiana's love for Onegin and her letter. (The completion of the third chapter's rough draft is dated 2 October 1824.) Pushkin would return to Lensky only in the middle of chapter 4, after Onegin's "confession" to Tatiana. He was still not entirely sure where to turn next (the motif of the Larins' departure for Moscow appears in the drafts; this means that the name-day party and the duel had not yet been planned), but it is clear from this that Tatiana took over Lensky's place as second protagonist, which untied Pushkin's hands as far as Lensky was concerned.[48]

Secondly, a significant event in literary polemics took place in the summer of 1824. Against the background of the predictable critical activity—which consisted of quarreling between "classicists" and "romantics," as well as unpleasant, but also predictable, reproaches aimed at the morals of the younger generation of poets—an article appeared by Wilhelm Küchelbecker called "On the Direction of Our Poetry, Especially Lyric, in the Past Decade," which questioned, point-blank, the Golden Age's predominant literary values: "Have we gained by exchanging the ode for the elegy and the epistle?"[49]

The essay staged a veritable battle scene between the genres of ode and elegy, in which the noble thundering of odes was destined to prevail over the pitiable and beggarly existence of elegies. In the plane of poetry's pragmatics, Küchelbecker proceeds from two different modes of verbal impact inherent in ode on the one hand and elegy on the other. The ode "soars, dins, and shines as it enthralls [*poraboshchaet*] the soul and ear of the reader," Küchelbecker expounds; whereas an elegy "only amuses us when, like a beggar, by begging and sobbing, it obtains (o miserable vocation!) the reader's condescension."[50] Throughout his essay, Küchelbecker mercilessly mocks doleful elegies, those of "lost youth" in particular.

While the impact of Küchelbecker's essay on the depiction of Lensky has been established in the scholarly literature, less attention has been paid to the fact that upon reading it, Pushkin went so far as to revise his early drafts. Lines like "He sang of life's faded bloom / At not quite eighteen years of age" ("Он пел поблеклый жизни цвет, / Без малого в осьмнадцать лет") were undoubtedly inspired by Küchelbecker's sarcastic formulations; only after Küchelbecker's article appeared was Lensky transformed into a doleful elegist and at the same time a semi-comic figure.

The poetic idiom in which Pushkin initially described Lensky—the idiom of sublime sensibility—is not endemic to the genre of the doleful elegy (*unylaia elegiia*). In the poetic output of the Friendly Literary Society (most famously, that of Andrei Turgenev and the early Zhukovsky), the elegy derives from German and English models and retains its proximity to the philosophical ode and high style. By the 1820s, the doleful elegy in middle style, which Küchelbecker writes about (or against) and Lensky really does imitate in chapter 6, was associated primarily with a different tradition—the French tradition of Nicolas Gilbert, Charles Hubert Millevoye, and Lamartine. In the draft versions of *EO*, Lensky is, first and foremost, a Schillerian,[51] and, as Schillerians must, exhibits an exalted ethical pathos: seethes, as we recall, at the very thought of "injustice and oppression"; demonstrates the "stirring of his blood" and even "an urge for vengeance" [*zhazhda mshchen'ia*]). All that is incompatible with the modesty of doleful elegy. ("In both the current and the ancient elegy, the poet speaks about himself, about *his* sorrows and delights," writes Küchelbecker.[52]) Pushkin accentuates the exalted character of Lensky's love poetry by organizing the tenth stanza around thrice repeating the solemn (in this context) verb "to sing": "Submissive to love, it was love that he sang. . . . He sang of parting and sadness. . . . He sang of distant lands" ("Он пел любовь, любви послушный. . . . Он пел разлуку и печаль. . . . Он пел те дальние страны"). The word "elegy" appears as such in the rough draft of chapter 2 only in the stanzas (crossed out in the first fair copy) where Pushkin sarcastically contrasts Lensky's sublime Platonism with "bards of blind pleasure" ("Bards of blind pleasure, / In vain for us do you render / The impressions of your wanton days / In vivid elegies" ["Певцы слепого упоенья / Напрасно дней <своих> блажных / Передаете впечатленья / Вы нам в элегиях живых"]).[53]

Tynianov is correct: in the draft of chapter 2, "[Lensky's] poetry is undoubtedly solemn,"[54] which makes it all the more striking how easily Pushkin transformed this sublime enthusiast into a "feeble elegiac minstrel." To do so, he had no need to rewrite entire stanzas—it only required a few new endings, mini-epilogues that retrospectively colored the sublime language of this stanza in ironic tones. Using what he had learned when working on "Liberty," Pushkin did not cross out the exaltedness trait from his Lensky but created a bimodal figure. Two modes remain relevant in Lensky: ethical pathos sits alongside the lowered plane of the doleful elegy. Thus did Lensky become Tynianov's "composite poet."[55] By combining, in his polemical ardor, his toppled idol Schiller with the "pygmies" Parny and Millevoye,[56] Küchelbecker had simplified Pushkin's task.

Lensky's compositeness had still other roots, which Pushkin put to use in *EO*. Russian Schillerianism of the early nineteenth century was in its own way experimental, assaying the combination, within a single lyric element, of the sphere of personal sensibility (put crudely, love and friendship), traditionally the province of the middle genres, and the sphere of the sublime (traditionally the subject of odes and psalms). The key text for this circle was Schiller's "Ode to Joy," which combines high and middle genres—the solemn hymn and the drinking song. This stylistic mixture was enabled by an ideological shift with neo-Platonic roots: by uniting people, friendship and love are a guarantee of harmony on earth. The joining together of people, the kinship of souls (friendship and love—platonic love, of course—are thus conflated here), is the work of the Creator, a condition of the world's creation.[57] The description of Lensky is given precisely from this perspective and in this lyric language.

In the beginning of chapter 2, Lensky is merely described; the moment he starts to act, metaphysically conceived notions of love and friendship acquire narrative agents (Ol'ga and Onegin, respectively), and the lyric ceases to work as lyric. Once wedded to a specific character, "I," "you," and "we" thus no longer act as "lyric shifters" or pronominal vacancies to be filled. This lyric tone's inadequacy vis-à-vis its object in the plot (that is, another character) is a powerful narrative force, which can be developed in two moods: the comic and the tragic. At the end of *EO*'s third chapter, it becomes clear that Pushkin walks both paths, distributing these moods across characters: Tatiana and her love story end up mainly in a tragic mood, while Lensky is mainly comic. "Mainly"—because Pushkin manipulates both moods in direct juxtaposition to one another. Thus, Tatiana's letter—a love elegy of uncommon lyric power—is accompanied by a half-comic dialogue with her nanny, while the parodic elegy by Lensky before his death is followed by his tragic demise.

Tatiana appropriates the functions originally earmarked for Lensky: the sincerity and naïveté of a "sensitive" person vis-à-vis the "cold" Onegin. The lovable properties of Lensky's heart ("He was, the dear, an ignoramus in matters of the heart" ["он сердцем милый был невежда"]; "He believed that a kindred soul / To him must be united" ["он верил, что душа родная / соединиться с ним должна"], and even the status of the lyric "I-in-love") are now equally applicable to Tatiana.⁵⁸ From this point on, *EO* becomes her bildungsroman.⁵⁹

Pushkin returns to revising Lensky's initial portrait in the rough draft for the middle of chapter 4 in early spring 1825.⁶⁰ Lensky as a character acquires comic traits; his poetry shifts to the realm of the doleful elegy. The sarcastic endings to stanzas VI, VII, VIII, and X of chapter 2 (quoted above) appear on the margins next to stanzas XXV and XXVI of chapter 4. This means that Pushkin came to his decision on Lensky's case in the middle of chapter 4.

Lensky is barely mentioned in chapter 3; the beginning of chapter 4 is devoted to Onegin's "confession" to Tatiana. Then, the "picture of happy love" between Lensky and Ol'ga beginning in stanza XXV is contrasted with Tatiana's woes. Part of the happy picture is, inevitably, Lensky's poetry: "Now on the souvenir pages [in Ol'ga's album] / Beneath the inscriptions of others / He leaves a tender verse, / Mute monument of reverie, / An instant thought's light trace / Still, after many years, the same" ("То на листках воспоминанья <в альбоме> / Пониже подписи других / Он оставляет нежный стих, / Безмолвный памятник мечтанья, / Мгновенной думы долгий след, / Все тот же после многих лет").⁶¹ The "sublime poet" Lensky transforms into a domestic versifier; the ideal of sensitive love easily allows for this. As we will see, Pushkin's decision to make of Lensky a scapegoat for literary polemic shifts the focus to poetry's pragmatics.

Ode or Elegy: "Come On, My Friend, What Is the Difference?"

The country graveyard, as we know from Gray, Zhukovsky, and Andrei Turgenev, was a constant topos of elegiac poetry and *the* place a good lyricist ought to visit. The narration of the second chapter ends with Lensky's visit to a graveyard. Predictably, the visit results in an appropriate verse, an epitaph to Ol'ga's late father: "full of sincere sadness / Vladimir [Lensky] there and then inscribed / A gravestone madrigal to him" ("и полный искренней печалью, / Владимир тут же начертал / Ему надгробный мадригал").⁶² In the same cemetery lie Lensky's own parents. In the canceled version, Pushkin mentions that Lensky's father died recently, which would have thus motivated the young man's arrival in the village.

In the draft version, Pushkin planned to introduce a contrast. Lensky would write an epitaph for Ol'ga's (presumably long-deceased) father, but not for his own: "My orphaned poet / Mourned his father's dust in silence (Mourned his father's dust without a rhyme")" ("Но мой поэт осиротелый / Оплакал молча отчий прах [Без рифм оплакал отчий прах]").⁶³ Only later does Pushkin arrive at a version close to the printed one: "He also honored with a sad inscription, / In tears, his mother and father's / Patriarchal dust" ("И там же надписью печальной / Отца и матери, в слезах, / Почтил он прах патриархальный").⁶⁴ No date of death here.

This shift is significant. Had Lensky mourned his recently deceased father "without a rhyme," he would have acted precisely in the spirit Pushkin decreed for himself at the end of the first chapter: keep your poetry at arm's length (or farther) from the emotion of the moment. Yet in the process of rewriting, the lyric poet Lensky evolved into a parody of a poet, a rhyming machine whose visit to a graveyard (especially the preferred, rural kind) must automatically result in a harvest of verses appropriate to the mood, and befitting a loyal son and future son-in-law. In other words, Lensky's poetic inspiration derives directly from his immediate environment: graveyard spells poetry.

Lensky's poetry makes its next appearance in the novel in chapter 4, in the form of "tender verse" written in an album. Pushkin pauses over albums for quite some time; the description of Lensky's album poetry, together with an "authorial" digression, takes up five whole stanzas. The two-stanza satirical digression is structured by a contrast between the albums of a "provincial miss" and a "splendid lady": the author prefers to write in the first type of album, which is unpretentious and formulaic, because his recipients "will not solemnly examine / Whether I lied wittily or not" ("не станут важно разбирать, / Остро иль нет я мог соврать").⁶⁵ In contrast, "whenever a splendid lady / Hands me her in-quarto [album], / I feel tremor and wrath, / I feel an epigram stirring in the bottom of my soul, / And yet, one is to write madrigals to them!" ("Когда блистательная дама / Мне свой in-quarto подает, / И дрожь и злость меня берет, / И шевелится эпиграмма / Во глубине моей души, / А мадригалы им пиши!").⁶⁶ This means that one must "lie" in either situation, as this is the standing order on the part of the album's owner. The following stanza opposes false "madrigals" to Lensky's sincere outpourings, which for the first time in the novel are referred to as elegies: "Whatever he notes, whatever he hears / About Ol'ga, this is what he writes about: / And full of vivid truth, / His elegies flow" ("Что ни заметит, ни услышит / Об Ольге, он про то и пишет: / И, полны истины живой, / Текут элегии рекой").⁶⁷ The ingenuousness of his lines follows directly from the sincerity of his feelings; this principle, we recall, was previously formulated by Karamzin in the same idiom in his "Epistle to Women": "No need for me to think: words flow like a river / When you converse with someone you love with all your soul." All of this, however, is a five-stanza prelude to Pushkin's argument with Küchelbecker:

XXXII.

Но тише! Слышишь? Критик строгий
Повелевает сбросить нам
Элегии венок убогий,
И нашей братье рифмачам
Кричит: "Да перестаньте плакать,
И всё одно и то же квакать,
Жалеть о *прежнем*, о *былом*:
Довольно, пойте о другом!"
—Ты прав, и верно нам укажешь
Трубу, личину и кинжал,
И мыслей мертвый капитал
Отвсюду воскресить прикажешь:
Не так ли, друг?—Ничуть. Куда!
"Пишите оды, господа,

XXXIII.

Как их писали в мощны годы,
Как было встарь заведено..."
—Одни торжественные оды!
И, полно, друг; не все ль равно?
Припомни, что сказал сатирик!
"Чужого толка" хитрый лирик
Ужели для тебя сносней
Унылых наших рифмачей?—
"Но всё в элегии ничтожно;
Пустая цель ее жалка;
Меж тем цель оды высока
И благородна..." Тут бы можно
Поспорить нам, но я молчу:
Два века ссорить не хочу.[68]

[But hush! You hear it? A stern critic / Commands us to throw off / The shabby wreath of elegies, / And shouts at us rhymesters: / "Come on, stop whining / And croaking all the same, / Lamenting what is *past* and *gone*; / Enough of that, sing of something else!" / —You are right, and I suppose you will point out to us / The trumpet, mask, and dagger, / And will order that there be revived, from wherever possible, / A dead capital of thoughts: / Is that right, my friend?— Nothing of the sort. No way! / "Write odes, gentlemen, // As they were written in the mighty age, / As was the custom in olden times . . ." / —Only celebratory odes! / Come on, my friend; what is the difference? / Recall what a satirist said! / Do you find the shrewd lyricist from "As Others See It" / More bearable than our doleful rhymesters?— / "But everything in an elegy is null; / Its empty aim is pathetic; / Compared to odes, whose aim is sublime / And noble . . ." We could argue / About that, but I'll refrain from saying anything: / I don't want to pit two ages against each other.]

The established reading of these much-discussed stanzas posits them as voicing Pushkin's ambivalence toward Küchelbecker's article. Lotman explains in his commentary, "While . . . standing in solidarity with the critical side of Küchelbecker's position, P[ushkin] could not agree with the archaizing pathos of the critic's program."[69] Indeed, Pushkin in *EO* highlights the regressive direction of Küchelbecker's program, paradoxically and parodically aligning its pathos with the elegiac mood of longing for *past* and *gone*. At the same time, Pushkin set himself a more complex task than just underscoring Küchelbecker's "archaizing pathos." His strategy was to take the two lyric genres polarized by Küchelbecker, elegy and ode, and polemically equate them ("Come on, my friend; what is the difference?") from the perspective of poetic pragmatics ("aim"), which consists in both cases of the degrading pragmatics of *being offered to the addressee in exchange for something*. This is why Pushkin also needed a long lead-up, depicting Lensky's elegies specifically in the context of albums (which imply a procedure of being offered). Just as the "shrewd lyricist" from Dmitriev's "As Others See It" ("Chuzhoi tolk") expected monetary benefits for his odes, so Lensky expects Ol'ga's favor in response to his elegies. The decisive blow against Lensky's poetic values comes at the beginning of the following stanza: "An admirer of fame and freedom, / In the excitement of his stormy thoughts, / Vladimir might have written odes, / Except that Ol'ga did not read odes" ("Поклонник славы и свободы, / В волненье бурных дум своих, / Владимир и писал бы оды, / Да Ольга не читала их").[70] A deadly parody of poetry's pragmatics.

In other words, Lensky's poetry is *entirely dependent* on its addressee and sole reader. She the reader, not he the poet, fully owns his poetry. The result is a closed circle: Lensky writes about Ol'ga for Ol'ga, and his poetry never goes beyond this circle and its primal courtship function. The pragmatic and stylistic downshifting that, as I discuss in part one of this book, engendered the verse culture of the Golden Age is here brought to its absurd limit and, to add insult to injury, is equated with the ode, to boot—a put-down because, after all, this downshifting had been undertaken in the highly *non*-odic interest of poetry's privateness and independence. In the case of Lensky, this aspired-to privacy and domesticity is degraded to a far-from-Horatian life in a provincial county, and its hard-won independence from officialdom to dependence on a future wife.

Ol'ga is not merely the addressee and reader but also the listener of Lensky's poetry:

Случалось ли поэтам слезным
Читать в глаза своим любезным
Свои творенья? Говорят,
Что в мире выше нет наград.
И впрям, блажен любовник скромный,
Читающий мечты свои
Предмету песен и любви,
Красавице приятно-томной!
Блажен... хоть, может быть, она
Совсем иным развлечена.[71]

[Have lachrymose poets ever chanced / To read their works / Before the eyes of their beloved ones? It is said, / There is no higher reward in the world. / And indeed, blessed is the humble lover, / Who reads aloud his dreams / To the subject of his songs and love, / A nicely soulful beauty! / Blessed is he ... though perhaps / It is something else entirely that she finds diverting.]

Here, another principle of the lyric culture Pushkin had grown up in is targeted—what Tynianov (as described in chapter 1) calls the "live address of the poetic word," that is, the situational and communicative proximity of poet to reader. A "lachrymose poet," Lensky is a practitioner of *dual felicity*, someone willing to kill two birds with one stone, make love and poetry at once. For his part, by contrast, the author is, by conviction, not one to take part in lyric deals:

XXXV.
Но я плоды моих мечтаний
И гармонических затей
Читаю только старой няне,

Подруге юности моей,
Да после скучного обеда
Ко мне забредшего соседа,
Поймав нежданно за полу,
Душу трагедией в углу,
Или (но это кроме шуток),
Тоской и рифмами томим,
Бродя над озером моим,
Пугаю стадо диких уток:
Вняв пенью сладкозвучных строф,
Они слетают с берегов.⁷²

[As for the fruits of my fancies / And [my] games with harmony, / I only read them to my old nanny, / The friend of my youth, / Or, after a boring dinner / Catching, by the flap of his coat, a neighbor / Who happened to wander in, / I choke him in a corner with my tragedy, / Or (no joking here) / Haunted by yearnings and rhymes, / Walking along the lake, / I scare a flock of wild ducks: / Having paid heed to my sweet-toned strophes, / They fly off from the banks.]

For Pushkin, random selection of listeners—down to the ducks—is a matter of principle: he discredits the very idea of a text aimed at a reader as a target of intentional action, regardless of whether it "soars" and "enthralls" the reader, like the ode, or "by begging and sobbing" obtains "the reader's condescension," like the elegy (according to Küchelbecker). That Pushkin rejected poetic impact and aim ("the aim of poetry is poetry," he wrote to Zhukovsky in 1825) did not mean he advocated "art for art's sake"; rather, he resented catering to readers' needs. *His* aim was independence from the reader.

Pushkin continually espoused this viewpoint from 1823 on, taking varied opportunities to do so. Tynianov was the first to highlight Pushkin's "struggle against the Karamzinian lady reader" (as manifested in statements like "I am not one of our eighteenth-century writers; I write for myself and publish for money, not for a smile from the fair sex").⁷³ Here could be added two comments showing a similar disdain for the pragmatics of the ode: "Not one of us would want the *magnanimous patronage of an enlightened grandee*; such a thing has been outmoded along with Lomonosov. Our contemporary literature is and must be noble and independent" (June 1824); "This is what that scoundrel Vorontsov does not understand. He imagines that a Russian poet will appear in his antechamber with a dedication to him or an ode, but the poet appears with a demand for respect as a member of the gentry with 600 years' standing—a devil of a difference!" (late spring 1825).[74] Significantly, Pushkin seems to make no distinction between the "*magnanimous patronage of an enlightened grandee*" and the idea of writing "for a smile from the fair sex." "Come on, my friend; what is the difference?" was his objection to Küchelbecker. Any "for"—*for* the grandee, *for* the beautiful woman, or *for* any possible addressee—equally diminishes and limits the author's freedom.

According to Tynianov, the reason Pushkin was not content with specifically targeting female readers had mainly to do with the stylistic and thematic limits that such an audience imposed. These note-ranges were too constricting for Pushkin; he demanded the full keyboard. He was scolded for his *Ruslan*'s not living up to the ideal of "reading material for women," but with *Boris Godunov*, completed in November 1825, he decisively exceeded all bounds ("They swear in all languages in my *Boris*. This tragedy is not for the fair sex"[75]). This was an important milestone for Pushkin: it was during his work on *Boris Godunov* that he overcame his old fear of "poetic captivity" when laboring over major works. "I feel my soul has completely developed, I can [now] create," he proudly wrote in an unsent letter to Nikolai Raevsky in 1825.[76] This was why, when Pushkin sat down to work on an uncompleted "<Objection to Küchelbecker's Articles Published in *Mnemozina*>," he used the notions of "labor" and "planning" in a positive sense hitherto unthinkable for him: "What freedom is there in Lomonosov's style and what plan can one require from a celebratory ode? . . . *Ode* rules out continuous labor, without which there is no true greatness."[77]

"Come, Oh, Come":
The Pyrrhic Victory of Pragmatics

In his objections to Küchelbecker, Pushkin reduced the entire genre of the ode to celebratory odes exclusively. The idea that the former craved a (hopeless, ridiculous) revival of eighteenth-century court poetry made a convenient straw man for Pushkin, but Küchelbecker's zeal for odes was in fact inspired by the avalanche of fiery poems called into being by the Napoleonic war. In the fifth chapter of *EO*, Pushkin once again returns to the celebratory ode for polemical purposes: the description of Tatiana's name-day party begins with a slightly reworked version of the opening of Lomonosov's "Ode on the Day of Her Sovereign Majesty Empress Elisaveta Petrovna's Accession to the Throne, 1748" ("Oda na den' vosshestviia na prestol Ee Velichestva Gosudaryni Imperatritsy Elisavety Petrovny 1748 goda"). In a footnote, Pushkin characterizes his quasi-quotation as "a parody of Lomonosov's famous lines," and cites the first three lines of Lomonosov's ode unaltered.[78]

But this is not so much a parody of Lomonosov's particular lines as a move to discredit the celebratory ode as a high genre in the plane of pragmatics; one celebration, the anniversary of a coronation, does not essentially differ from another, a provincial name-day party. In chapter 5, Pushkin delegates to a "resourceful poet," Monsieur Triquet, the act of offering a congratulatory poem to Tatiana. Triquet does not compose anything, instead finding an old song (*kuplet*) in an almanac and reworking it for the event. An occasional poet like Lensky, Triquet is also a *poet-performer*.

I have already discussed the function of performance for poetry in the Golden Age. A poem befitting the reader's situation (be it everyday-communicative, emotional, or any other) could be appropriated by this reader for their own needs: the more often this occurs, the more successful the text. A poem invested with musical form (that is, a poem-turned-song) has especially high chances of success; such a work literally gets to be performed (to the accompaniment of a piano or guitar). This affords the performer the opportunity to tap into the principle of dual felicity: a song, when sung, may act both as a vocal work and as a speech act. This is precisely what Sofia Del'vig was counting on when she sang Baratynsky's "Dissuasion" to Aleksei Vul'f. Monsieur Triquet is a performer in both senses: he both adapts someone else's text to his own celebratory needs and sings it for the name-day celebrant and her guests as a toast:

XXXIII.

Освободясь от пробки влажной,
Бутылка хлопнула; вино
Шипит; и вот с осанкой важной,
Куплетом мучимый давно,
Трике встает; пред ним собранье
Хранит глубокое молчанье.
Татьяна чуть жива; Трике,
К ней обратясь с листком в руке,
Запел, фальшивя. Плески, клики

Его приветствуют. Она
Певцу присесть принуждена;
Поэт же скромный, хоть великий,
Ее здоровье первый пьет
И ей куплет передает.[79]

[Ridding itself of the damp cork, / The bottle pops; the wine / fizzes; then, striking a solemn pose, / Long tortured by his song, / Triquet stands; before him, the whole gathering / Maintains a deep silence. / Tatiana is barely alive; Triquet, / Addressing her, a sheet of paper in his hand, / Starts singing, out of tune. Applause and shouting / greet him. She / Is compelled to make a curtsy to the singer; / The poet, modest although great, / Is first to drink her health / And hands to her his song.]

Along with epitaphs, congratulatory verses comprised one of the broadest categories of occasional verse and were a constant object of poetic commissions and other engaged poetry-making practices. (Populating the lowest niche of this category were, as Viazemsky put it, "versifiers wandering door to door" offering their poems for tips.[80]) Triquet was most likely a tutor, and in the provincial household probably also served as local master of ceremonies, distributing (or composing) poems for the children to learn and recite at household festivities. Preparing a song for Tatiana was as much part of Triquet's job as writing an ode to the empress was for Lomonosov.

As a representation of poetry's everyday pragmatics, this portrait of the household toastmaster is demeaning enough—but Pushkin has taken it a step further. As Lotman suggests, the Frenchman's name (spelled in Russian throughout) is telling: "Triqué (French, informal) means 'beaten with a stick'; beating someone with a stick signified a means of demeaning humiliation for a person who was unworthy of being challenged to a duel and consequently excluded from the circle of decent people. This is how a swindler or lowly con-artist might have been dealt with."[81] Or, we might add: a Russian poet. Pushkin included the following anecdote in his "Excerpts from Letters, Thoughts, and Observations" (1827): "Trediakovsky had more than one occasion to be beaten.... It is said that [State Secretary] Volynsky once ordered an ode from the court poet Vasily Trediakovsky on the occasion of a certain celebration, but the ode was not completed in time, and the zealous state secretary punished the negligent versifier with his cane."[82] Trediakovsky indeed wrote and performed celebratory songs for the court. The "certain celebration" of which Pushkin speaks was the notorious jesters' wedding in the Ice Palace; as punishment for his misstep, Trediakovsky, dressed as a jester, was forced to recite his verses during the ceremony.[83] Behind the image of Triquet, which seems to be entirely comic, we see a flicker of the tragically humiliated poet.

Pushkin does not have Lensky write congratulatory songs. His behavior at the name-day party is pathetic enough without verses. It is worth noting that this behavior is likely explained by Lensky's jealousy not only as a man but also as an author; Ol'ga blushes, pleased by the "vulgar madrigal" that Onegin, one more *performer*, "tenderly whispers" to her during the mazurka. "Madrigal" here might simply mean a compliment, as Lotman notes, not necessarily written in verse but in any case living up to the "wittiness" standards of the bon mot.[84] It produces the same effect on Ol'ga as did the elegies of the enamored Lensky; the impact on the addressee is independent of who is speaking. In courtship situations, the speaker—including Lensky with all his poetry and love—remains to some extent interchangeable. Social dancing, after all, implies the alternation of partners. The sensitive Lensky refuses to accept this basic convention; hence, his absurd behavior.

Contemplating the upcoming duel, Onegin pinpoints Lensky's conduct: "Let a poet / Fool around; at the age of eighteen / It's excusable" ("пускай поэт / Дурачится; в осьмнадцать лет / Оно простительно").[85] Just like the English "fool," the Russian *durak* used to refer to both a "stupid man" and a "buffoon" or "jester." In my view, Pushkin foregrounds the latter meaning. In chapter 8 he brings back the figure of the poet in love as a buffoon (now designated by the unequivocal Russian word *shut*), matching the allusion to Lensky by adding his keywords "elegy" and "ideal": "One sorrowful buffoon / Finds his ideal in her / And, leaning against the door, / Prepares an elegy for her" ("Один какой-то шут печальный / Ее находит идеальной / И, прислонившись у дверей, / Элегию готовит ей").[86]

Fittingly for a poet, Lensky cannot restrain himself from writing an elegy the night before the duel, and the author emphasizes that the general thrust of this elegy is, above all, amatory: "his verses / Full of love's nonsense / Resound and flow" ("его стихи, / Полны любовной чепухи, / Звучат и льются").[87] It begins as a common doleful elegy (so common that Tynianov correctly defines it as a *semi-parody* of doleful elegy),[88] with the "yearning for lost youth" (as Küchelbecker put it) characteristic thereof: "Whither, whither have you departed / My springtime's golden days?" ("Куда, куда вы удалились, / Весны моей златые дни?"); it then discusses the uncertainty of the coming day and the possibility of imminent death and oblivion. But following smoothly thus in the rut of elegy ultimately leads Lensky to do something unexpected—direct an imperative exclamation right at Ol'ga:

". . . но ты
Придешь ли, дева красоты,
Слезу пролить над ранней урной
И думать: он меня любил,
Он мне единой посвятил
Рассвет печальный жизни бурной! . . .
Сердечный друг, желанный друг,
Приди, приди: я твой супруг! . . ."⁸⁹

["But you, / Will you come, maiden of beauty, / To drop a tear onto the early urn / And think to yourself: he loved me, / To me alone did he dedicate / The sorrowful dawn of his stormy life! . . . / Friend of my heart, my desired friend, / Come, oh, come: I am your spouse! . . ."]

Proskurin insightfully comments: "The lines on which Pushkin breaks off his citation of the elegy . . . hint at a further ('off-screen') progress of Lensky's poetic thought . . . in the direction of the erotic and the sexual."⁹⁰ I would only hypothesize that it is not Pushkin who breaks off the elegy but Lensky, because his "poetic thought" has reached its logical end and collapsed into a cry of invitation, if not a mating call. This is a subtle transition: in the lines "Will you come, maiden of beauty, / To drop a tear onto the early urn," Lensky is speaking about his grave; this is the potential elegiac future and the address to Olga comes across as an apostrophe; in "Come, oh, come" the "erotic line" has matured to direct speech; he wants her here and now. In poetry, the invitational imperative "come" most often refers to the muse and comes at the beginning of the text; in contrast, Lensky uses it to end his elegy, laying bare the sole, wholly carnal reason for his inspiration. As a matter of fact, it is not only Lensky's poem that breaks off here but his whole poetic career; not because he will die the next day but because the pragmatics of "live address" have finally taken precedence over poetics and poetry. If the final aim of the poetry turns out to be "the mystery of the conjugal bed" with his sole addressee/reader, which the author promised him at the end of chapter 4, Lensky's poetry is no longer needed. His poetic downshifting has at last brought him to the ground.

Whither?

Lensky's early death retrospectively alters his profile, not merely converting a quasi-comic character into the victim of a tragic event but also reconnecting him to the poetry of sublime sensibility through association with Zhukovsky's "Country Graveyard."[91] The author's meditation on Lensky's fate begins on a high note: "His martyred shade, / Has perhaps carried off with it / A sacred mystery, and / A quickening voice is dead to us" ("Его страдальческая тень, / Быть может, унесла с собою / Святую тайну, и для нас / Погиб животворящий глас").[92] At the same time, we are given to understand that Lensky's extant (as opposed to prospective) poetry has no chance of surviving its author. As a would-be alternative, Pushkin paints a parodic version of the *aurea mediocritas* ideal:

XXXVIII. XXXIX.

А может быть и то: поэта
Обыкновенный ждал удел.
Прошли бы юношества лета:
В нем пыл души бы охладел.
Во многом он бы изменился,
Расстался б с музами, женился,
В деревне, счастлив и рогат,
Носил бы стеганый халат;
Узнал бы жизнь на самом деле,
Подагру б в сорок лет имел,
Пил, ел, скучал, толстел, хирел,
И наконец в своей постеле
Скончался б посреди детей,
Плаксивых баб и лекарей.[93]

[It may also be that / Our poet was destined for an ordinary lot. / The years of his youth would have passed: / The fire of his soul would have cooled. / He would have changed in many ways, / Would have parted with his muses, got married, / In the countryside, happy and cuckolded, / He'd be wearing a quilted dressing gown; / Would have known real life, / Would have suffered from gout at forty, / Would have drunk, eaten, got bored, gained weight, fallen ill, / And then, finally, in his bed / He would have died among his children, / Tearful peasant women, and healers.]

No one is found at Lensky's rural grave, save for a bast-plaiting shepherd, hardly a reader of Lensky's poetry.[94] Eventually, a "maiden of beauty" appears at the graveside:

> И горожанка молодая,
> В деревне лето провождая,
> Когда стремглав верхом она
> Несется по полям одна,
> Коня пред ним останавливает,
> Ремянный повод натянув,
> И, флер от шляпы отвернув,
> Глазами беглыми читает
> Простую надпись—и слеза
> Туманит нежные глаза.[95]

[And a young woman from the city, / Summering in the countryside, / Amid dashing on horseback / Across the fields, alone / Halts her steed in front of it / Tightening a belt rein / And turning up the veil from her hat / She reads with cursory eyes / The simple inscription—and a tear / Dims her tender eyes.]

The late poet does, after all, find a sensitive reader, but, alas, she is the reader of his epitaph, not his poetry. Worse yet, as we discover in the next stanza, she is also the reader of the novel in verse *Eugene Onegin*, and as such is interested not in the deceased poet but in what will happen next.[96]

The author solemnly promises his equestrian reader he will leave no character unaccounted for in due time, and immediately grants himself an extension—on the grounds of his advancing age (Pushkin was twenty-seven when he wrote this), which leaves him too little energy to "flirt with a rhyme" and makes him, overall, colder and more dour, thus more inclined to "austere [*surovoi*] prose."

Having confessed this, Pushkin delivers a blow to elegy—the cornerstone genre of the Golden Age, and the target of Küchelbecker's more ponderous attack. A comic treatment, it appears, works better than the latter's solemn indignation.

XLIV

> Познал я глас иных желаний,
> Познал я новую печаль;

Для первых нет мне упований,
А старой мне печали жаль.
Мечты, мечты! где ваша сладость?
Где, вечная к ней рифма, *младость*?
Ужель и вправду наконец
Увял, увял ее венец?
Ужель и впрям и в самом деле
Без элегических затей
Весна моих промчалась дней
(Что я шутя твердил доселе)?
И ей ужель возврата нет?
Ужель мне скоро тридцать лет?[97]

[I have come to know the voice of other desires, / I have come to know a new sadness; / I put no trust in the former, / And I regret the old sadness. / Dreams, O dreams—where is your sweetness [*sladost'*]? / Where is the stock rhyme to it: *youth* [*mladost'*]? / Can it really be that at last / The garland [of my youth] has wilted? / Can it really be, in actual fact, that / Without elegiac tricks, / The springtime of my life has passed / (As I used to say all the time in jest)? / And can it really never return? / Will I really soon be thirty?]

Having "really, in actual fact" killed off his young poet, who had (as is wont in doleful elegies) equated "youth" with "life," Pushkin, like his readers, is eager to learn what's next:

XLV

Так, полдень мой настал, и нужно
Мне в том сознаться, вижу я.
Но так и быть: простимся дружно,
О юность легкая моя!
Благодарю за наслажденья,
За грусть, за милые мученья,
За шум, за бури, за пиры,
За все, за все твои дары;
Благодарю тебя. Тобою,
Среди тревог и в тишине,
Я насладился . . . и вполне;
Довольно! С ясною душою

Пускаюсь ныне в новый путь
От жизни прошлой отдохнуть.[98]

[So, the midday of my life has come. / And I must admit, I see it. / But let it be: let's part as friends, / O my light youth! / I thank you for all the joys, / For the sadness, the dear torments, / For the clamor, the storms, the feasts, / For all your gifts; / I thank you. / Among troubles and in calmness / Have I enjoyed you ... to the fullest; / Enough! With a clear soul / I set out now on a new path, / To rest from my old life.]

Here, Pushkin both follows a tradition and goes against its grain. Farewell to youth—the central theme of doleful elegies—dictated hackneyed formulas (down to specific rhymes), and was wildly popular among poets in their late teens. In the above two stanzas, Pushkin turns against the elegiac tradition by bidding farewell to his bygone youth in a light and optimistic key, with the foretaste of a "new path." This "new path" gestures toward Baratynsky's "Confession." As discussed in chapter 5, to the extent that Baratynsky in this poem casts parting with a lover as a parting with youth, "Confession" represents a loveless, libertine breakup masquerading as a doleful elegy. Pushkin, in turn, parts with his youth as a libertine might with a lover, carefree and without looking back. Thus, the end of *EO*'s sixth chapter works just as an epilogue might: it gives the author freedom to slip out of his poetic skin and move on. The question is, to put it in Lensky's vocabulary—whither?

Epilogue as Dialogue

Before answering this question, I will briefly sum up several key contentions of this book. The verse culture of the Golden Age—which, of course, Pushkin came of age in, and was steeped in directly in its prime—was undergirded by a certain system of relations within the triangle *author—text—reader*. These relations presumed proximity: of the author to the text (the sincerity condition), of the text to the reader (relatability condition), and of the author to the reader ("live address of the poetic word"). It should be emphasized once again that this *orientation toward proximity* is often misidentified with "salon culture." Such a designation is reductionist; for instance, neither the fictional Larins from *EO*, nor the typical real-life rural album owner could ever have hosted anything like a full-fledged salon. Proximity as a literary value is independent of physical or personal distance between author and reader. Lyric truly did not set itself the goal of "enthralling the reader's soul," as Küchelbecker characterized the function of the ode; much the opposite, it was supposed to cater to readers' needs. The pragmatics of lyric was twofold. First, it was attuned to readerly participation, allowing readers to replace the authorial voice in the text with their own ("This is my life," as the forlorn E. B. wrote beside Pushkin's elegy); second, it follows the principles of aim and impact: the text was expected to have a specific effect (moral, emotional, and so on) on a reader.

All the components of this pragmatic proximity began to weigh on Pushkin as soon as he had mastered versification. The convention that required poetry to hinge upon readership (writing for a smile), and the common understanding of the lyric text as a performative act—as if such works came with the implied tagline: "I am Pushkin, and I approve this message"—repelled him alike as forms of dependency. As we have seen, Pushkin continually works on distancing his lyric "I" from the text (beginning with "Liberty"), and the text from the reader (in his attacks on both Karamzinian "lady readers" and the "enlightened grandee," as well as in his rejection of "poetry's aim").

Nonetheless, this distancing does not mean that Pushkin moved toward lyric in John Stuart Mill's sense of a soliloquy "overheard" by the reader. He drifts in the opposite direction, distancing himself from lyric as such. Küchelbecker's article, as well as Pushkin's internal dialogue with it, helps Pushkin formulate this position; the ode could not provide salvation from the elegy because, for him, the opposition between these two lyric genres is contrived. In Küchelbecker's view, the ode is "disinterested" or "impartial" (*beskorystna*), unlike the elegy or epistle, for two reasons: first, because the "feelings" expressed by the author are inspired by lofty causes; and second, because the ode, on account of its exalted style and subject, is distanced from the reader. Küchelbecker's is a markedly vertical construction; the odist rises above the "language of the crowd," "everyday events," and even above himself ("he neither rejoices at, nor complains over, the insignificant events of his own life"), in order to "enthrall the reader's ear and soul."[99]

For Pushkin, this proposal—to reorient poetry from the horizontal axis to the vertical—implied trading one type of dependency for another. The new sublime entailed no fewer stylistic and thematic limitations than those imposed by elegy; the imperial past of the ode in Russia spelled poetic servility, down to outright buffoonery. Most importantly, Küchelbecker's avowed impact on the reader, even an "enthralled" reader, left the *felicity* of impact the decisive criterion of poetic work. Even having *risen above* readers, the poet remained subordinate to them. It was precisely this situation that Pushkin describes in his 1828 poem "The Poet and the Mob" ("Poet i chern'"). Here, the mob directs the poet:

> Нет, если ты небес избранник,
> Свой дар, божественный посланник,
> Во благо нам употребляй:
> Сердца собратьев исправляй.
> Мы малодушны, мы коварны,
> Бесстыдны, злы, неблагодарны;
> Мы сердцем хладные скопцы,
> Клеветники, рабы, глупцы;
> Гнездятся клубом в нас пороки.
> Ты можешь, ближнего любя,
> Давать нам смелые уроки,
> А мы послушаем тебя.[100]

[No, if you are heaven's chosen one, / A divine messenger, use your gift / For our good: / Correct the hearts of your brethren. / We are cowards, we are treacherous, / Shameless, vile, ungrateful; / In our hearts, we are cold as eunuchs, / [We are] Slanderers, slaves, fools; / We contain nests of balled-up vice. / You can, loving thy neighbor, / Give us bold [moral] lessons, / And we will listen to you.]

In other words, moving along the scale from the "lowly" to the "sublime" essentially changed nothing.

In his above-cited article on the "Direction of Our Poetry," Küchelbecker pits two lyric "directions" or tendencies against one another: the odic on the one hand and elegiac on the other. But, says Pushkin, a plague on both your houses. His response to Küchelbecker is to dispute the assumed benefits of poetry's lyric direction as such, whether in elegiac or odic form. As to the tendency of Russian literature, what "direction" it should take, Pushkin had his own program. Its generic constituents were announced in *EO* in the author's dispute with the "stern critic": "You are right, and I suppose you will point out to us / The trumpet, mask, and dagger, / And will order that there be revived, from wherever possible, / A dead capital of thoughts." Tynianov deciphers these lines thus: "The time of elegies has passed; its place will be taken not by lyric genres, and in any case, certainly not by the archaic ode, but by other genres—the trumpet, mask, and dagger—drama in verse."[101]

Pushkin had indeed just finished his drama *Boris Godunov*, which, for the first time, gave him occasion to declare "I can create." For him, "to create" stood for more than to write poems; drama was one of the antidotes to the self-serving "report on [*izlozhenie*] the poet's own feelings," as Küchelbecker, following the critical standard, defined lyric. Another antidote was prose. The "dead capital of thoughts" must be revived; this is what prose is for: "Precision and brevity are the main merits of prose. It requires thoughts and more thoughts—without them, brilliant expressions lead nowhere. ... Reminiscences of bygone youth won't do much to advance our literature."[102] Pushkin's positive program has to do with intellectual work; such work presupposes an emotional distance between author and text.

In the history of *EO*'s making, Lensky's demotion to the rank of archetypal elegist began in the latter half of September 1824. This process, as noted above, was linked with, if not triggered by, Pushkin's polemics with Küchelbecker, whose essay is ironically quoted in the foreword to *EO*'s first chapter. Soon after drafting this foreword, Pushkin wrote his "Conversation between a Bookseller and a Poet" ("Razgovor knigoprodavtsa s poetom"), to be used as a poetic preface to that same first chapter. In terms of Pushkin's literary doctrine, this "Conversation" presents a solution to the problem of literary pragmatics that had been Lensky's undoing as a poet, and ultimately as a (diegetically) living character.

This dialogue has been traditionally interpreted as a clash.[103] The bookseller, in this reading, represents economic pragmatism; the poet, conversely, protects the rights of lyric. There is, indeed, a stark contrast between the former's crudely commercial language and the latter's exalted tone, but the two never disagree in essence. Rather, the dialogue is marked by a significant repetitiveness: each time the bookseller, with sarcastic cynicism, cites some new pragmatics for writing poetry—*for* fame, *for* women, *for* love—the poet rejects it. But there is no clash, because neither of the two really takes these *for*'s for a serious reason. In the end, they make a deal.

To begin with, the bookseller offers to convert the poet's leaflets (*listochki*) filled with verses into a bundle (*puk*) of banknotes; the latter veers into idyllic reminiscences of those times when, in proud solitude, he kept his poetry to himself. Slyly, the bookseller reminds the poet of the fame visited upon him since that time. The poet's rejoinder, about the vanity of fame, involves a phrase familiar to us, namely, "Blessed is he":

Блажен, кто про себя таил
Души высокие созданья
И от людей, как от могил,
Не ждал за чувство воздаянья!
Блажен, кто молча был поэт
И, терном славы не увитый,
Презренной чернию забытый,
Без имени покинул свет!¹⁰⁴

[Blessed is he who has kept to himself / The sublime creations of his soul / And never expected rewards for feeling / Neither from people nor from graves! / Blessed is he who was a poet while keeping silent / And who, not wreathed with the thorns of fame, / Forgotten by the despicable mob, / Left the world without leaving his name to it.]

Pushkin once again employs the Horatian device from the second epode, with its signature final twist laying bare the blatant discrepancy between the speaker and the spoken. (This fiery retort on the subject of fame's vanity, after all, is given by a man who, as we learn in the poem's final line, has brought his manuscript to market.)

The consideration of fame having been rejected, the bookseller offers a new reason and a new audience for his interlocutor's poetry: "Praise to you is but a tiresome jingling; / But ladies' hearts require fame: / Write for them" ("Хвала для вас докучный звон; / Но сердце женщин славы просит: / Для них пишите"). The poet's answer to this is to relegate such pragmatics to juvenilia by the likes of Lensky:

Уста волшебные шептали
Мне звуки сладкие мои...
Но полно! в жертву им свободы
Мечтатель уж не принесет;
Пускай их юноша поет,
Любезный баловень природы
. . . .
Когда на память мне невольно
Придет внушенный ими стих,
Я так и вспыхну, сердцу больно:
Мне стыдно идолов моих.¹⁰⁵

[Enchanting lips used to whisper / My [poetry's] sweet sounds to me . . . / But enough! The dreamer / Will no longer sacrifice his freedom to them; / Let some youngster sing of them, / Some kindly fair-haired boy of nature / . . . / When I chance to recall / A line inspired by ["charming eyes" and "enchanting lips"], / I flush [with anger], my heart feels pain: / I am embarrassed by my idols.]

As in the first movement of "Conversation," the poet accentuates temporal distance: at one time he didn't write for publication, at one time he wrote for women. Both statements are about the past. The next turn of dialogue refines the preceding *for*; the bookseller wonders whether there is some "one and only" among the "fair ladies." Through an emotionally loaded response, the poet makes it clear that his love was hopeless. Having gone through every available model of poetic pragmatics, the bookseller inquires:

Итак, любовью утомленный,
Наскуча лепетом молвы,
Заране отказались вы
От вашей лиры вдохновенной.
Теперь, оставя шумный свет,
И муз, и ветреную моду,
Что ж изберете вы?

Поэт

Свободу.[106]

[So then, weary of love, / Bored by the babbling of fame, / You have rejected in advance your inspired lyre. / Now, having left behind the noisy world, / As well as muses and flighty fashion, / What will you choose?—Poet:—Freedom.]

This is the key moment in "Conversation." The word "freedom," marked off as a single line, is loaded with maximal semantic weight. In his response, the bookseller does not object; instead, he recommends that the poet not disdain money; the poet immediately agrees, transitioning from verse to prose: "You are completely right. Here is my manuscript. Let's make a deal."[107]

In the bookseller's final response, Pushkin includes a recipe for estrangement. Selling his manuscript entails its author's alienation from the manuscript's text. Mutatis mutandis, this is the same temporal distancing that Pushkin had discovered back when working on his "Liberty":

Предвижу ваше возраженье;
Но вас я знаю, господа:
Вам ваше дорого творенье,
Пока на пламени труда
Кипит, бурлит воображенье;
Оно застынет, и тогда
Постыло вам и сочиненье.
Позвольте просто вам сказать:
Не продается вдохновенье,
Но можно рукопись продать.[108]

[I anticipate your objection; / But I know you gentlemen well: / Your creation is dear to you, / Whilst heated on labor's flame / Your imagination boils and seethes; / It will cool and harden, and then / Likewise will you cool toward your composition. / Let me tell you simply: / Inspiration is not for sale, / But you can sell your manuscript.]

What freedom does Pushkin's poet have in mind when, responding to the bookseller, he chooses it over his lyre, flighty fashions, and the noisy world? The answer becomes clear in light of Pushkin's unsent letter regarding his upcoming resignation from state service in the summer of 1824:

What am I to regret? My unsuccessful career? I am at peace with this thought now. My salary? Since my literary endeavors bring me more money, it is only natural to sacrifice my service duties, etc. . . . The only thing I long for is independence. . . . I have already overcome my aversion to writing poetry and selling it in order to make my living—the hardest step has already been taken. If I still write on a free whim of inspiration, then, once I complete a poem, I see a commodity in it, with this or that price for a piece.[109]

In Pushkin's case, the "freedom" his poet speaks of in "Conversation" acquires a dual meaning. This freedom is not only poetic but also personal: the freedom to make a living without relying on the government, that is, without serving.[110]

In the autumn of 1824, while in the humiliating position of being confined to his family estate (albeit at least free from service), Pushkin paints a utopian picture of full independence: the independence of the author from the text, the independence of the text from the reader, the independence of the noble from serving the tsar. Independence from the reader means neither enmity nor disaffection. On the contrary, as soon as the reader ceases to be the addressee and the aim of impact, the relationship between author and reader can become "noble and independent" for both parties. The poetic pragmatics formerly constraining the author's and the reader's freedom is replaced by healthy relations of exchange, in which no one is obligated to oblige. The dangers Pushkin sensed as lurking in too familiar a relationship between author and reader (such as that of Lensky and Ol'ga) were averted by the presence of a middleman—the bookseller. This middleman also guaranteed the author's personal independence—through purchasing his works to publish them.

On the one hand, much of what Pushkin wished for future literature eventually came true. On the other, as every kid learns from cautionary tales like Pushkin's own about the golden fish, be careful what you wish for. After Pushkin's conversation with the imagined bookseller, when the literary market began its rapid development, it became clear that readers did want, after all, to be catered to. (The law of supply and demand, of course, entails nothing like independence of the sort Pushkin had envisioned.) The culture of lyric entered a decline proportional to the growth of the market for books and magazines. This was not a decline in the quantity of verse produced. On the contrary, as Aleksandr Bestuzhev summed up in 1833: "No one wanted to listen to verse any more once everyone started writing it. Finally, scattered complaints merged in a general call! 'Prose, prose! Water, simple water!'"[111] In line with Tynianov's law of literary evolution, Golden Age poetic culture was destined to fall precisely because it had won so decisive and universal a victory. When everyone speaks, no one listens.

"Your imagination boils and seethes; / It will cool and harden, and then . . ." For good reason does Pushkin use a metallurgic metaphor for his bookseller's final pitch to the poet. The choice of metal here is key. What was golden in the Golden Age, whether that of Russian literature or the mythic past, was gold's absence from the picture. Once there is gold, it multiplies, as in the bookseller's lines: "Our age is a huckster; in this iron age, / There is no freedom without money / . . . / We need gold, gold, gold: / Lay up as much gold as you can!" ("Наш век—торгаш; в сей век железный / Без денег и свободы нет / ... / Нам нужно злата, злата, злата: / Копите злато до конца!").[112] The presence of gold makes the age iron, not golden. Rather than offer some objection to the bookseller's friendly advice, the poet in his response readily switches from poetry to prose.

Fortunately for us, Pushkin never entirely switched from poetry to prose; nor did his "Conversation between a Bookseller and a Poet" imply any intention to do so. Quite the opposite: "Conversation" was published as a preface to the opening chapter of what would be a poetic labor of seven years and more than five thousand lines. Yet, by the time he wrote "Conversation," Pushkin, to use Mandel'shtam's line, had "learned well the art of parting"—the art of epilogue. He had learned that epilogue was what gives an author freedom from his or her written past, makes this past "*plusqueparfait.*" The dialogue of the bookseller and the poet is, thus, an epilogue to the poet's poetry. In a sense, every epilogue is a dialogue: of the author with his or her work, once *this* work is completed and the two part ways, each on their own new path. The true art of epilogue lies not in concluding the work but in the freedom to exit from it and look ahead.

Notes

Preface

1. Ostrovskii, "U istokov 'Biblioteki poeta,'" 180.

Introduction

1. Pletnev, "Pis'mo k grafine," 244.
2. Okudzhava, *Stikhotvoreniia*, 343.
3. For a different attribution of this (apocryphal?) philological anecdote, see Zholkovskii, "S Lotmanom na druzheskoi noge."
4. Merzliakov, *Kratkoe nachertanie*, 173–74.
5. Rachinskii, *Tatevskii sbornik*, 111.
6. As discussed in Reitblat, *Kak Pushkin vyshel v genii*.
7. See, for example, Iser, *The Implied Reader*.
8. See, for instance, Timenchik, "Azy i uzy kommentariia."
9. Shklovskii, "O pisatele i proizvodstve," 199.
10. Eliot, *The Use of Poetry*, 18.
11. Jakobson, "Poetry of Grammar"; Empson, *Seven Types of Ambiguity*; Fenollosa and Pound, *The Chinese Written Character*.
12. See, in particular, Jakobson, "Linguistics and Poetics."
13. Boratynskii, *Polnoe sobranie sochinenii*, 2:1:90.
14. A. N. Poliakov suggested in 1918 that the poem refers to Aleksandra Voeikova, whose salon both Baratynsky and Lev Pushkin frequented in the early 1820s (cited ibid., 93), but based on what is known about Voeikova, it is hard to see her in the role of the light-hearted Charis of Baratynsky's poem.
15. See Todd, *The Familiar Letter*, 57, 135.
16. Pletnev, "Pis'mo k grafine," 244.
17. Cohen, *Social Lives of Poems*, 13–14, 17–59.
18. Legoy, "Le siècle."

19. Bestuzhev, "Vzgliad na russkuiu slovesnost'," 488.
20. Eckermann, *Conversations of Goethe*, 18.
21. Mill, *Autobiography and Literary Essays*, 348.
22. Pushkin, *Polnoe sobranie sochinenii*, 13:167. All citations from Pushkin's *Polnoe sobranie sochinenii* refer to the sixteen-volume edition (Leningrad: AN SSSR, 1937–59), unless otherwise noted.

Chapter 1. Lyric as Speech Act and Literary Fact

1. V. A. Olenina. Tetrad' s gazetnymi vyrezkami i vospominaniiami. Otdel rukopisei Rossiiskoi Natsional'noi Biblioteki (Manuscript Division of the Russian National Library, Saint-Petersburg), f. 542, ed. kh. 877, l. 51. The emperor's poem contains a pun. In period Russian the preposition *dlia* (for) could signify both "to" and "in exchange for."
2. James, *Pragmatism*, 46. While Peirce did not, as James misremembers, use the term *pragmatism* in the specific essay quoted, the coinage's attribution to him is correct.
3. Ibid., 45.
4. Ibid., 274. Actually, James recited eight stanzas of the original eleven.
5. Ibid., 276.
6. Ibid., 277.
7. Ibid., 278.
8. Austin, *How to Do Things*, 5.
9. Ibid., 22.
10. Culler, *Theory of the Lyric*, 130.
11. Culler, *Literary Theory*, 75–77.
12. As was famously discussed, with examples from English literature, in Frye, "Theory of Genres" (1957), 38–39; in the 1910s and 1920s the importance of chants, spells, and other magic genres for understanding poetry was discussed by the formalists; see Shklovsky, "On Poetry," 3–24; Jakobson, "Modern Russian Poetry," 58–82.
13. Culler, *Theory of the Lyric*, 131.
14. Culler, *Literary Theory*, 76.
15. Tynianov, "Literary Fact."
16. Derzhavin, *Sochineniia Derzhavina*, 1:1:665–69.
17. See Kuznetsova and Mel'tsin, "Preobrazhenie real'nosti," 492.
18. Ivan Liprandi, "Iz dnevnika i vospominanii," 323.
19. Culler, *Theory of the Lyric*, 128.
20. See Sandler, *Distant Pleasures*, 18–19.
21. Bakhtin, "Discourse in the Novel," 278–88; for a survey of New Criticism views on poetry (lyric, in particular), see Culler, *Theory of the Lyric*, 263–75.
22. Tynianov, "Oda kak oratorskii zhanr," 251.
23. Pushkin, *Polnoe sobranie sochinenii*, 15:80.
24. Vatsuro, "Poeticheskii manifest Pushkina."

25. Ibid., 28.

26. See *Ostaf'evskii arkhiv kniazei Viazemskikh*, 3:643.

27. Viazemskii, *Zapisnye knizhki (1813–1848)*, 214.

28. For more on the political and generic aspects of this poem, see Wachtel, *A Commentary*, 227.

29. Viazemskii, *Stikhotvoreniia* (1986), 84.

30. Batiushkov, *Sochineniia v dvukh tomakh*, 2:255.

31. Viktor Shklovsky's term *ostrannenie* was derived from *strannyi* and should be spelled with two *n*'s (not one as had become customary). The original "*-nn-*" spelling is now coming back both in Russian and English. See a recent book: Oever, *Ostrannenie*.

32. Tihanov, "Marxism and Formalism Revisited."

33. Aronson and Reiser, *Literaturnye kruzhki i salony*; Grits, Trenin, and Nikitin, *Slovesnost' i kommertsiia*; Todd, *Fiction and Society*; Peschio, *The Poetics of Impudence*.

34. To the essays already mentioned—"Literary Fact," "On Literary Evolution," and "Ode as an Oratorical Genre"—we should also add Tynianov's seminal "Arkhaisty i Pushkin."

35. To my knowledge, no specific evidence of odes being recited in the eighteenth century exists. Still, the "oratory orientation" of the genre, to my mind, can hardly be disputed, given that all functionally neighboring genres, that is, speech types employed on court and state occasions—*kanty* (canticles), sermons, and manifestos, in chronological order—were undoubtedly presented orally.

36. See Golburt, *The First Epoch*, 72–113.

37. See Maiofis, *Vozzvanie k Evrope*, 97–157; Vinitsky, *Vasily Zhukovsky's Romanticism*, 179–236.

38. Quoted after Proskurina, *Mify imperii*, 218, 198. While the first of these quotations comes from the memoir of Senator Osip Kozodavlev, the latter reflects Catherine's own critical opinion of odes, Proskurina believes.

39. This thought, expressed in Kozodavlev's story of the success of "Felitsa," is supported in Proskurina, *Mify imperii*, 195–236.

40. For an excellent recent discussion of "Felitsa" and Derzhavin's balance of odic and conversational principles, see Golburt, *The First Epoch*, 47–59.

41. See Pogosian, "Uroki imperatritsy," 241–68.

42. Todd, *Fiction and Society*, 55–56.

43. *Ostaf'evskii arkhiv kniazei Viazemskikh*, 2:226.

44. See Vinitskii, "Poeticheskaia semantika Zhukovskogo." On reservations regarding Zhukovsky's court poetry on the part of Viazemsky and others, see Vinitsky, *Vasily Zhukovsky's Romanticism*, 190–91.

45. Quoted in Grech, *Opyt kratkoi istorii Russkoi literatury*, 307–8.

46. See a recent comprehensive collection of studies on French-Russian bilingualism: Offord et al., *French and Russian in Imperial Russia*.

47. See Lotman and Uspenskii, "Spory o iazyke"; Uspenskii, *Iz istorii russkogo literaturnogo iazyka*; Zhivov, *Language and Culture*, 346–80; Gasparov, *Poeticheskii iazyk Pushkina*, 25–60.

48. Vigel', *Zapiski*, 1:186–87.

49. One verse from Alexis Piron's 1738 *La Métromanie* in particular—"La mère en prescrira la lecture à sa fille" (The mother will prescribe reading to her daughter)—became something of a meme among Russian poets, from Dmitriev, who used it to praise Mikhail Murav'ev's writings, and later to express his disdain for Pushkin's *Ruslan i Liudmila*, to Pushkin himself, who in his comments to *Eugene Onegin* notes the irony that this popular moralistic motto derives from the writings of Piron, of all people, who was particularly known for his obscene poetry.

50. Vigel', *Zapiski*, 1:301–2.

51. For a valuable discussion of the "axiological miniaturization" of Russian literature in the last quarter of the eighteenth century, see Hammarberg, *From the Idyll to the Novel*, 93–127.

52. Vigel', *Zapiski*, 301–2.

53. Turgenev, "Pis'ma A. I. Turgeneva k I. I. Dmitrievu," 654.

54. Cited from Bazanov, *Uchenaia respublika*, 123.

55. Peskov, *Letopis' zhizni i tvorchestva*, 226.

56. Batiushkov, *Opyty v stikhakh i proze*, 200.

57. Karamzin, *Polnoe sobranie stikhotvorenii*, 169–70; full text of the poem is in ibid., 169–70. Further page references in the text are to this edition.

58. On balancing poetry and service, see Reyfman, *How Russia Learned to Write*; Velizhev, "'Senator' vs. 'Poet'"; Zorin, *Poiavlenie geroia*, 180–97.

59. For a discussion of Karamzin's life-building, see Lotman, *Sotvorenie Karamzina*.

60. Karamzin, *Polnoe sobranie stikhotvorenii*, 391–92.

61. Pavlova, *Polnoe sobranie stikhotvorenii*, 77.

62. Maiakovskii, *Polnoe sobranie sochinenii*, 10:282.

Chapter 2. Functions

1. Tynianov, "Literaturnyi fakt," 257–58.
2. [Ushak]ov, "Gospodinu izdateliu *Literaturnykh listkov*," 95.
3. Del'vig, *Sochineniia*, 133.
4. Viazemskii, *Stikhotvoreniia* (1958), 75–79.
5. Bowring, *Specimens of the Russian Poets*, 1:51.
6. Ibid., 48.
7. Ibid., 48–49.
8. Rachinskii, *Tatevskii sbornik*, 111.
9. Del'vig gave the version published after Sofia Ponomareva's death a different title: "Na smert' sobaki Amiki." Ponomareva's album is brilliantly analyzed in Vadim Vatsuro's book-length study *S. D. P. Iz istorii literaturnogo byta*; on this contribution by Del'vig, see 187–89.

10. Batiushkov, *Sochineniia v dvukh tomakh*, 2:219.
11. Pushkin, *Polnoe sobranie sochinenii*, 1:238.
12. Batiushkov, *Opyty v stikhakh i proze*, 200.
13. Ibid., 11–12. The most comprehensive study of Russian light poetry remains Zorin, "Vsled shestvuia Anakreonu."
14. On the sociopolitical dimension of Batiushkov's speech, see Greenleaf, "Found in Translation," 56–57.
15. See Batiushkov, *Opyty v stikhakh i proze*, 495.
16. Stael, *Germany*, 1:102–3.
17. See Dmitriev, *Vzgliad na moiu zhizn'*, 14; and Lotman, *Besedy o russkoi kul'ture*, 86–87.
18. See Izmailov, "Pushkin v dnevnike gr. D.F. Fikel'mon," 34.
19. On oral speech in its relation to literature and culture of the Golden Age, see Lotman, "K funktsii ustnoi rechi"; Paperno, "O rekonstruktsii ustnoi rechi."
20. Zhukovskii, *Sobranie sochinenii*, 4:639.
21. Ibid.
22. Ibid.
23. There is a venerable tradition of publishing the conversations of poets, from such eyewitness accounts as Thomas Medwin's *Journal of the Conversations of Lord Byron* (1824), Henry Nelson Coleridge's *Specimens of the Table Talk of the Late Samuel Coleridge* (1835), and Johann Peter Eckermann's *Gespräche mit Goethe* (1836) to scholarly compilations like Sergei Gessen's *Razgovory Pushkina* (1929).
24. One of these was the poet-improviser Sergei Neelov, whom Petr Viazemsky called "the Russian Aeolian harp, the popular ribald balalaika," and Pushkin, less euphemistically yet lovingly, *chantre de la merde*. Viazemskii, *Polnoe sobranie sochinenii*, 8:361; Pushkin, *Polnoe sobranie sochinenii*, 13:184.
25. *Ostaf'evskii arkhiv kniazei Viazemskikh*, 3:552.
26. Viazemskii, *Polnoe sobranie sochinenii*, 2: 286–87.
27. Grech, *Chteniia o russkom iazyke*, 2:32.
28. Vigel', *Zapiski*, 1:132.
29. Dolgorukov, *Povest' o rozhdenii moem*, 1:58.
30. Ibid., 604.
31. *Ostaf'evskii arkhiv kniazei Viazemskikh*, 2:317.
32. Ibid., 1:286.
33. See Todd, *The Familiar Letter*, 85–94. Todd draws his examples mostly from the correspondence of Arzamas members; many more could be added, from Dmitriev to Iazykov.
34. Batiushkov, *Sochineniia v dvukh tomakh*, 2:74.
35. Ibid., 75.
36. Jackson, *Dickinson's Misery*, 90.
37. "Pis'mo Denisa Vasil'evicha Davydova k Zhukovskomu," 975.

38. See Peschio, *The Poetics of Impudence*, 15–16; and Bowers, "Unpacking Viazemskii's *Khalat*."
39. Peschio, *The Poetics of Impudence*, 44–45.
40. Jackson, *Dickinson's Misery*, 90–100.
41. Todd, *The Familiar Letter*, 76–77. See also a more recent study of Russian epistolary culture: Atanasova-Sokolova, *Pis'mo kak fakt*.
42. Del'vig, *Sochineniia*, 134.
43. Pil'shchikov, "Nomina si nescis . . . ," 70.
44. For an excellent case study of early nineteenth-century poetic circulation, see Bowers, "Unpacking Viazemskii's *Khalat*."
45. See Vinitsky, *Vasily Zhukovsky's Romanticism*, 185–97.
46. Viazemskii, *Stikhotvoreniia* (1958), 132–34.
47. *Ostaf'evskii arkhiv kniazei Viazemskikh*, 2:7, 9–10. Indeed, the poem was published the same winter, with a semitransparent camouflage thrown over the when and where of the matter. The author's name is omitted; while "Warsaw" is given as the place of the poem's departure, nothing is said of its destination; and the recipient's identity is hidden under "T. . . . ." (a cryptogram easy to crack knowing the syllabo-tonic flow of Russian verse).
48. Dmitriev, *Pis'ma I. I. Dmitrieva*, 3.
49. The existence of this opinion is alluded to in "Pis'mo A. E. Izmailova I. I. Dmitrievu," 971.
50. Batiushkov, *Sochineniia v dvukh tomakh*, 2:492.
51. Zeidlits, *Zhizn' i poeziia*, 114.
52. Ong, *Orality and Literacy*, 11.
53. Bartenev, "Pushkin v iuzhnoi Rossii," 1094.
54. *Ostaf'evskii arkhiv kniazei Viazemskikh*, 1:162.
55. Goethe, *The Autobiography of Goethe*, 386.
56. Ong, *Orality and Literacy*, 14.
57. See Tynianov, "Arkhaisty i Pushkin"; Lotman and Uspenskii, "Spory o iazyke"; Zhivov, *Language and Culture*, 346–80.
58. *Noveishii, samyi polnyi i podrobnyi pis'movnik*, 3, 2; further page references in the text are to this edition. Published anonymously, this manual presented a compilation of exemplary letters, some in verse, with two theoretical prefaces, one based, in part, on French sources.
59. An accessible and helpful exposition of turn-taking in (literary) speech situations is found in Pratt's study *Toward a Speech Act Theory*, 100–109. The book is less trustworthy in the section that deals with the Russian formalist legacy, which seems over-reliant on a mere handful of translated articles plagued by misrendered terms.
60. Peschio, *The Poetics of Impudence*, 47–49.
61. Cited from Modzalevskii, "Pushkin," 277.
62. Peskov, *Letopis'*, 268.

63. "Vyderzhki iz starykh bumag Ostaf'evskogo arkhiva," 894.
64. Batiushkov, *Sochineniia v dvukh tomakh*, 2:177.
65. Vigel', *Zapiski*, 1:195.
66. Cited from Culler, *Theory of the Lyric*, 131.
67. For a useful survey of such studies from the 1890s to the 1990s, see Debreczeny, *Social Functions of Literature*, 11–12; a more recent discussion of memory and literature is found in Gronas, *Cognitive Poetics*.
68. "Much morass in Ober-Issel makes the good land awful." Goethe, *Aus meinem Leben*, 1:57.
69. As Stepan Zhikharev recalls, Krylov's recital of his fables at a sitting of Shishkov's literary society was "articulate, simple . . . and incredibly expressive: every line cut itself into your memory"; Petr Karabanov, in a discussion that followed, uses the same image to defend those playwrights who persisted in writing comedies in verse rather than prose: "The sharp words of verse cut themselves quicker into memory, and characters' actions appear more salient in verse than they do in prose." Zhikharev, *Zapiski sovremennika*, 506.
70. *Ostaf'evskii arkhiv kniazei Viazemskikh*, 2:148.
71. Pushkin, *Polnoe sobranie sochinenii*, 13:117.
72. Cited from Eikhenbaum, *Lermontov*, 41.
73. Boratynskii, *Polnoe sobranie sochinenii*, 2:99.
74. Zhukovskii, *Sobranie sochinenii*, 2:161.
75. In this respect, the *pointe* in Zhukovsky's poem appears to be inspired by Baratynsky more than by Schiller's "Morgen können wir's nicht mehr, / Darum laßt uns heute leben!" (Tomorrow, we will probably not be around, / So then, let us live today!)."
76. *Ostaf'evskii arkhiv kniazei Viazemskikh*, 4:9.
77. Galinkovskii, *Utrennik prekrasnogo pola*.
78. Petina, "Ob al'bomnom kharaktere russkikh izdanii."
79. *Vospominaniia Bestuzhevykh*, 28–29.
80. Batiushkov, *Sochineniia v dvukh tomakh*, 2:178.
81. Karamzin, *Pis'ma N. M. Karamzina*, 93.
82. Cited from Eikhenbaum, *Lermontov*, 40.
83. Petina, "Ob al'bomnom kharaktere russkikh izdanii," 145.
84. The specific authorship remains unknown; the slogan was set to music by Irving Berlin for a Disney-produced short used by the 1952 Eisenhower campaign.
85. "Sovremennaia russkaia bibliografiia," 243. As Boris Eikhenbaum shows, copying, imitating, and rearranging verse lines from elder poets was how young Lermontov learned his craft. See Eikhenbaum, *Lermontov*, 21–75.
86. Pushkin, *Polnoe sobranie sochinenii*, 16:135.
87. Shklovskii, "O pisatele i proizvodstve," 199.
88. Such, for instance, were the rules in the Free Society of the Lovers of Russian Letters, whose members included Del'vig and Baratynsky.

89. Viazemskii, *Stikhotvoreniia* (1986), 452–53.
90. Batiushkov, *Sochineniia v dvukh tomakh*, 2:315.
91. Cited from Lotman and Al'tshuller, *Poety 1790–1810-kh godov*, 658.
92. *Ostaf'evskii arkhiv kniazei Viazemskikh*, 2:148.
93. On the effects of misremembering in literary studies, see Dolinin, "Tsena odnoi bukvy."
94. Cited from Gorchakov, "Vyderzhki," 259.
95. Vatsuro, "Literaturnye al'bomy," 40–41.
96. Derrida, "Che cos'è la poesia?," 230; Culler, *Theory of the Lyric*, 130.

Chapter 3. Situations and Occasions

1. R, "Vesna," 62 (dated 1821), emphasis in original. Following Mikhail Longinov's attribution of the elegy to Batiushkov, it was included in the latter's *Works*, as *presumably* Batiushkov's: Longinov never explained his attribution and no evidence was found to support it.
2. *Arkhiv brat'iev Turgenevykh*, 2:364.
3. Ibid., 365.
4. See Reitblat, *Kak Pushkin vyshel v genii*; Rebecchini and Vassena, *Reading in Russia*; Hoogenboom, "Sentimental Novels and Pushkin."
5. *Arkhiv brat'iev Turgenevykh*, 2:72.
6. Merzliakov, *Kratkoe nachertanie*, 173–74.
7. -R-, "Pis'mo k izdateliu," 79–80.
8. Brodskii, *Sochineniia Iosifa Brodskogo*, 1:61.
9. See Culler, "Why Lyric?"; and Jackson, "Who Reads Poetry?"
10. See Peskov, *Letopis' zhizni i tvorchestva*, 21–22; Vatsuro, *S. D. P. Iz istorii literaturnogo byta*, 182–200, 259–61, 289–90.
11. The album inscription is a copy of the journal version (published in *Novosti literatury* in 1823). The text I quote reinstates Pushkin's punctuation as it appeared in the above journal and corrects one misremembered word.
12. See Tabakova, "Pushkin v al'bomakh sovremennikov," 288–90.
13. As Robert Darnton has shown, projecting the read upon one's private life has been a widespread mode of reading since Rousseau; see Darnton, *The Great Cat Massacre*, 215–56.
14. Fried, *Absorption and Theatricality*.
15. Franklin, "Mapping the Graphosphere"; see also Reitblat, "Pis'mennaia literatura."
16. Ivanitskii, "Avtobiografiia," 228.
17. Glagoleva, *Tul'skaia knizhnaia starina*, 78.
18. Andronikov, *Lermontov*, 186.
19. Dmitriev, *Vzgliad na moiu zhizn'*, 69.
20. *Russkaia sentimental'naia povest'*, 91.
21. See Mel'ts, "Pesni i romansy"; and Hodge, *A Double Garland*.

22. See O. Proskurin, "Pop-kul'tura (2)."
23. [Dmitriev], *Karmannyi pesennik*.
24. Tynianov, "Ode as an Oratorical Genre."
25. Derzhavin, *Sochineniia Derzhavina*, 7:570.
26. Ibid.
27. Ibid.
28. Ibid.
29. Here and elsewhere I quote "Finland" as translated by Rawley Grau in Baratynsky, *A Science Not for the Earth*, 13.
30. Boratynskii, *Polnoe sobranie sochinenii*, 1:140–41.
31. Quoted in Peskov, *Boratynskii*, 162–63; other than the section set off by square brackets, from Grau's translation of Konshin's text (Baratynsky, *A Science Not for the Earth*, 483–84).
32. *Vospominaniia Bestuzhevykh*, 156–58.
33. Aksakov, *Polnoe sobranie sochinenii*, 3:78.
34. Gordin and Gordin, *I. A. Krylov*, 194–95.
35. Zhikharev, *Zapiski sovremennika*, 259, 445–46.
36. Ibid., 279.
37. Aksakov, "Pis'ma k M. G. Kartashevskoi," 76.
38. "Pis'mo V. A. Zhukovskogo," 1070.
39. Aksakov, "Pis'ma k M. G. Kartashevskoi," 75.
40. *Russkaia sentimental'naia povest'*, 296.
41. Zorin, *Poiavlenie geroia*, 44.
42. Batiushkov, *Opyty v stikhakh i proze*, 56.
43. Fontenelle, *Conversations*, xiv.
44. Batiushkov, *Sochineniia v dvukh tomakh*, 2:177.
45. See Golovina, "Gazeta dlia odnogo chitatelia"; Antonova, *Ordinary Marriage*, 17–19.
46. See Golovina, "Eshche odin spisok."
47. Cited in ibid., 31.
48. *Ostaf'evskii arkhiv kniazei Viazemskikh*, 2:65.
49. Zorin, *Poiavlenie geroia*, 44.
50. Vinitsky, *Vasily Zhukovsky's Romanticism*, 12; for an in-depth analysis of Zhukovsky's "domestic utopia," see also pages 111–22, 147–52.
51. Zhiliakova, *Perepiska V. A. Zhukovskogo*, 642; Zhukovskii, *Polnoe sobranie sochinenii*, 13:62.
52. Zhukovskii, *Polnoe sobranie sochinenii*, 65; for clarity's sake, I have restored the words and sentences written in shorthand in the original to their full forms.
53. Ibid., 63.
54. Ibid., 65.
55. Ibid.
56. Ibid., 92.

57. Ibid., 107.

58. Ibid., 63; on the role of poetic "self-quotations" in Zhukovsky's diaries and notebooks, see Lebedeva, "Printsipy romanticheskogo zhiznetvorchestva," 423–24.

59. See the description of the notebook, quoted from Pavel Simoni, in Zhukovskii, *Polnoe sobranie sochinenii*, 468.

60. Zhukovskii, *Polnoe sobranie sochinenii*, 68–69.

61. Ibid., 69.

62. Ibid.

63. Ibid., 75.

64. Kern, *Vospominaniia, dnevniki, perepiska*, 181.

65. Zhukovskii, *Polnoe sobranie sochinenii*, 13:92–93.

66. Simoni, "Pis'ma-dnevniki V. A. Zhukovskogo."

67. Translated by Andrey Kneller.

68. Vatsuro, *Lirika pushkinskoi pory*, 21.

69. Vol'pert, *Pushkin v roli Pushkina*, 42–43.

70. See Pushkin, *Rukoiu Pushkina*, 179–84. Tati'ana Zenger's 1935 attribution remains tentative.

71. "We must not, of course, succumb either to vulgar *biographism*, which takes a literary work for a reproduction of the situation from which it originated and infers an unknown situation from a work, or to vulgar *antibiographism*, which dogmatically denies any connection between the work and the situation" (Jakobson, *Selected Writings*, 5:239). "We must never confuse—as has been done up to now and as is still often done—the *represented* world with the world outside the text (naïve realism); nor must we confuse the author-creator of a work with the author as a human being (naïve biographism); nor confuse the listener or reader of multiple and varied periods, re-creating and renewing the text, with the passive listener or reader of one's own time (which leads to dogmatism in interpretation and evaluation).... But it is also impermissible to take this [crucial] boundary line as something absolute and impermeable.... However forcefully the real and represented world resist fusion, however [irrevocable] the presence of that [crucial] line between them, they are nevertheless indissolubly tied up with each other and find themselves in continual mutual interaction; uninterrupted exchange goes on between them, similar to the uninterrupted exchange of matter between living organisms and the environment that surrounds them" (Bakhtin, *The Dialogic Imagination*, 253–54; I have made two slight amendments in square brackets to this translation to bring the quotation closer to the original).

72. Tomashevsky, "Literature and Biography," 49.

73. Lotman, "The Decembrist in Daily Life"; Lotman, "The Poetics of Everyday Behavior."

74. Sandler, *Distant Pleasures*, 39–77.

75. *Ostaf'evskii arkhiv kniazei Viazemskikh*, 2:333–34.

76. Cited from Peskov, *Letopis' zhizni i tvorchestva*, 196.

77. Pushkin, *Polnoe sobranie sochinenii*, 13:334.
78. First published in *Severnye tsvety na 1832 god* (St. Petersburg, 1831). The poem was only published after Del'vig's untimely death in 1831, with the following foreword: "Written in Revel in 1827, the 'Sonnet to the Russian Fleet' remained a secret, even from the poet's friends, until his demise."
79. Cited from Peskov, *Letopis' zhizni i tvorchestva*, 181.
80. Mirskii, "Baratynskii," xxv.
81. Boratynskii, *Polnoe sobranie sochinenii*, 2:237–38.
82. Viazemskii, *Sochineniia v dvukh tomakh*, 1:93–94.
83. Cited from Batiushkov, *Sochineniia v trekh tomakh*, 3:706.
84. Davydov, *Stikhotvoreniia*, 58.
85. *Ostaf'evskii arkhiv kniazei Viazemskikh*, 1:305
86. Cited from Savkina, *Razgovory s zerkalom*, 294.
87. Cited from Tsiavlovskii, "Pushkin," 702.
88. Viazemskii, *Zapisnye knizhki*, 412.
89. Ibid.
90. Pushkin, *Polnoe sobranie sochinenii*, 16:160.
91. Dolgorukov, *Povest' o rozhdenii moem*, 2:303.
92. Ibid., 2:416.
93. Stepanov, "Neizdannye teksty," 427.
94. Iazykov, "Pis'ma k rodnym," 174.
95. See Tsiavlovskii, *Stat'i o Pushkine*, 218.
96. Zorin, *Poiavlenie geroia*, 338.
97. Goethe, *Novels and Tales*, trans. R. D. Boylan, 297.
98. Zorin, *Poiavlenie geroia*, 338. For a close reading of Turgenev's entry (of which the fragment quoted here is but a minor part), see Vinitskii, "Posviashchenie v poeziiu."
99. Tomashevskii, *Pushkin i Frantsiia*, 78.
100. Cited from Tynianov, "Arkhaisty i Pushkin," 48.
101. Batiushkov, *Sochineniia v trekh tomakh*, 3:78.
102. Lebedeva and Ianushkevich, *Zhukovskii v vospominaniiakh sovremennikov*, 102.
103. Zhukovskii, *Sobranie sochinenii v chetyrekh tomakh*, 1:396, emphasis in original.
104. See Fraiman, *Tvorcheskaia strategiia*, 12–35.
105. Zhukovskii, *Sobranie sochinenii*, 4:544.
106. Zorin, *Poiavlenie geroia*, 44.
107. As discussed in her two conference papers, "Effekt Arcimbol'do" and "'Osen'' Baratynskogo."
108. Zhukovskii, *Sobranie sochinenii*, 1:264, 262.
109. Boratynskii, *Polnoe sobranie sochinenii*, 2:301; translation by Rawley Grau in Baratynsky, *A Science Not for the Earth*, 147.

110. Pecherin, "Zamogil'nye zapiski," 154.
111. Glinka, *Zapiski*, 146.
112. See, among others, his already-mentioned works: "The Decembrist in Daily Life" and "The Poetics of Everyday Behavior."
113. *Noveishii polnyi pis'movnik*, 55.

Part II. One, Two, Many

1. Wolf, "The Lyric."
2. Tynianov, "Ode as an Oratorical Genre."
3. Ramazani, *Poetry and Its Others*, 15.
4. Wales, *Personal Pronouns*, 7.
5. See Todd, *The Familiar Letter*; Todd, *Fiction and Society*, 45–104; and Peschio, *The Poetics of Impudence*.
6. Batiushkov, *Opyty v stikhakh i proze*, 367.

Chapter 4. The Extended Self

1. *Vospominaniia Bestuzhevykh*, 18, 25.
2. Abrams, *The Mirror and the Lamp*, 14–21.
3. Aksakov, "Pis'ma k M. G. Kartashevskoi," 87.
4. Kutuzov, "Apollon s semeistvom," 93.
5. Levin, "Lirika s kommunikativnoi tochki zreniia"; Lotman, "Avtokommunikatsiia."
6. Levin, "Lirika s kommunikativnoi tochki zreniia," 472.
7. Ibid., 466.
8. The absence of "I" in "Graveyard" is discussed in Toporov, "Sel'skoe kladbishche," 225; and Ciepiela, "Reading Russian Pastoral," 36.
9. Fraiman, *Tvorcheskaia strategiia*, 24–25.
10. Ciepiela, "Reading Russian Pastoral," 38.
11. Pushkin, *Polnoe sobranie sochinenii*, 3:250.
12. Mazur, "O myshinoi begotne," 251–53.
13. Wachtel, *Cambridge Introduction to Russian Poetry*, 77.
14. See Grigorieva, "'Mne ne spitsia . . . ,'" 209–12; a similar interpretation is given in Jakobson, "O 'Stikhakh . . .'"
15. Wachtel, *Cambridge Introduction to Russian Poetry*, 77.
16. Clark and Chalmers, "The Extended Mind," 7.
17. Ibid., 18.
18. Mazur, "O myshinoi begotne," 254.
19. See, among others, Liamina and Samover, *Bednyi Zhozef*; "Diaries and Intimate Archives," 561–629; Paperno, "Who, What Am I?," 9–29; Zorin, *Poiavlenie geroia*.
20. Zorin, *Poiavlenie geroia*, 46–52, 214–99.
21. Cited from Liamina and Samover, *Bednyi Zhozef*, 103.
22. Ianushkevich, "Dnevniki V. A. Zhukovskogo," 399–405, 417–19.

23. Vatsuro, *Lirika pushkinskoi pory*, 21.
24. Eikhenbaum, *Molodoi Tolstoi*, 26–31.
25. Paperno, "Who, What Am I?," 12.
26. Begichev, *Semeistvo Kholmskikh* (1841), 4:319.
27. Zhikharev, *Zapiski sovremennika*, 65.
28. Ibid., 63.
29. Karamzin, *Izbrannye sochineniia*, 1:498.
30. Mikhailova, "Pis'ma V. L. Pushkina," 221.
31. Karamzin, *Izbrannye sochineniia*, 1:571.
32. Ibid.
33. Peskov, *Letopis' zhizni i tvorchestva*, 275–76.
34. Eikhenbaum, "Literaturnaia domashnost'," 82–86; Aronson and Reiser, *Literaturnye kruzhki i salony*; Peschio, *The Poetics of Impudence*. For an important discussion of the unstable boundary between private and public life in Russian culture of the period, see Schönle, "The Scare of the Self."
35. Aronson and Reiser, *Literaturnye kruzhki i salony*, 37.
36. Peschio, *The Poetics of Impudence*, 42.
37. For memoiristic accounts of literary societies in provincial gymnasiums, see Ivanitskii, "Avtobiografiia," 238; Galakhov, *Zapiski cheloveka*, 60–63.
38. Peschio, *The Poetics of Impudence*, 24–33.
39. Lotman, *Sotvorenie Karamzina*, 295.
40. Todd, *The Familiar Letter*, 40–42.
41. Peskov, *Letopis' zhizni i tvorchestva*, 231.
42. *Vospominaniia Bestuzhevykh*, 209.
43. Zhukovskii, *Polnoe sobranie sochinenii*, 13:18–19.
44. Pushkin, *Polnoe sobranie sochinenii*, 12:218.
45. Vatsuro, *Lirika pushkinskoi pory*, 21–36.
46. Rashkov, "Zhizn' Shillera," 137–38.
47. Ancillon, *Nouveaux essais*, 2:70.
48. Aizikova, "Dialog russko-nemetskikh traditsii."
49. Zhukovskii, *Polnoe sobranie sochinenii*, 13:147.
50. Ibid., 124.
51. Khagi, *Silence and the Rest*.
52. Zhukovskii, *Polnoe sobranie sochinenii*, 10:2:272.
53. Kiukhel'beker, *Puteshestvie*, 36.
54. Kiukhel'beker, *Izbrannye proizvedeniia*, 1:147.
55. Senderovich, "Simpozium poetov," 482.
56. Pushkin, *Polnoe sobranie sochinenii*, 2:969.
57. Zhukovskii, *Polnoe sobranie sochinenii*, 1:186.
58. Ibid., 343.
59. See Vatsuro, *Lirika pushkinskoi pory*, 180.
60. Davydov, *Stikhotvoreniia*, 57.
61. Derzhavin, *Sochineniia Derzhavina*, 1:1:665–66.

62. Batiushkov, *Opyty v stikhakh i proze*, 22.
63. Senderovich, "Simpozium poetov," 486.
64. Batiushkov, *Opyty v stikhakh i proze*, 275.
65. For a brief but insightful discussion of the role of friendly epistles in the structure of *Eugene Onegin*, see Skachkova, "Druzheskoe poslanie."
66. Pushkin, *Polnoe sobranie sochinenii*, 13:180.
67. Peschio, *The Poetics of Impudence*, 28.
68. Davydov, *Stikhotvoreniia*, 57.
69. Vatsuro, *Lirika pushkinskoi pory*, 178.
70. Gasparov, *Poeticheskii iazyk Pushkina*, 42–117.
71. Cited from *Ostaf'evskii arkhiv kniazei Viazemskikh*, 1:67.
72. Zhukovskii, *Polnoe sobranie sochinenii*, 1:599 (commentary on "Bard . . ." by A. S. Ianushkevich).
73. Pushkin, *Polnoe sobranie sochinenii*, 11:143.
74. Zhukovskii, *Polnoe sobranie sochinenii*, 1:244.
75. Ibid., 237–38.
76. Ibid., 239–40.
77. Batiushkov, *Opyty v stikhah i proze*, 200.
78. Batiushkov, *Sochineniia v trekh tomakh*, 3:408.
79. Hall, *The Silent Language*.
80. Pil'shchikov, "Nomina si nescis . . . ," 70; see also Pil'shchikov and Peschio, "The Proliferation of Elite Readerships."
81. "Ot budushchikh zhurnalistov k Redaktoru V.E.," 311.
82. Pil'shchikov, "Nomina si nescis . . . ," 78.
83. Baratynskii, *Polnoe sobranie sochinenii*, 2:198.
84. Translation by Rawley Grau in Baratynsky, *A Science Not for the Earth*, 85.
85. Kireevskii, *Kritika i estetika*, 237.
86. Zhukovskii, *Polnoe sobranie sochinenii*, 1:346–48.
87. Mandelstam, "On the Addressee," 69.
88. The essay's original title in Russian is "O sobesednike."
89. *"Ty" Bal'monta nikogda ne nakhodit adresata* (Mandel'shtam, *Sobranie sochinenii*, 1:185).
90. Mandelstam, "On the Addressee," 70.
91. See Mandel'shtam, *Sochineniia v dvukh tomakh*, 1:399.
92. Mandelstam, *Hope Abandoned*, 25.

Chapter 5. You and I

1. See the two essays in which Jakobson discusses Pushkin's "Ia vas liubil": "Poetry of Grammar and Grammar of Poetry" and "Two Poems by Puškin."
2. Shklovskii, *Izbrannoe v dvukh tomakh*, 2:196.
3. Shklovsky, *Zoo*, 3.
4. Viazemskii, *Stikhotvoreniia* (1958), 72.

5. Galakhov, *Zapiski cheloveka*, 106–7.
6. [Begichev], *Semeistvo Kholmskikh* (1832), 2:115.
7. Pushkin, *Polnoe sobranie sochinenii*, 3:100.
8. Dostoevsky, *Demons*, 131.
9. Cited from Savkina, *Razgovory s zerkalom*, 258.
10. Galakhov, *Zapiski cheloveka*, 107–8. On the role of albums in courtship, see Hammarberg, "Flirting with Words."
11. Bestuzhev, "Roman v semi pis'makh," 450.
12. Galakhov, *Zapiski cheloveka*, 107–8.
13. Ibid.
14. Ibid.
15. Ibid., 451.
16. Pushkin, *Polnoe sobranie sochinenii*, 3:103. For an analysis of this poem in the broader context of personal pronouns in Pushkin's love lyric, see Etkind, *Bozhestvennyi glagol*, 112–25. As has been noted more than once, there existed a rich tradition of Tu-versus-Vous poems in eighteenth-century French literature.
17. Translation, with my slight adjustments, from Arndt, *Pushkin Threefold*, 223.
18. Pushkin, *Polnoe sobranie sochinenii*, 13:301.
19. Istrin, "Mladshii turgenevskii kruzhok," 56.
20. Zorin, *Poiavlenie geroia*, 300–466.
21. Darnton, *The Great Cat Massacre*, 229–33.
22. Dolgorukov, *Povest' o rozhdenii moem*, 1:99.
23. Barthes, *A Lover's Discourse*.
24. See, for instance, Millevoye, "Sur l'élégie," 29. A certain Abbé D* encountered by Karamzin's "Russian traveler" in Paris voices the same opinion, only in a negative way ("He wrote dramatic elegies, but never tragedies"); see Karamzin, *Izbrannye sochineniia*, 1:466.
25. Valmont uses the plural ("élégies") despite the fact that, as he confesses to someone else, since his love letters to the unapproachable Madame de Tourvel return to him unopened, he sends the same letter again and again, only changing the envelope (Choderlos de Laclos, *Les Liaisons dangereuses*, 2:379).
26. Proskurin, *Poeziia Pushkina*, 56–139.
27. For a discussion of role-playing based on literary models in Russian culture of the Golden Age, see Lotman, "Theater and Theatricality"; Vol'pert, *Pushkin v roli Pushkina*.
28. Boratynskii, *Polnoe sobranie sochinenii*, 1:236.
29. Translation by Rawley Grau in Baratynsky, *A Science Not for the Earth*, 21.
30. Pushkin, *Polnoe sobranie sochinenii*, 14:33. On the libertine models in Pushkin and Vul'f, see Vol'pert, *Pushkin v roli Pushkina*, 33–59; Pil'shchikov, "Aleksandr Pushkin," 58–69.
31. *Liubovnye pokhozhdeniia*, 48.

32. Ibid., 64. Most of Vul'f's diary entries covering his affair with Sofia Del'vig come from late 1828, during the relationship itself, but several of those I cite were written in 1829 and 1830, when, languishing in a remote military camp, the bored Vul'f would kill time by recapping his past love life in written form.
33. Ibid.
34. Ibid.
35. Ibid., 41.
36. Ibid., 42.
37. Ibid., 43.
38. Ibid.
39. Ibid.
40. Ibid., 43–44.
41. Ibid., 50.
42. Ibid., 53.
43. Ibid.
44. Ibid.
45. Ibid., 75.
46. See Zhivov, *Language and Culture*, 418–23. According to Zhivov, this etymology applies to Russian love vocabulary in general.
47. *Liubovnye pokhozhdeniia*, 44.
48. Baratynsky, *Polnoe sobranie stikhotvorenii*, 2:33.
49. Cited in Peskov, *Letopis' zhizni i tvorchestva*, 166.
50. Modzalevskii, "Roman dekabrista Kakhovskogo," 212–13.
51. See Peskov, *Letopis' zhizni i tvorchestva*, 242.
52. Boratynskii, *Polnoe sobranie sochinenii*, 2:202.
53. *Liubovnye pokhozhdeniia*, 74.
54. Cited from Boratynskii, *Polnoe sobranie sochinenii*, 2:202.
55. *Liubovnye pokhozhdeniia*, 146; I hasten to note that Pushkin gave this advice with regard to women generally, *not* in the context of how Vul'f might win the wife of their mutual friend Del'vig.
56. Peskov, *Letopis' zhizni i tvorchestva*, 213.
57. Khitrova, "Literaturnaia pozitsiia Baratynskogo."
58. Shvartsband, *Pushkin*, 19–45.
59. Pushkin, *Polnoe sobranie sochinenii*, 12:303.
60. Ibid., 2:209.
61. See the commentary provided in the newest Pushkin edition: Pushkin, *Polnoe sobranie sochinenii v 20-ti tomakh*, 2:2:635–36.
62. *Liubovnye pokhozhdeniia*, 147.
63. Pushkin, *Polnoe sobranie sochinenii*, 13:34; the situation was actually "more dire" than the "compare-despairing" Pushkin realized—Baratynsky at the time was twenty-*one*.

64. Ibid., 13:239.
65. Ibid., 2:228.
66. Ibid., 13:74.
67. Ibid., 13:84.
68. Ibid., 13:88.
69. Boratynskii, *Polnoe sobrabie sochinenii*, 2:63–64.
70. The early (1823) text of "Confession" I quote here differs significantly from the revised—canonical—version published in 1835. Wherever the two versions overlap, I use Rawley Grau's translation of the latter in Baratynsky, *A Science Not for the Earth*, 31–33.
71. For an excellent analysis of Baratynsky's "Confession," see Nilsson, "Baratynskij's Elegiac Code." A brief but important insight on how the ethical dimension of Baratynsky's elegies ranges beyond "conventional morality" is found in Proskurin, *Poeziia Pushkina*, 80–81. Lazar Fleishman briefly discusses "ethical neutrality" in Baratynsky's elegies in his "Iz istorii elegii," 37–38.
72. See Ginzburg, *O lirike*, 77; Bocharov, *O khudozhestvennykh mirakh*, 84.
73. Bocharov, *O khudozhestvennykh mirakh*, 83.
74. See Dobritsyn, "Libertinskaia model' povedeniia."
75. The scholarship on libertine literature is vast. Particularly important for my study was Versini, *Le Roman le plus intelligent*.
76. *Liubovnye pokhozhdeniia*, 62.
77. Kern, *Vospominaniia, dnevniki, perepiska*, 53.
78. Pushkin, *Polnoe sobranie sochinenii*, 2:437; the libertine genealogy of these lines is noted in Dobritsyn, "Libertinskaia model' povedeniia," 150, 160.
79. Choderlos de Laclos, *Les Liaisons dangereuses*, 2:487.
80. Ibid.
81. Ibid.
82. Pushkin, *Polnoe sobranie sochinenii*, 11:185.
83. Ibid., 13:278.
84. Ibid., 11:60.
85. Fleishman insightfully calls Baratynsky's elegies "extended aphorisms"; "Iz istorii elegii," 38.
86. See, for instance, Dornier, *Le Discours*, 73–97, 185–253.
87. Diderot, *Contes et romans*, 897.
88. La Bruyère, *The Characters*, 90.
89. Chamfort, *Maximes*, 69.
90. Cited from Vatsuro, Fomichev, and Larionova, *Pushkin v prizhiznennoi kritike*, 123.
91. Ibid., 219.
92. On the genre structure of *Prisoner*, and particularly its role in elegy, see Proskurin, *Poeziia Pushkina*, 108–22; and Proskurin, "Kommentarii."

93. Proskurin, "Kommentarii," 163.
94. Pushkin, *Polnoe sobranie sochinenii*, 13:8.
95. Ibid., 127.
96. Ibid., 11:187.
97. Ibid.
98. Baratynsky, *Polnoe sobranie stikhotvorenii*, 2:5.
99. Ibid., 166.
100. Ibid., 19–20.
101. Pushkin, *Polnoe sobranie sochinenii*, 4:106.
102. Baratynsky, *Polnoe sobranie stikhotvorenii*, 2:163.
103. Ibid.
104. Pushkin, *Polnoe sobranie sochinenii*, 4:262. On Pushkin's reaction to *Eda*, see Bodrova, "K istorii pushkinskoi epigrammy."
105. Baratynsky, *Polnoe sobranie stikhotvorenii*, 2:163.
106. Ibid.
107. Pushkin, *Polnoe sobranie sochinenii*, 6:65.
108. Translations from *Eugene Onegin* here and in the next chapter are mine, although I have consulted Vladimir Nabokov's translation and used several lines from it.
109. Pushkin, *Polnoe sobranie sochinenii*, 6:98.
110. Proskurin, *Poeziia Pushkina*, 168–69.
111. As Lotman has observed, there is strong, if circumstantial, evidence that Pushkin read *Eda*, or at least parts of it, before its publication in 1826. Lotman suggests this took place in late 1824 (see Lotman, *Pushkin*, 633).
112. Ibid., 80.
113. Pushkin, *Eugene Onegin*, 2:150–51.
114. Pushkin, *Polnoe sobranie sochinenii*, 6:75.
115. For an analysis of this device in Onegin's response to Tatiana, see Hasty, *Pushkin's Tatiana*, 124.
116. Pushkin, *Polnoe sobranie sochinenii*, 6:76.
117. Hasty, *Pushkin's Tatiana*, 125–26.
118. Boratynskii, *Polnoe sobranie sochinenii*, 2:38.
119. Pushkin, *Polnoe sobranie sochinenii*, 3:188. Of the many scholarly works on "I loved you," I would single out the subtle analysis in Senderovich, "Vnutrenniaia rech'."
120. Pushkin, *Polnoe sobranie sochinenii*, 3:1193.
121. This attribution remains generally accepted, despite being disputed in 1958 by Tat'iana Tsiavlovskaia who, using pop-psychological insights to bolster her argument, traced "I loved you" to Pushkin's affair with Karolina Sobańska (see Tsiavlovskaia, "Dnevnik A. A. Oleninoi," 289–92). In Tsiavlovskaia's view, Pushkin later readdressed the poem to Olenina by inscribing it in her album.
122. Cited in ibid., 290. Olenina's album is now lost.

Chapter 6. The Art of Epilogue

1. Tynianov, "O parodii," 310. Translated by Ainsley Morse and Phil Redko.
2. Proskurin, "Kommentarii," 18–144.
3. As Proskurin writes: "Upon [*Ruslan and Liudmila*'s] appearance, the 'fairy-tale-like' epic poem practically disappeared from Russian literature as a productive genre" (ibid., 60).
4. For the most recent, to my knowledge, contribution to this debate, see Proskurin, "'Zlodeiskaia porfira.'"
5. Pushkin, *Polnoe sobranie sochinenii v 20-ti tomakh*, 2:1:12.
6. Translation from Arndt, *Pushkin Threefold*, 165.
7. See the commentary (by V. E. Vatsuro, E. O. Larionova, and A. I. Rogova) in Pushkin, *Polnoe sobranie sochinenii v 20-ti tomakh*, 2:1:475–76.
8. Ibid., 17.
9. Translation (with my adjustments) from Binyon, *Pushkin*, 85.
10. Parsamov, *Dekabristy*, 143–45.
11. For a brief but rich description of the fate of the *Beatus ille* . . . formula on Russian soil, see Mazur, "'Pora, moi drug, pora!,'" 387–96, 405–19. As Georgii Levinton observes ("'Blazhen, kto . . . '"), the *Blazhen kto* . . . formula in Russian poetry has at least three main sources: Horace's second epode, the Bible, and an ode of Sappho translated by Boileau. In most of the cases I discuss in this chapter, I believe, Pushkin alludes to Horace. For a different reading of Pushkin's use of the *Blazhen, kto* . . . formula in *EO*, see Bozovic, *Nabokov's Canon*, 20–25.
12. Pushkin, *Polnoe sobranie sochinenii*, 6:169.
13. As mentioned in the previous chapter, translations from *Eugene Onegin* are mine, although I have consulted Vladimir Nabokov's translation and used several lines from it.
14. From their manuscript circulation to recent editions, the two texts have lived separately. One reason for this is evident: "Liberty" was among the poems that cost Pushkin his southern exile. This magnified the political explosiveness of his ode in the eyes of those who read and copied it and thus overshadowed the madrigal.
15. Pushkin, *Polnoe sobranie sochinenii v 20-ti tomakh*, 1:476.
16. Ibid.
17. Ibid., 481.
18. Oksman, "Pushkinskaia oda 'Vol'nost'," 5.
19. Proskurin, "Pushkin and Politics," 106–7; Pushkin, *Polnoe sobranie sochinenii v 20-ti tomakh*, 2:1:486.
20. Maiofis, *Vozzvanie k Evrope*, 320–47.
21. Pushkin, *Polnoe sobranie sochinenii v 20-ti tomakh*, 2:1:6–7.
22. Cited in ibid., 468 (commentary by E. O. Larionova).
23. Of the enormous bibliography on *EO* the most relevant for my study are: Tynianov, "On the Composition of *Eugene Onegin*"; Tynianov, "Arkhaisty i Pushkin"; Tynianov, "Pushkin," 155–58; and Proskurin, *Poeziia Pushkina*, 140–98; see also

Lotman's study of *EO* in his *Pushkin*, 391–762; Bocharov, "The Stylistic World of the Novel"; and Greenleaf, *Pushkin and Romantic Fashion*, 205–86. See also important contributions to the discussion of smaller lyric genres in *EO* in Baevskii, "Traditsiia 'legkoi poezii'" and N. I. Mikhailova, "'Evgenii Onegin.'"

24. Fomichev, *"Evgenii Onegin,"* 16. A different explanation is suggested in Shvartsband, *Istoriia tekstov*, 127–33.

25. Among the voluminous scholarship on the character/author relationship as it unfolds in *EO*, I would single out here Sergei Bocharov's contribution in "Forma plana."

26. Tynianov, "Pushkin," 156.

27. Proskurin, *Poeziia Pushkina*, 149.

28. Samuil Shvartsband argues ("Istoriia tekstov," 136–41) that Pushkin originally meant to cut off chapter 1 at stanza LVI, and convincingly points to Pushkin's intention to create a parallel structure of two types of narrations: one about the character, the other about the author, which led Pushkin to conclude the chapter with more stanzas of the latter type, to preserve this balance.

29. Pushkin, *Polnoe sobranie sochinenii*, 6:28–29.

30. Ibid., 6:29.

31. See Bocharov, "The Stylistic World of the Novel," 133–38.

32. Tynianov, "Arkhaisty i Pushkin," 121.

33. Pushkin, *Eugene Onegin*, 2:245.

34. Lotman, *Pushkin*, 594–95. See also the detailed analysis in Lotman, "K evoliutsii postroeniia kharakterov," 143–50.

35. Proskurin, *Poeziia Pushkina*, 150.

36. Pushkin, *Polnoe sobranie sochinenii*, 6:267–73. A photocopy of the notebook (PD 834) Pushkin used when working on the second chapter of *EO* is available in volume 4 of the 1996 *Rabochie tetradi* edition (the draft of stanzas VI to X is found on ll. 25ob.–27). For a detailed description of Pushkin's work on these stanzas in this notebook, see Levkovich, "Rabochaia tetrad'," 219–20.

37. Vatsuro, *Lirika pushkinskoi pory*, 33–36.

38. See ibid.; and Zorin, *Poiavlenie geroia*, 214–513.

39. See Nabokov's commentary in Pushkin, *Eugene Onegin*, 2:228; Lotman, *Pushkin*, 592.

40. Pushkin, *Polnoe sobranie sochinenii*, 6:267. For a detailed analysis of Pushkin's work on this line, see Teletova, "Dushoi filister gettingenskii."

41. Nabokov cites this letter in his commentary (Pushkin, *Eugene Onegin*, 2:229; I have adjusted his translation).

42. D'iakonov, "Ob istorii zamysla 'Evgeniia Onegina,'" 85; Lotman, "K evoliutsii postroeniia kharakterov," 143.

43. Traditional dating for this first fair copy (in or after January 1824) has been recently challenged by Proskurin ("Iz istorii odesskogo teksta," 210–11), who maintains that Pushkin began work on the first fair copy of chapter 2 in September 1824,

after arriving in Mikhailovskoe from Odessa and after, in early September, having prepared the copy of chapter 1 for publication. It is not entirely clear, then, why, if indeed Pushkin worked on the first fair copy and on the fragment to be sent to Del'vig essentially at the same time, in mid-September, the versions of the first fair copy and those published in *Severnye tsvety* are different and, in particular, why he did not cross out the endings, missing in the publication, from the first fair copy (as he had crossed out the entire three stanzas IXa, IXb, and IXc—see Pushkin, *Polnoe sobranie sochinenii*, 6:559). I am inclined to think that preparation of the fragment for *Severnye tsvety* presented the next stage of Pushkin's editing work, after the first fair copy. When he returned to it, in the second fair copy in the spring of 1825, the missing endings were completely rewritten.

44. Pushkin, *Polnoe sobranie sochinenii*, 6:558–60.

45. Ibid., 108.

46. Cf. the first fair copy versions, respectively, of stanzas VII and X, which are still quite close to the draft versions: "He knew both labor and inspiration / And refreshing repose / Young life's inexplicable urge / *For something* / A riotous feast of wild passions / And tears, and the heart's peace" ("Он знал и труд и вдохновенье / И освежительный покой / *К чему-то* жизни молодой / Неизъяснимое влеченье / Страстей мятежных буйный пир / И слезы и сердечный мир"); "He sang of the groves where he used to meet / His eternal lovely ideal" ("Он пел дубравы где встречал / Свой вечный, милый идеал") (Pushkin, *Polnoe sobranie sochinenii*, 6:558–60).

47. Sidiakov, "K istorii raboty Pushkina."

48. D'iakonov, "Ob istorii zamysla 'Evgeniia Onegina,'" 89–90.

49. Kiukhel'beker, "O napravlenii nashei poezii," 455.

50. Ibid., 454–55.

51. As M. F. Mur'ianov has shown, Lensky followed Schiller even in his hairdo ("Portret Lenskogo," 82–85).

52. Kiukhel'beker, "O napravlenii nashei poezii," 454.

53. Pushkin, *Polnoe sobranie sochinenii*, 6:271–72, 558–59; angle brackets indicate words crossed out by Pushkin.

54. Tynianov, "Arkhaisty i Pushkin," 119.

55. Bocharov calls "Lensky's world . . . *unconsciously heterostylistic*" ("The Stylistic World of the Novel," 145).

56. Kiukhel'beker, "O napravlenii nashei poezii," 455, 458.

57. See Vatsuro, *Lirika pushkinskoi pory*, 28–36.

58. Shvartsband, *Istoriia tekstov*, 166–67.

59. See Todd's section on *Eugene Onegin* as "life's novel" in *Fiction and Society*, 106–36.

60. Sidiakov, "K istorii raboty Pushkina." For the photocopy, see Pushkin, *Rabochie tetradi*, 4: PD 835, l. 58.

61. Pushkin, *Polnoe sobranie sochinenii*, 6:84–85.

62. Ibid., 48.
63. Ibid., 571.
64. Ibid., 571–72.
65. Ibid., 85. In the period Russian, *vrat'* not only meant "to lie," as it does now, but also "to chat" or "babble." Pushkin clearly refers to both meanings in this line.
66. Ibid., 86.
67. Ibid.
68. Ibid., 86–87.
69. Lotman, *Pushkin*, 637. See also the insightful analysis found in Gasparov, *Poeticheskii iazyk Pushkina*, 64–72; Greenleaf, *Pushkin and Romantic Fashion*, 245–46; and Proskurin, *Literaturnye skandaly pushkinskoi epokhi*, 229–59. For the most recent elaborate discussion of these and neighboring stanzas, see Mazur, "Maska neistovogo stikhotvortsa."
70. Pushkin, *Polnoe sobranie sochinenii*, 6:87.
71. Ibid., 88.
72. Ibid.
73. Tynianov, "Arkhaisty i Pushkin," 64–67. The quote comes from Pushkin's letter to Viazemsky of 8 March 1824 (Pushkin, *Polnoe sobranie sochinenii*, 13:89).
74. Pushkin, *Polnoe sobranie sochinenii*, 13:96, 179. The translation of the second quote is from Todd, *Fiction and Society*, 107.
75. Pushkin, *Polnoe sobranie sochinenii*, 13:266. On the reception of *Ruslan*, see Peschio, *The Poetics of Impudence*, 94–114.
76. Pushkin, *Polnoe sobranie sochinenii*, 13:198.
77. Ibid., 11:41–42; angle brackets indicate the title was given by the editors of *Polnoe sobranie sochinenii*. For a detailed analysis of this draft article, see Krasnoborod'ko and Khitrova, "Pushkinskii nabrosok vozrazheniia Kiukhel'bekeru."
78. Pushkin, *Polnoe sobranie sochinenii*, 6:194.
79. Ibid., 112.
80. Viazemsky came up with the term *shinel'nye stikhi* ("overcoat verses") to refer to this practice (*Zapisnye knizhki*, 212).
81. Lotman, *Pushkin*, 662.
82. Pushkin, *Polnoe sobranie sochinenii*, 11:53.
83. See Reyfman, *Vasilii Trediakovsky*, 27–28, 202, 220–21.
84. Lotman, *Pushkin*, 666.
85. Pushkin, *Polnoe sobranie sochinenii*, 6:121.
86. Ibid., 160.
87. Ibid., 125.
88. Tynianov, "Arkhaisty i Pushkin," 120–21.
89. Pushkin, *Polnoe sobranie sochinenii*, 6:126.
90. Proskurin, *Poeziia Pushkina*, 175–76.
91. Zhukovsky's presence in chapters 6 and 7 of *EO* is analyzed in Nemzer, *Pri svete Zhukovskogo*, 215–27.

92. Pushkin, *Polnoe sobranie sochinenii*, 6:133.
93. Ibid., 133–34.
94. On the bast shoe the peasant is plaiting, and the role of Zhukovsky in this episode, see Proskurin, *Poeziia Pushkina*, 177; and Nemzer, *Pri svete Zhukovskogo*, 217–20.
95. Pushkin, *Polnoe sobranie sochinenii*, 6:134.
96. On this reader's lack of interest in the fate of Lensky, see Greenleaf, *Pushkin and Romantic Fashion*, 281.
97. Pushkin, *Polnoe sobranie sochinenii*, 6:136.
98. Ibid.
99. Kiukhel'beker, *Puteshestvie*, 454. Natal'ia Mazur also discusses the notion of "interest" (*koryst'*) as used by Küchelbecker and Pushkin; in her view, both use *koryst'* as a Russian equivalent for Helvetius's concept of "l'intérêt" ("Maska neistovogo stikhotvortsa," 175–77).
100. Pushkin, *Polnoe sobranie sochinenii*, 3:142.
101. Tynianov, "Arkhaisty i Pushkin," 116.
102. Pushkin, *Polnoe sobranie sochinenii*, 11:19.
103. For the most recent detailed analysis of "Conversation," see Kahn, *Pushkin's Lyric Intelligence*, 175–87.
104. Pushkin, *Polnoe sobranie sochinenii*, 2:326.
105. Ibid., 327.
106. Ibid., 329.
107. Ibid., 330.
108. Ibid., 329–30.
109. Pushkin, *Polnoe sobranie sochinenii*, 13:95.
110. For a recent analysis of Pushkin's complicated service career, see Reyfman, *How Russia Learned to Write*, 44–85.
111. Bestuzhev, "O romane N. Polevogo," 134.
112. Pushkin, *Polnoe sobranie sochinenii*, 2:329.

Bibliography

Abrams, Meyer Howard. *The Mirror and the Lamp: Romantic Theory and the Critical Tradition*. London: Oxford University Press, 1971.
Aizikova, I. A. "Dialog russko-nemetskikh traditsii filosofsko-istoricheskoi mysli v mirovozzrenii i tvorchestve V. A. Zhukovskogo (O retseptsii filosofii istorii F. Ansil'iona)." *Vestnik Tomskogo gosudarstvennogo universiteta* 296 (2017): 7–13.
Aksakov, K. "Pis'ma k M. G. Kartashevskoi: Publikatsiia E. I. Annenkovoi." *Ezhegodnik Rukopisnogo otdela Pushkinskogo Doma na 1973 god* (1976): 74–89.
Aksakov, S. T. *Polnoe sobranie sochinenii*. St. Petersburg: N. G. Martynov, 1886.
Ancillon, Jean Pierre Frédéric. *Nouveaux essais de politique et de philosophie*. 2 vols. Paris: Egron, 1824.
Andronikov, I. L. *Lermontov: Issledovaniia i nakhodki*. Moscow: Khudozhestvennaia literatura, 1977.
Antonova, Katherine Pickering. *An Ordinary Marriage: The World of a Gentry Family in Provincial Russia*. Oxford: Oxford University Press, 2012.
Arkhiv brat'iev Turgenevykh. 7 vols. St. Petersburg: Tipografiia Akademii nauk, 1911–21.
Arndt, Walter. *Pushkin Threefold: Narrative, Lyric, Polemic, and Ribald Verse*. New York: Dutton, 1972.
Aronson, M., and S. Reiser. *Literaturnye kruzhki i salony*. Edited by Boris Eikhenbaum. Leningrad: Priboi, 1929.
Atanasova-Sokolova, Deniz. *Pis'mo kak fakt russkoi kul'tury XVIII–XIX vekov*. Budapest: EFO, 2006.
Austin, J. L. *How to Do Things with Words*. Cambridge, MA: Harvard University Press, 1975.
Baevskii, Vadim. "Traditsiia 'legkoi poezii' v 'Evgenii Onegine.'" *Pushkin: Issledovaniia i materialy* 10 (1982): 106–20.
Bakhtin, Mikhail. *The Dialogic Imagination*. Edited by Michael Holquist. Translated by Caryl Emerson and Michael Holquist. Austin: University of Texas Press, 1981.

———. "Discourse in the Novel." In Bakhtin, *The Dialogic Imagination*, 259–422.
Baratynskii, Evgenii. *Polnoe sobranie stikhotvorenii*. Edited by E. Kupreianova and I. Medvedeva. Leningrad: Sovetskii pisatel', 1936.
Baratynsky, Yevgeny. *A Science Not for the Earth: Selected Poems and Letters*. Translated by Rawley Grau. Edited by Rawley Grau and Ilya Bernstein. Brooklyn, NY: Ugly Duckling Presse, 2015.
Bartenev, P. A. "Pushkin v iuzhnoi Rossii." *Russkii arkhiv*, nos. 8–9 (1866): 1089–1214.
Barthes, Roland. *A Lover's Discourse: Fragments*. Translated by Richard Howard. New York: Hill and Wang, 2001.
Batiushkov, Konstantin. *Opyty v stikhakh i proze*. Edited by Irina Semenko. Moscow: Nauka, 1977.
———. *Sochineniia v dvukh tomakh*. Edited by Andrei Zorin. Moscow: Khudozhestvennaia literatura, 1989.
———. *Sochineniia v trekh tomakh*. Edited by Leonid Maikov and Vladimir Saitov. St. Petersburg: P. N. Batiushkov, 1885–87.
Bazanov, Vasilii. *Uchenaia respublika*. Leningrad: Nauka, 1964.
[Begichev, Dmitrii]. *Semeistvo Kholmskikh: Nekotorye cherty nravov i obraza zhizni, semeinoi i odinokoi, russkikh dvorian*. Moscow: Avgust Semen, 1832.
———. *Semeistvo Kholmskikh: Nekotorye cherty nravov i obraza zhizni, semeinoi i odinokoi, russkikh dvorian*. Moscow: Avgust Semen, 1841.
Bestuzhev, Aleksandr. "O romane N. Polevogo 'Kliatva pri grobe gospodnem.'" In *Dekabristy: Estetika i kritika*, edited by R. G. Nazar'ian and L. G. Frizman, 133–87. Moscow: Iskusstvo, 1991.
———. "Roman v semi pis'makh." In *Poliarnaia zvezda, izdannaia A. Bestuzhevym i K. Ryleevym*, edited by V. A. Arkhipov, V. G. Bazanov, and Ia. L. Levkovich, 447–55. Moscow: Izdatel'stvo Akademii nauk SSSR, 1960.
———. "Vzgliad na russkuiu slovesnost' v techenie 1824 i nachale 1825 godov." In *Poliarnaia zvezda, izdannaia A. Bestuzhevym i K. Ryleevym*, edited by V. A. Arkhipov, V. G. Bazanov, and Ia. L. Levkovich, 488–99. Moscow: Izdatel'stvo Akademii nauk SSSR, 1960.
Binyon, T. J. *Pushkin: A Biography*. New York: Vintage Books, 2004.
Bocharov, Sergei. "Forma plana (nekotorye voprosy poetiki Pushkina)." *Voprosy literatury* 12 (1967): 115–36.
———. *O khudozhestvennykh mirakh*. Moscow: Sovetskaia Rossiia, 1985.
———. "The Stylistic World of the Novel." In *Russian Views of Pushkin's* Eugene Onegin, edited by Sona Hoisington, 122–68. Bloomington: Indiana University Press, 1988.
Bodrova, Alina. "K istorii pushkinskoi epigrammy 'Stikh kazhdyi v povesti tvoei...'" In *Philologica* 9, nos. 21–23 (2012): 104–20.
Boratynskii, Evgenii. *Polnoe sobranie sochinenii i pisem*. Moscow: Iazyki slavianskoi kul'tury, 2002–.

Bowers, Katherine. "Unpacking Viazemskii's *Khalat*: The Technologies of Dilettantism in Early Nineteenth-Century Russian Literary Culture." *Slavic Review* 74, no. 3 (2015): 529–52.
Bowring, John, trans. *Rossiiskaia Antologiia: Specimens of the Russian Poets*. 2nd ed. 2 vols. London: R. and A. Taylor, 1821.
Bozovic, Marijeta. *Nabokov's Canon: From* Onegin *to* Ada. Evanston, IL: Northwestern University Press, 2016.
Brodskii, Iosif. *Sochineniia Iosifa Brodskogo*. St. Petersburg: Pushkinskii fond, 1992.
Brooks, Cleanth. *The Well Wrought Urn: Studies in the Structure of Poetry*. New York: Harcourt, 1947.
Chamfort, Nicolas. *Maximes, Pensées, Anecdotes, Caractères & Dialogues*. Paris: Lévy, 1857.
Choderlos de Laclos, Pierre. *Les Liaisons dangereuses*. Translated by Ernest Dowson. London, 1898.
Ciepiela, Catherine. "Reading Russian Pastoral: Zhukovsky's Translation of Gray's Elegy." In *Rereading Russian Poetry*, edited by Stephanie Sandler, 31–57. New Haven, CT: Yale University Press, 1999.
Clark, Andy, and David Chalmers. "The Extended Mind." *Analysis* 58, no. 1 (1998): 7–19.
Cohen, Michael. *The Social Lives of Poems in Nineteenth-Century America*. Philadelphia: University of Pennsylvania Press, 2015.
Culler, Jonathan. *Literary Theory: A Very Short Introduction*. Oxford: Oxford University Press, 1997.
———. *Theory of the Lyric*. Cambridge, MA: Harvard University Press, 2015.
———. "Why Lyric?" *PMLA* 123, no. 1 (2008): 201–6.
Darnton, Robert. *The Great Cat Massacre: And Other Episodes in French Cultural History*. New York: Basic Books, 1984.
Davydov, Denis V. "Pis'mo Denisa Vasil'evicha Davydova k Zhukovskomu." *Russkii arkhiv*, no. 6 (1868): 975.
———. *Stikhotvoreniia*. Leningrad: Sovetskii pisatel', 1984.
Debreczeny, Paul. *Social Functions of Literature: Alexander Pushkin and Russian Culture*. Stanford, CA: Stanford University Press, 1997.
Del'vig, Anton. *Sochineniia*. Edited by Vadim Vatsuro. Leningrad: Khudozhestvennaia literatura, 1986.
Derrida, Jacques. "Che cos'è la poesia?" In *A Derrida Reader: Between the Blinds*. Edited by Peggy Kamuf, 221–37. New York: Columbia University Press, 1991.
Derzhavin, Gavriil. *Sochineniia Derzhavina s ob"iasnitel'nymi primechaniiami Ia. Grota*. St. Petersburg: Izd. Imp. Akademii nauk, 1864–83.
D'iakonov, I. M. "Ob istorii zamysla 'Evgeniia Onegina.'" *Pushkin: Issledovaniia i materialy* 10 (1982): 70–105.
"Diaries and Intimate Archives." *Russian Review* 63, no. 4 (2004): 561–629.
Diderot, Denis. *Contes et romans*. Edited by Michel Delon. Paris: Gallimard, 2004.

[Dmitriev, I. I.] *Karmannyi pesennik, ili Sobranie luchshikh svetskikh i prostonarodnykh pesen*. Moscow: Tip. Ponomareva, 1796.

Dmitriev, I. I. *Pis'ma I. I. Dmitrieva k kniaziu P. A. Viazemskomu*. Edited by Nikolai Barsukov. St. Petersburg: Stasiulevich, 1898.

———. *Vzgliad na moiu zhizn'*. Moscow: V. Got'e, 1866.

Dobritsyn, Andrei. "Libertinskaia model' povedeniia i iazyk frantsuzskogo libertinazha v 'Evgenii Onegine.'" In *Vremennik Pushkinskoi komissii* 32, 145–70. St. Petersburg: Rostok, 2016.

Dolinin, Aleksandr. "Tsena odnoi bukvy." In *Shipovnik: Istoriko-filologicheskii sbornik k 60-letiiu Romana Davidovicha Timenchika*, edited by Iu. Leving, A. L. Ospovat, and Iu. Tsivian, 82–90. Moscow: Vodolei, 2005.

Dolgorukov, Ivan. *Povest' o rozhdenii moem . . .* 2 vols. St. Petersburg: Nauka, 2005.

Dornier, Carole. *Le Discours de maîtrise du libertinage: Étude sur l'oeuvre de Crébillon fils*. Paris: Klincksieck, 1994.

Dostoevsky, Fyodor. *Demons: A Novel in Three Parts*. Translated by Richard Pevear and Larissa Volokhonsky. New York: Vintage Classics, 1995.

Eckermann, Johann Peter. *Conversations of Goethe with Eckermann and Soret*. Translated by John Oxenford. London: George Bell & Sons, 1874.

Eikhenbaum, Boris. *Lermontov: Opyt istoriko-literaturnoi otsenki*. Leningrad: Gosudarstvennoe isdatel'stvo, 1924.

———. "Literary Environment." In Matejka and Pomorska, *Readings in Russian Poetics*, 56–65.

———. "Literaturnaia domashnost'." In *Moi vremennik: Marshrut v bessmertie*, by Boris Eikhenbaum, 83–87. Moscow: Agraf, 2001.

———. *Molodoi Tolstoi*. Petersburg: Izd-vo Z. I. Grzhebina, 1922.

Eliot, T. S. *The Use of Poetry and the Use of Criticism: Studies in the Relation of Criticism to Poetry in England*. Cambridge, MA: Harvard University Press, 1961.

Empson, William. *Seven Types of Ambiguity: A Study of Its Effects in English Verse*. London: Chatto and Windus, 1930.

Etkind, Efim. *Bozhestvennyi glagol: Pushkin, prochitannyi v Rossii i vo Frantsii*. Moscow: Iazyki russkoi kul'tury, 1999.

Fenollosa, Ernest, and Ezra Pound. *The Chinese Written Character as a Medium for Poetry*. New York: Fordham University Press, 2008.

Fleishman, L. "Iz istorii elegii v pushkinskuiu epokhu." In *Pushkinskii sbornik*, 24–53. Riga: Latviiskii gosudarstvennyi universitet, 1968.

Fomichev, Sergei. *"Evgenii Onegin": Dvizhenie zamysla*. Moscow: Russkii put', 2005.

Fontenelle, Bernard de. *Conversations on the Plurality of Worlds*. Translated by Elizabeth Gunning. London: J. Cundee, 1803.

Fraiman, Tat'iana. *Tvorcheskaia strategiia i poetika V. A. Zhukovskogo (1800–pervaia polovina 1820-kh godov)*. Tartu: Tartu Ülikooli Kirjastus, 2002.

Franklin, Simon. "Mapping the Graphosphere: Cultures of Writing in Early 19th-Century Russia (and Before)." *Kritika* 12, no. 3 (2011): 531–60.

Fried, Michael. *Absorption and Theatricality: Painting and Beholder in the Age of Diderot*. Berkeley: University of California Press, 1980.

Frye, Northrop. "Theory of Genres." In *The Lyric Theory Reader: A Critical Anthology*, edited by Virginia Jackson and Yopie Prins, 30–39. Baltimore, MD: Johns Hopkins University Press, 2014.

Galakhov, A. D. *Zapiski cheloveka*. Moscow: Novoe literaturnoe obozrenie, 1999.

Galinkovskii, Iakov. *Utrennik prekrasnogo pola, ili vsegdashnii damskii calendar'*. St. Petersburg: Tipografiia Imperatorskago teatra, 1807.

Gasparov, Boris. *Poeticheskii iazyk Pushkina kak fakt istorii russkogo literaturnogo iazyka*. St. Petersburg: Akademicheskii proekt, 1999.

Ginzburg, Lidiia. *O lirike*. Leningrad: Sovetskii pisatel', 1974.

Glagoleva, O. E. *Tul'skaia knizhnaia starina*. Tula: Izdatel'stvo Tul'skogo gosudarstvennogo pedagogicheskogo instituta, 1992.

Glinka, Sergei. *Zapiski*. Moscow: Zakharov, 2004.

Goethe, Johann Wolfgang. *Aus meinem Leben: Dichtung und Wahrheit*. Tübingen: Cotta'sche Buchhandlung, 1811.

———. *The Autobiography of Goethe: Truth and Poetry; From My Own Life*. Translated by John Oxenford. Cambridge: Cambridge University Press, 2013.

———. *Novels and Tales by Goethe*. Translated by R. D. Boylan. London: Henry G. Bohn, 1854.

Golburt, Luba. *The First Epoch: The Eighteenth Century and the Russian Cultural Imagination*. Madison: University of Wisconsin Press, 2014.

Golovina, T. N. "Eshche odin spisok 'Goria ot uma.'" In *Potaennnaia literatura*, 4–5:27–33. Ivanovo: Ivanovskii gos. universitet, 2004.

———. "Gazeta dlia odnogo chitatel'ia." In *Potaennnaia literatura*, 2:26–33. Ivanovo: Ivanovskii gos. universitet, 2000.

Gorchakov, Vladimir. "Vyderzhki iz dnevnika ob A. S. Pushkine." In *Pushkin v vospominaniiakh sovremennikov*, edited by Vadim Vatsuro et al., 1:229–63. St. Petersburg: Akademicheskii proekt, 1998.

Gordin, A. M., and M. A. Gordin, eds. *I. A. Krylov v vospominaniiakh sovremennikov*. Moscow: Khudozhestvennaia literatura, 1982.

Grech, Nikolai. *Chteniia o russkom iazyke*. St. Petersburg, 1840.

———. *Opyt kratkoi istorii Russkoi literatury*. St. Petersburg: Tipografiia N. Grecha, 1822.

Greenleaf, Monika. "Found in Translation: The Subject of Batiushkov's Poetry." In *Russian Subjects: Empire, Nation, and the Culture of the Golden Age*, edited by Monika Greenleaf and Stephen Moeller-Sally, 51–80. Evanston, IL: Northwestern University Press, 1998.

———. *Pushkin and Romantic Fashion: Fragment, Elegy, Orient, Irony*. Stanford, CA: Stanford University Press, 1996.

Grigor'eva, A. D. "'Mne ne spitsia . . .' (K voprosu o poeticheskoi traditsii)." *Izvestiia Akademii nauk SSSR: Seriia literatury i iazyka* 33, no. 3 (1974): 207–15.

Grits, T., V. Trenin, and M. Nikitin. *Slovesnost' i kommertsiia (Knizhnaia lavka A. F. Smirdina)*. Edited by V. B. Shklovskii and B. M. Eikhenbaum. Moscow: Federatsiia, 1929.

Gronas, Mikhail. *Cognitive Poetics and Cultural Memory: Russian Literary Mnemonics*. New York: Routledge, 2011.

Hall, Edward T. *The Silent Language*. Garden City, NY: Doubleday, 1959.

Hammarberg, Gitta. "Flirting with Words: Domestic Albums, 1770–1840." In *Russia—Women—Culture*, edited by Helena Goscilo and Beth Holmgren, 297–320. Bloomington: Indiana University Press, 1996.

———. *From the Idyll to the Novel: Karamzin's Sentimental Prose*. Cambridge: Cambridge University Press, 1991.

Hasty, Olga Peters. *Pushkin's Tatiana*. Madison: University of Wisconsin Press, 1999.

Hodge, Thomas P. *A Double Garland: Poetry and Art-Song in Early Nineteenth-Century Russia*. Evanston, IL: Northwestern University Press, 2000.

Hoogenboom, Hilde. "Sentimental Novels and Pushkin: European Literary Markets and Russian Readers." *Slavic Review* 74, no. 3 (2015): 553–74.

Ianushkevich, A. S. "Dnevniki V. A. Zhukovskogo kak literaturnyi pamiatnik." In Zhukovskii, *Polnoe sobranie sochinenii*, 13:397–419.

Iazykov, N. M. "Pis'ma k rodnym: Publikatsiia A. A. Karpova." *Ezhegodnik Rukopisnogo otdela Pushkinskogo doma na 1976 god* (1978): 147–78.

Iser, Wolfgang. *The Implied Reader: Patterns of Communication in Prose Fiction from Bunyan to Beckett*. Baltimore, MD: Johns Hopkins University Press, 1978.

Istrin, V. M. "Mladshii turgenevskii kruzhok i Aleksandr Ivanovich Turgenev." In *Arkhiv brat'ev Turgenevykh*, 2:3–134.

Ivanitskii, N. I. "Avtobiografiia Nikolaia Ivanovicha Ivanitskogo." In *Shchukinskii sbornik*, 8:218–358. Moscow: Sinodal'naia tipografiia, 1909.

Izmailov, A. E. "Pis'ma A. E. Izmailova I. I. Dmitrievu. 1816–1830." *Russkii arkhiv*, nos. 7/8 (1871): 961–1014.

Izmailov, Nikolai. "Pushkin v dnevnike gr. D. F. Fikel'mon." *Vremennik pushkinskoi komissii*, no. 1 (1962): 32–37.

Jackson, Virginia. *Dickinson's Misery: A Theory of Lyric Reading*. Princeton, NJ: Princeton University Press, 2005.

———. "Who Reads Poetry?" *PMLA* 123, no. 1 (2008): 181–87.

Jackson, Virginia, and Yopie Prins, eds. *The Lyric Theory Reader*. Baltimore, MD: Johns Hopkins University Press, 2014.

Jakobson, Roman. "Linguistics and Poetics." In Jakobson, *Selected Writings*, 3:18–51.

———. "Modern Russian Poetry: Velimir Khlebnikov." In *Major Soviet Writers: Essays in Criticism*, edited by E. J. Brown, 58–82. Oxford: Oxford University Press, 1973.

———. "O 'Stikhakh, sochinennykh noch'iu vo vremia bessonnitsy.'" In Jakobson, *Selected Writings*, 3:378–87.

———. "Poetry of Grammar and Grammar of Poetry." In Jakobson, *Selected Writings*, 3:87–97.
———. *Selected Writings*. The Hague: Mouton, 1981.
———. "Two Poems by Puškin." In *Verbal Art, Verbal Sign, Verbal Time*, by Roman Jakobson, edited by Krystyna Pomorska and Stephen Rudy, 47–58. Minneapolis: University of Minnesota Press, 1985.
James, William. *Pragmatism: A New Name for Some Old Ways of Thinking*. New York: Longmans, Green, and Co., 1921.
Kahn, Andrew. *Pushkin's Lyric Intelligence*. Oxford: Oxford University Press, 2008.
Karamzin, Nikolai. *Izbrannye sochineniia v dvukh tomakh*. Moscow: Khudozhestvennaia literatura, 1964.
———. *Pis'ma N. M. Karamzina k kniaziu P. A. Viazemskomu: 1810–1826*. St. Petersburg: Stasiulevich, 1897.
———. *Polnoe sobranie stikhotvorenii*. Moscow: Sovetskii pisatel', 1966.
Kern, Anna. *Vospominaniia, dnevniki, perepiska*. Moscow: Pravda, 1989.
Khagi, Sofya. *Silence and the Rest: Verbal Skepticism in Russian Poetry*. Evanston, IL: Northwestern University Press, 2013.
Khitrova, D. "Literaturnaia pozitsiia Baratynskogo i esteticheskie spory kontsa 1820-kh godov." In *Pushkinskie chteniia v Tartu 3*, edited by Liubov' Kiseleva, 149–80. Tartu: Tartu Ülikooli Kirjastus, 2004.
Kireevskii, Ivan. *Kritika i estetika*. Moscow: Iskusstvo, 1979.
Kiukhel'beker, V. K. *Izbrannye proizvedeniia v dvukh tomakh*. Moscow: Sovetskii pisatel', 1967.
———. "O napravlenii nashei poezii, osobenno liricheskoi, v polednee desiatiletie." In Koroleva and Rak, *Puteshestvie, Dnevnik, Stat'i*, 453–59.
———. *Puteshestvie, Dnevnik, Stat'i*. Edited by N. V. Koroleva and V. D. Rak. Leningrad: Nauka, 1979.
Krasnoborod'ko, Tatiana, and Daria Khitrova. "Pushkinskii nabrosok vozrazheniia Kiukhel'bekeru." In *Russian Literature and the West: A Tribute for David M. Bethea*, edited by Aleksandr Dolinin, Lazar Fleishman, and Leonid Livak, 66–116. Stanford, CA: Stanford University Press, 2008.
Kutuzov, N. I. "Apollon s semeistvom." In Vatsuro et al., *Pushkin v prizhiznennoi kritike*, 91–94.
Kuznetsova, N. V., and M. O. Mel'tsin. "Preobrazhenie real'nosti v 'Povesti . . .' kn. I. M. Dolgorukova." In Dolgorukov, *Povest' o rozhdenii moem*, 2:491–513.
La Bruyère, Jean de. *The Characters*. Translated by Henri Van Laun. London: J. C. Nimmo, 1885.
Lebedeva, O. B. "Printsipy romanticheskogo zhiznetvorchestva v dnevnikakh V. A. Zhukovskogo." In Zhukovskii, *Polnoe sobranie sochinenii*, 13:420–42.
Lebedeva, O. B., and A. S. Ianushkevich, eds. *Zhukovskii v vospominaniiakh sovremennikov*. Moscow: Nauka, 1999.

Legoy, Corinne. "Le siècle de la 'métromanie': Usages sociaux et politiques de la poésie dans la France de la Restauration." *Romantisme* 140, no. 2 (2008): 9–20.
Levin, Iurii. "Lirika s kommunikativnoi tochki zreniia." In *Izbrannye Trudy*, by Iurii Levin, 463–80. Moscow: Iazyki russkoi kul'tury, 1998.
Levinton, Georgii. "'Blazhen, kto . . .': K istorii formuly." In *Russkaia sud'ba krylatykh slov*, edited by V. E. Bagno, 141–239. St. Petersburg: Nauka, 2010.
Levkovich, Ia. "Rabochaia tetrad' Pushkina PD No. 834: (Istoriia zapolneniia)." *Pushkin: Issledovaniia i materialy* 15 (1995): 201–34.
Liamina, Ekaterina, and Natal'ia Samover. *Bednyi Zhozef: Zhizn' i smert' Iosifa Viel'gorskogo*. Moscow: Iazyki russkoi kul'tury, 1999.
Liprandi, Ivan. "Iz dnevnika i vospominanii." In *Pushkin v vospominaniiakh sovremennikov*, edited by Vadim Vatsuro et al., 1:285–343. St. Petersburg: Akademicheskii proekt, 1998.
Lotman, Iu. "Avtokommunikatsiia: 'Ia' i 'Drugoi' kak adresaty (O dvukh modeliakh v sisteme kul'tury)." In *Semiosfera* by Iurii Lotman, 163–77. St. Petersburg: Iskusstvo-SPB, 2010.
——. *Besedy o russkoi kul'ture: Byt i traditsii russkogo dvorianstva (XVIII–nachalo XIX veka)*. St. Petersburg: Iskusstvo-SPB, 1994.
——. "K evoliutsii postroeniia kharakterov v romane 'Evgenii Onegin.'" *Pushkin: Issledovaniia i materialy* 3 (1960): 131–73.
——. "K funktsii ustnoi rechi v kul'turnom bytu pushkinskoi epokhi." In *Izbrannye stat'i*, 3:430–8. Tallinn: Alexandra, 1993.
——. *Pushkin: Biografiia pisatelia; Stat'i i zametki, 1960–1990; "Evgenii Onegin": kommentarii*. St. Petersburg: Iskusstvo-SPb, 1995.
——. *Sotvorenie Karamzina*. Moscow: Kniga, 1987.
Lotman, Iurii, and Mark Al'tshuller, eds. *Poety 1790–1810-kh godov*. Leningrad: Sovetskii pisatel', 1971.
Lotman, Ju. "The Decembrist in Daily Life: Everyday Behavior as a Historical-Psychological Category." In Lotman and Uspenskij, *The Semiotics of Russian Culture*, 71–123.
——. "The Poetics of Everyday Behavior in Eighteenth-Century Russian Culture." In *The Semiotics of Russian Cultural History*, edited by Alexander D. Nakhimovsky and Alice Stone Nakhimovsky, 67–94. Ithaca, NY: Cornell University Press, 1985.
——. "The Theater and Theatricality as Components of Early Nineteenth-Century Culture." In Lotman and Uspenskij, *The Semiotics of Russian Culture*, 141–64.
Lotman, Ju., and B. A. Uspenskij. *The Semiotics of Russian Culture*. Edited by Ann Shukman. Ann Arbor: University of Michigan Press, 1984.
——. "Spory o iazyke v nachale XIX veka kak fakt russkoi kul'tury." In *Izbrannye Trudy*, by B. A. Uspenskii, 2:331–467. Moscow: Gnozis, 1994.

Luria, A. R. *The Mind of a Mnemonist: A Little Book about a Vast Memory*. Translated by Lynn Solotaroff. Cambridge, MA: Harvard University Press, 1987.

Maiakovskii, V. V. *Polnoe sobranie sochinenii*. Moscow: Khudozhestvennaia literatura, 1955–61.

Maiofis, Maria. *Vozzvanie k Evrope: Literaturnoe obshchestvo "Arzamas" i rossiiskii modernizatsionnyi proekt 1815–1818 godov*. Moscow: Novoe literaturnoe obozrenie, 2008.

Mandelstam, Nadezhda. *Hope Abandoned*. New York: Atheneum, 1974.

Mandelstam, Osip. "On the Addressee." In *Collected Critical Prose and Letters*, by Osip Mandelstam, edited and translated by Jane Gary Harris, 67–73. London: Collins Harvill, 1991.

———. *Sobranie sochinenii v chetyrekh tomakh*. Edited by P. Nerler and A. Nikitaev. Moscow: Art-Biznes-Tsentr, 1993–94.

———. *Sochineniia v dvukh tomakh*. Moscow: Khudozhestvennaia literatura, 1990.

Matejka, Ladislav, and Krystyna Pomorska, eds. *Readings in Russian Poetics: Formalist and Structuralist Views*. Cambridge, MA: MIT Press, 1971.

Mazur, Natal'ia. "Effekt Archimbol'do v opisatel'noi lirike: 'Osen'' Baratynskogo." Conference paper presented at Izobrazhenie i slovo: Formy ekfrasisa v literature. Institute of Russian Literature, St. Petersburg, 2008.

———. "Maska neistovogo stikhotvortsa v 'Evgenii Onegine': Polemicheskie funktsii." *Pushkin i ego sovremenniki* 5 (2009): 141–208.

———. "O myshinoi begotne, Pushkine, Marke Avrelii i ob uslovno-funktsional'nykh kontekstakh." In *Shipovnik: Istoriko-filologicheskii sbornik k 60-letiiu Romana Davidovicha Timenchika*, edited by Iu. Leving, A. L. Ospovat, and Iu. Tsivian, 250–60. Moscow: Vodolei, 2005.

———. "'Osen'' Baratynskogo: Rekonstruktsiia kanona." Conference paper presented at Pushkinskie chteniia V. Tartu University, Estonia, 2010.

———. "'Pora, moi drug, pora! Pokoia serdtse prosit': Istochniki i kontekst." *Pushkin i ego sovremenniki* 4 (2005): 364–419.

Mel'ts, Mikaela. "Pesni i romansy na stikhi Pushkina." *Pushkin i ego sovremenniki* 2 (2000): 138–58.

Merzliakov, Aleksei. *Kratkoe nachertanie teorii iziashchnoi slovesnosti*. Moscow: Universitetskaia tipografiia, 1822.

Mikhailova, N. I. "'Evgenii Onegin' i al'bomnaia kul'tura pervoi treti XIX veka." *Izvestiia Rossiiskoi Akademii nauk, Seriia Literatury i Iazyka* 55, no. 6 (1996): 15–22.

———. "Pis'ma V. L. Pushkina k P. A. Viazemskomu." *Pushkin: Issledovaniia i materialy* 11 (1983): 213–49.

Mill, John Stuart. *Autobiography and Literary Essays*. Vol. 1 of *Collected Works of John Stuart Mill*. Edited by John M. Robson and Jack Stillinger. London: Routledge, 1981.

Millevoye, Charles-Hubert. "Sur l'élégie." In *Oeuvres*, by Charles-Hubert Millevoye, 1:3–41. Paris: Furne, 1833.

Mirskii, D. "Baratynskii." In *Polnoe sobranie stikhotvorenii*, by E. A. Baratynskii, 1:v–xxxiv. Leningrad: Sovetskii pisatel', 1936.

Modzalevskii, Boris. "Pushkin, Del'vig i ikh peterburgskie druz'ia v pis'makh S. M. Del'vig." In *Pushkin i ego sovremenniki: Izbrannye trudy (1898–1928)*, 227–338. St. Petersburg: Iskusstvo-SPB, 1999.

———. "Roman dekabrista Kakhovskogo." In *Pushkin i ego sovremenniki: Izbrannye trudy (1898–1928)*, 152–226. St. Petersburg: Iskusstvo-SPB, 1999.

Mur'ianov, M. F. "Portret Lenskogo v 'Evgenii Onegine.'" *Wiener Slavistisches Jahrbuch* 40 (1994): 75–90.

Nemzer, Andrei. *Pri svete Zhukovskogo: Ocherki istorii russkoi literatury*. Moscow: Vremia, 2013.

Nilsson, Nils Åke. "Baratynskij's Elegiac Code." In *Russian Romanticism: Studies in Poetic Codes*, edited by Nils Åke Nilsson, 144–66. Stockholm: Almqvist & Wiksell International, 1979.

Noveishii polnyi pis'movnik, ili Vseobshchii sekretar'. St. Petersburg: Pri 1-m Kadetskom korpuse, 1810.

Noveishii, samyi polnyi i podrobnyi pis'movnik. Part 1. St. Petersburg: Tipografiia Imperatorskikh teatrov, 1822.

Oever, Annie van den, ed. *Ostrannenie: On "Strangeness" and the Moving Image; The History, Reception, and Relevance of a Concept*. Amsterdam: Amsterdam University Press, 2010.

Offord, Derek, Lara Ryazanova-Clarke, Vladislav Rjeoutski, and Gesine Argent, eds. *French and Russian in Imperial Russia: Language Use among the Russian Elite*. Edinburgh: Edinburgh University Press, 2015.

Ohmann, Richard. "Speech Acts and the Definition of Literature." *Philosophy & Rhetoric* 4, no. 1 (1971): 1–19.

Oksman, Iulian. "Pushkinskaia oda 'Vol'nost'": (K voprosu o datirovke)." *Problemy istorii kul'tury, literatury, sotsial'no-ekonomicheskoi mysli* 5, no. 2 (1989): 3–33.

Okudzhava, Bulat Sh. *Stikhotvoreniia*. St. Petersburg: Akademicheskii proekt, 2001.

Ong, Walter J. *Orality and Literacy: The Technologizing of the Word*. London: Routledge, 2002.

Ostaf'evskii arkhiv kniazei Viazemskikh. 5 vols. Edited by V. I. Saitov and P. N. Sheffer. St. Petersburg: Stasiulevich, 1899–1913.

Ostrovskii, Arsenii. "U istokov 'Biblioteki poeta.'" In *Vospominaniia o Iu. Tynianove: Portrety i vstrechi*, edited by Veniamin Kaverin, 173–87. Moscow: Sovetskii pisatel', 1983.

"Ot budushchikh zhurnalistov k Redaktoru V.E." *Vestnik Evropy* 188, nos. 7/8 (1821): 306–13.

Paperno, Irina. "O rekonstruktsii ustnoi rechi iz pis'mennykh istochnikov (Kruzhkovaia rech' i domashniaia literatura v pushkinskuiu epokhu)." In *Semantika nominatsii i semiotika ustnoi rechi: Lingvisticheskaia semantika i semiotika*, edited by B. Gasparov, A. Dulichenko, and M. Sheliakin, 122–34. Tartu: Tartu Ülikooli Kirjastus, 1978.

———. *"Who, What Am I?": Tolstoy Struggles to Narrate the Self*. Ithaca, NY: Cornell University Press, 2014.

Parsamov, Vadim. *Dekabristy i russkoe obshchestvo 1814–1825 gg*. Moscow: Algoritm, 2016.

Pavlova, Karolina. *Polnoe sobranie stikhotvorenii*. Moscow and Leningrad: Sovetskii pisatel', 1964.

Pecherin, Vladimir. "Zamogil'nye zapiski." In *Russkoe obshchestvo 30-kh godov XIX v.: Liudi i idei; Memuary sovremennikov*, edited by A. I. Fedosov, 148–311. Moscow: MGU, 1989.

Peschio, Joe. *The Poetics of Impudence and Intimacy in the Age of Pushkin*. Madison: University of Wisconsin Press, 2012.

Peskov, Aleksei. *Boratynsky: Istinnaia povest'*. Moscow: Kniga, 1990.

———, ed. *Letopis' zhizni i tvorchestva E. A. Boratynskogo*. Moscow: Novoe literaturnoe obozrenie, 1998.

Petina, Larisa. "Ob al'bomnom kharaktere russkikh izdanii pervoi poloviny XIX veka." In *Literaturnyi byt pushkinskoi pory*, edited by N. I. Mikhailova, 141–60. Moscow: Nestor-Istoriia, 2012.

Pil'shchikov, Igor'. "Aleksandr Pushkin mezhdu libertinazhem i dendizmom." In *Russian Literature* 86, nos. 1–2 (2014): 35–84.

———. "Nomina si nescis... (Struktura auditorii i 'domashniaia semantika' u Pushkina i Baratynskogo)." In *Na mezhe mezh Golosom i Ekhom*, edited by L. O. Zaionts, 70–81. Moscow: Novoe izdatel'stvo, 2007.

Pil'shchikov, Igor', and Joe Peschio. "The Proliferation of Elite Readerships and Circle Poetics in Pushkin and Baratynskii (1820s–1830s)." In *The Space of the Book: Print Culture in the Russian Social Imagination*, edited by Miranda Remnek, 82–107. Toronto: University of Toronto Press, 2011.

Pletnev, P. A. "Pis'mo k grafine S. I. S. o russkikh poetakh." In Vatsuro et al., *Pushkin v prizhiznennoi kritike*, 244–47.

Pogosian, Elena. "Uroki imperatritsy: Ekaterina II i Derzhavin v 1783 godu." In *Na mezhe mezh Golosom i Ekhom*, edited by L. O. Zaionts, 241–68. Moscow: Novoe izdatel'stvo, 2007.

Pratt, Mary Louise. "Ideology and Speech-Act Theory." *Poetics Today* 7, no. 1 (1986): 59–72.

———. *Toward a Speech Act Theory of Literary Discourse*. Bloomington: Indiana University Press, 1977.

Proskurin, Oleg. "Iz istorii odesskogo teksta poemy Pushkina 'Tsygany' (k metodike chteniia pushkinskikh rukopisei)." In *Permiakovskii sbornik*, edited by Natal'ia Mazur, 2:186–214. Moscow: Novoe Izdatel'stvo, 2010.

———. "Kommentarii." In Pushkin, *Poemy i povesty*, 18–363.

———. *Literaturnye skandaly pushkinskoi epokhi*. Moscow: OGI, 2000.
———. *Poeziia Pushkina, ili Podvizhnyi palimpsest*. Moscow: Novoe literaturnoe obozrenie, 1999.
———. "Pop-kul'tura (2)." *Livejournal*, 3 May 2006. http://o-proskurin.livejournal.com/49378.html.
———. "Pushkin and Politics." In *The Cambridge Companion to Pushkin*, edited by Andrew Kahn, 105–17. Cambridge: Cambridge University Press, 2007.
———. "'Zlodeiskaia porfira' (Eshche raz o datirovke i politicheskom kontekste ody Pushkina 'Vol'nost')." In *Russko-frantsuzskii razgovornik ili ou Les Causeries du 7 Septembre: Sbornik statei v chest' Very Arkad'evny Milchinoi*, edited by Oleg Lekmanov and Ekaterina Liamina, 273–86. Moscow: Novoe literaturnoe obozrenie, 2015.
Proskurina, Vera. *Mify imperii: Literatura i vlast' v epokhu Ekateriny II*. Moscow: Novoe literaturnoe obozrenie, 2006.
Pushkin, A. S. *Eugene Onegin: A Novel in Verse*. Translated by Vladimir Nabokov. Bollingen Series 72. New York: Pantheon, 1964.
———. *Poemy i povesti*. Vol. 1 of *Sochineniia*. Edited by David Bethea and Nikita Okhotin. Moscow: Novoe izdatel'stvo, 2007.
———. *Polnoe sobranie sochinenii v 16-ti tomakh*. Leningrad: AN SSSR, 1937–59.
———. *Polnoe sobranie sochinenii v 20-ti tomakh*. St. Petersburg: Nauka, 1999–.
———. *Rabochie tetradi*. St. Petersburg and London: Institut russkoi literatury (Pushkinskii dom), 1997.
——— *Rukoiu Pushkina: Nesobrannye i neopublikovannye teksty*. Edited by M. A. Tsiavlovskii, L. B. Modzalevskii, and T. G. Zenger. Moscow: Academia, 1935.
R. "Vesna." *Novosti literatury*, no. 17 (1822): 62–63.
-R-. "Pismo k izdateliu," *Moskovskii vestnik*, no. 1 (1827): 76–82.
Rachinskii, S. A., ed. *Tatevskii sbornik*. St. Petersburg: Stasiulevich, 1899.
Ram, Harsha. *The Imperial Sublime: A Russian Poetics of Empire*. Madison: University of Wisconsin Press, 2006.
Ramazani, Jahan. *Poetry and Its Others: News, Prayer, Song, and the Dialogue of Genres*. Chicago: University of Chicago Press, 2014.
Rashkov, N. A. "Zhizn' Shillera." *Nevskii zritel'* 1, no. 1 (1820): 128–39.
Rebecchini, Damiano, and Raffaella Vassena, eds. *Reading in Russia: Practices of Reading and Literary Communication (1760–1930)*. Milano: di/segni, 2014.
Reitblat, A. I. *Kak Pushkin vyshel v genii*. Moscow: Novoe literaturnoe obozrenie, 2001.
———. "Pis'mennaia literatura v Rossii v XIX veke." In Rebecchini and Vassena, *Reading in Russia*, 79–97.
Reyfman, Irina. *How Russia Learned to Write: Literature and the Imperial Table of Ranks*. Madison: University of Wisconsin Press, 2016.
———. *Vasilii Trediakovsky: The Fool of the "New" Russian Literature*. Stanford, CA: Stanford University Press, 1990.

Russkaia sentimental'naia povest'. Edited by P. A. Orlov. Moscow: Izdatel'stvo Moskovskogo universiteta, 1979.

Sandler, Stephanie. *Distant Pleasures: Alexander Pushkin and the Writing of Exile*. Stanford: Stanford University Press, 1989.

Savkina, Irina. *Razgovory s zerkalom i Zazerkal'em: Avtodokumental'nye zhenskie teksty v russkoi literature pervoi poloviny XIX veka*. Moscow: NLO, 2007.

Schönle, Andreas. "The Scare of the Self: Sentimentalism, Privacy, and Private Life in Russian Culture, 1780-1820." *Slavic Review* 57, no. 4 (1998): 723-46.

Senderovich, Savelii. "Simpozium poetov: K istorii i teorii poeticheskikh zhanrov." In *Figura sokrytiia: Izbrannye raboty*, 1:472-509. Moscow: Iazyki slavianskikh kul'tur, 2012.

———. "Vnutrenniaia rech' i terapevticheskaia funktsiia v lirike: O stikhotvorenii Pushkina 'Ia vas liubil.'" *Revue des études slaves* 59, nos. 1-2 (1987): 315-25.

Shklovskii, Viktor. *Izbrannoe v dvukh tomakh*. Moscow: Khudozhestvennaia literatura, 1983.

———. "O pisatele i proizvodstve." In *Literatura fakta: Pervyi sbornik materialov rabotnikov LEFa*, edited by N. F. Chuzhak, 194-200. Moscow: Zakharov, 2000.

———. "Togda i seichas." In *Literatura fakta: Pervyi sbornik materialov rabotnikov LEFa*, edited by N. F. Chuzhak, 129-30. Moscow: Zakharov, 2000.

Shklovsky, Viktor. "On Poetry and Trans-Sense Language." Translated by Gerald Janecek and Peter Mayer. *October* 34 (1985): 3-24.

———. *Zoo, or Letters Not about Love*. Translated by Richard Sheldon. Normal, IL: Dalkey Archive Press, 2001.

Shvartsband, Samuil. *Istoriia tekstov: "Gavriiliada," "Podrazahaniia Koranu," "Evgenii Onegin" (gl. I-IV)*. Moscow: RGGU, 2004.

———. *Pushkin: Opyty v stikhakh i proze*. St. Petersburg: Dmitrii Bulanin, 2014.

Sidiakov, Lev. "K istorii raboty Pushkina nad vtoroi glavoi 'Evgeniia Onegina.'" *Vremennik pushkinskoi komissii 1973* (1975): 5-11.

Simoni, P. K., ed. "Pis'ma-dnevniki V. A. Zhukovskogo 1814 i 1815 godov." In *Pamiati V. A. Zhukovskogo i N. V. Gogolia*, 1:145-213. St. Petersburg: Tip. Imp. Akademii nauk, 1907.

Skachkova, O. N. "Druzheskoe poslanie A. S. Pushkina i 'Evgenii Onegin.'" In *Problemy pushkinovedeniia: Sbornik nauchnykh trudov*, edited by Lev Sidiakov, 5-15. Riga: Latviiskii gos. universitet, 1983.

"Sovremennaia russkaia bibliografiia." *Moskovskii telegraf*, no. 2 (1828): 235-252.

Stael Holstein, Baroness [Anna Louise Germaine de Staël-Holstein]. *Germany*. Translated from the French. London: John Murray, 1813.

Stepanov, V. P. "Neizdannye teksty I. M. Dolgorukova." In *XVIII vek: Sbornik 22*, edited by N. D. Kochetkova, 409-30. St. Petersburg: Nauka, 2002.

Tabakova, N. A. "Pushkin v al'bomakh sovremennikov." In *Pamiati Anny Ivanovny Zhuravlevoi: Sbornik statei*, edited by G. V. Zykova and E. N. Penskaia, 282-96. Moscow: Tri kvadrata, 2012.

Teletova, N. K. "Dushoi filister gettingenskii." *Pushkin: Issledovaniia i materialy* 14 (1991): 205–13.

Tihanov, Galin. "Marxism and Formalism Revisited: Notes on the 1927 Leningrad Dispute." *Literary Research/Recherche littéraire* 19, nos. 37–38 (2002): 69–77.

Timenchik, R. D. "Azy i uzy kommentariia." In *The Real Life of Pierre Delalande: Studies in Russian and Comparative Literature to Honor Alexander Dolinin*, edited by David M. Bethea, L. S. Fleishman, and A. L. Ospovat, 175–85. Stanford, CA: Stanford University Press, 2007.

Todd, William Mills. *The Familiar Letter as a Literary Genre in the Age of Pushkin*. Princeton, NJ: Princeton University Press, 1976.

———. *Fiction and Society in the Age of Pushkin: Ideology, Institutions, and Narrative*. Cambridge, MA: Harvard University Press, 1986.

Tomashevskii, Boris. *Pushkin i Frantsiia*. Leningrad: Sovetskii pisatel', 1960.

Tomashevsky, Boris. "Literature and Biography." In Matejka and Pomorska, *Readings in Russian Poetics*, 47–55.

Toporov, Vladimir. "'Sel'skoe kladbishche' Zhukovskogo: K istokam russkoi poezii." *Russian Literature* 10 (1981): 209–86.

Tsiavlovskaia, T. "Dnevnik A. A. Oleninoi." *Pushkin: Issledovaniia i materialy* 2 (1958): 247–92.

Tsiavlovskii, Mstislav. "Pushkin po materialam arkhiva M. P. Pogodina." *Literaturnoe nasledstvo*, nos. 16–18 (1934): 679–724.

———. *Stat'i o Pushkine*. Moscow: Izdatel'stvo Akademii nauk SSSR, 1962.

Turgenev, A. I. "Pis'ma A. I. Turgeneva k I. I. Dmitrievu." *Russkii arkhiv*, no. 3 (1867): 639–70.

Tynianov, Iurii. "Arkhaisty i Pushkin." In *Pushkin i ego sovremenniki*, 23–121. Moscow: Nauka, 1969.

———. "Literary Fact." In *Modern Genre Theory*, edited by David Duff, 29–49. New York: Longman, 2000.

———. "Literaturnyi Fakt." In *Poetika, Istoriia literatury, Kino*, 255–70. Moscow: Nauka, 1977.

———. "Oda kak oratorskii zhanr." In *Poetika, Istoriia literatury, Kino*, 227–52. Moscow: Nauka, 1977.

———. "The Ode as an Oratorical Genre." Translated by Ann Shukman. *New Literary History* 34, no. 3 (2003): 565–96.

———. "O literaturnoi evoliutsii." In *Poetika, Istoriia literatury, kino*, 270–81. Moscow: Nauka, 1977.

———. "On Literary Evolution." In Matejka and Pomorska, *Readings in Russian Poetics*, 68–78.

———. "On the Composition of *Eugene Onegin*." In *Russian Views of Pushkin's Eugene Onegin*, edited by Sona Hoisington, 71–90. Bloomington: Indiana University Press, 1988.

———. "O parodii." In *Poetika, Istoriia literatury, Kino*, 284–310. Moscow: Nauka, 1977.
———. "Pushkin." In *Pushkin i ego sovremenniki*, 122–65. Moscow: Nauka, 1969.
[Ushak]ov, [Vasil]y. "Gospodinu izdateliu Literaturnykh listkov." *Literaturnye listki*, nos. 21–22 (1824): 90–100.
Uspenskii, Boris. *Iz istorii russkogo literaturnogo iazyka XVIII–nachala XIX veka: Iazykovaia programma Karamzina i ee istoricheskie korni*. Moscow: Izdatel'stvo Moskovskogo universiteta, 1985.
Vatsuro, Vadim. *Lirika pushkinskoi pory: Elegicheskaia shkola*. St. Petersburg: Nauka, 1994.
———. "Literaturnye al'bomy v sobranii Pushkinskogo doma (1750–1840-e gody)." *Ezhegodnik Rukopisnogo otdela Pushkinskogo doma na 1977 god* (1979): 3–54.
———. "Poeticheskii manifest Pushkina." *Pushkin: Issledovaniia i materialy* 14 (1991): 65–72.
———. *S. D. P. Iz istorii literaturnogo byta pushkinskoi pory*. Moscow: Kniga, 1989.
Vatsuro, Vadim, S. A. Fomichev, and E. O. Larionova, eds. *Pushkin v prizhiznennoi kritike, 1820–1827*. St. Petersburg: Gos. pushkinskii teatral'nyi tsentr, 1996.
Velizhev, Mikhail. "'Senator' vs. 'Poet': (Avto)biograficheskaia mifologiia i literaturnaia reputatsiia I. I. Dmitrieva." *AvtobiografiЯ* 5 (2016): 117–50.
Versini, Laurent. *Le Roman le plus intelligent: Les Liaisons dangereuses de Laclos*. Paris: Honoré Champion, 1998.
Viazemskii, Petr. *Sochineniia v dvukh tomakh*. Edited by Maxim Gillel'son. Moscow: Khudozhestvennaia literatura, 1982.
———. *Polnoe sobranie sochinenii*. 12 vols. Edited by S. D. Sheremetev. St. Petersburg: Stasiulevich, 1878–96.
———. *Stikhotvoreniia*. Edited by Kseniia Kumpan. Leningrad: Sovetskii pisatel', 1986.
———. *Stikhotvoreniia*. Edited by Lidiia Ginzburg. Leningrad: Sovetskii pisatel', 1958.
———. *Zapisnye knizhki (1813–1848)*. Moscow: Izdatel'stvo Akademii nauk SSSR, 1963.
Vigel', Filipp. *Zapiski*. Moscow: Krug, 1928.
Vinitskii, Il'ia. "Poeticheskaia semantika Zhukovskogo, ili Rassuzhdenie o vkuse i smysle 'Ovsianogo kiselia.'" *Novoe literaturnoe obozrenie* 61 (2003): 119–51.
———. "Posviashchenie v poeziiu." *Russian Studies* 2, no. 1 (1996): 53–77.
Vinitsky, Ilya. *Vasily Zhukovsky's Romanticism and the Emotional History of Russia*. Evanston, IL: Northwestern University Press, 2015.
Vol'pert, Larisa. *Pushkin v roli Pushkina: Tvorcheskaia igra po modeliam frantsuzskoi literatury; Pushkin i Stendal'*. Moscow: Iazyki russkoi kul'tury, 1998.
Vospominaniia Bestuzhevykh. Edited by Mark Azadovskii. Moscow: Izdatel'stvo Akademii nauk SSSR, 1951.
Vul'f, A. N. *Liubovnye pokhozhdeniia i voennye pokhody A. N. Vul'fa: Dnevnik 1827–1842*. Edited by E. N. Stroganova and M. V. Stroganov. Tver: Vsia Tver', 1999.

"Vyderzhki iz starykh bumag Ostaf'evskogo arkhiva." *Russkii arkhiv*, no. 6 (1866): 859–903.

Wachtel, Michael. *The Cambridge Introduction to Russian Poetry*. Cambridge: Cambridge University Press, 2004.

———. *A Commentary to Pushkin's Lyric Poetry, 1826–1836*. Madison: University of Wisconsin Press, 2011.

Wales, Katie. *Personal Pronouns in Present-Day English*. Cambridge: Cambridge University Press, 1996.

Wolf, Werner. "The Lyric: Problems of Definition and a Proposal for Reconceptualisation." In *Theory into Poetry: New Approaches to the Lyric*, edited by Eva Müller-Zettelmann and Margarete Rubik, 21–56. Amsterdam: Rodopi, 2005.

Zeidlits, Karl. *Zhizn' i poeziia V. A. Zhukovskogo: 1783–1852*. St. Petersburg: Vestnik Evropy, 1883.

Zhikharev, Stepan. *Zapiski sovremennika*. Edited by Boris Eikhenbaum. Moscow and Leningrad: Izdatel'stvo Akademii nauk SSSR, 1955.

Zhiliakova, E. M., ed. *Perepiska V. A. Zhukovskogo i A. P. Elaginoi, 1813–1852*. Moscow: Znak, 2009.

Zhivov, Viktor. *Language and Culture in Eighteenth-Century Russia*. Boston: Academic Studies Press, 2009.

Zholkovskii, Aleksandr. "S Lotmanom na druzheskoi noge." In *Memuarnye vin'etki i drugie non-fictions*, 83–85. St. Petersburg: Zvezda, 2000.

Zhukovskii, Vasilii. "Pis'mo V. A. Zhukovskogo." *Russkii arkhiv*, no. 7 (1866): 1070–77.

———. *Polnoe sobranie sochinenii i pisem v 20 tomakh*. Moscow: Iazyki russkoi kul'tury, 1999–2013.

———. *Sobranie sochinenii v chetyrekh tomakh*. Moscow and Leningrad: GIKhL, 1959–60.

Zorin, Andrei. *Poiavlenie geroia: Iz istorii russkoi emotsional'noi kul'tury kontsa XVIII–nachala XIX veka*. Moscow: NLO, 2016.

———. "Vsled shestvuia Anakreonu." In *Tsvetnik: Russkaia legkaia poeziia kontsa XVIII–nachala XIX v.*, 5–53. Moscow: Kniga, 1987.

Index

Page numbers in italics indicate the illustration.

Abrams, M. H., 106–7, 125
Aksakov, Konstantin, 93–94, 126
Aksakov, Sergei, 93–94
albums, 8, 22, 29; drawing in album, 177, *178*, 180, 183, 187; handwritten texts (graphosphere) and, 82–83, 96, 119, 192, 238, 254n13; love practices and, 164–65; memory/memorability of text and, 69, 73–74; oral literature and, 74–75; poetry and, 15–16, 29, 73–74, 77, 81–84, 96, 192–93, 201–2, 224–26, 268n65; reader and writer co-experience and, 82–83
Alekseev, Nikolai, 184
Alexander I (emperor of Russia), 21–22, 35, 85
Alexandra Fedorovna (Grand Duchess), 35, 58–59
allo-speaking (*inakogovorenie*), 24, 133, 144, 147, 161, 162, 164
ancestral (family) homes, 31–32, 48–49, 58, 117. *See also* domestic spaces
Ancillon, Jean Pierre Frédéric, 143
aphorism(s), 68, 73, 96, 190, 191, 199, 216, 263n85
Ariosto, Ludovico, 113

Aronson, Mark, 139, 140
Arzamas literary society, 57, 139–40, 141, 144–45, 209, 210, 251n33
Austin, J. L., 23–24, 95
author/authorship, 207, 211–12, 216, 217, 228, 229, 238, 240; ownership of text and, 70–75, 253n85, 253n88; proxemics and, 237–38; reader and, 156, 157, 159, 237–38, 244; text and, 240, 244
auto-communication, 126–38, 144

Bakhtin, Mikhail, 28, 29, 33, 104, 116, 122, 256n71
Bakhtin, Nikolai, 113
Bal'mont, Konstantin, 159
Baratynsky, Evgeny, 5, 29, 41, 64, 68, 70–72, 78–79, 81, 104–6, 117, 139, 141, 143, 154–55, 253n75, 253n88, 262n63, 263n85, 264n111; *The Ball*, 176; "Confession," 184–91, 194, 195, 197, 198, 237; "Desolation," 117; "Dissuasion," 86, 124, 162, 168, 169, 171–77, *178*, 183, 187, 196, 201, 230, 262n46; *Eda*, 191, 193–98, 212, 264n111; "A Falling Out," 200; "Feasts," 156; "Finland," 89–91,

Baratynsky, Evgeny (*continued*) 93, 115–16; "To Lida," 181; "The Little Imp," 180–81; "To L. Pushkin," 11–13, 247n14; "My gift is meager...," 156–59; "Russian Song," 181; "The Skull," 68–69, 253n75; "With the tender tongue of heart...," 179, 180

Barkov, Ivan, 39

Bartenev, Petr, 61

Barthes, Roland, 167

Batiushkov, Konstantin, 5, 28, 31–32, 36, 38, 41, 47, 50, 55, 56, 60, 65, 69–72, 95, 103, 105, 114, 138–39, 144, 155, 157, 176, 183, 204, 214, 219, 254n1; "A Bard in the Colloquium of Friends of Russian Letters," 124; "To a Friend," 159; "To Friends," 51, 154; "My Penates," 48–49, 58, 145–50, 153; "Speech on the Influence of Light Poetry...," 51–52; "To Zhukovsky," 150

Baudelaire, Charles, 66

Begichev, Dmitrii, 135–36, 162–63

Bely, Andrei, 177

Berlin, Irving, 253n84

Bestuzhev, Aleksandr, 16, 141, 142, 184, 185, 244; *Novel in Seven Letters*, 164–67

Bestuzhev, Mikhail, 90

Bestuzhev, Nikolai, 125

Blake, William, 132

Bludov, Dmitry, 60

Bocharov, Sergei, 187

Boileau-Despréaux, Nicolas, 27, 265n11

Bolotov, Andrei, 84–85

Bowring, John, 49

Brodsky, Joseph, 79, 144

Bukharina-Annenkova, Vera, 85

Bunina, Anna, 69

Bürger, Gottfried August, 113

Burtsov, Aleksei, 147–48, 151

Byron, George Gordon, 104, 195, 214, 215, 217

Catherine II (Catherine the Great, empress of Russia), 35, 36, 37, 45, 64, 249n38

Catullus, Gaius Valerius, 50

celebratory odes, 30, 35, 229–31

censorship, 72–73, 84, 109–11, 180

Chalmers, David, 132, 133

Chamfort, Nicolas, 191

Chernavin, Iakov, 96

Chikhachev, Andrei, 96, 97, 101, 111

Ciepiela, Catherine, 129

Clark, Andy, 132, 133

Cohen, Michael, 16

Coleridge, Henry Nelson, 251

community-building, 123–24, 138, 150, 151

complicity, participation (*souchastie*), 7, 79, 81, 107–8, 118, 119

confession(s): "Confession" (Baratynsky), 184–91, 194, 195, 197, 198, 237; confessional diaries, 134–35; *Eugene Onegin* (Pushkin), 188, 197, 198, 199, 220, 223; love elegies and, 188, 197, 198, 199

congratulatory poetry, 30, 229–31

Constant, Benjamin, *Adolphe*, 41, 187

conversation(s): as a literary fact, 11, 26–29, 53; poetry and, 36, 37, 41, 43–44, 122; turn-taking techniques and, 64–66; as verbal performance, 52–54, 61, 85, 251nn23–24

Cranach, Lucas, the Elder, 14

Crébillon, Claude Prosper Jolyot de, 174

Culler, Jonathan, 6, 24, 25, 26, 27, 45, 75, 132

Dante Alighieri, 126

Darnton, Robert, 166, 254n13

Davydov, Denis, 56–57, 71, 104, 108, 151; "A Call to Punch," 147–48; "The Female Eagle, Ruff, and Blackcock," 85

Del'vig, Anton, 5, 49–50, 64, 141, 144, 155–56, 168, 170, 176, 179, 180, 184, 219, 253n88, 257n78, 266–67n43; "On the Death of Lesbia's Sparrow," 50, 250n9; "My Hut," 48, 58, 145; "Revel', in July 1827," 105–6, 257n78

Del'vig, Sofia, 168–77, 183, 187, 230, 262n32, 262n46

Derrida, Jacques, 75

Derzhavin, Gavriil, 30, 37, 39, 52, 84, 94; "Discourse on Lyric Poetry," 88–89; "Felitsa," 35–36, 249n39; "Invitation to Dinner," 27, 28, 147–48; "Waterfall," 87–88

diaries, 96, 102–3, 128, 133–37

Dickinson, Emily, 56, 57

Diderot, Denis, 190

dinners (feasts), 27–28, 145–52

Dlia Nemnogikh (For the Few) (journal), 58–59

Dmitriev, Ivan, 37–40, 42–43, 48, 60, 64–65, 85, 87, 141, 250n49; *Fashionable Wife*, 85; *My Trifles Too*, 47; "As Others See It," 226

doleful (*unylaia*) elegies, 117, 176, 182, 188, 198, 200, 220–23, 232–33, 236–37

Dolgorukov, Ivan, 27, 55, 110, 111, 137, 166–67

domestic spaces, 15, 31–32, 48–50, 58, 117, 147–48, 150, 250n9

domestic stage, 54–55, 118; in love practices, 162–63, 167; oral delivery of poetry, 91

Dostoevsky, Fedor, 16, 163

dramatic stage, 64, 90, 91, 92–93, 177

drinking songs, 108, 123–24, 138, 146, 152, 156, 204

dual felicity of poetry, 27, 28, 163, 173, 196, 227, 230

Dubiansky, Fedor, 85

Duclos, Charles Pinot, 188

Eikhenbaum, Boris, 70, 135, 253n85; "Literary Domesticity," 139–40; "Literature's Everyday Environment," 33–36, 139–40

Eisenhower, Dwight D., 26, 67, 70, 253n84

Eisenstein, Sergei, 207

Elagina, Avdotia (Duniasha), 101–2

elegy(ies), 76, 78, 83, 114–15, 119, 128–29, 132, 135, 167–68, 217, 223, 254n1, 261nn24–25; albums, 192–93, 224, 226; *Eugene Onegin* (Pushkin) and, 217, 221, 224, 226, 232–33, 235–37, 239–40; odes versus, 34, 121–22, 220–21, 225–27, 231, 232, 238, 239, 240; parody of, 222, 226; reader and writer co-experience and, 79, 119; reading-cum-writing spaces and, 114–15; *souchastie* and, 7, 79–80. See also doleful (*unylaia*) elegies; love poetry; poetry set to music; *romans*; specific authors

Eliot, T. S., 10

emotions: elegies and, 79–80; poetry's impact on, 106–8, 125–26; reader and writer co-experience and, 77, 227

Engelgardt (Baratynskaia), Anastasia, 81

Engelgardt, Boris, 33

epilogues, 192, 209, 213, 216, 237, 245

epistles, 11–12, 29–32, 42–45, 103, 138, 151; community-building and, 124, 150; dinners and, 145–49; domestic spaces and, 150; on friendship, 138–45; love practices and, 165–67; private/public spheres and, 57; style perfection and, 72

epitaphs, 177, 223–24, 231, 235

Evreinov, Nikolai, 93

fables, 65, 66, 85, 108, 164, 253n69

family (ancestral) homes, 31–32, 48–49, 58, 117. See also domestic spaces

feasts (dinners). *See* dinners
Ficquelmont, Dolly de, 53
Fleishman, Lazar, 263n85
Fomichev, Sergei, 212
Fontenelle, Bernard Le Bovier de, 95
Fraiman (Stepanishcheva), Tatiana, 128–29
Franklin, Benjamin, 135, 136
Franklin, Simon, 84, 104
French language, 38–39, 60, 114, 118, 165–66, 250n49, 261n16
French literature, 16, 55; elegies and, 167–68, 261nn24–25; libertinism and, 167, 168, 171, 187, 189, 195; love poetry and, 261n16; moralistic maxims and *pensées*, 190–91; translations of poetry and, 113. *See also specific authors*
Fried, Michael, 83
Friendly Literary Society, 112, 144–45, 218
friendship, 77, 117, 141–47; epistles and, 138–40; readership as, 152–60; with women through poetry, 41–42, 43
Fuchs, Aleksandra, 29
Fuchs, Karl, 29
functions of poetry, 4, 41, 47–48, 53, 58, 119, 121, 167, 211, 218; authorship and ownership of text and, 70–75, 253n85, 253n88; conversations as verbal performance and, 52–54, 61, 251nn23–24; domestic spaces and, 48–50, 250n9; domestic stage and, 54–55; dual felicity of poetry and, 51, 59, 60, 65, 216, 238; letters and, 55–57, 59, 63–65, 252n58; light poetry and, 41, 50–52, 54, 55, 65; memory/memorability of text and, 65–68, 69, 70, 73–75, 253n69, 253n75; oral literature and, 60–62, 74–75; *pointe* and, 58, 68–70, 73, 253n75

Galakhov, Aleksei, 162, 164
Galinkovsky, Iakov, 69
Garve, Christian, 99
Gasparov, Mikhail, 6
Georgievsky, Ivan, 70
Germany: German-language texts, 86, 118; German-language translations, 58–59, 114; influences in literature and philosophy, 204, 218, 221; national literature and, 16. *See also specific authors*
Gilbert, Nicolas Joseph Laurent, 221
Glinka, Fedor, 168
Glinka, Mikhail, 205
Gluck, Christoph Willibald, 86
Gnedich, Nikolai, 27, 30, 36, 90–93; *The Iliad* (Homer) translation, 90, 92, 204; "To A. S. Pushkin," 29
Goethe, Johann Wolfgang von, 16, 17, 61, 67; *The Sorrows of Young Werther*, 112–13, 116, 168
Gogol, Nikolai, 115
Golburt, Luba, 35
Golenishchev-Kutuzov, Pavel, 30
Golitsyna, Evdokiia, 209
Golovina, T. N., 96
Gombrich, E. H., 10
Gorchakov, Vladimir, 73–74
graphosphere (handwritten texts). *See* handwritten texts
Gray, Thomas, 113, 114–16, 128, 130, 223
Green Lamp literary society, 139–40, 144–45
Griboedov, Alexander: *The Student* (Griboedov and Katenin), 146–47; *Woe from Wit*, 65, 66, 84, 92, 96, 110, 111
Grigorieva, A. D., 130

Hall, Edward T., 155
handwritten texts (graphosphere), 16, 32, 76, 84–85, 99–101, 104, 112, 134,

154; in albums, 82–83, 96, 119, 192, 238, 254n13; censorship and, 84, 110, 111; diaries and, 96, 102–3; love practices and, 164–65; peer corrections in, 71, 72, 149–50; poetry and, 3, 6, 14, 82–83, 96, 119, 192, 208, 238, 254n13, 265n14; productive reading and, 96, 97, 110, 111
Hasty, Olga Peters, 199
Hesiod, 14
Homer, *The Iliad*, 90, 92, 204
Horace, 13, 48, 49, 108, 207–8, 214, 265n11
Houdar de La Motte, Antoine, 87
Hugo, Victor, 15

Iazykov, Nikolai, 5, 104, 111–12, 139, 184
Illichevsky, Aleksey, 141
inakogovorenie (Shklovsky). *See* allospeaking
Ingres, Jean-Auguste-Dominique, 14
Istrin, V. M., 166
Ivanitsky, Nikolai, 84

Jackson, Virginia, 16, 56, 57
Jakobson, Roman, 6, 23, 26, 66, 67, 70, 104, 122, 132, 161, 202, 256n71
James, William, 22–23, 248n2, 248n4

Kaisarov, Petr, 166
Kakhovsky, Petr, 177
Kapodistrias, Ioannis, 53, 60
Karabanov, Petr, 253n69
Karamzin, Nikolai, 15, 38–41, 48, 53, 55, 57, 60, 65, 70, 78, 114, 140–41, 143, 144, 159, 164, 188, 204, 228, 238; "Epistle to Women," 42–45, 224–25; "Evgenii and Iulia," 85–86; *Letters of a Russian Traveler*, 137–39, 261n24; *My Trifles*, 47; *Poor Liza*, 193
Karazin, Vasily, 40, 41
Kartsev, Fedor, 136–37

Katenin, Pavel, 91, 113, 146–47
Keats, John, 132
Kern, Anna, 27, 101, 103, 104, 187–88
Khagi, Sofya, 144
Khitrovo, Elizaveta, 31
Khvostov, Dimitrii, 27, 150
Kireevsky, Ivan, 139, 141–42, 157, 158
Kireevsky, Vasily, 141–42
Klopstock, Friedrich Gottlieb, 86
Kokoshkin, Fedor, 52, 91
Kolosova, Aleksandra, 91
Konshin, Nikolai, 89–90, 91, 106, 115–16, 184
Kozlov, Vasily, 76, 104
Kozlovsky, Petr, 53–54, 251n24
Kozodavlev, Osip, 249nn38–39
Krasovsky, Aleksandr, 109, 110
Krylov, Ivan, 36, 65, 66, 164, 253n69
Küchelbecker, Wilhelm, 48, 141, 144, 147, 155–56; "On the Direction of Our Poetry, Especially Lyric, in the Past Decade," 203, 220–22, 225–29, 231–32, 238–40, 269n99; "To Friends, on the Rhine," 145
Kutuzov, Nikolai, 126

La Bruyère, Jean de, 190–91
Laclos, Pierre Choderlos de, *Dangerous Liaisons*, 166–71, 175–77, 183, 189–90, 192, 261n25
Lamartine, Alphonse de, 38, 126, 221
language(s): Church Slavonic, 38, 39, 92; French, 38–39, 53, 60, 250n49; German, 86, 118; Italian, 86, 113; letters and, 44–45; love practices and, 165–66, 261n16; poetic function of, 26, 66, 67, 122; Russian as a literary language, 38–41, 53, 60, 63
Lavater, Johann Caspar, 43
Le Bovier de Fontenelle, Bernard, 95
Legoy, Corinne, 16
Lermontov, Mikhail, 5, 68, 187, 253n85

letters (postal and hand-to-hand correspondence): Arzamas literary society and, 57; community-building and, 124; diaries and, 102–3, 134, 135; dual felicity of poetry and, 59, 63–64, 65, 163; of friendship, 141; functions of poetry and, 55–57, 59, 63–64, 65; letter writing manuals, 63–65, 118–19, 252n58

Levin, Yuri, 126–27, 128, 135

Levinton, Georgii, 265n11

libertinism, 179–80, 188, 198, 199, 200, 201; in French literature, 167, 168, 171, 187, 189, 195; in love practices, 169–70, 173, 174, 176, 183, 187–88; in love elegies, 174, 176, 187–95, 201, 237; parody of, 193–94

light poetry, 41–43, 50–52, 54, 55, 65, 150, 211

Liprandi, Ivan, 27

literary language. See language(s)

literary societies, 95, 140; Arzamas, 57, 139–40, 141, 144–45, 209, 210; Friendly Literary Society, 112, 144–45, 218; Green Lamp, 139–40, 144–45; peer corrections in, 71

literary templates: fiction as template for love affairs, 166, 167, 169, 170, 171, 175, 176; letters and, 119; love elegy as template for love affairs, 168, 169, 171–72, 173–77, 187, 262n46; reading poetry and, 80, 83

live address (Tynianov), 27–32, 36, 37, 122, 133, 150, 227–28, 233

Lomonosov, Mikhail, 30, 37–39, 123–24, 228; "Evening Reflection on God's Majesty," 133–34; "Morning Reflection on God's Majesty," 133–34; "Ode on the Day of Her Sovereign Majesty Empress Elisaveta Petrovna's Accession to the Throne, 1748," 229–31

Longfellow, Henry Wadsworth, 15

Longinov, Mikhail, 254n1

Lotman, Yuri, 6, 45, 104, 118, 135, 136, 141, 226, 231, 232

Louis XIV (king of France), 16

love poetry, 161–63, 181; live address and, 32, 36; love elegies, 120, 123–24, 167–77, 180, 183–84, 187–201, 222, 232–33, 237; love practices and, 163–64; madrigals, 165, 166, 206, 207, 208–9, 211–12, 216, 265n14; personal pronouns in, 165, 261n16; poetry set to music and, 86–87, 89, 168, 172, 176, 177, 183, 201; *pointe* and, 174, 176; textual versus contextual semantics and, 173–77, 262n46

love practices, 161–71, 173–74, 175, 183, 187, 261n16, 262n46

Lucian of Samosata, 95

Lunacharsky, Anatoly, 33

Luria, Aleksandr, 66

Lutkovskaia, Anna (Annette), 81

lyceum, 8, 138, 140, 141, 152, 210, 219

MacLeish, Archibald, 13

madrigals, 29, 71, 74, 166, 206–12, 216, 223–24, 232, 265n14

Magritte, René, 181

Maikov, Vasily, 39

Maiofis, Maria, 209

Mandel'shtam, Nadezhda, 144, 159–60

Mandel'shtam, Osip, 159

Manzoni, Alessandro, 53

Marcus Aurelius, 130

Maria Fedorovna (Dowager Empress), 35

Mayakovsky, Vladimir, 46

Mazdorf, Aleksandr, 67

Mazur, Natalia, 116, 130, 134, 269n99

memorization, of poetry, 75,

memory/memorability of text(s), 6, 26, 66–71, 73–75, 111, 118, 253n69, 253n75

Merzliakov, Aleksei, 7, 79, 91–92, 107–8, 112, 118–19; "Amid the Level Vale," 86–87
Meyerhold, Vsevolod, 101, 177
Mill, John Stuart, 17, 133, 238
Miller, Perry, 16
Millevoye, Charles Hubert, 221, 222
Mirsky, D. S., 106
"Modest and Sofia," 94, 95, 97
Moretti, Franco, ix
Moskovskii telegraf (Moscow telegraph) (journal), 70
Moskovskii vestnik (Moscow herald) (journal), 79
Mounet-Sully, Jean, 101, 119
Mozart, Wolfgang Amadeus, 9–10, 81, 119
Mukhanov, Aleksandr, 176
Muraviev, Mikhail, 42–43, 95, 250n49, 267n51

Nabokov, Vladimir, 198, 217, 219
Napoleonic wars, 66, 105, 107–8, 151, 152, 204, 229
Neelov, Sergei, 251n24
Neledinsky-Meletsky, Yuri, 64–65
New Criticism, American, 24, 28, 80
Novikov, Nikolai, 39
Novosti literatury (The literary news), 76, 116

occasional poetry, 15–16, 17, 130, 231, 268n80
odes, 32, 35, 37, 38, 45, 48, 121–22, 204–11, 249nn38–39; congratulatory poetry and, 30, 229–30; elegies versus, 220–21, 225–27, 231, 232, 238, 239, 240; functions of, 152; handwritten texts and, 208, 265n14; oral delivery of poetry, 30, 87, 231–32; as oratory, 28–29, 30, 34–37, 87, 88, 121–22, 249nn34–35; parody of, 146–47, 230

Odoevsky, Aleksandr, 70
Oksman, Iulian, 209
Okudzhava, Bulat, 5, 6, 138–39
Olenin, Alexei, 36
Olenina, Anna, 103, 163, 165, 166, 201–2, 264n121
Olenina, Varvara, 21
Olin, Valerian, "Stanzas to Eliza," 109–10
Ong, Walter, 60–62
operas, 93, 205
oral delivery of poetry, 30, 87–88, 94, 116; on domestic stage, 91; on dramatic stage, 90, 91, 92–93. *See also* poetry set to music; *romans*
oral literature, 60–62, 74–75
Ostrovsky, Aleksandr, 177
Ovid, 14, 27, 80, 105, 115, 184
Ozeretskovsky, Nikolai, 118
Ozerov, Vladislav, 142

Panina, Varvara (Varia), 83
Paperno, Irina, 135
Parny, Évariste de, 113, 114, 167–68, 183, 222
Parry, Milman, 60
Parsamov, Vadim, 206, 207
participation, complicity (*souchastie*), 7, 79, 81, 107–8, 118, 119
Pasternak, Boris, 13
patronage, 36, 37, 105, 152, 228–29
Paul I (emperor of Russia), 85, 209
Pavlova, Karolina, 46
Pecherin, Vladimir, 118
peer corrections, 71, 72, 149–50
Peirce, Charles, 22–23, 248n2
perfection: poetry and, 52, 72, 136, 184, 187; self-perfection, 72, 97–99, 135–37
personal pronouns, 123–24, 126, 127, 132, 151–53, 154, 160, 165, 195, 201, 261n16. *See also* auto-communication
Peschio, Joe, 34, 57, 64, 139, 140, 150

Petina, Larisa, 69, 70
piiticheskaia dietika. See poetic dietetics
Pilshchikov, Igor', 156
Pindar, 48, 146, 152
Piron, Alexis, 70–71, 250n49
Pletnev, Petr, 5, 15–17, 37–40, 91, 164, 191, 193, 195, 198, 203
poetic dietetics (*piiticheskaia dietika*), 148, 214
poetry set to music, 85–89, 122; congratulatory poetry and, 230–32; love poetry and, 168, 172, 176, 177, 183, 201; love practices and, 172, 176, 177, 230. See also *romans*; songs
Pogodin, Mikhail, 109
pointe, 58, 68–70, 73, 174, 176, 253n75
Poliarnaia zvezda (The polar star), 184, 185
Ponomareva, Sofia, 50, 81, 250n9
prayers: auto-communication and, 133–34, 135, 136; diaries and, 134–36; poetry and, 78, 122, 123, 128; as a type of speech, 25, 92, 143–44
private/public spheres, 57–60
productive reading, 3, 94–96; handwritten texts and, 96, 97, 110, 111; reading-cum-writing spaces and, 112–15; self-perfection and, 97–99; translations of poetry and, 114–15, 118
Proskurin, Oleg, 87, 168, 192, 204–5, 218, 233, 265n3, 266n43
Proskurina, Vera, 249nn38–39
Protasova, Alexandra (Sasha), 98. See also Voeikova, Alexandra
Protasova, Ekaterina, 98–100
Protasova, Maria (Masha), 98–102
proxemics, 154–60, 237–38
Pushkin, Alexander, 3–5, 8–9, 16–17, 53, 56–57, 61, 66, 69–72, 82–85, 87, 88, 90, 96, 103–5, 111, 115, 116, 119, 142, 145, 147, 152, 155, 163, 166, 168, 169, 177–82, 184–85, 189–93, 195, 251n24, 254n13, 262n55, 262n63, 264n111, 264n121, 265n11; "19 October 1825," 146; *Boris Godunov*, 110–12, 229, 240; "A confession of love . . . ," 163; 191, 199; "Conversation between a Bookseller and a Poet," 146, 240–45; "To Dorida," 73–74, 81; "Epistle to the Censor," 57; *Eugene Onegin*, 8, 109, 149, 156, 187–88, 196–201, 203–45, 250n49, 266n43, 267n46, 268n65, 267n51, 267n55; "Excerpts from Letters, Thoughts, and Observations," 231–32; *The Fountain of Bakhchisarai*, 212; "To Gnedich," 27, 29, 30; *The Gypsies*, 212; "I loved you," 161–62, 200–202, 264n121; "To Kaverin," 51; "My friend, I have forgotten," 181–83; "Objection to Küchelbecker's Articles Published in *Mnemozina*," 229; "Ode to Liberty," 121, 205–12, 216, 221, 238, 243, 265n14; "One Rainy Autumn Evening," 87; "Parting," 141; "To Princess Golitsyna. Sending Her the Ode 'Liberty,'" 206, 207, 208–9, 211–12, 216, 265n14; *The Prisoner of the Caucasus*, 191–93, 194–96, 198, 212; *Ruslan and Liudmila*, 126, 181, 204–5, 210, 211, 213, 229, 250n49, 265n3; "Scene from Faust," 188; "To the Sea," 67; "To the Slanderers of Russia," 31; "Thou and You," 165, 201; "Verses Composed at Night during Insomnia," 123, 128–32, 134, 137, 144
Pushkin, Lev, 11–13, 67, 106, 247n14
Pushkin, Vasily, 50, 55, 72, 138, 145, 147, 150, 158

Rachinsky, Sergei, 50
Racine, Jean, 55, 167
Raevsky, Andrei, 107, 108
Raevsky, Nikolai, 229
Ram, Harsha, 40

Ramazani, Jahan, 122
reader and writer co-experience, 6, 76–80, 82, 83, 119, 227–28
readership, 3–10, 15, 36, 42–45, 76, 97, 99, 134, 154–59, 228, 235, 237–41, 244
reading-cum-writing spaces, 112–15
reading poetry, 3, 16, 75, 77–83, 87, 97, 99, 105–9, 113, 115, 118–20, 254n13; conversations and, 85; emotions and, 108; literary templates and, 80, 83; memorization and, 111, 118; oral delivery of poetry, 30, 87–94, 116; reader as speaker, 80, 81–83. *See also* productive reading; reader and writer co-experience
Reiser, Solomon, 139
Richardson, Samuel, *Clarissa, or, the History of a Young Lady*, 64, 94, 169, 170, 183, 190, 198
romans (song), 36, 84, 108, 152, 164, 172, 177, 201, 204
Rostopchina, Evdokiia, 85
Rousseau, Jean-Jacques, 64, 94, 116, 166, 167, 188, 254n13
Rozen, Egor, 205
Ryleev, Kondraty, 69, 125

Saint-Lambert, Jean-François de, 65, 95, 155
salons, 28–29, 34, 50, 53, 90, 122, 139–40, 237
Sandler, Stephanie, 28, 104–5
Sappho, 27, 265n11
Saussure, Ferdinand de, 61
Schiller, Friedrich, 142, 149, 156, 166; "An die Freude" ("Ode to Joy"), 78, 143, 222; "Das Siegesfest," 68–69, 253n75
Schillerians, 142, 144–45, 218, 221, 222, 267n51
Semenova, Ekaterina, 91
Senderovich, Savely, 145–46, 148

Severnye tsvety (journal), 38, 179, 180, 219, 257n78, 266–67n43
Shelley, Percy, 24, 25, 132
Shevyrev, Stepan, 68
Shishkin, Mikhail, 83
Shishkov, Aleksandr, 40, 41
Shklovsky, Viktor, 8–9, 33, 71, 144, 161–62, 201, 249n31
Shvartsband, Samuil, 181
Sidiakov, Lev, 219
Simoni, Pavel, 102
Sobańska, Karolina, 264n121
Sobolevsky, Sergei, 106
Society of Lovers of Russian Literature, Moscow University, 52, 90, 253n88
Socrates, 43, 61
Sokhanskaya, Nadezhda, 163–64
Sokolov, Grigory, 109, 200
Sokovnina, Anna, 112
Sokovnina, Katerina, 166
Somov, Orest, 172, 173
songs, 15, 83, 87, 122; community-building and, 123–24; congratulatory poetry and, 230–32; drinking songs, 108, 123–24, 138, 146, 152, 156; song-books, 85, 87. *See also* poetry set to music; *romans*
souchastie (complicity, participation), 7, 79, 81, 107–8, 118, 119
Sovremennik (The contemporary) (journal), 71
Staël, Madame de, 52, 218
Stroganov, Mikhail, 179
Sullivan, Louis H., 10, 167
Sumarokov, Aleksandr, 38
Sumarokov, Pankratii, 40
Suvorov, Aleksandr, 30, 152
Syn otechestva (Son of the fatherland) (journal), 36, 59–60, 73, 181

Talleyrand, Charles Maurice de, 54
Tasso, Torquato, 113, 204

templates. *See* literary templates
theaters: domestic stage, 54–55, 64, 118; dramatic stage, 64, 90, 91, 92–93, 177
Tiutchev, Fedor, 5, 123, 143, 144
toasts, 11, 68, 122–24, 133, 145–54, 230–31
Todd, William Mills III, 36, 57–58, 103
Tolstoy, Lev, 16, 135, 205
Tomashevsky, Boris, 104, 113
Trediakovsky, Vasily, 124, 231–32
Trotsky, Leon, 33
Tsiavlovskaia, Tatiana, 264n121
Tsoi, Viktor, 138–39
Tsvetaeva, Marina, 177
Tsvetnik (The flower garden), 94
Turgenev, Aleksandr, 29–30, 40, 55–56, 72, 76–77, 97, 105, 115, 116, 134, 145, 150, 206, 208–11, 218–19, 252n47
Turgenev, Andrei, 76–78, 103–4, 112–15, 135, 166, 218, 221, 223
Turgenev, Nikolai, 116, 206, 208–10, 218–19
Tynianov, Yuri, ix, 26–30, 32–35, 44, 45, 55, 64–65, 87, 88, 103, 104, 121, 122, 203, 217–19, 221, 222, 227, 244, 249nn34–35

unylaia (doleful) elegies. *See* doleful (*unylaia*) elegies
Ushakov, Vasily, 48

Vatsuro, Vadim, 30, 74, 103, 135, 151, 218
verbal performance, and conversations, 52–54, 61, 85, 251nn23–24
Viazemskaia, Vera, 31–32, 49, 166, 176
Viazemsky, Petr, 5, 31–32, 36, 37, 54, 55, 58, 61, 64–65, 67, 69–70, 97, 106–9, 142, 147, 149, 162, 174, 183, 189, 193, 206, 208–9, 211, 231, 251n24, 268n80; "Epistle to Turgenev with the Pie," 29–30, 145, 150, 252n47; "To My Soulmate," 48, 49, 71–72, 150
Vigel', Filipp, 39–40, 55

Vinitsky, Ilya, 98, 104
Voeikov, Aleksandr, 76, 98, 191, 192, 193, 195, 198, 204
Voeikova (Protasova), Aleksandra, 247n14
Voltaire, 55, 71
Volynsky, Artemii, 231
Vorontsov, Mikhail, 105, 228–29
Vorzhsky, Aleksei, 92–93
Vul'f, Aleksei, 168–80, 183, 187, 230, 262n32, 262n46

Wachtel, Michael, 130–32
Wales, Katie, 123
Whitman, Walt, 23, 248n4

Young, Edward, 116

Zakrevskaya, Agrafena, 106
Zhikharev, Stepan, 91–93, 134, 136, 137, 253n69
Zhivov, Victor, 262n46
Zhukovsky, Vasily, 5, 15, 37–38, 53, 55–56, 60–61, 70–73, 77, 84, 93, 97–104, 112–15, 117, 124, 128, 133, 135, 141–42, 147, 149–50, 158, 164, 218, 223; "A Bard in the Camp of Russian Warriors," 36, 107, 108, 138–39, 151–54, 204; "The Bard's Song at the Tomb of Victorious Slavs," 107; "To Batiushkov," 146, 148; "Country Graveyard," 114–16, 118, 123, 128–32, 134, 144, 153–54, 234; "Epistle to Emperor Alexander," 37, 72; "Epistle to Voeikov," 204; "On Friendship and Friends," 143–44; "Summer Evening," 36, 58–59; "Twelve Sleeping Maidens," 204; "Triumph of the Victors," 68–69, 253n75; *Vladimir*, 204
Zorin, Andrei, 94, 97, 104, 112, 116, 134
Zrazhevskaia, Aleksandra, 109
Zubov, Platon, 28

PUBLICATIONS OF THE WISCONSIN CENTER
FOR PUSHKIN STUDIES

Realizing Metaphors: Alexander Pushkin and the Life of the Poet
David M. Bethea

The Pushkin Handbook
Edited by David M. Bethea

The Uncensored "Boris Godunov": The Case for Pushkin's Original "Comedy," with Annotated Text and Translation
Chester Dunning with Caryl Emerson, Sergei Fomichev, Lidiia Lotman, and Antony Wood

Alexander Pushkin's "Little Tragedies": The Poetics of Brevity
Edited by Svetlana Evdokimova

Taboo Pushkin: Topics, Texts, Interpretations
Edited by Alyssa Dinega Gillespie

Pushkin's Tatiana
Olga Hasty

Lyric Complicity: Poetry and Readers in the Golden Age of Russian Literature
Daria Khitrova

Derzhavin: A Biography
Vladislav Khodasevich; Translated and with an introduction by Angela Brintlinger

The Poetics of Impudence and Intimacy in the Age of Pushkin
Joe Peschio

The Imperial Sublime: A Russian Poetics of Empire
Harsha Ram

How Russia Learned to Write: Literature and the Imperial Table of Ranks
Irina Reyfman

Challenging the Bard: Dostoevsky and Pushkin, a Study of Literary Relationship
Gary Rosenshield

Pushkin and the Genres of Madness: The Masterpieces of 1833
Gary Rosenshield

Pushkin's Rhyming: A Comparative Study
J. Thomas Shaw

A Commentary to Pushkin's Lyric Poetry, 1826–1836
Michael Wachtel

www.ingramcontent.com/pod-product-compliance
Lightning Source LLC
Chambersburg PA
CBHW070837160426
43192CB00012B/2217